THE UNIVER

ESSAYS IN LATER MEDIEVAL
FRENCH HISTORY

The archbishop's hall, Tours, where the Estates of 1468 were held.

ESSAYS IN LATER MEDIEVAL FRENCH HISTORY

P. S. LEWIS

THE HAMBLEDON PRESS

LONDON AND RONCEVERTE

The Hambledon Press 1985

35 Gloucester Avenue
London NW1 7AX (U.K.)

309 Greenbrier Avenue,
Ronceverte, West Virginia 24970 (U.S.A.)

ISBN 0 907628 41 9

British Library Cataloguing in Publication Data

Lewis, P.S.
    Essays in later medieval French history. —
    (History series; 29)
    1. France — History — 15th century
    I. Title   II. Series
    944'. 026   DC101.9

Library of Congress Cataloging in Publication Data

Lewis, P.S. (Peter Shervey)
    Essays in later medieval French history.

    A collection of the author's essays, many of which
have been previously published.
    English and French.
    Includes bibliographical references and index.
    1. France — History — 15th century — Addresses, essays,
    lectures. 2. Great Britain — History — Lancaster and
    York, 1399-1485 — Addresses, essays, lectures. I. Title.
    DC101. 9. L47 1985   944'.026   85-5551
    ISBN 0 907628 41 9

Printed and Bound in Great Britain
by Robert Hartnoll Ltd., Bodmin, Cornwall

CONTENTS

Acknowledgements   vi

1   Introduction   1

2   France in the Fifteenth Century: Society and
    Sovereignty   3

3   Une devise de chevalerie inconnue, créée par un
    comte de Foix?   29

4   Le dragon de Mauvezin et Jean I, Comte de Foix (1412-36)   37

5   Decayed and Non-Feudalism in Later Medieval France   41

6   Of Breton Alliances and Other Matters   69

7   The Pensioners of Louis XI   91

8   The Failure of the French Medieval Estates   105

9   Breton Estates   127

10 The Estates of Tours   139

11 The Centre, the Periphery, and the Problem of Power
    Distribution in Later Medieval France   151

12 Jean Juvenal des Ursins and the Common Literary
    Attitude towards tyranny in Fifteenth-Century
    France   169

13 Two Pieces of Fifteenth-Century Political
    Iconography
              (a) Clovis Touches for the King's Evil   189
              (b) The English Kill their Kings   191

14 War Propaganda and Historiography in Fifteenth-
    Century France and England   193

15 Sir John Fastolf's Lawsuit over Titchwell 1448-55   215

16 The Growth of the Nation State   235

17 Conclusion   241

Index   242

ACKNOWLEDGEMENTS

The following chapters were originally published elsewhere and are reprinted by the kind permission of the original publishers.

2   *Europe in the Late Middle Ages*, ed. J.R. Hale, J.R.L. Highfield and B. Smalley (Fabers, London, 1965) 466-94.

3   *Annales du Midi*, 66 (1964), 77-84.

5   *Bulletin of the Institute of Historical Research*, xxxvii (1964), 157-84.

6   *War, Literature and Politics in the Late Middle Ages: Essays in Honour of G.W. Coopland*, ed. C.T. Allmand (Liverpool, 1976), 122-43.

8   *Past and Present*, 23 (1962), 3-24. World Copyright: The Past and Present Society, Corpus Christi College, Oxford, England.

11   *The Crown and Local Communities in England and France in the Fifteenth Century*, ed. J.R.L. Highfield and R. Jeffs (Alan Sutton, Gloucester, 1981), 33-50.

12   *Medium Aevum*, xxxiv (1965), 103-21.

13   *Journal of the Warburg and Courtauld Institutes*, xxvii (1964), 317-20.

14   *Transactions of the Royal Historical Society*, 5th series, 15 (1965), 1-21.

15   *The Historical Journal*, 1 (1958), 1-21.

16   *Britain and France: Ten Centuries*, ed. D. Johnson, F. Bédarida and F. Crouzet (Dawson, Folkestone, 1980), 32-6, 366-7.

INTRODUCTION

To write an Introduction to a collection of one's own essays is, I suppose, rather like writing one's own obituary: one is afraid of overdoing it. The papers here collected are the work of about a quarter of a century, of discovery and of excitement about French later medieval history: finding out things, explaining, *devising*, as they'd say then. I thought to put two general pieces at beginning and end, one comparatively old, one comparatively recent. In between, the essays fall into two general groups: on political structure in later medieval France, and on mental structure. Political structure again divides, into three fields. One concerns informal power structures. Two papers here are unpublished: one marginally frivolous, one much more important. The second concerns representative institutions: a meritorious subject, if a bit well-worn: here there are two unpublished papers, one which deals with an 'eccentric' regional assembly, the other an attempt to understand what, if one were someone actually at a meeting of an Estates general, one would have made of it all. What would one have made of it all: coming from the periphery, what did one make of the centre; in a different sense, this is what the last paper in this section is about.

Second, *mentalités*. Someone, once, said that he saw the ghost of Jean Juvenal des Ursins behind me. I wish it were: I know what he looked like, I have tried to see through his mind in editing his writing: but I am still not certain that I see him – Jean Juvenal – plain in the hôtel des Ursins in Paris, now buried under the Hôtel Dieu.

After that, a minor if not too unimportant piece, and then something reasonably important, on comparable reactions to the use of historical material in France and in England during the later middle ages. And finally, an out-of-kilter, but not irrelevant essay, in the sense that it is about the making of historiography, but in England. If only one had this kind of material in France; but when Pierre Charbonnier can turn up the material for his *Guillaume de Murol*, what might one expect?

To begin, then.

FRANCE IN THE FIFTEENTH CENTURY:

SOCIETY AND SOVEREIGNTY

'Tout', thought Michelet, 'influe sur tout'; and this resounding observation is, though still respectable, now only too plainly a truism. The politics of a particular society, for instance, are most clearly and most fully understood as an emanation of it; and it is the purpose of this paper to discuss in these terms the internal politics of fifteenth-century France.

But what does one mean by 'politics' in the France of the later Middle Ages? Naturally they were limited in scope, since the number of questions which had to be discussed and the number of those who were important enough to discuss them, the members of the 'political society', were limited; and government, though ideally it concerned itself with such concepts as justice and the good administration of the whole community, was often more vitally concerned with the management of the political society on questions other than these. And what does one mean by 'society'? Not only were there in it the divisions of the group, the class; there were the divisions of the region, the *pays*, the locality. This localization was a function partly of geography, partly of historical development. The boundaries of these local compartments were as difficult (or as easy) to over-leap as those of class. There was nothing to stop (though there were things to hinder) a determined bourgeois or a determined peasant from rising into at least the lower ranks of the nobility; there was nothing to stop a member of one of those local communities, those micro-societies, from entering, through seigneurial or royal service, through the Church, through a simple acceptance of the wider world, the macro-society of the great, of the government, of the cosmopolitan; but there was much to hinder it and much that was regional remained in the thinking of even the most cosmopolitan.

These boundaries, immunities in a loose sense, were re-inforced by the often frail formalities of privileges, of charters, of immunities in a strict sense: of liberties for regions, of liberties for social groups, of liberties for individuals. There were people who thought in terms of a unity, as there were people who thought tenderly of classes other than their own. There were people who acted for the common good and there were more who said that they did; but the latter were often found out, as Louis XI and Thomas Basin (on opposite sides) found out the leaguers self-styled of the Public Weal. Between such in-dividualists conflict could naturally be acute. Royal officers attacked noble and clerical immunists; they and the immunists attacked each other. Social conflict in later medieval France was not essentially one of class: it was of every individual immunist, whatever his class, against his immediate enemies, occasionally in alliance with his peers or with his neighbours. Against the kingdom, the unity, the macro-society, was set the micro-society, the *pays*; and against both was set the individual.

The fragile unity had its most potent expression in the idea of the king, in the image of a perfect government, and to some extent in the actual efficacy of the king, the person, in the con-troller, more or less, of a far from perfect government. The image of sovereignty[1] naturally differed for different people: a *juponnier* in Orléans might deny the king outright and cry 'Kings, kings, kings: we have no king but God!'; an elderly inhabitant of the *Massif central* might have strange superstitions about the Royal Mark. The views of those who were inarticu-late on paper, peasant or noble, are hard to discover. Some may have seen the king only in the most general terms, as the most impressive figure in an impressive cortège on the road, a 'royal ceremony', indulged in by Charles V, according to Christine de Pisan, only to impress 'the most worthy status of the high crown

---

[1] The sources of material given without reference in this and the three following paragraphs will be found in 'Jean Juvenal des Ursins and the Common Literary Attitude towards Tyranny in Fifteenth-Century France', *Medium Aevum*, xxxiv (1965). See below 169-88.

of France' upon his successors[1]—and also, presumably, upon the bystander. A mere royal presence could be terrifying enough, even to an experienced Italian ambassador.[2] But the image of government of those who were articulate on paper, the men of letters, was more formal than this. It was compounded of notions legal, theological, moral, some indeed from a remote past and some concocted in a less respectable present. Its ingredients could, according to taste or to disingenuousness, be so treated as to produce an image of royal right or of royal duty; its theories so handled as to exhort resistance or to deny resistance utterly. In so far as people thought about politics abstractedly at all in later medieval France, it was in its terms that they made plain their views.

The king was a spiritual and a public being as well as a private one. The Gallican controversy had reinforced his original divinity. A number of popular miracles, now attached to Clovis, illustrated the particular regard with which the Crown of France was held in Heaven: the origin of the *fleurs-de-lys*, the origin of the oriflamme, the miraculous descent of the *Sainte-ampoule* and the power which, it was generally held, its chrism conferred upon the king to touch for the evil found ready pictorial expression in popular abbreviated chronicles.[3] In more extravagant moments it might be held that, in touching for the evil, the king performed miracles in his own lifetime. The king was the head of the body politic and, it could be argued by Jean de Terre-Vermeille about 1420, resistance was thus unnatural as well as sacrilegious. It could be argued, *quia quod principi placuit legis habet vigorem,* that the king was above the law. The very misfortunes of France had reinforced the image of the saviour of France,

> *For his loss is our ruin*
> *And our safety with him lies.*

The misfortunes of war had indeed weakened the willingness of the articulate to think of resistance. The English, who killed their kings, were regarded with a fascinated and rather formal

---

[1] *Le Livre des fais et bonnes meurs du sage roy Charles V,* ed. S. Solente, [Société de l'histoire de France], i (Paris, 1936), 51.

[2] *Dépêches des ambassadeurs milanais en France,* ed. B. de Mandrot and C. Samaran, [Société de l'histoire de France], i (Paris, 1916), 238.

[3] 'Two Pieces of Fifteenth-century Political Iconography', *Journal of the Warburg and Courtauld Institutes,* xxvii (1964), 317-19. See below 188-91.

horror: a horror, again, expressed in pictorial form.[1] Resistance had once been preached, as late as the first decade of the fifteenth century by the doctors of the university of Paris; it was to be preached again after its end. But in the course of the century only Thomas Basin, who had been involved in the war of the Public Weal, justified rebellion; for the rest, the literary, though they made their distinctions between king and tyrant, though they preached the moral duty of the anointed of heaven and the head of the body politic, though they pointed to the customary awful warnings of scripture, antiquity and even recent history, though they fulminated against tyranny, for the rest the literary refused to countenance resistance. The intellectual victors were the king's lawyers in *parlement*. For them it was temerarious 'to talk of the king's authority, it's sacrilege to debate it . . .; for the authority of the king . . . is greater than advocates could express it and it is not subject to the opinions of doctors'. The latter, with other literary men, adopted an elegiac attitude and said, with Commynes, 'when all's said and done, our only hope should be in God'.

The king, then, 'has no other control over him than the fear of God and his own conscience'. It was to be hoped that these were efficacious; but too often hope was deferred. If sovereignty was never challenged, the actions of the sovereign and, more often, of his servants were accused in diatribe and in action. A hopeful reluctance to tarnish the image of sovereignty led in the former to a reluctance to accuse the person of the sovereign; in the latter there was no such inhibition. Charles VI and Charles VII had the example of Richard II of England before their eyes; Louis XI in his later days cowered behind remarkable systems of physical defences. While the men of letters, a peaceful crew on the whole, regarded the *voye de faicte*, the way of action, with abhorrence, others less peaceable might not. The ideas of the articulate, even the notions of the inarticulate, did not create the political movement of late medieval France: they were its creation. The motivity of politics and the motivity of political theory had a more practical source.

Why did people behave as they did? First we must ask how they did behave. Charles VI was mad, Charles VII at least politically inexpert until comparatively late in his reign (though he became very dexterous), Louis XI, though a remarkable

[1] Ibid., pp. 319–20. See below 191-2.

man, not necessarily a very efficient one.[1] The English war, and with it the problem of all those who had accepted the sovereignty of the king of England and France, dragged on until the 1450s and the threat of renewed war remained. The revenue from the *domaine*, the royal estates, was far too low for the purposes for which it was intended. And yet Charles VII and Louis XI could at times act with considerable authority. But perhaps we should distinguish between the groups or the individuals to whose detriment such strength was shown. What were the power relationships between the king, the government, and these groups or individuals? What was this interplay of sovereignty and society?

The question of the king's income gives us our first set of problems. A rich king with a taste for power can buy troops to browbeat the unbribable and can bribe the unbeatable. But first he must get the money; and if he lack the strength that comes from wealth to do so his position is, understandably, impossible. Extraordinary revenue came from taxation; and taxation, in principle, was granted by representative assemblies.[2] 'What touches all should be approved by all' had and still did echo from one end of France to another. Specific privileges protected the rights of specific *pays*; some were dearly cherished. But privileges and laws were, like the political theory of later medieval France, *ex post facto* things: a king who needed not to consult the estates for practical reasons needed very rarely (unless the idea had been ingrained even in him by long years of practice) to consult them for theoretical reasons. For what practical reasons did Charles VII (for it was he alone in the fifteenth century who consulted assemblies with any regularity) feel it necessary to allow his subjects their rights?

He had not (and neither had that paragon Charles V) any special affection or reverence for representative assemblies: he and his entourage seem to have thought, as Charles V and earlier kings had thought, that public opinion needed to be wooed in, preferably, as large an assembly as possible. Now late-medieval Frenchmen had on the whole a profound dislike of general assemblies, of the whole kingdom, say, or of Langue-

---

[1] R. Doucet, 'Le Gouvernement de Louis XI [X]', *Revue des cours et conférences*, (1923–4), 661–9.

[2] The sources of material given without reference in this and the seven following paragraphs will be found in 'The Failure of the French Medieval Estates', *Past and Present*, xxiii (1962), 3–24. See below 105-26.

doil or of a Languedoc larger than the three *sénéchaussées* of Toulouse, Carcassonne and Beaucaire-Nîmes. Though a number of rationalizations of this phobia could be produced (the hazards of the roads in wartime, the cost of travelling vast distances in France, the language barrier between north and south, the difficulties of accommodating a large assembly) its essential cause lay in the long-standing particularism of provincial France. Why should Rouergue be dealt with in the same assembly as the rest of the kingdom, or even in the same assembly as the rest of the Midi? Why should the representatives of the *sénéchaussée* of the Landes (the problem was the same for the duke of Aquitaine) be in the same assembly as those of the Bordelais? It was, in any case, impossible to expect a large assembly like that of the kingdom or that of Languedoil to make a final grant. Charles VII and his entourage, like Charles V and others before them, seem to have wanted large assemblies more for political reasons than anything else: general support was necessary in order to woo the smaller regional assemblies which actually granted the taxes into granting them. Such general support seems to have been necessary primarily in times of defeat, under Charles V as under Charles VII. But large assemblies had a tendency to become tiresome with their grievances; and Charles VII, like Charles V before him, was quite prepared to let general assemblies slip out of existence with the first upsurge of returning victory. They began to slip after the coronation at Reims; they finally vanished after the estates of Orléans in 1439; and they left very few wracks behind.

There remained the regional assemblies, possibly more fervent in defence of local liberty. Some, indeed, remained so. But none presented much obstacle to a determined ruler out for income. 'Charles VII', wrote Commynes, 'never raised more than eighteen hundred thousand francs a year; and King Louis, his son, was raising at the time of his death forty-seven hundred thousand francs, without counting the artillery and other things like that':[1] and, painfully, he was right. The rectitude of using what were in origin taxes for the war for comparatively peaceful purposes was still disputable in the mid-century; but even the reformers of the Cabochian movement in 1413 had

[1] P. de Commynes, *Mémoires*, ed. J. Calmette and G. Durville, [Classiques de l'histoire de France], ii (Paris, 1925), 220.

allowed Charles VI half his extraordinary revenue for non-military purposes.[1] It was upon taxation that the wealth of the king depended; and that taxation he got with very little trouble.

The pressing need of war presumably encouraged the tax-payer while the war remained: 'defence of the realm' was a well-established criterion for subvention.[2] The threat of war remained after 1453, though some people at least were not convinced that it was enough to justify permanent taxation.[3] There was indeed local resistance from some of the regional assemblies that survived: from those of the Dauphiné, for instance, or from those of Rouergue. Various forms of pressure could be exerted; but determined and independent estates like those of the Dauphiné could still extract a soft answer from Louis XI in the 1470s and ensure that the taxes of the *pays* rose by two-thirds instead of by one and two-thirds. But the estates of the Dauphiné were rather exceptional. Elsewhere the regional assemblies, where they survived, were less successful. Why was there so little resistance?

Methods of coercion could be successful. In 1462 the Millavois were threatened with a fine of 'a hundred marks of silver and with the seizure and sale of our goods and with the arrest of our persons and on top of that with the penalty of being rebels and disobedient to the king our lord' if they did not accede to a 'particular demand' made by royal commissioners in the face of resistance and wholesale bribery by the estates of Rouergue. The habit of backstairs representations in which a number of towns indulged could hoist them with their own petard. A lack of cohesion amongst the members of the same order in an assembly, that essential individualism, might provide a general ground for the weakness of the regional assemblies. For what interest had they in co-operation? Rodez during the English occupation had run an intelligence service for the count of Armagnac out of urban revenues; Millau in 1369 had carried its doubts about the sovereignty of Charles V to Montpellier, Avignon and Bologna, had held a service for Sir Thomas Wettenhall, English seneschal of Rouergue who died of wounds at Montlaur, and had replaced the arms of England with those of France only on the orders of his French

---

[1] 'Jean Juvenal des Ursins', op. cit.,
[2] J. R. Strayer, 'Defense of the Realm and Royal Power in France', *Studi in onore di Gino Luzzatto*, (Milan, 1949) i, 289–96.
[3] 'Jean Juvenal des Ursins', op. cit.,

successor.[1] At an individual level the same divergence of interest could be found in members of every order of an Estates. The concept of co-operation, of common action (though it existed) developed very slowly in France. There were so few pressures to foster it.

Why should one engage in united action? As a landowner, ecclesiastical or lay, what interest had one in uniting to oppose taxation? One was on the whole oneself exempt: one attended an assembly in order to consent to the taxation of one's tenants. It could be argued that one had an interest in protecting the source of one's own revenue, that one could be more valiant in defence of this than the bourgeoisie which claimed to represent the *tiers-état*. Some landowners may have been, if only for reasons of prestige, solicitous of their subjects; but the remoteness of the sting of taxation provides at least a *prima facie* case for the apparent lack of resistance of the first two orders to the abolition or coercion of their assemblies. And bourgeois, too, could become exempt from taxation. 'A very large number of the richest people are exempt and don't pay anything', complained the *mairie* of Dijon in 1452, '. . . the merchants and smaller people pay all.'[2] Whole towns could opt out of the taxation system (but with this we will deal later). It can be argued that in the end the taxpayer was left unprotected before the ravening wolf. A Jean Juvenal des Ursins could raise his voice in their protection; but few would raise a hand.

Grievances against the government, infringements of the privileges of the *pays*, these, certainly, might lead the members of an assembly to voice a common complaint. But (however much they might recognize piously their duty of justice) kings did not call assemblies to listen to grievances against themselves and their officers. Since no assembly summoned by the Crown in France acted as a law court or had anything to do with the process of legislation (other than presenting its *cahiers de doléances*) the sole reason for the summoning of an assembly was to raise money. And to his doing this arbitrarily rather too few

[1] *Comptes consulaires de . . . Rodez*, ed. H. Bousquet, I, *Cité*, ii, [Archives historiques du Rouergue, xvii], (Rodez, 1943), *passim*; *Documents sur la ville de Millau*, ed. J. Artières, [Archives historiques du Rouergue, vii], (Millau, 1930), 145–95 *passim*; P. Chaplais, 'Some Documents regarding the Fulfilment and Interpretation of the Treaty of Bretigny 1361–1369', *Camden Miscellany*, xix, [Camden Third Series, lxxx], (London, 1952), 51–78.

[2] F. Humbert, *Les Finances municipales de Dijon du milieu du xive siècle à 1477*, (Paris 1961), 247.

potential members of an assembly seem to have been prepared to object strongly enough to make it advisable for a king to summon them.

Why did they object strongly enough in the areas in which estates survived? This is the most puzzling question. One is forced to answer it in terms of the general historical development of a particular *pays* which gave its inhabitants some will for an assembly which those of other areas lacked. Any more particular common reasons seem impossible to divine. And properly, of course, one should go below the *pays* and its general social composition to the actual individuals who, at all the moments in the life of an assembly, made its existence. But the biographical method is difficult, if not impossible, to apply to these estates. The reasons for action of a Jean Juvenal des Ursins, archbishop duke of Reims and *premier pair* of France, at the estates general of Tours in 1468 are clear enough from his speech itself and from the voluminous collected works in which it survives;[1] the reasons for action of someone more obscure at an obscure local assembly are silent in the silence of the inarticulate.

But in any case Charles VII and Louis XI got their money. They also, in the same fit of absence of mind, got a standing army. How much this was regarded as the seal of despotism is disputable. Jean Juvenal, who had a ready eye for tyranny, at least overlooked it.[2] We know too little about the composition of the companies of *gens d'ordonnance*, too little about their loyalties, too little about the loyalties of their commanders. The claim made in the same military *ordonnance* of 1439 that only the king could raise a private army clearly was ignored by magnates in times of stress. The military situation remained at least open: the battle of Montlhéry in 1465, for instance, was very nearly a draw with the advantage, if any, on the side of the rebels. But at least Charles VII and Louis XI were rich enough to invest in military power which forced the discontented of the Praguerie and the Public Weal in turn to resort to arms; and, as we shall see, to invest in the tacit bribery which softened the winter of their original discontent.

These kings, then, were comparatively wealthy; the strength which they needed to take their taxes on the whole arbitrarily

---

[1] Bibliothèque nationale, ms. fr. 2701.
[2] 'Jean Juvenal des Ursins', op. cit.

was the strength of victory and of the essential unwillingness to object if those non-taxpayers who were in principle the guardians of the unfortunate contributor. And with the disappearance of assemblies the king was left even more clearly *vis-à-vis* a kingdom composed of individuals or of groups of individuals. These, privileged, immune, with rights in principle irrefrangible, now played essentially a lone game with the government. They made (occasionally successfully) attempts at coalition; but the game was essentially an open one, with a ruler who was quite prepared to print his own aces. He made the law, despite the theory that some laws were fundamental; the courts were his, despite the view that they acted as a check upon arbitrary action. An idea in the air, such as that of the priority of the duty of the subject (who owed obedience) over that of the vassal (who had his rights), investigated by Jean de Terre-Vermeille about 1420, could bear fruit in Louis XI's dealings with François II of Brittany.[1] Religion, Claude de Seyssel's third curb[2] upon monarchy, was, though these men were pious, hardly much of a check upon them. In 1465 Louis XI was alleged to have said 'that he needed to do as the brothers of St Francis did, that is, to play the hypocrite'. This, though Louis could also deny that duplicity was his custom,[3] was hardly encouraging for those who wished to put their trust in princes.

How was the game played? One must remember its complication. No king could act alone: he had his entourage, his counsellors, his 'favourites'; he had his civil servants. In this welter of governance the individual will of the king might be hard to identify: the members of the entourage and the civil servants naturally had their own games to play. The great, too, had their entourages, their counsellors, their civil servants; the interplay of interests quickens. And there could at times be a confusing lack of hostility between major protagonists: politics could be a curious love-hate relationship. To a certain extent the bickerings were the bickerings of the members of a single team who might, on the whole, agree about many things but who disagreed about who was to play where. And though to our hindsight men's interests *vis-à-vis* the government might seem fairly clear, in the immediacy of the royal presence, in the

[1] Ibid.
[2] *La Monarchie de France*, ed. J. Poujol, (Paris, 1961), 115–19.
[3] *Dépêches des ambassadeurs milanais*, op. cit., iv (Paris, 1923), 156, 74.

interplay of interest and personality, strange things could happen: the actions of a moment need not be wholly calculated, nor wholly rational.

The structure of government was on the whole simple enough. The king, like every magnate, had a council to help him rule; he had an administration to deal with his estates and with the collection of extraordinary revenue. The last and the central financial and judicial organizations were naturally more complicated than those of a simple magnate; they and the royal chancery, though its methods and its diplomatic might be copied closely by those of the princes, naturally dealt with a far greater body of business than those of a magnate; but royal and seigneurial administrations were sufficiently alike for their personnel to be interchangeable. These officers naturally had their own fortunes to look to. Their shortcomings, the failure of 'justice', figured largely in the lamentations of reformers; the king's tolerating their malefactions was bitterly attacked.[1] But to what extent were his own servants under his control? Did he indeed encourage them to create his 'tyranny' for him? Or did the civil servants create the king's tyranny for their own ends? Was royal lawyers' eagerness to defend the rights of the Crown, for instance, simply a natural lawyer's eagerness to create long and lucrative lawsuits as, it was argued in 1484, magnates' apparent eagerness for estates stemmed from a desire to collect their expenses as commissioners to them? How could a king[2] control his officers? Stability in office, though eagerly claimed by the officers, was not yet an assured thing; venality of office, though practised, not yet wholly approved of; plurality and non-residence, though common enough to be normal, still formally frowned upon.[3] The Crown still had in principle at least some hold over its servants; but whether the final sanction of dismissal or even of condemnation was exercised may have depended more upon the political position of the officer than upon the degree of his malefaction. Given the nature of government, whose men were the civil servants? Could any man rely upon an attachment to the person of the king alone?

[1] 'Jean Juvenal des Ursins', op. cit.
[2] J. Masselin, *Journal des Etats généraux de France tenus à Tours en 1484*, [Documents inédits sur l'histoire de France], (Paris, 1835), 636.
[3] The latest and in some ways the most searching discussion of these problems and of the position of lawyers in later medieval France in general may be found in B. Guenée, *Tribunaux et gens de justice dans le bailliage de Senlis à la fin du moyen âge (vers 1380–vers 1550)*, (Paris, 1963).

Certainly the need for patronage in acquiring office seems to have been a considerable one. The rivalry of patrons, egged on by their own civil servants to find them royal office, has been seen as prodromic of civil war;[1] and patronage was required not only by those who hoped for office but by those already royal officers who hoped for seigneurial service to increase their income or who hoped for advancement in that of the Crown or who needed protection in keeping the places they had already acquired. Some, admittedly, suffered from the conflict of loyalty thus created. Jean Cadier, royal *élu* in the Bourbonnais, who was also a household servant of Jean II, duke of Bourbon, and then auditor of accounts for him at Moulins, was attacked during the onslaught on the duke in 1480 for infidelity to the Crown which could hardly be thought extensive.[2] But if there was danger in serving too loyally a patron there was also danger in serving too loyally the Crown: the punishment of Jean de Doyat, *bailli* of Montferrand, who had led the local attack on Jean II de Bourbon, was an awful warning to those too zealous in the interests of the Crown of what might happen when, on the accession of a minor king, a magnate's influence might again be formidable.[3] A civil servant had naturally to judge his chances in the same way as minor *seigneurs* caught between greater powers had to judge theirs. In 1457 maître François Hallé, *conseiller du roy*, was appointed judge of the *chambrerie* by the *chambrier* of France, Jean II de Bourbon.[4] Twenty-three years later he was his most implacable opponent as king's advocate in *parlement*.[5] He, certainly, had not made the mistake of Jean Cadier. In the same way as their actions in defending the king's interests might be independent of the will or even of the knowledge of the king, so the civil servants' actions as clients could not be wholly subservient to the interests of their patrons. If extreme conflict arose between their masters, they had to choose; but only when their seigneurial patron was pretty firmly defeated were they likely to lose his protection. And such open conflict was not on the whole normal. Much more

[1] E. Perroy, 'Feudalism or Principalities in Fifteenth-Century France', *Bulletin of the Institute of Historical Research*, xx (1945), 184.

[2] H. de Surirey de St.-Remy, *Jean II de Bourbon, duc de Bourbonnais et d'Auvergne (1426–1488)*, (Paris, 1944), 188–90.

[3] A. Bossuat, *Le Bailliage royal de Montferrand (1425–1556)*, (Paris, 1957), 55–6, 79–80.

[4] Letters of 17th March, 1457, Archives nationales, P.1358[2] cote 536.

[5] Surirey, op. cit., 184–7, 195.

characteristic possibly was an uneasy neutrality in which it was possible to serve both or, indeed, many masters.

But too much generalization on this subject is probably unwise. The precise interplay of patronage and the civil service is all too little known. A civil servant, especially a courtier civil servant might become himself important; he might so embed himself at court that his patron might almost become his client. Arguably the *épuration* of officers in 1461 could be seen as the product of the accession to power with Louis XI of a party of 'outs'; arguably there was a riposte of the disinherited in 1465 with the war of the Public Weal. Admittedly the mortality in 1461 in the class of courtier civil servants *par excellence*, the *baillis*, was considerable; but it was very much less in 1465. Michel Juvenel des Ursins, who went out as *bailli* of Troyes with his brother the chancellor of France in 1461 and came back with him in 1465 is one of the few clear cases of the return of the old 'ins'; but Guillaume Juvenel des Ursins in 1461–5 was far from completely 'out'. The higher civil servant himself was an integer in the problem: he might still retain some independence of both patron and Crown.

But for these men friends, if no particular friend, were still essential. Guillaume Juvenel des Ursins was advised when he became chancellor by his brother Jean 'not to think you can resist the will of those who will be at court: because that will only have you suppressed and thrown out. It's much better to have patience and dissemble and be the cause of making less trouble, since one can't profit by being too firm and losing one's job: messire Arnault de Corbie used to . . .'.[1] To deplore the nervous strain of being a courtier was an established literary affectation. 'The court', wrote Alain Chartier, 'is an assembly of people who under the pretence of acting for the good of all, come together to diddle each other; for there's scarcely anyone there who isn't engaged in buying and selling and exchanging, sometimes their income, sometimes their old clothes—for we of the court are high-class merchants, we buy the other people— and sometimes for their money we sell *them* our own precious humanity.' The corruption of the court was deplorable. 'The abuses of the court and the habits of courtiers are such that no one lasts there without being corrupted and no one succeeds

[1] 'Jean Juvenal des Ursins', op. cit.

there without being corruptible.'[1] But corrupt, nerve-racking, or not, the court was nevertheless the source *par excellence* of political power. The problem of the control of this nuclear reactor was naturally a considerable one: it depended primarily on the personality of the king and upon the ability of the men to whom, inevitably, he was forced to delegate power. Charles VI's incapacity caused a civil war; the way in which Charles VII in the 1420s and early '30s was captured by 'favourites' has led to recondite speculation upon the state of his mental health. But in the end Charles learned how to manage the court, to choose the best man for a particular job, 'one at the war, another in the financial departments, another in the council, another running the artillery'. 'Eventually', wrote the Burgundian chronicler Chastellain, 'since he had an expert knowledge of the people around him and since he had everything under his eye, misdeeds as well as virtuous actions, it became so dangerous to be in his entourage that no one, however great he was, had the faintest idea where he stood; and so everybody watched their step very carefully, in case, if they put a foot wrong, they should be caught on the hop.'[2] This was the essence of personal rule: it was impossible to avoid the employment of men who would be remarked upon as 'most accepted the most familiar in speaking to the king';[3] it was imperative to keep them under control. Kings, Louis XI once told Commynes, do not naturally love those to whom they are beholden;[4] and certainly Louis XI was not without ingratitude. It was little wonder courtiers' nerves suffered.

But while they kept their nerve (and their place) courtiers could prosper themselves and could prosper the affairs of others. The inter-relation of the court and the powerful outside interests has not been studied for the fifteenth century:[5] but clearly such an inter-relationship existed. Amongst the *alliances* of Gaston IV, count of Foix, are two in which intimate servants of the dauphin promised to maintain him in the good graces of

[1] Alain Chartier, *Le Curial*, ed. F. Heuckenkamp, (Halle, 1899), 22, 23, 6,7.

[2] *Oeuvres de Georges Chastellain*, ed. Kervyn de Lettenhove, ii (Brussells, 1863), 183–4.

[3] Malletta on Josselin du Bois, *Dépêches des ambassadeurs milanais*, op. cit., ii (Paris, 1919), 364–5.

[4] Commynes, op. cit., i (Paris, 1924), 251–2.

[5] For a discussion of it in an earlier period, see R. Cazelles, *La Société politique et la crise de la royauté sous Philippe de Valois* (Paris, 1958).

their master:[1] such services were part of courtly existence. But the powerful outside interests, the great, had themselves a place at court; and in the same way as kingship demanded the management of the entourage, so it demanded the management in personal terms of the great. It was when such management failed, when the great left the court to nourish their grievances and dream of revenge, that the drums of war were heard. But how were these men to be managed?

The most powerful group were the magnates. They, and all nobles, faced a number of problems.[2] Their income from land had probably fallen as a result of the demographic crisis of the Black Death and the subsequent epidemics and as a result of the war; holdings abandoned to the enemy[3] might increase the enemy's spoils of war but they were clearly of little use to oneself. And the very conditions of seigneurial existence brought their own difficulties. A noble must live nobly, he must live magnificently, he must dispend. The dispendiousness of Jean, duke of Berry, 'in his time a worthy prince and honourable', who 'delighted greatly in precious stones, entertained strangers most willingly and gave them his own most liberally'[4] was legendary and the inventory of his goods after his death fabulous; but others, too, had their minor Aladin's caves; and for others, too, the claims of prestige demanded considerable expenditure. Then there were the problems of the family. The dower interests of one's mother, the claims to marriage-portions and inheritances of, especially, one's possible numerous younger sons and daughters, legitimate or illegitimate, warred in the dutiful seigneurial breast with the interest of the principal heir, the maintainer of the line. Then there were the problems of one's soul and those of one's friends and relations. Not only did prestige demand a distinguished funeral: the establishment of chaplainries, masses, perpetual lamps might lead to the nibbling away of the patrimony. Then there were the problems of living in the practice of arms: capture and ransom could be costly and

---

[1] See the article cited below (p. 20, n. 4), p. 172.

[2] For a discussion of those faced by the nobility of the south-west, see R. Boutruche, *La Crise d'une société: seigneurs et paysans du Bordelais pendant la guerre de cent ans* (Paris, 1947), 233–94.

[3] Even if the results of such patriotism could be mitigated: A. Bossuat, 'Le Rétablissement de la paix sociale sous le règne de Charles VII', *Le Moyen Age*, lx (1954), 143–44.

[4] Jean Juvenal des Ursins, *Histoire de Charles VI*, ed. Michaud and Poujoulat, [Nouvelle collection des mémoires, ii], (Paris, 1857), 532b.

even disastrous for oneself and for those loyal friends whom one could persuade to stand surety for one.[1] All of these problems could lead to dispute: with creditors, with one's indignant family and with others with some legal claim to a part of one's property, with one's indignant captors; and in the same way a conflict over one's judicial rights could arise with one's neighbours and with neighbouring royal officers. Dispute and conflict meant lawsuits; and lawsuits were costly and tiresome. The web of his own existence was something every seigneur had to come to terms with.

Not all, of course, failed to do so. The mortality rate of seigneurial families may seem to be high in the fifteenth century; but one has to allow in it for the normal failure of families due to failure to produce a male heir.[2] And there could be compensations within the web of seigneurial existence itself. Prosperous marriages might balance disastrous births and deaths: the trade in marriage-portions was not all one way. The Church was a repository made for unwanted sons and daughters; informed manipulation of customs of seigneurial inheritance might allow one to disinherit the unwanted and to create, as the Albrets created, a family inheritance custom. If the balance in the ransom and booty trade was tilted firmly in favour of the invader and his adherents at least the latter prospered amongst Frenchmen; and some loyal patriots might make a lucky windfall. An intelligent administration of one's estates might still bring in something from this failing source. But one source more might salvage especially the powerful: the patronage of the Crown, those pensions, those gifts, those offices, the struggle for which became only too clearly a large part of the content of the seigneurial attitude towards politics.

In the same way as the king pensioned the civil servants and for the same reasons of weakness as kings in France had always allowed the nobility exemption from taxation, the king pensioned the great. Up to half the revenue of the dukes of Burgundy at the turn of the fourteenth century came from such extraordinary sources; up to half the revenue of the dukes of

---

[1] A. Bossuat, 'Les Prisonniers de guerre au xvᵉ siècle: la rançon de Jean, seigneur de Rodemack', *Annales de l'Est*, 5, ii (1951), 145–62.
[2] E. Perroy, 'Social Mobility among the French *Noblesse* in the Later Middle Ages', *Past and Present*, xxi (1962), 31–2.

Bourbon in the later fifteenth century.[1] But those very acquisitions from an impotent Crown could hinder their recipients' action. At what stage, pressed possibly by the king or by his servants with or without his knowledge or consent, did one adopt the *voye de faicte*? Dunois, the Italian ambassador pointed out with his usual shrewdness in 1465, 'has lost an excellent position and eighteen thousand francs which he had from the king of France between offices and pension'[2] through his participation in the war of the Public Weal; one might easily be led to submit for gains rather less than one had hoped for when one realized that one might lose all. The unreality of politics in the later fifteenth century, the curiously ambiguous attitudes of government and magnates, stemmed from the nature of the things over which there was conflict.

The nature of the pressure the magnates felt from the 'government' naturally varied precisely from person to person. Conflict over the duke of Brittany's royal rights, conflict over the propriety of the count of Foix's ruling by the grace of God, the interminable pressure of the royal officers of the *bailliage* of Montferrand upon those of the duke of Bourbon's *sénéchaussée* of Riom, conflicts essentially of prestige and position and to a certain extent of the income which maintained both, purely human dislike between persons: these were the pressures that might drive a magnate into open resistance. The *douceurs* of favour, the settlement of conflict (temporarily) in one's terms, an increase in one's pension, even the apparent proffer of purely human affection: these were the pressures that might bring one back into the fold. Though their revolt in the 1460s might bear the proud name of the Public Weal, nothing, it could be argued, was further from its participants' minds. Any theoretical approach to politics other than the crudest seems to have passed the magnates by;[3] not because they were unsophisticated, incapable, uncultured, unintelligent, but because their position was very much one of the *status quo*, interpreted in their favour. They were rebels; but they were hardly revolutionary.

How much of a danger were they to a king determined, like Louis XI, say, not to have 'an equal in his kingdom'?[4] In time

---

[1] M. Mollat, 'Recherches sur les finances des ducs Valois de Bourgogne', *Revue historique*, ccxix (1958), 314; Surirey, op. cit., 92–7.

[2] *Dépêches des ambassadeurs milanais*, op. cit., iii (Paris, 1920), 90–91.

[3] 'Jean Juvenal des Ursins', op. cit.

[4] *Dépêches des ambassadeurs milanais*, op. cit., ii, 204.

of open conflict much depended on their wealth and their ability to raise forces; in 1465 Malletta thought 'all these *seigneurs* are short of cash or have no men except their gentlemen and subjects under their command'.[1] But what was the nature of the political pyramid beneath each prince, which might be useful not only in war but also in the no less complicated games of peace? To a certain extent there still seems to have been in France some reliance upon the purely feudal nexus: the duke of Bourbon still seems to have thought it worth while to call out his vassals and rear-vassals in Forez in April 1465.[2] But there were also more sophisticated means of linking seigneur and seigneur, seigneur and servant. Most spectacular of these, it has been alleged, were the princely orders of chivalry; but though the Burgundian *Toison d'or*, the Breton *Hermine* and the Orléans *Porc-épic* may have had a clearly political purpose, the purely chivalric seems to predominate in such exercises in an eccentric social convention as the *Ecu d'or*, the *Ecu vert à la dame blanche*, the *Fer de prisonnier*, the *Dragon* and the *Croissant*.[3] There were less cumbersome ways of collecting allies.[4] The feudal nexus had, with such things as the money fee for term of life, become etiolated enough; but with the final collapse of the idea of homage as an additional security to mutual interest it was still imagined that stability could be given to the shifting sands of interest by different oaths or by new methods of providing reward. The formal contracts, the *alliances*, which bound together on equal terms the princes of the fifteenth century are notorious; and some magnates at least experimented with the use of *alliances* with inferiors and created a diplomatic parallel to that of the English 'bastard feudalism'. In those who dealt with the administration of his estates a magnate might find a loyal nucleus for his affinity; and some seigneurs at least wooed clients with sinecure household office and pensions on the royal pattern. The acquisition of allies by these methods seems naturally to have been most rapid when magnates were faced, in the time of incompetent kings and of civil war, with the need to defend their interests: the evidence, for instance, for *alliances*

---

[1] Ibid., iii, 161.

[2] Letters of 27th April, 1465, Archives nationales, P.1402¹ cote 1225.

[3] 'Une Devise de chevalerie inconnue, créé par un comte de Foix? Le *Dragon*', *Annales du Midi*, lxxvi (1964), 77–82. See below 28–35.

[4] The sources of material given without reference in this and the following paragraph will be found in 'Decayed and Non-Feudalism in Later Medieval France', *Bulletin of the Institute of Historical Research*, xxxvii (1964), 157–84. Below 41-68.

with subordinates seems to get thinner after about 1450, though the princes had no less need to defend their interests against Louis XI than they had had against each other in earlier days. But we know all too little about French 'non-feudalism'; and how the leaguers of the Public Weal really raised their forces is throughly obscure.

How valid had these created loyalties been? Some of the *allié* families of the house of Foix seem to have shown considerable tenacity in fidelity between the 1370s and the 1440s. One should possibly not underestimate the ability of a seigneur paramount in his *pays* to command local loyalty. Of the contracts made with men further removed from the epicentre of his power one may have more doubt; their validity probably grew less as they approached those agreements of temporary convenience, the contracts in which the princes of the civil war confessed their eternal devotion to each other. For the *allié* the problem was much the same as for the client civil servant whom he resembled closely in position: at what stage was it prudent to stop risking all for one's lord? Loyalty was naturally a business much more complicated than simple apparent interest for men whose families had long attachment to those of their patrons: interest ran much deeper than the advantage of a moment. Loyalty to a seigneur in his *pays* might become inherent: in the south-west, in the north-east it might supplant the claim of sovereignty. How was a king to deal with this? The claim to rule by the grace of God was the first thing to be attacked: sovereignty was not mocked. And even loyalties apparently inherent could be sapped. Garsias du Faur, member of a loyal family of comital servants, chancellor of Jean V, count of Armagnac, expert negotiator of difficult matters, found happy employment as a president of the *parlement* of Toulouse after the fall of Lectoure.[1] The career of Philippe Pot, godson of Philippe le Bon, member of the *Toison d'or*, who abandoned the duke's grand-daughter for the novel office of *grand sénéchal* of Burgundy and a pension of 4,000 *livres tournois* from Louis XI and who was quite prepared to preach, in the interests of the Beaujeux, the doctrine of popular sovereignty at the estates general of 1484; or of Philippe de Commynes, who abandoned Charles le Téméraire for Louis in 1472 (but who ended up on the opposite

[1] A. Viala, *Le Parlement de Toulouse et l'administration royale laique (1420–1525 environ)*, (Albi, 1953) i, 124–5.

side in 1484) illustrated the way in which at times the most devoted servant might seem to be in the game for money rather than for love. The arrogation of superior interest, the creation of a greater loyalty to the Crown, were clearly necessary acts for a determined monarch. The great military *ordonnance* of 1439 forbade private armies: how much notice of it was taken by prospective commanders and prospective troops depended largely on the weight with which the royal hand was felt in their locality. Naturally a king could not rule his country without the co-operation of its magnates; but co-operation had degrees. In 1465 Malletta, who had a healthy respect for the mere force of suzerainty, thought 'the subjects of these lords [of the Public Weal] have nevertheless great fear to contradict the king':[1] a king's rule, too, had degrees.

A king must rule: the greatest trouble comes when he does not, not when he does. Chastellain clearly thought that in the end Charles VII could rule; and that Louis XI could do so many thought during his lifetime: long after his death the testimony that he was feared above all is formidable. Both he and his father faced magnate revolt; the fact that this occurred might be evidence of their failure as kings but their success in suppressing it, or in avoiding its consequences, is at least tribute to their ability after the event. 'In the kingdom of France,' wrote Sir John Fortescue with some justice, 'they've never changed their king, right from the time the country was first inhabited by the French, except through the rebellion of such mighty subjects':[2] French magnates, at least, sometimes tried like the English to kill their kings. Charles VII and Louis XI escaped assassination, death in civil war, usurpation; the *voye de faicte* succeeded only in acquiring for those who undertook it the most temporary of extra advantages. The problem of the overmighty subject was to haunt many other kings than these; and each was to fence with the spectre according to his own skill. Charles VII and Louis XI may be judged on theirs.

If the major struggles of politics were thus personal rather than 'constitutional', if the government could avoid 'constitutional' assemblies and could, on the whole, deal successfully with magnates and their political pyramids, how did those inhabitants of the kingdom who had no assembly to protect them and

---

[1] *Dépêches des ambassadeurs milanais*, op. cit., iii, 161.
[2] *The Governance of England*, ed. C. Plummer (Oxford, 1885), 129.

no wish to adopt the *voye de faicte* fare in their relations with it? Churchmen, in principle, might be pacifists *par excellence*: what was the relationship of their section of society with the Crown? Essentially, in this political context, one thinks of the upper clergy as the political group *par excellence*. Certainly it is their interests which come out most clearly in the 'Church's' dealings with the government. Their relationship was a complicated one, involved in the complexities of ecclesiastical and, later, of Italian politics. Two objects of conflict may be isolated in the three-cornered struggle of pope, king and clergy: benefices and taxation. Essentially the greater clergy were out for the maximum independence they could get; and they fought for it enshrined in the liberties of the Gallican Church, classically expressed in the Pragmatic Sanction of Bourges of 1438 but current long before, occasionally in a more violent form. The attitude of the government varied. Briefly, Charles VII accepted the Gallican Pragmatic and wooed the pope with breaches of it; Louis XI accepted submission to the pope and bullied him with threats of the Pragmatic. On the whole there was more to be got for the Crown from the second process.

But as well as having problems *vis-à-vis* the pope—and the king—*qua* taxpayers and collators, the upper clergy had their problems *vis-à-vis* the king alone *qua* tenants, immunists and mere subjects. In the estates general of 1484 they might dwell long on the Pragmatic and the 'rights and liberties' of the Gallican Church, which 'king Clovis, St Charlemagne, St Louis, Philippe le Bel, king Jean, Charles V, Charles VI and latterly Charles VII', so they imagined, had defended: but they also dwelt on its 'prerogatives, privileges, rights, immunities, liberties and franchises', grievously diminished by the government of Louis XI.[1] A considerable amount of heated information on this problem under Charles VII (to whose reputation distance lent enchantment) is provided by Jean Juvenal des Ursins, successively *évêque-comte* de Beauvais, *évêque-duc* de Laon, *archévêque-duc* de Reims.[2] The two problems of the temporal and of temporal and spiritual jurisdiction were to a certain extent confounded in that they might both be 'grieved' by the actions of the *parlement* of Paris: a court which since the earlier

---

[1] Masselin, op. cit., 663, 665.
[2] Especially in the treatise, Verba mea auribus percipe, Domine, of the 1450's [Bibliothèque nationale, ms. fr. 2701, fols. 107vb–113vb].

fourteenth century had been extending its competence over ecclesiastical affairs and whose actions created one particular aspect of 'gallicanism'.[1] *Parlement* was not necessarily prejudiced against ecclesiastics, any more than Louis XI was prejudiced against nobles; but its actions and possibly more direct ones of the government provided the stuff of ecclesiastical complaint. That the king should provide remedy 'in preserving the name *most Christian*'[2] fell on the whole on the deaf ears of those who were prepared to use sweeping theories of sovereignty to limit the jurisdiction of the Church; however much they were prepared at the same time to uphold its Gallican liberties.

Under such pressure what could an ecclesiastic do? He could complain bitterly of such tyranny; he could threaten the sanctions of moral law; he could excommunicate. But the penalties of excommunication could be avoided[3] and moral sanctions and bitter complaints broke no bones. There remained the personal influence of each churchman; but this of necessity remains obscure. Few became more openly political in defence of their liberties. There were political bishops: Martin Gouge, bishop of Clermont, Guillaume de Champeaux, bishop of Laon, Thomas Basin, bishop of Lisieux, Jean Balue, bishop of Evreux, for example; but these men were politicians, members of a political entourage, rather than ecclesiastics forced into politics by intolerable interference with the rights of the Church. They belonged to the world of the court, not essentially to that of the Church; and although it could be argued that many high ecclesiastics might have passed through the court, it is as courtiers that those who remained politicians *par excellence* should be thought of, not as churchmen oppressed by tyranny. For these there was little remedy; and their moral views provided little danger for the government.

The upper bourgeoisie, were they much danger? Again one must probably exclude the courtiers, the politicians amongst them and think only of those whom their towns thought of as 'notable people and of some rank, who would be bold enough to talk in person'[4] to the king. Jacques Coeur apart, there were

[1] G. Mollat, 'Les Origines du gallicanisme parlementaire aux xive et xve siècles', *Revue d'histoire ecclésiastique*, xliii (1948), 90–147.

[2] Masselin, op. cit., 666.

[3] M. Morel, *L'Excommunication et le Pouvoir civil en France du droit canonique classique au commencement du xve siècle* (Paris, 1926).

[4] *Registres consulaires de la ville de Lyon*, ed. M. C. and G. Guigue, i (Lyon, 1882), 331.

few great bourgeois who lived, as it were, 'bourgeoisly' in the practice of trade. Their interests on the whole were those of their town: it is as bourgeois of Lyon or of Tours or of Rodez that one should think of them in this political context. What were the interests of their towns? Again, one defines them as liberties and immunities: the privileges of the town jealously guarded against infringement, prudently reconfirmed at regular intervals, the immunities of the town in matters of jurisdiction, the liberty of the town from some forms or all forms of taxation. It was these that sent the notable bourgeois on long and perilous journeys through France at the town's expense, to the king's courts and the king's courtiers. It was in defence of these that towns offered shy (or not so shy) presents to influential people, as Millau offered its congratulations to a newly appointed official of the *parlement* of Toulouse because he 'can do a great deal of good to the commons and in particular to the inhabitants of the town' or as Lyon gave ten *livres tournois* to the dauphin's secretary in 1420 'so that he should speak well of the town to monseigneur le dauphin' when the town had failed to send him troops.[1] The backstairs representations of such urban communities were an established thing by the fifteenth century;[2] and so were remissions of taxation for such virtuous causes as urban fortifications. But such representations brought, as we have seen, their own dangers: towns delivered themselves into the hands of the wolf.

A wolf capable, like Louis XI, of ravening ravened. Remissions were still made of taxation; but the private milking of important towns was continuous.[3] And the influence of the government was not confined to this. In so far as the upper bourgeoisie, superior members of the guilds, members of that mystical *maior et sanior pars* which provided the members in turn of the smaller and upper councils of the town, felt any pressure from the inferior artisans, from the lower bourgeois of the larger and lower councils or from those who were not bourgeois at all but simple 'inhabitants', royal support in the form of favourable theoretical regulations and practical support if the *menu peuple* broke into open violence was all too desirable to them. The government had no interest in proletarian revolt; but protection, against such things as combinations, for instance, was

---

[1] Viala, op. cit., i, 158; Guigue, op. cit., i, 252.
[2] 'The Failure of the French Medieval Estates', op. cit., 14. See below 116.
[3] R. Gandilhon, *Politique économique de Louis XI* (Rennes, 1940), 286–91.

still desirable.[1] Caught between the inevitable millstones, the upper bourgeoisie had every interest in the end in playing in with the Crown.

And the *menu peuple*, in the towns, in the country, were they much danger? A combination of violent Parisians and left-wing university theorists could force a reforming ordinance out of the government in 1413. But although urban revolt was sporadic throughout the fifteenth century and although Jean Juvenal des Ursins could make dark hints of uprisings, more general insurrection is hard to find;[2] nor, even if it had come about, is it easy to see that it would have been of more danger than the *Jacquerie* or the *Tuchins*. Although it is not very likely that in 1422 the *populaires*' 'purse is like the cistern which has collected and still collects the waters and the drains of all the riches in this kingdom',[3] it still remained true that—allowing for a delay because of the war—in France as elsewhere labourers agrarian and industrial were very much better off than they had been before or, before very long, than they were to be again.[4] The seigneurial reaction of the later years of Louis XI's reign, the bad harvests of the last years: these might have been predisposing causes of revolt; but none seems to have occurred. For those who had suffered so much and who still suffered a little, it may have been that peace was worth it at any price. But peasant and urban revolts were not, in later medieval terms, serious political things.

There were those who thought tenderly of the *menu peuple*; there were forces—and not only theories of general subjection—which tended towards the unity of the orders of society (and it must be remembered that the orders were the upper orders); there were contradictory interests which cut across the stark lines which we have described; there were nobles of perhaps unusual loyalty to the Crown; there were royal officers who were prepared, on the surface at least, to protect those whom they administered from their more rapacious colleagues. On the surface of things the submarine currents are blurred, confused, less visible. And it is hard, perhaps, to justify an analysis which

---

[1] H. Sée, *Louis XI et les villes* (Paris, 1891), 30–7; Gandilhon, op. cit., 161 ff.

[2] Sée, op. cit., 176–83; 'Jean Juvenal des Ursins', op. cit.

[3] Alain Chartier, *Le Quadrilogue invectif*, ed. E. Droz, [Classiques français du moyen age], 2nd edn. (Paris, 1950), 34.

[4] E. H. Phelps Brown and S. V. Hopkins, 'Wage-rates and Prices: Evidence for Population Pressure in the Sixteenth Century', *Economica*, new series, xxiv (1957), 289–306.

shows an awareness of politics in terms of which very few people in the fifteenth century would have thought. But there are vivid flashes of insight recorded on the surface into motive and behaviour, into attitude and interest: one may perhaps make an approximation to the fifteenth-century way of thinking and the fifteenth-century way of action valid in modern terms. And perhaps as a result a number of problems are clarified.

They concern primarily the development of tyranny in France, the collapse of formal 'opposition', the birth of the *Ancien régime*. Arbitrary taxation and the over-notorious standing army were achieved essentially because of its weakness: the 'opposition' had no interest in opposing. Hostility to the government was aroused primarily by the more direct action of the king or his entourage or his servants upon some fairly powerful political figure or body. One should not underestimate the initiative of the entourage or the servants: to a considerable extent the tyrant was incapable of controlling the instruments of his tyranny. Since there was no peaceful means of expressing this hostility, if one could not remove its cause by counter-influence or counter-action in the courts, one was left with the *voye de faicte*, the way of direct action. For some groups in society this was unthinkable for practical reasons which the articulate, the literary, rationalized into principle. For some, who did not think in terms of political theory, it was thinkable: and with these rebels—or at least with their leaders—the unwieldy tyranny had, on the whole, to deal softly. Popular revolts, on the other hand, were negligible. But no one, except possibly members of the *menu peuple*, objected overmuch to the system. The practice of arbitrary rule in France was too deep-rooted for this. Yet it terrified Sir John Fortescue,[1] who had spent eight long and impoverished years in exile on the Meuse. The English were different, thought Fortescue; but for the causes of the difference between English and French society in the later Middle Ages one must retreat to the dimmest confines of their history, as one must advance into later periods to understand the consequences of the political *conjoncture* of the fifteenth century. Michelet's *vie intégrale* is not only '[ne] véritablement la vie qu'autant qu'elle est complète'; dominated by its past, it dominates its future.

---

[1] *Governance,* op. cit., 113–16; *De Laudibus Legum Anglie,* ed. S. B. Chrimes (Cambridge, 1942), 80–6.

The *Dragon* of Mauvezin-en-Bigorre, in the Pyrenees, put into the gateway in the time of Jean I de Foix, probably between 1412 and 1419, when his brother Mathieu became comte de Comminges, comte de Bigorre. Above, the banner of Béarn-Foix; below, the crest of Béarn; beneath, the celebrated motto, 'J'ay bela dama', translatable perhaps as 'I have a fine lady', or more colloquially. Gaston IV, Jean I's son, took the *devise*, 'C'est moi qui l'a'.

3

UNE DEVISE DE CHEVALERIE INCONNUE, CRÉÉE PAR UN COMTE DE FOIX?

L'érudition connaît déjà un catalogue impressionnant d' « ordres » de chevalerie établis, entre 1350 et 1450, par des princes français. La *Pomme d'or*[1], l'*Écu d'or*[2], l'*Écu vert à la dame blanche*[3], le *Fer de prisonnier*[4], le *Porc-épic*[5], le *Croissant*[6], l'*Hermine*[7], la *Toison d'or*[8], ont tous pendant quelque partie de cette période orné divers membres des corps de ceux qu'ils voulaient honorer ou attirer. Doit-on, cependant, appeler ordres de chevalerie tous ces groupements? Tel n'était pas l'avis du vieil Olivier de La Marche. « Quant ung prince donne quelque devise à plusieurs nobles hommes sans nombre et sans chapitres, écrit-il, cela ne se doit point nommer ordre, mais devises seullement », et c'est à ce titre que le fier champion de la *Toison d'or* refuse cette distinction au *Croissant*, au *Porc-épic* et à l'*Hermine*, dont le

1. Statuts : A. Jacotin, *Preuves de la maison de Polignac*, II, Paris, 1899, p. 172-73; A. Bossuat, *Un Ordre de chevalerie auvergnat : l'ordre de la Pomme d'or*, dans *Bull. hist. et scientique de l'Auvergne*, 1944, p. 83-98.
2. Statuts : *La Chronique du bon duc Loys de Bourbon*, éd. A.-M. Chazaud, Société de l'histoire de France, Paris, 1876, p. 8-15; P. Dumont, *L'Ordre de l'Écu d'or*, dans *Bull. de la Société d'émulation du Bourbonnais*, 1923, p. 46-49.
3. Statuts : *Le Livre des faicts du bon messire Jean le Maingre, dit Boucicaut*, éd. Michaud et Poujoulat, Nouv. Coll. des mémoires, II, Paris 1857, p. 255 b-257 b.
4. Statuts : *Choix de pièces inédites relatives au règne de Charles VI*, éd. L. Douet-d'Arcq, Soc. de l'histoire de France, I, Paris, 1863, p. 370-74
5. A. Favyn, *Le Theâtre d'honneur*, I, Paris, 1620, p. 730 ff. L'original du texte de Favyn était « une petite chronique manuscrite françoise composée par un herauld d'Orléans, nommé Hennotin de Cleriaux natif de Blois », que je n'ai pas pu identifier.
6. Statuts : *Œuvres complètes du roi René*, éd. de Quatrebarbes, I, Angers, 1845, p. 51-75.
7. Guillaume de St-André, *Histoire de Jean IV*, éd. dom H. Morice, *Mémoires pour servir de preuves à l'histoire ecclésiastique et civile de Bretagne*, II, Paris, 1744, col. 356-57.
8. Statuts : *Chronique de Jean Le Févre*, éd. F. Morand, Soc. de l'histoire de France, II, Paris, 1881, p. 210-54. Nous taisons ici la *devise* de l'*Echarpe d'azur*, établie par Nompar II, seigneur de Caumont, à Jérusalem en 1419 (voir ci-dessous, n. 26).

premier même n'était rien plus qu'une « confrairie ou devise »[9]. Qu'il ait cru nécessaire d'exprimer ces critiques, cela porte à croire que la discussion du sujet n'allait pas sans quelque imprécision de pensée. Certes, les statuts du *Croissant* parlent d' « ordre », comme font d'ailleurs, à propos de l'*Écu d'or* et de l'*Écu vert*, Jean Cabaret et l'auteur inconnu du *Livre des faicts*; en outre les colliers du *Porc-épic* et de l'*Hermine* étaient pour les contemporains des colliers d' « ordre »[10]. Olivier de La Marche a tenu à distinguer, semble-t-il, les ordres formels des ordres non formels, les permanents des éphémères, et ses précisions auraient été approuvées par quelques-uns du moins de ses contemporains. Le *Fer de prisonnier* n'a duré que deux ans, l'*Écu vert* cinq; et dans les deux cas les compagnons du maréchal Boucicaut et de Jean Iᵉʳ de Bourbon se sont abstenus de donner à leur association le nom d'*ordre*. L'*Écu vert* n'avait pas de titre particulier, le *Fer de prisonnier* s'appelait « compaignie »; de même le curieux « ordre » auvergnat de la *Pomme d'or* était qualifié de « alliance » : bien que ses membres appelaient leur signe « un ourdre ».

La plupart de ces groupes étaient pourtant limités quant au nombre; et parmi les plus imprécis quelques-uns ont joui d'une longue existence. Favyn en 1620 dit avoir vu des membres du *Croissant* vêtus de leurs insignes[11]. L'*Hermine,* avec de surplus le collier de l'*Épi* dont François Iᵉʳ de Bretagne l'avait dotée, a duré jusqu'en 1532 au plus tôt[12]. Charles d'Orléans, bien que sa manière négligée fasse contraste avec le protocole de la *Toison d'or,* a donné à Philippe le Bon le collier de son « ordre » quarante-quatre ans après la date supposée de la fondation du *Porc-épic*[13]. Le *Croissant* avait des officiers aux titres solennels[14] et semble avoir tenu un nombre de conseils[15]. Il se peut donc que les nuances qui séparent « ordre » et « devise » aient été trop complexes pour se tenir à l'aise dans les catégories rigides d'Olivier de La Marche. Mais la nécessité même qu'il a sentie de les établir, nous en dit long sur la matière et nous convie à lui emboîter le pas.

9. Olivier de La Marche, *Espitre pour tenir et celebrer la noble feste du Thoison d'or,* éd. H. Beaune et J. d'Arbaumont, *Mémoires d'Olivier de La Marche,* Société de l'histoire de France, IV, Paris, 1888, p. 161-62.

10. Lettres citées ci-dessous, n. 28; dom G. A. Lobineau, *Histoire de Bretagne,* Paris, 1707, II, *Preuves,* col. 628-29.

11. Favyn, *op. cit.,* I, p. 868.

12. Lobineau, *op. cit.,* I, p. 630. Un collier de l' « ordre » de l'*Hermine* était porté par le dauphin François III, duc de Bretagne, à son couronnement, le 14 août 1532 (B. Pocquet, *Histoire de Bretagne,* V, Rennes, 1913, p. 21).

13. Enguerran de Monstrelet, *Chronique,* éd. L. Douet-d'Arcq, Société de l'histoire de France, V, Paris, 1861, p. 443-44. Cf. Olivier de La Marche, *op. cit.,* IV, p. 162. Le duc d'Orléans semble avoir conféré son « ordre » à un grand nombre de personnes pendant les années 1430 et 1440 (Bibl. nat., ms. Clairambault 1241, p. 693-711).

14. « Senateur », chapelain, chancelier, vice-chancelier, trésorier, greffier, roi d'armes, poursuivant d'armes.

15. On trouvera des copies des actes des conseils tenus en 1450-52 dans Bibl. nat., ms. Clairambault 1241, p. 905-20.

Il est évident que, parmi ces associations, certaines ont été plus formellement constituées que d'autres et certaines ont duré plus longtemps. Certaines aussi ont comporté un élément politique plus important. Il est possible que la *Toison d'or* ait été, comme dit M. Pocquet du Haut-Jussé, « destinée, sous l'apparat mondain qui la décorait, à gagner au duc [de Bourgogne] une clientèle de seigneurs qui n'étaient plus ses vassaux »[16]; et que l'*Hermine,* dont le personnel semble si nombreux et si éclectique, ait été conçu dans le même but; quant au *Porc-épic* il est plus que probable que son fondateur s'en est servi pour raffermir les liens de la clientèle[17]. Les statuts de la *Pomme d'or* soulignaient que les rapports entre les membres étaient d'égal à égal, ce que répétait moins fortement Louis II de Bourbon dans son instruction à l'*Écu d'or.* Mais un prince avait bien d'autres moyens, plus commodes, d'assembler des clients et des *alliés*[18]; il avait bien d'autres options que l'ordre de chevalerie. Qui plus est, la mention du rapport d'égal à égal lui aussi se trouve ailleurs, par exemple parmi les groupements gascons et quercinois qu'ont étudiés M. Morel et M. d'Alauzier[19]. Dans les « ordres » politiques, les éléments politique et chevaleresque constituent un mélange ni harmonieux ni sans doute efficace. Il ne fait pas de doute qu'on regardait la possession de l' « ordre » d'un seigneur comme témoignage éclatant de dévouement envers sa personne; mais le dévouement peut chanceler. Comme un plein soleil qui fait irruption sur un théâtre illuminé, les réalités de la politique rendaient encore plus irréelles les mimes de l'*emprise* chevaleresque.

La dévotion religieuse, la protection des dames (des classes supérieures) et le combat à outrance : tels étaient les buts que plusieurs associations entendaient servir. L'élément religieux était particulièrement insistant dans l'ordre du *Croissant*; il réapparaît en proportion descendante dans le *Fer de prisonnier* et la *Pomme d'or.* Le service des dames infortunées, honoré au-dessus de tout par le Maréchal Boucicaut (les membres de l'*Écu vert* y étant dévoués presque exclusivement) était loin d'être négligé par Jean Ier de Bourbon et par les membres de la *Pomme d'or.* Mais c'était surtout la lice dont les joies dominaient le *Fer de prisonnier* et dont les devoirs s'imposaient à l'*Écu d'or.* Et alors que Louis II de Bourbon sommait (assez mollement) ses chevaliers de l'accompagner « là ou nous porrons trover et conquester honneur par fait de chevalerie », son fils faisait agir sur les membres du *Fer de prisonnier* des pressions autrement fortes.

---

16. B. A. Pocquet du Haut-Jussé, *Les Pensionnaires fieffés des ducs de Bourgogne de 1352 à 1419,* dans *Mémoires de la Soc. pour l'histoire du droit et des institutions des anciens pays bourguignons, comtois et romands,* 1942, p. 150.

17. Lobineau, *op. cit.,* II, p. 628-29; lettres citées ci-dessous, n. 28.

18. *Decayed and Non-Feudalism in Later Medieval France,* dans *Bull. of the Institute of Historical Research* . See below 41-68.

19. H. Morel, *Une Association de seigneurs gascons au XIVe siècle,* dans *Mélanges... Louis Halphen,* Paris, 1951, p. 523-24; L. d'Alauzier, *Une Alliance de seigneurs du Quercy en 1380,* dans *Annales du Midi,* 1952, p. 149-50.

Ce ne fut pas là la première tentative de Jean Ier de Bourbon pour s'aiguillonner lui-même et pour aiguillonner les autres à la poursuite de l'honneur. En 1406, étant alors comte de Clermont, avec Jean de Foix, vicomte de Castelbon — le futur Jean Ier, comte de Foix — il avait fait vœu, comme il dit, « pour le tresgrant desir que nous avions & avons davancer nos corps en bonne renomme par le mestier darmes... pour lamour de noz dames de porter sur nous une rondelle, un bracelet & un solleret de fer », jusqu'à ce qu'ils eussent chacun trouvé quelqu'un du côté anglais qui les acquitterait de leur vœu. En juillet, Jean de Bourbon et Jean de Foix, avec onze autres « chevaliers & escuiers, gentilzhommes de noms & darmes & sans reprouche », proposèrent une rencontre d'armes avec un semblable compagnonnage sous Thomas de Lancastre[20]. Il ressort clairement de ceci que la rondelle, le bracelet et le solleret ont été en quelque sorte les devanciers du fer de prisonnier. Mais il est possible aussi que cet incident de 1406 ait eu de l'influence non seulement sur Jean de Bourbon, mais aussi sur son « compaignon... darmes »[21] Jean Ier de Foix.

Le défi de 1406 se lit dans le ms. British Museum Add. 18840, dont les quatre feuilles de parchemin apparemment détachées sont de 266 × 196 mm et dont la lettre de forme pourrait dater du dernier quart du xve siècle[22]. La première feuille comprend le défi de 1406; la deuxième un défi des membres du *Fer de prisonnier* du 16 septembre 1414[23]; et dans les deux dernières on trouve les statuts d'une *devise* du *Dragon,* fondée par « le conte de Fouix », que nous reproduisons ci-dessous. Le ms. est une copie parfois un peu maladroite; l'orthographe de *Foix,* quoique inconnue par ailleurs, n'est pas impossible. Le texte ne nous fournit aucune indication qui permettrait de le dater. Étant donnée l'association avec les défis de 1406 et 1414, il semble raisonnable d'attribuer la *devise* à Jean Ier de Foix. Le symbole du dragon lui semble avoir été particulièrement cher. En sa jeunesse il jouta sous l'enseigne du dragon[24]; ce fut selon toute vraisemblance lui qui fit sculpter le dragon trop notoire du château de Mauvezin-en-Bigorre : un dragon qu'on retrouva au xviie siècle encore[25] dans la

20. Lettres du 6 juillet 1406 (British Museum, Add. ms. 18840, f° 1^{r.-v.}).

21. Quand Charles de Bourbon, comte de Clermont, rédigait son *alliance* avec Jean 1er de Foix, le 19 octobre 1425, il fit mention du fait que son père et Jean Ier « pour plus grant singularite de amour & aliance ilz soient compaignons darmes » (Arch. dép. Basses-Pyrénées, E 432).

22. Les quatre feuilles ont été brochées en deux paires qui étaient ensuite brochées dans le livre comme deux assemblages. Il n'y a aucune réclame sur les folios 1^v ou 2^v ; il y a une réclame gribouillée « compais [?] » à côté du dernier mot sur le folio 3^v. La reliure est moderne. Le Museum a acheté le manuscrit de Boone, le 10 janvier 1852.

23. La date de ce défi (aux fils du roi de Portugal, qui répondaient après un délai considérable, le 23 octobre 1415 qu'ils étaient, malheureusement, trop occupés en Afrique) paraît rendre nécessaire une révision de la date du 1er janvier 1415, donnée par Douet, d'après Dupuy, pour la création de l' « ordre ».

24. Miguel del Verms, *Cronique dels comtes de Foix et senhors de Béarn,* éd. J.A.C. Buchon, *Choix de chroniques et mémoires...,* Paris, 1838, p. 591 a.

25. *Le Vraye Et Parfaite Science des armoiries de feu Louvan Géliot,* éd P. Paillot, Dijon, 1661, p. 656.

chapelle du cardinal de Foix aux Célestins d'Avignon parmi un blason attribué à Jean « XV ». Ces données circonstancielles ne prouvent rien, bien entendu; mais la *devise* du Dragon n'aurait pas certainement manqué d'à propos chez le chevalier du *J'ay bela dama*[26].

Cette *devise* du *Dragon* portait plus loin encore le sentiment qui inspirait le *Fer de prisonnier*. Comme ce dernier, elle était au fond une *emprise d'armes* qui visait secondairement à encourager la conduite chevaleresque envers les dames de condition. L'idée d'aide réciproque n'affleure qu'en quelques mots du dernier article. Mais la complexité des faits d'armes est ici sans pair, tandis que l'idée d'un insigne qui augmenterait en gloire à mesure que son détenteur avancerait en prouesse n'est que du boy-scoutisme avant la lettre. Les membres du Dragon ne sont pas connus; j'ai peine à croire cependant à un élément politique de quelque importance. Quand Jean Ier de Foix (si c'est à lui que nous avons affaire) voulait lever des *alliés*, il usait de méthodes bien plus directes, les ducs de Bourbon de même[27]. Néanmoins une méthode n'en écarte pas forcément d'autres : témoins deux au moins des adhérents de Louis d'Orléans qui lui étaient liés par un triple lien, *alliance*, fonctions d'hôtel, « ordre »[28]. Il reste pourtant que le but du *Fer de prisonnier* et du *Dragon* semble plus militaire que celui de la plupart des autres « ordres ».

Peut-être convient-il de souligner que les « ordres » de chevalerie (surtout quand ils ne se sont pas ainsi nommés) n'ont pas toujours eu des buts nécessairement politiques, que l'apparat mondain n'a pas nécessairement été de pure décoration, et qu'aucune visée sérieuse ne soutient nécessairement toutes ces manifestations d'un bizarre code social. Les listes des membres de l'*Écu d'or,* de l'*Écu vert,* de la *Pomme d'or* et du *Fer de prisonnier* présentent des coïncidences remarquables : leur rayonnement géographique a été sans doute assez

26. A ce propos les épaves des statuts d'une *devise* de l'*Echarpe d'azur,* « leve » en 1419, lorsqu'il était en pèlerinage à Jérusalem, par Nompar II de Caumont, le protégé de Jean Ier de Foix, ne manquent pas d'intérêt. Elles se trouvent au British Museum, ms. Egerton 890; le texte a été publié par le marquis de La Grange, *Voyaige d'oultremer ou Jhérusalem par le seigneur de Caumont, l'an MCCCCXVIII,* Paris, 1858, mais malheureusement cet érudit n'a pas pris le soin d'indiquer qu'il y a dans la partie du ms. qui contient les règlements de l'*Echarpe d'azur* beaucoup de rayures et d'insertions faites dans une autre écriture que celle du texte, et surtout que le texte paraît ne pas contenir, soit par la faute du copiste, soit par la faute de son original, le folio qui semble avoir donné la plupart de ces règlements. Le ms. Egerton 890 semble être l'unique ms. survivant de cette partie du livre de Caumont; et puisque les statuts de Nompar II pour les membres de sa *devise,* tels qu'ils survivent, ont une ressemblance très forte avec ceux de la *devise* du *Dragon,* nous avons cru devoir les reproduire ci-dessous en marge des statuts qui étaient peut-être l'œuvre de son patron Jean Ier de Foix.

27. *Decayed and Non-Feudalism,* déjà cité.

28. *Henricus de Rothemberch miles, Barolis curie magister* est devenu non seulement l'*allié* et chambellan de Louis d'Orléans, le 20 février 1405, mais aussi membre de son « ordre » (lettres Arch. nat. K 57[a] n° 9[25]); de même Jean de La Baume, seigneur de « Valussin », le 17 mars 1405 (*Ibid.,* n° 9[26]).

étroit, mais étroit aussi le monde chevaleresque au dedans de ces limites régionales. L'existence est indéniable des ordres politiques, des ordres dont la raison d'être a été de lier le récipiendaire au seigneur patron; mais en revanche, pourquoi nier l'existence d'un monde où l'on accomplissait des faits d'armes et de chevalerie extravagants et romanesques, monde peuplé d'hommes qui avaient envie d'en accomplir et qui voulaient payer cher les récits des prouesses d'autrui? Voilà le milieu qui a quelques chances d'être celui de la *devise* du *Dragon;* c'est ce milieu qu'éclairent ses statuts, l'œuvre peut-être d'un grand seigneur méridional.

PIÈCE JUSTIFICATIVE*

British Museum, Add. ms. 18840.

fo. 3ʳ   [J]e le conte de Fouix faiz assavoir que il ma este commande de par celle que nullement escondire ne doy ne veuil que je porte sur moy en divise ung dragon dor pour emprinse darmes & aultres choses, et veult aussi que je la donne a porter a certain nombre de dames & de damoisselles, de chevaliers & descuiers[29]; auquel dragon a ungne perle au plus hault de son elle senestre, et vait ensuivant en la mesme[30] elle a ix scieges vuys, ou pluseurs aultres pierres pourront estre; et chacun qui ladicte divise portera en lieu et en temps pourra acomplir par son bon heur & travail lesdiz scieges lun apres lautre desdictes pierres, chacun en son *capitulo*[31], ainsi que apres sensuist, et ce pour aconpaignier et faire hon-

---

* Dans la transcription de ce document nous avons suivi l'usage moderne quant aux majuscules, quant à la ponctuation (sauf dans l'usage des accents et de l'apostrophe) et quant aux lettres *i* et *j*, *c* et *t*, *v* et *u*.

29. British Museum, ms. Egerton 890, f° 57ᵛ (cf. La Grange, *op. cit.*, p. 75-76) : ... comence a parler de le divize de le Eschirpe dazur que je prins a pourter audit voyatge Jerusalem. [*Dans une deuxième écriture :*] Cest le devise de lEschirpe dazur que le seigneur de Caumont a leve au voyeige Jerusalem.

[*Dans l'écriture du texte :*] Noper seigneur de Caumont, de Chasteauneuf, de Chasteaucullier & de Berbeguieres [a tous ceulx qui sont & advenir seront *rayé*] fais assavoir [« a tous presens & av(enir) » *dans une autre écriture, effacé*] que jay en « ter » pris [*l'insertion est dans la deuxième écriture*] de porter sur moy en divise une eschirpe dazur qui est une couleur que signifie loyaute a memoyre & tesmoign que « ge » [*dans la deuxième écriture*] le vueill maintenir; et en icelle eschirpe a une targe blanche a une croix vermeille, pour [ce que *rayé*] mieux [aye *rayé*] « avoir » [*dans la deuxième écriture*] en remenbrance le passion nostre sr. et aussi en honneur & souvenance de monsr. saint George [comme le plus souverain chevallier que onques fust ne jamais sera *rayé*], par tel quil luy plaise moy estre en toute bonne ayde; et hault en le targe ha escript **ferm**, en [sig *rayé*] [f° 58ʳ].

30. Ms. « mesure ».

31. Les lettres « ca » sont suivies d'un signe d'abréviation indéterminé.

neur a ladicte perle; et celles ou ceulx qui ladicte divise porteront convient avant toutes choses que elles promectent & eulx jurent de tenir les choses & articles qui sensuivent.

Premierement que les dames & damoisselles promecteront quant prendront ladicte emprinse quelles feront leurs povoirs de honnorablement recepvoir, festoier & faire bonne chiere a tous gentilz hommes chevaliers & escuiers, ou elles ne sauront aucun villain reprouche.

Item seront tenues & tenus toutes celles & ceulx qui porteront ladicte emprinse que sy le cas advenoit que len diffamast & deist mal daucune gentille femme ou gentil homme, que chacun doye dire et prier que len se veuille taire de tel langaige, car il nest ne bel ne bon ne honnorable; et ce ilz ne sen veuillent taire, qui sen departent par telle maniere que len puisse cognoistre que nul mal dire ne leurs plaist.

Item que se a nulle dame ou damoisselle len metoit sus aucun mauvais & deshonneste cas, ou que len fist aucun magnifeste & esvident tort en deshonneur ou en heritaiges, & elle se voulsist deffendre par aucun de nostre emprinse, que chacun soit tenu de prendre sa querelle & la deffendre par son corps; & par telle condition, que elle lasseurera par haulx sermens quelle ne seroit couppable de ce que len luy mectroit sus & du tort que on luy voldroit faire ou feroit.

Item que dedens ung an apres que ilz prendroient ladicte divise ilz auront a leurs requestes faictes les armes qui sensuivent, ou sen / seront mis raisonnablement en leurs devoirs.

fo. 3ᵛ   [I]tem que chacun deux requerra ung gentil homme de nom et darmes pour jouster de fer de lance, tant que lun ou lautre soit porte a terre ou navre, ou que deux lances soient brisees ou fers rompuz de droicte encontre; et apres conbatront a pye de leurs espees deux assaulx, sans hurter des corps a leurs poictrirs ne prendre aux poings: lesquelz conbatront tant que lun ou lautre soit porte a terre ou blesse, ou lespee rompue ou perdue des mains, ou que xxv coups soient feruz de[32] bort des plates en amont.

Item que les lances seront de telles longueurs comme len a acoustume de jouster en guerre.

Item que quant chacun aura acomplies cesdictes armes pourra meptre ung dyament au siege tout seul & derriere les autres.

Item que celuy qui aura conbatu en champ clos corps a corps pourra meptre pour acompaignier ladicte perle, au plus hault sciege & plus pres delle, ung rubi; et pour combatre ou champ en nombre de gentilz hommes pourra mectre un aultre ruby en la place audessoubz du premier.

---

32. Il y existe ici une petite lacune dans le texte.

Item et mesmement quil aura este en bataille sur mer pourra meptre ungne esmeraulde en la plus haulte place empres; et qui aura este en bataille sur terre pourra meptre une aultre esmeraulde audessoubz decelle.

Item pareillement celuy qui sera en guerre ou en armee sur Sarrazins pourra meptre un saphi au plus hault sciege empres; et pour aller au Saint Sepulcre pourra meptre ung aultre saphi ou sciege apres cestuy.

Item & quiconques sera en assault de place fermee poura meptre une tourquoyse au sciege ensuivant; et qui le darrain acomplir vouldra, en emcontre de guerre de 1 hommes ou plus luy conviendra trouver.

Item seront tenues lesdictes dames & damoisselles de porter ledit dragon ung an par la maniere quilz lont repceu; et au bout de lan pourront emplir les scieges desdictes pierres, ainsy que les chevaliers ou escuiers feroient quant par leurs bons heurs & travail aroient acompli les armes & voyages dessusdiz.

Item se aucun de ladicte devise fasoit aucun vil ou mauvais cas (ce que Dieu ne veuille), par lequel il ne fust digne de porter nostredicte devise, je retiens que je la luy puisse oster par plains & conseil des aultres mes / compaignons.

fo. 4ʳ   Item seront tenues toutes celles et ceulx de ladicte devise pourchasser lun a lautre bien & honneur a leurs povoirs; et quant aucun de ladicte devise yra de vie a trespas que chacun & chacune fera chanter sept messes & moy xxx pour lame de luy ou delle[33].

---

33. British Museum, ms. Egerton 890, fᵒ 58ʳ (cf. La Grange, *op. cit.*, p. 76) : [le *rayé*] « Ite » m « se » dieu « x » [*les insertions sont dans la deuxième écriture au-dessus d'un grattage*] faisoit son comandement daucun de ceux de leditte eschirpe [& ilz le saurront que *rayé*] « sceu quilz laient » [*dans la deuxième écriture*] chacun fera chanter trois messes, deux de Requiem & une de monsr. saint George pour larme dycelluy, & moy xx.
Et [apres ces choses susdit ( ) *rayé*] « oultre ce j » [*dans la deuxième écriture*] ay establi & ordonne que se null de leditte eschirpe perdoit son heritatge & navoit de quoy vivre [je soys *rayé*] « suy » [*dans la deuxième écriture*] tenus la que par luy seray requis [de *rayé*] ly [*remanié de* lui *dans la deuxième écriture*] donner & tenir son estat sellon quil « 1 » [*dans la deuxième écriture au-dessus d'un grattage*] appertiendra.

4

LE DRAGON DE MAUVEZIN
ET JEAN I COMTE DE FOIX (1412-36)

La dalle héraldique qui décore le château-fort de Mauvezin[1] en Bigorre a été, on le sait, assez discutée. Mais il y a des données, dont quelques-unes, je crois, sont restées jusqu'ici inutilisées, qui permettent de délimiter un peu le champ des spéculations: je voudrais les énumérer dans cette brève note.

Sur la dalle se trouvent trois symboles, dont chacun occupe un tiers de la hauteur. Le premier, en bas, est un dragon héraldique. Le deuxième, au milieu, est un casque vu de profil à gauche, surmonté du cimier de la maison de Foix-Béarn. Le troisième, en haut, est la bannière carrée de cette maison. Sur le fond de la dalle, de chaque coté du cimier, se trouvent les mots 'J'ay bel/le dame'.

Il paraît difficile de nier que ces mots aient formé la devise de Jean I de Foix. Il la prit dans sa jeunesse, atteste Michel du Bernis;[2] elle se retrouve, écrite après coup, sur une copie manuscrite du *Livre de chasse* de Gaston III Fébus comte de Foix,[3] qui date elle-même de la fin du quatorzième siècle; la renommée de cette devise parvint aux oreilles d'Alain Chartier;[4] Mauvezin était, rappelons-le, en la possession de Jean I depuis 1412. On a suggéré, il y a cinquante ans, que la dalle avait été placée au-dessus de la porte du château par Jean I:[5] cette hypothèse paraît tout à fait raisonable.

Cependant elle a été récemment mis en question. Une bête sculptée sur le tombeau d'Yvain de Béarn était, nous dit-on 'étrangement semblable au

---

[1] Mauvezin, Hautes-Pyrénées, ar. Bagnères-de-Bigorre, c. Lannemezan. Cette dalle fut préservée du vandalisme révolutionnaire par le lierre qui la recouvrait.

[2] 'Miguel del Verms', *Cronique dels comtes de Foix et senhors de Béarn*, éd. J. A. C. Buchon, [Choix de chroniques et mémoires sur l'histoire de France, xive siècle] (Paris, 1838), p. 590b.

[3] Bibliothèque nationale, ms. francais 619; P. Tucoo-Chala, *Gaston Fébus et la vicomté de Béarn, 1343–1391*, (Bordeaux, 1960), p. 19.

[4] Le Debat des deux fortunés d'amours, ed. J. C. Laidlaw, *The Poetical Works of Alain Chartier* (Cambridge, 1974), p. 194.

[5] A. Claverie, 'Au Château de Mauvezin-en-Bigorre', *Revue de Gascogne*, nouv. sér., xiv (1914), p. 78.

dragon vaincu et terrassé' de Mauvezin.[6] En fait, l'animal foulé sous les pieds du gisant d'Yvain de Béarn, et dont nous avons le dessin dans un manuscrit qui provient de Gaignières,[7] est bel et bien un lion, et non pas un dragon. Il n'y a donc nulle raison d'attribuer la dalle de Mauvezin au bâtard de Gaston Fébus.

Par contre, la présence du dragon peut servir à raffermir le lien avec Jean I. Dans sa jeunesse, quand il 'concebet en so coratge la sua ensenha . . .: "J'ay bela dama'"', il 'conquistet la lissa' contre un comte de Mendoza 'per lo dragon per lo qual se fazia'.[8] Le témoignage de Michel du Bernis a été repris par Arnaud Esquerrier et par Miégeville: Jean I 's'en anec en Navarra, se combatec ab lo comte de Mendossa y gasanhec la enseigna del Dragon'.[9] Il est fort probable q'un blason qui au milieu du XVIIe siècle se trouvait dans la chapelle du cardinal de Foix aux Célestins d'Avignon était celui de Jean I de Foix: un dragon aux ailes élevées, et portant lui même le casque au cimier de Foix-Béarn, y tenait contre son corps l'écu de la maison.[10] De plus, il est bien possible que ce comte de Foix ait établi une espèce d''ordre' de chevalerie à terme limité, et à fonctions purement chevaleresques, la 'devise' du Dragon.[11] Le type du dragon de Mauvezin pourrait bien avoir été celui de l'enseigne de ce groupement. Car ce fier dragon n'est ni foulé, ni écrasé. Le chef élevé, il tient dans sa griffe droite la hampe de la bannière de Foix-Béarn, qui s'étend du haut en bas de la dalle héraldique; il est couronné du casque de cette fougueuse maison. C'est un dragon avec lequel il faut compter: un dragon tout à fait approprié à Jean I comte de Foix.

Et la 'bela dama', qui était-elle? Il est probable qu'on ne le saura jamais. Le fils de Jean I, Gaston IV comte de Foix, avait, lui aussi, une belle dame. La devise, 'C'est moy qui l'a', qu'il porta aux joutes de Nancy et de Chalons en 1445,[12] complète à merveille le 'J'ay bela dama' de son père.[13] Etant donné les bizarreries du code chevaleresque, on ne peut guère prêter grande importance à une telle donnée. Quand Richard Beauchamp earl of Warwick jouta à Constance en 1414 devant l'empereur Sigismund, 'the

---

[6] M. et G. de Béarn, 'Du "Lion des Pyrénées" au Dragon de Mauvezin. Découverte de la sépulture d'Yvain de Lescar et la clef de l'énigme du "Jay belle Dame", *Revue régionaliste des Pyrénées*, xliii (1959), p. 176.

[7] Bodleian Library, ms. Gough Drawings Gaignières 5, fo. 90[r].

[8] Michel du Bernis, *op. cit.*, pp. 590b, 591a.

[9] *Chroniques romanes des comtes de Foix composées au xve siècle par Arnaud Esquerrier et Miégeville*, éd. F. Pasquier et H. Courteault, (Foix-Paris-Toulouse-Pau, 1895), pp. 67, 140.

[10] L. Galiot, *La Vraye et Parfaite Science des Armoiries,* éd. P. Palliot (Dijon, 1661), p. 656. Malheureusement l'auteur de ce livre attribue le blason à Jean XV comte de Foix.

[11] 'Une "Devise" de chevalerie inconnue, créée par un comte de Foix? Le Dragon', *Annales du Midi*, lxxvi (1964), pp. 77–84; voyez ci-dessus, pp. 29-36.

[12] Guillaume Leseur, *Histoire de Gaston IV, comte de Foix*, ed. H. Courteault, [Sociéte de l'histoire de France], i (Paris, 1893), pp. 152, 185.

[13] Claverie, *op. cit.*, p.

emperesse toke the erles lyvere, a bere, from a knyghtes shuldre, and for greet love and favour she sette hit on her shuldre'.[14] De telles amours, purement formalistes, n'étaient pris au sérieux par personne, à commencer par le chevalier-amant. Cependant, Jean I de Foix semble avoir été un peu plus fidèle à l'objet de sa devise, et peut-être son fils l'était-il aussi. Cette fidelité semble écarter l'amour chevaleresque conventionnel et fugitif, sans désignant nécessairement la femme légitime.[15] A en croire Guillaume Leseur, Gaston IV, à sa mort, fut transporté 'au haut palais'

> Lá oú fameuse Renommée le couronne
> En hault renom de gloire perennable,
> A tousjours mais, maulgré mort, perdurable.[16]

Son père lui-meme était-il devoué à cette dame à la fois exigeante et généreuse? Jean I, si c'est vraiment lui qui a établi la 'devise' du Dragon, l'a fait parce qu'il 'a este commande de par celle que nullement escondire ne doy ne veuil'.[17] C'est peut-être bien dame Renommée qui l'avait requis de créer son 'ordre' pour la conquérir; elle pourrait bien avoir cédé aux prouesses et du père et du fils. En tout cas, il n'est pas prouvé que la belle dame de Mauvezin ait été une femme en chair et en os; ne nous acharnons pas à chercher des candidates physiques à ce titre.[18]

Le problème de la dame de Mauvezin est, d'ailleurs, d'interêt secondaire. Le dragon reste l'élément le plus intéresant de la dalle héraldique du château. Comme le porc-épic de Louis duc d'Orléans,[19] cette bête était l'insigne d'un 'ordre' chevaleresque, donc distinguée de cette foule d'insignes personnels, comme pour Louis d'Orléans le loup et

---

[14] *Pageant of the Birth Life and Death of Richard Beauchamp Earl of Warwick K. G. 1389–1439*, éd. viscount Dillon and W. H. St. John Hope (London, 1914), pl. xxxiv.

[15] Rappelons, cependant, que Jean duc de Berry, à en croire René d'Anjou, était assez fidèle à son amour anglais:

> Jehan duc de Berry suis, ce de vérité saige,
> Qui en tenant prison, et pour mon père ostaige
> Le roy Jehan qui estoit ès mains des Angloiz pris,
> Je fu si ardamment d'estre amoureux espris
> D'une dame Englaische, servante au dieu d'Amours,
> Que vaincu me senty per ses gracieux tours.
> Pour elle pris ung mot, et mis soubz mon escu
> Le cygne blanc navré.

[Le Livre du Cuer d'amours espris, éd. de Quatrebarbes, *Oeuvres complètes du roi René*, iii (Angers, 1846), p. 117.]

[16] Leseur, *op. cit.*, i. 171.

[17] 'Une "Devise" de chevalerie inconnue . . .' *op. cit.*, p. 82.; ci-dessus, p. 33.

[18] Cependant, Alain Chartier regarde la devise de Jean I comme indiquant la prouesse du comte en matière d'amour plutôt qu'en matière d'honneur [*op. cit.*, p. 194].

[19] 'Une "Devise" de chevalerie inconnue . . .', *op. cit.*, pp. 77f.; voyey ci-dessus, p.29f.

l'arbalète,[20] comme pour Jean duc de Berry l'ourson et le cygne navré,[21] dont les seigneurs du quinzième siècle se servaient pour décorer leurs livres, leurs couteaux, leurs signets, et, peut-être, leurs serviteurs.[22] Les alliés de Jean I de Foix guerroyaient-ils, comme le faisaient les *retainers* des grands seigneurs anglais, en portant son insigne, soit sur leurs vêtements, soit à leur cou? Etant donné que le dragon était sans doute réservé à la 'devise', cet insigne n'était probablement pas un dragon. Mais alors quel était-il? Ou bien une *livery* de cette espèce était-elle inconnue à l'époque dans le Midi? C'est cela qu'on voudrait savoir: et voici un nouveau problème posé par le Dragon de Mauvezin.

---

[20] *Quelques Pièces relatives à la vie de Louis I, duc d'Orléans, et de Valentine Visconti, sa femme*, éd. F. M. Graves, (Paris, 1913), pp. 109, 110.

[21] J. J. Guiffrey, *Inventaires de Jean duc de Berry (1401–16)*, (Paris, 1894–96), ; voyez ci-dessus, n. 15.

[22] *Quelques Pièces relatives à la vie de Louis I, duc d'Orléans, op. cit.*, pp. 109, 110.

DECAYED AND NON—FEUDALISM IN LATER MEDIEVAL FRANCE[1]

ILLEGITIMATED by Charles Plummer and dissected by Mr. McFarlane,[2] the 'bastard feudalism' of later medieval England is comparatively well known.[3] Though late Victorian historians thought with horror of its methods compared with the purer forms of an earlier age, essentially the function of both 'true' and 'bastard' feudalism was the same. Their purpose was the acquisition of service in return for reward. They differed only in the form of the reward and in the means employed in attempting to ensure that service was indeed done in return for it. Land ceased to be the way *par excellence* of acquiring followers; payment and sometimes mere assumption of interest supplanted it. The traditional loyalties of tenure and neighbourhood were not wholly overwhelmed; but they became perhaps more obviously mingled with loyalties engendered by power and by ability. The oath and the confirmatory document were still thought of as important in ratifying a loyalty now clearly based upon self-interest; the forms and the formulae of the earlier period remained prominent in men's minds. But the idea of homage palled; a variety of oaths and documents were more to the taste of those who swore and those who contracted; and with their aid the patrons of the fourteenth and fifteenth centuries attempted to assure at least the core of that service, support and following which practical necessity and the claims of prestige demanded.

The patrons of later medieval France had no less need of service, support and following; but their attitude to the problem has not received analysis. For M. Perroy, some twenty years ago, 'contracts of retinue . . . do not seem to have existed on the other side of the Channel'.[4] But even if this were true there are enough tantalizing clues to whet one's appetite to discover some of the means by which this later medieval political society in France was put

---

[1] The following abbreviations have been used in giving references: ABP, Archives des Basses-Pyrénées, Pau; *AHG, Archives historiques du département de la Gironde*; AN, Archives nationales, Paris; ATG, Archives de Tarn-et-Garonne, Montauban; BN, Bibliothèque nationale, Paris; PRO, Public Record Office, London; SHF, Société de l'histoire de France.

In identifying *seigneuries* the conventions of the Berger-Levrault *Dictionnaire des Communes* (Paris, 1956) have been followed.

[2] K. B. McFarlane, 'Bastard feudalism', *BIHR*, xx (1943-5), 161-80.

[3] An exhaustive bibliography may be found in B. D. Lyon, *From Fief to Indenture: the Transition from Feudal to Non-Feudal Contract in Western Europe* (Cambridge, Mass., 1957), p. 252 n. 15.

[4] E. Perroy, 'Feudalism or principalities in fifteenth-century France', *BIHR*, xx (1943-5), 181.

together. It is the purpose of this article to present the results of such a preliminary investigation; and while no investigation of this subject can safely claim to be exhaustive it may at least pretend to some interest for those concerned with later medieval society both in France and in England.

To begin with that question of contract. The existence of a short-term military agreement in France has long been recognized. The existence of a 'non-feudal' agreement for life service in peace and war, a far more significant form of contract, is far less well known.[1] Admittedly its origins are obfuscated by remnants of forms more purely 'feudal'. In England the gap between the feudal contract creating a fee secured on land and the contract of service secured by indenture seems to have been crossed in one bold leap at the end of the thirteenth century. The fee secured on land was clearly essentially feudal; the contract secured by indenture equally clearly essentially non-feudal. As far as English denizens were concerned there was no stepping-stone in between. The money fee, the fee secured on an annuity, was known to the English royal chancery, though not to that of any magnate; but it appears to have been used by the Crown primarily for 'external' as opposed to 'internal' purposes.[2] In France the money fee, the *fief-rente*, was used by both king and magnates for both internal and external ends. It has, like the English indenture, been dealt with comparatively fully; its edges have been carefully defined. Even its most fragile forms, the *fief-rente* for term of life predominant in France from the thirteenth century on, the conditional *fief-rente*, may, it is argued, with propriety be called feudal.[3] But there does exist a half-world of the decayed *fief-rente* to which the description 'feudal' is almost denied. The problem is raised first by the question of the *fief-rente* for term of life created, apparently, by the grant of a lump sum.[4] Can there be a *fief-rente* without a *rente*? M. Sczaniecki did not think so; such contracts, he felt, 'appartiennent déjà à une nouvelle époque où l'on ne se soucie plus du droit et du vrai sens des institutions féodales'.[5] The shadows of this new epoch merit closer examination.

A group of some forty contracts made with Louis duc d'Orléans and his son Charles in the period 1397–1412, for instance, survives in the Archives Nationales.[6] The greater number of them were made with nobles in Germany and the Low Countries; a majority of them created straightforward *fiefs-rentes* for the term of a single life. One or two created *fiefs de reprise*: Reginald, *secundo genitus* of Juliers, for instance, surrendered on behalf of himself and his heirs a piece of property and received it again as a vassal of Louis d'Orléans.[7] Nine contracts attempted to create a fee in return for a lump

---

[1] Mr. Lyon deals with the military contract (pp. 254–61) but neither he nor M. Sczaniecki (*Essai sur les fiefs-rentes* (Paris, 1946)) touch more than very briefly upon the contract for term of life.

[2] Lyon, pp. 43, 32.

[3] *Ibid.*, pp. 61–8.

[4] *Ibid.*, pp. 71–9.

[5] Sczaniecki, p. 164.

[6] AN K 54, 56[A–B], 57[A–B].

[7] Undated letters, AN K 57[A], no. 9[8].

sum[1]; three of these, a hereditable fee.[2] Of these three, two provided for the return of the lump sum in case of default. But how precisely were Louis d'Orléans and his heirs to constrain Johann V herr von Reifferscheid in the Rhineland and his to return the 2,000 *francs d'or* granted to him and to pay damages for default, 'super quibus simplici verbo ipsius domini nostri Aurelianensis vel deputatorum ab ipso seu suorum heredum' was to be believed ?[3] As a means of control over one's vassal this provision was, to say the least, roundabout.

All that remained in this kind of contract was initial mutual interest, an initial payment hopefully revocable and the act of fidelity and homage. The only element essentially 'feudal' was the last. And if it, too, disappeared with what was one left ? On 9 July 1404 Waleran de Luxembourg, comte de Ligny and de St.-Pol, received a money fee of 6,000 *livres tournois* from Louis d'Orléans. In return, he became his man and servant and did him faith and homage. As well as this he promised him by the faith and oath of his body to help him against all men (with a few carefully defined exceptions), to preserve his interests, to warn him of trouble in store, to give him good counsel and to keep that of Louis d'Orléans secret.[4] On 23 August Edouard de Bar, marquis de Pont, promised much the same to Louis d'Orléans; he, too, received a pension of 6,000 *livres tournois*; but he did not do him faith and homage, and he did not become his vassal.[5] The chancery clerks of the duc d'Orléans endorsed Waleran de Luxembourg's letters 'Lomage monsr. de St. Pol'. They endorsed those of Edouard de Bar simply 'lettre de messr. Edouart de Bar marquis du Pont'. This distinction they were careful to preserve in their endorsement of other letters by which men became simply the *alliés*, and not the vassals, of the ducs d'Orléans.[6] In the endorsement of only one of the eight such contracts which survive did they slip up, that of Jean de La Baume in 1405.[7] But things were so confused in the matter of contracts at that time that they might well be excused.

A later hand classed all these Orléans documents as *alliances*. The term is probably best used rather more strictly, to describe documents clearly

[1] AN K 57[A], nos. 9[10, 11, 13, 15, 22, 28–31]. [2] *Ibid.*, nos. 9[11, 13, 15].

[3] Letters of 2 June 1401, *ibid.*, no. 9[11]. The provision for damages seems to rule out the possibility here of a parallel contract more purely feudal of the kind discussed by Mr. Lyon (pp. 77–9).

[4] Below, p. 178, document 1.

[5] Letters, AN K 56[A], no. 9. It is unlikely that the sentence recording homage was omitted by accident.

[6] AN K 57[A], no. 9[[1]]: 'Lettres de monsr. de Clicon par lesquelles il promet servir monsr. le duc dOrls. contre touz except. le roy nostresr. & monsr. le dalphin' [18 Oct. 1397]; AN K 56[B], no. 25[[1]]: 'Lettres du conte de Foix touch. le service quil a promis faire a monsr. le duc' [4 Apr. 1401]; AN K 57[A], no. 9[25]: 'Lettres du serement de feaulte fait a monsr. le duc dOrliens par messire Henry de Rothemberc chevalier' [20 Feb. 1405]; *ibid.*, no. 9[33]: 'Lettre de messr. Pons de Castillon par laquelle il promet service a monsr. parmi la some de C l.t. de pension quil prent chacun an de monsr.' [29 Jan. 1410].

[7] AN K 57[A], no. 9[26]: 'Lettres de lommage fait a monsr. le duc par le seigneur de La Baume' [17 Mar. 1405].

non-feudal. In that confusing period between 1397 and 1412 the ducs d'Orléans were creating money fees, fees secured by homage and a lump sum, and *alliances* in the strict sense pell-mell. The purpose of all these actions was the same. It was only the form of the contract that differed. Why one form rather than another should have been chosen is not at all clear. Some clue is perhaps given by the contracts of Bernard d'Armagnac with the successive dukes in 1403 and 1410. Of the formidable Louis d'Orléans 'Bernart conte dArmignac' became the vassal for a money fee of 6,000 *livres tournois* on much the same terms as Waleran de Luxembourg seven months later[1]; of the sixteen-year-old orphan Charles 'Bernard par la grace de Dieu conte dArmignac, de Fesen[ac], de Roudes et de Pardiac, viscomte de Fesen[et], de Bruilles et de Creissel et seigneur dez terres de Riviere, dAure et dez Montaignes de Rouuergue' became the *allié* on equal terms,[2] exchanging practically identical letters-patent and announcing with Charles d'Orléans their *alliance* to the world in letters-patent issued under both their names.[3] Bernard d'Armagnac had not only escaped from a vassalitic subordination to a son to whom he had promised Louis d'Orléans in 1403 to do homage; in entering into the grandest form of the new contracts he had escaped from all subordination whatsoever.

The difference between the old, the 'feudal' form of contract, and the new, the 'non-feudal' form, seems to find its crux simply in the question of whether or not homage was done. This may seem utterly to lack a distinction. But in lacking that distinction it provides a crossing almost without a jar from the old world of the feudal relationship to the new world of the non-feudal: from the firmest of relationships based on land and homage to the most flexible of relationships based upon a contractual expression of mutual interest. The phrases remained the same: in the least observed of those grandest of the new contracts, the *alliances* between equals which gave diplomatic form to the manoeuvrings of the princes of France in the first half of the fifteenth century, the new *alliés* promised each other much the same services as the vassal had promised his lord.[4] The only thing that changed, essentially, was the form of the obligation. Just how far the spirit of the contract had changed, at least from that of the money fee, is another matter. The real distinction was in men's attitudes to their contractual obligations and in whether they intended to keep them, not in the form of the document in which these were enshrined.

In England the break between the old and the new was abrupt. The statute *Quia Emptores* had made difficult a relationship based upon tenure[5]; the money fee had no vogue; the indenture seemed a reasonable means of reinforcing the relationship of contracting lord and man. In France 'feudalism' was more elastic: the final insignificant fracture did not come

---

[1] Letters of 17 and 18 Nov. 1403, AN K 56[B], nos. 25[2 and 3].
[2] Letters of 24 Feb. 1410, *ibid.*, no. 25[4].
[3] Letters of 29 Oct. 1409, 24 Feb. 1410 and Feb. 1410, *ibid.*, nos. 25[7, 5, 6 and 8].
[4] Below, p. 63, document 2.
[5] T. F. T. Plucknett, *Legislation of Edward I* (Oxford, 1949), pp. 107–8.

until the end of the fourteenth century. For it is not only in the administration of Louis d'Orléans that confusion is apparent. In that of the Valois dukes of Burgundy from the middle thirteen-eighties on, a flight from the purely feudal is equally evident.[1] But it is perhaps to the administration of the comté de Foix and the vicomté de Béarn that we should turn for our clearest picture both of the end of the old and of the new. For when Archambaud de Grailly comte de Foix and his two sons, the future Jean I de Foix and Gaston captal de Buch, became the servants of Louis d'Orléans in 1401,[2] the sort of contract into which they entered had long been known in the south-west.[3]

On the roll of the army which mustered at Morlaas in August 1376, addressed as 'dear friends', wooed with blandishments of honour and vague promises by the formidable Gaston III Fébus comte de Foix, were 161 'valedors de Mossenhor qui no son soos sosmes': the 'supporters' of Gaston Fébus 'who are not his subjects'.[4] Of the obligation of one at least of these men we may be quite clear. Gaillard de Lamothe had contracted to become the 'companhoo & alliat' of Fébus on 11 December 1375 and his contract survives on the register of the notary-general of Béarn.[5] No such document seems to exist in the earliest remaining register of the notary-general, for 1347-9[6]; no document of this straightforward kind appears before this contract in the second surviving register, which begins in 1371; no such document seems to survive in the Trésor des chartes de Pau. The nature of the obligation of the other 160 *alliés* of Gaston Fébus in 1376 will probably have to remain dark. But the nature of the obligation of a number of his *alliés* after 1376 and of many others of the *alliés* of his successors as comtes de Foix and vicomtes de Béarn need not remain obscure.

The origins of the non-feudal *alliance* in Béarn are probably safely enough placed in the time of Gaston Fébus. The first surviving contract seems to be that made with a group of Commingeois *seigneurs* in January 1375.[7] The original form of document seems to have been letters-patent recording

---

[1] See below, p. 57.

[2] Letters of 4 Apr. 1401, AN K 56[B], no. 25[1].

[3] The earliest such contract known to me is that by which the unfortunate Guillaume Sans seigneur de Pommiers promised to serve the father of the ultimate cause of his downfall, Arnaud Amanieu sire d'Albret, on 13 May 1358 (his condemnation in 1377 by the Court of Sovereignty of Guyenne (PRO E 101/181/6) is printed, from a copy, in *AHG*, xxvi (1888-9), 149-63: below, p. 65, document 3. The next surviving contract is apparently that between Bertrand seigneur de Montagut in the Agenais and Jean I comte d'Armagnac of 26 July 1370: below, p. 65, document 4.

[4] 'Rôles . . . de l'armée rassemblée . . . par Gaston Phoebus, comte de Foix (1376-78),' *AHG*, xii (1870), 141, 167-73.

[5] Below, p. 65, document 5.

[6] ABP III E 857.

[7] Register of the notary-general of Béarn, ABP E 302 fo. 94 r-v; printed by P. Tucoo-Chala, *Gaston Fébus et la vicomté de Béarn, 1343-91* (Bordeaux, 1960), pp. 354-5.

both sides of the contract, a copy of which was held by each of the parties to it.[1] This form continued to have a limited popularity[2]; and, indeed, under Archambaud de Grailly the mechanism of the indenture was used briefly as a vehicle for it.[3] A number of simpler forms appeared in the thirteen-eighties[4]; but the document which finally emerged triumphant as the main means of expressing the Foix *alliances* was the letter-patent, issued under a single name and seal, usually but not always recording a counter-promise to the *allié* by the comte, exchanged with the comte for one in which his obligations were presumably more fully and those of the *allié* perhaps more succinctly recorded. The earliest surviving example of this kind of document in its full form seems to be that in which Arnaud Roger de Comminges made public his obligations to Jean I de Foix in 1413.[5] A considerable number of them survive for the period before 1445.[6] There are slight variations in form; but their proliferation gives good ground for a diplomatic of the sort of relationship which they enshrine.

The *fief-rente* was, of course, well known in Foix-Béarn as elsewhere; and there was, again, a considerable amount of similarity between the duties imposed upon the *vassal* and those imposed upon the *companhon*, *aliat*, *servidor* or *valedor*.[7] But never, except possibly in one rather curious

---

[1] The document quoted above, p. 45, n. 7, takes this form as do letters of Bertrand de Lamothe seigneur de Bruch and de Clermont, of 19 Nov. 1380 (Register of the notary-general of Béarn, ABP E 304 fo. 30 r–v).

[2] *Alliances* of Nompar I seigneur de Caumont, with Mathieu de Castelbon comte de Foix, below, p. 66, document 6; of Beaumont d'Astarac with Jean I comte de Foix, 4 March 1412, in ABP E 424; of Jean bâtard d'Astarac his brother, 20 Apr. 1415, endorsed upon his brother's contract; of Guillaume Ramon seigneur de Caumont, 29 Aug. 1417, in ABP E 427; of Jean de Lamothe seigneur de Castelnau de Mesmes and de Noaillan, 26 May 1421, in ABP E 429; of Nompar II seigneur de Caumont, 30 July and 12 Aug. 1428, in ABP E 434; of Jean de Lamothe seigneur de Castelnau de Mesmes, with Gaston IV comte de Foix, 11 July 1436, in ABP E 438.

[3] Indentures of Ramon Roger de Comminges with Archambaud de Grailly and Isabelle de Foix, 11 Sept. 1398; and of Guillaume Arnaud de Lamothe seigneur de Roquetaillade with Archambaud de Grailly, 18 Sept. 1398, in ABP E 416.

[4] On 3 Sept. 1380 the notary-general of Béarn recorded that 'lo noble mossr. Ar. Guill., senhr. de Sent Blancat caualer prometo & jura sus lautar de Sent Martij en leglisie de Pau seruir "& adjudar" a mossr. lo comte contre totz homjs exceptat soos senhors, du tuut la vite deudit mossr. lo comte' (ABP E 304 fo. 25r). For other transient forms of the same decade see *ibid.* fos. 77v, 79r, 82r, 84r.

[5] Below, p. 67, document 7. On 8 Sept. 1413 Guilheis Unaut de Lanta seigneur de 'Mausac', had made a contract in this form with Jean I comte de Foix; but it omits two important clauses (in ABP E 425).

[6] In ABP E 425, 427–9, 432, 434, 435, 437–9. Numbers by years, including renewals: for 1413, 3; 1414, 1; 1415, 1; 1418, 1; 1420, 2; 1421, 1; 1422, 5; 1423, 1; 1424, 2; 1425, 4; 1426, 5; 1427, 4; 1428, 1; 1429, 1; 1431, 5; 1432, 3; 1434, 3; 1436, 4; 1437, 1; 1438, 9; 1439, 3; 1440, 1; 1441, 1; 1444, 1.

[7] The text recording the grant of a *fief-rente* printed by Tucoo-Chala, pp. 361–2, is typical of a number to be found in the registers of the notary-general of Béarn, ABP E 302 and 304.

case,[1] were the terms which implied vassality allowed to become anything other than completely distinguishable from those which implied *alliance*; never was the formal difference between the manners of their obligation allowed to become blurred. The precise form of homage was regarded as stereotyped in Béarn[2]; and the precision of the common form was carefully observed.[3] Although some of the ritual of homage took place at the making of one or two of the earlier contracts[4] it appears to die out at least of the documents recording them. The oaths which accompanied the *alliance* in Foix-Béarn seem to have been distinct from those which accompanied homàge.[5] The reign of Gaston Fébus seems again to have been the period of experiment[6]; but it was the common oath upon the Gospels that won in the end. Other

---

[1] The indenture of Guillaume Arnaud de Lamothe seigneur de Roquetaillade of 18 Sept. 1398 in ABP E 416 is endorsed, 'Carta de Guilhem Ar. sr. de Rochatalhade dijt lo homj de La Mota cum ses feyt homi de mossr. lo comte per ij^c floris darrenda que eg la promes de dar cascun an a la festa de Totz Santz'. His contract with Jean I comte de Foix of 2 Aug. 1422 in ABP E 432 is endorsed 'Liansse de lomj de La Mota'. The insistence upon the title of Guillaume Arnaud de Lamothe seems to point at least to its being unusual.

[2] The forms of homage in Béarn do not seem to have changed very radically between the late 1300s and the early 1400s (see those recorded in ABP E 300, 302, 304, 314 and 321). Of the documents recording them the notary-general of Béarn noted simply 'fiat in forma juxta cursum generale[m] &c' (ABP E 302 fo. 4v), 'fiat in bona forma juxta cursum generalem' (*ibid.* fo. 9v), 'fiat in forma &c' (*ibid.* fo. 75v), 'fiat in forma' (ABP E 304 fo. 3r), 'sie feites segont lestil comu de las cartes deus homenatges' (*ibid.* fo. 33v).

[3] Of a homage taken on 24 Feb. 1376 the notary-general noted 'fiat in bona forma juxta cursum excepto osculo & fo lo sus "sus" "[en Crotz *crossed out*] los Santz Euuangelis de Diu" [en vn breujari "en abscencie de missau & de Crotz" *crossed out*]' (ABP E 302 fo. 131r).

[4] Gaillard de Lamothe in 1375 obliged himself 'tocan sa maa dextre en la maa deudijt mossr. de Foixs e baisan en sa boque' (below, p. 66., document 5); Ramon Roger de Comminges vicomte de Couserans and Archambaud de Grailly comte de Foix 'sen toquan la j a lautre ab lors maas dretas e sen baysan en lors bocas' (indenture of 11 Sept. 1398 in ABP E 416).

[5] Again there are a few exceptions: the contracts of Ramon Roger de Comminges vicomte de Couserans of 11 Sept. and of Guillaume Arnaud de Lamothe seigneur de Roquetaillade of 18 Sept. 1398 were made 'sus lo libre missau e la Crotz benedite desus lo Te igitur pausada' (indentures in ABP E 416); those of Huc vicomte de Caraman and his eldest son Jean of 22 Sept. 1427 (letters in ABP E 434) and of the señor de Gavin and his sons of 6 Sept. 1434 and of 18 Aug. 1436 (letters in ABP E 437 and 438) were made upon the Cross and the *Te igitur*.

[6] Guillaume Sans seigneur de Pommiers swore to Bernard Ezi II in 1358 upon an altar (below, p. 64, document 3); and so did Arnaud Guillaume seigneur de St.-Blancard to Gaston Fébus on 3 Sept. 1380 (ABP E 304 fo. 25r) and a number of other seigneurs (on a number of different altars) to Fébus in the 1380s (*ibid.* fos. 28r, 33r, 82r, 84r). Bertrand de 'St.-Artemie' of Quercy promised 'sus la fee de son cors & sus pene destre faus & mauuat & sus totes las penes que hom li poyra metre sus' and swore upon the altar of the chapel of Orthez castle on 2 Jan. 1389; Jean de 'Chombile' of Quercy promised and swore on the *Te igitur* as well as on the Gospels on 12 March 1389 (letters in ABP E 412).

forms of promise and oath appeared later[1]; but they did not shake the pre-eminence of the *Saints-Evangiles*.[2]

The comtes de Foix expected from their *alliés* much the same sort of general agency and informal intelligence service as they and others had expected from their vassals.[3] And in their general obligation of this kind to their lord the *alliés* of the comtes de Foix stood to him much as the retainers in England of, for instance, Lord Hastings in the fourteen-seventies, who promised 'to be unto him faithful and true servant[s] and to do him faithful, true and diligent service and his part to take against all men',[4] stood to theirs. And much as most of the Hastings indentures had a more or less strong military flavour so did most of the Foix *alliances*.[3] Some contracts were more specific than others on the question of harbouring, of payment for harbouring and of payment for the *allié*'s own contingent in the comte de Foix's service[5]; but most were content to leave the question of obligation in war, like that of obligation in peace, in general terms. In their obligation in turn to their retainers the comte de Foix and Lord Hastings again matched very closely. As Lord Hastings promised Henry Willoughby in 1477 'to be his good, loving and favourable lord and him aid, help, succour and sup-

---

[1] For example: upon God: Gaillard de Durfort (letters of 17 Sept. 1414, in ABP E 425 and of 17 Aug. 1436, in ABP E 348), a unique example; 'sus ma bone fe cum a leyau caualer': Arnaud Roger de Comminges (below, p. 67, document 7); 'sus pene destre faus et maubat': Nompar seigneur de Caumont (letters of 30 July and 12 Aug. 1428, in ABP E 434); 'sur la foy et serement de mon corps et sur mon honneur': Aymerigon seigneur d'Estissac (below, p. 67, document 8); 'sur ma part de Paradis': Pierre de Louvain (letters of 13 Nov. 1438, in ABP E 438). The last four oaths were used in Foix-Béarn only to reinforce those upon God or the Gospels. Cf. the oaths taken by some of the Hastings retainers in England (W. H. Dunham jr., 'Lord Hastings' indentured retainers 1461–83', *Transactions of the Connecticut Academy of Arts and Sciences*, xxxix (1955), 48).

[2] Although proctors could negotiate and swear on their principals' behalf to observe the conditions of the contract, ratification and an oath in person seem to have been usual: an *alliance* made in Apr. 1415 by the proctors of Bertrand seigneur de Montferrand, for instance, was sworn to by him upon the Gospels on 31 July (letters in ABP E 427). In the case of Nompar de Caumont's *alliance* with Mathieu de Castelbon comte de Foix in 1394 a proper seal was regarded as important (below, p. 66, document 6) but a number of cases of a borrowed seal occur: Jean de 'Chombile' on 12 March 1389, for instance, borrowed that of his fellow-Quercynois the seigneur de Puycornet (letters in ABP E 412). There appear to have been no rules about signature or about witnesses.

[3] See, for instance, the obligations of Aymerigon d'Estissac (below, p. 67, document 8).

[4] Indenture of Henry Willoughby of 28 Feb. 1478 (Dunham, *ubi supra*, p. 129).

[5] Payment for harbouring occurred mainly in documents of the 1430s; see, for instance, the contract of Aymerigon d'Estissac (below, p. 67, document 8). The contract arranged by the proctors of Bertrand seigneur de Montferrand in 1415 stipulated that Jean I de Foix should pay 'audiit sr. de Monferran et assas gens qui menera los guages aixi cum fare aus autres sons aliatz' (letters of 19 Apr. 1415, in ABP E 427). Payment seems in fact to have been so normal a thing since at least the time of Gaston Fébus (see the arrangements for payment in 1376, 'Rôles de l'armée', *AHG*, xii. 142) that not much mention was made of it.

port in all his matters according to the law',[1] so Gaston IV de Foix, according to Pierre de Louvain, promised him 'de soccourer et aydier, se besoing me faisoit, selon semblant seigneur que vous estez doit soccourir et aydier assemblable alie & serviteur que je suis'.[2] There is an echo here from an earlier age[3]; but good-lordship was not confined to England.

But, admittedly, unlike the Hastings indentures (and more, indeed, in conformity with the general run of English contracts) a minority of the Foix *alliances* provided for more specific reward. For the grander of the comte de Foix's clients the contemplation of the ancient friendship shown and honour done by the comital house to theirs may have been, as they claimed,[4] reason enough for them to continue in that relationship with him; others possibly needed to be attracted with lures more substantial. Pensions seem to have been given throughout the period covered by the surviving contracts, from Beaumont d'Astarac's annuity of 200 *florins béarnais* in 1412[5] to François de Montferrand's of 200 *francs bordelais* in 1440.[6] In 1431 Bernard Aubert of Roussillon received 'la rende & emolmentz apperthientz a la baronie de Castelbielh estiem de La Marque en Penedes qui bos me auetz donat a tote ma vite'.[7] A lump sum was occasionally given, again throughout the period: that of 1,800 *moutons* granted to Jean vicomte d'Uzès in 1431[8] remained capped by one of 2,000 *écus* given in 1429 to Jean comte d'Astarac on top of a pension of 500 *florins aragonais*.[9] But, on the whole, the nature of the client's interest, like that of the lord, was left in general terms. The *alliés* of the comtes de Foix knew what their duty was; and when they in turn claimed his 'amparance, protection, socors, ajude e deffensse',[10] they knew what they required of his good-lordship. Further reward was hardly necessary, for instance, for those who followed Jean I to court in 1425. For Jean Roger de Comminges seigneur de Tarride,[11] or for Jean comte d'Astarac,[12] the profits of good-servantship were obvious to all.

But did the *alliés* of south-west France incur that stigma of infidelity which characterized the retainer in England? Was the characteristic of the non-

---

[1]See p. 48, n. 4.

[2]Letters of 13 Nov. 1438, in ABP E 438.

[3]See, for instance, the obligations of Gaston Fébus to his vassal the seigneur de Curton (Tucoo-Chala, p. 361).

[4]As, for instance, did Arnaud Roger de Comminges (below, p. 167, document 7).

[5]Letters of 4 March 1412, in ABP E 424.

[6]Letters of 29 March ' 1439' (= 1440 ?), in ABP E 438.

[7]Letters of 2 Sept. 1431, in ABP E 435.

[8]Letters of 27 Aug. 1431, *ibid.*

[9]His heir was to return the 2,000 *écus* to Jean I's heir if he failed to keep the *alliance* (letters of 28 March ' 1428' (= 1429 ?) in ABP E 434).

[10]Letters of Jeanne de Voisins dame de Mirepoix and de Lagarde, as guardian of Philippe de Lévis-Mirepoix her son, of 5 Sept. 1418, in ABP E 428.

[11]*Alliance* with Jean I comte de Foix, 15 Dec. 1413, in ABP E 425; pension of 1,000 *livres tournois* from the Crown, 15 Dec. 1425 (G. Du Fresne de Beaucourt, *Histoire de Charles VII* (Paris, 1881–91), ii. 119 n. 3).

[12]*Alliance* with Jean I comte de Foix, 18 June 1423, in ABP E 432; gift of 2,000 *livres tournois* from the Crown, 1 Dec. 1425 (Du Fresne de Beaucourt, ii. 119).

feudal contract in France, too, a disrespect for irrefrangibility ?[1] Some clauses in the documents creating the Orléans *fiefs-rentes* might allow one to doubt that of the last feudal form of contract. 'Pierre sire de Cronebec & de Neufchastel', for instance, was quite prepared to serve Louis d'Orléans against those to whom he had previously done similar homage or of whom he held in fee; he simply wanted to be indemnified for any damage this infidelity might cause.[2] As an *allié* of Charles d'Orléans, Jean comte d'Alençon was equally prepared to disregard any *alliances* that he might have with his dearly beloved brother the duke of Brittany.[3] But the breach of an *alliance* might in principle be actionable at law: one made between Louis II duc de Bourbon and Humbert seigneur de Villars in 1402 offered the latter a remarkable though perhaps not unusual list of courts ecclesiastical and secular in which a case concerning it might be brought.[4] Yet a royal command could in principle at least dissolve an *alliance*: in this way Charles VI attempted to annul a web of magnate contracts in 1412[5]; in this way he attempted to annul the obligations of Agne III de La Tour seigneur d'Olliergues in 1413 and attach him to himself.[6] And an *allié* could be released from his oath by an ecclesiastical relaxation: Bernard d'Armagnac comte de Pardiac and Jean I de Foix promised each other that such relaxation should be null in their *alliance* of 1432.[7] But at least it was felt necessary that such tiresome manoeuvres should be gone through. When François de Montferrand seigneur d'Uza was in the process of arranging a contract with Gaston IV de Foix in 1440 he had to promise to release himself from an anterior *alliance*

---

[1] McFarlane, *ubi supra*, pp. 174 ff.

[2] Letters of 21 Apr. 1401, AN K 57[A], no. 9[9].

[3] Letters of 26 Feb. 1411, *ibid.*, no. 1[6].

[4] 'Et a voulu & vuelt ledit monsr. le duc estre compelli et contraint par les cours, juridicions & compulsions de lempereur de Rome, du roy nostre sr., de la chambre du pape, du petit seel de Montpellier & de toutes autres cours espirituelles & seculieres que ledit monsr. de Villars vouldra eslire, & par chascune dicelles conjonctement ou particulierement, a tenir, garder & acomplir les choses dessusdictes; et quant a ce a soubsmis & obligie lui & ses biens, terres & seignories quelxconques a la cohercion desdictes cours & juridicions & de chascune dicelles; et voulu que par lexecution de lune lautre ne soit empeschee ou retardee' (letters of 18 Aug. 1402, AN P 1391[1], cote 529). The contract of Archambaud de Grailly and his sons with Louis d'Orléans (cited above, p. 49;) was made specifically obliging their goods, as were, amongst the Foix *alliances*, those of Jeanne de Voisins (cited above, p. 45, n. 10) and of Nompar II de Caumont of 21 May 1439 (letters in ABP E 438; cf. ABP E 319 fos. 113v–114v).

[5] Letters of 22 Aug. 1412, AN K 57[B], no. 20 (printed in *Choix de pièces inédites relatives au règne de Charles VI*, ed. L. Douët d'Arcq (SHF, Paris, 1863–4), i. 352–3, hereafter referred to as Douët d'Arcq). The *alliances* of the Orléans princes with the English were renounced the following day (letters of the duc d'Orléans, AN K 57[B], no. 22; of the comte de Vertus, *ibid.*, no. 21).

[6] Agne III had become the *allié* of Jean I duc de Bourbon on 28 May 1413 (letters, AN P 1358[2], cote 588[(1)]). He was released also 'pour ceste foiz et quant a ce cas tant seulement' from any tie of liege homage (letters of 11 Nov. 1413, AN R[2] 3, no. 68).

[7] Letters of 7 July 1432, in ABP E 435; printed by L. Flourac, *Jean I comte de Foix* (Paris, 1884), pp. 295–8.

with Charles II d'Albret.[1] One could not be entirely informal in one's treachery.

The *alliances* of the comtes de Foix were normally made for life: that is, no shorter term is ever mentioned. But renewal of the *alliance* after the death of the party on either side was far from uncommon. Aymerigon d'Estissac, the *allié* of Jean I in 1425,[2] became the *allié* of his son Gaston IV in 1439;[3] and he was by no means alone in his fidelity.[4] The interest of the patron's heir could be protected in an *alliance*;[5] and an *allié* could promise in turn the service of his. A contract made by the seigneurs de Duras, de Lesparre and de Montferrand with Archambaud de Grailly as captal of Buch in 1394 was made for themselves and for their sons.[6] The son of the seigneur de Duras ratified it with Jean I de Foix in 1414, made another *alliance* with Gaston IV in 1436 and in 1440 promised to have it ratified by his son in turn when he reached a proper age.[7] In the same way the contract with the seigneurs de Montferrand was ratified and renewed in 1415 and in 1429.[8] The house of Caumont seems to have served that of Foix as steadily from at least 1394 onwards as those of Durfort and Montferrand.[9] The pious preambles of the grander clients were thus not wholly without content; and the stability of some of their relationships with the comtes de Foix does not seem to be doubtful.

Fidelity and infidelity was not in any case a matter of stark black and white. The *alliance* had inherited from the *fief-rente* a capacity for being conditional. A considerable number of sovereign *seigneurs*, patrons, friends and relations could live together in all amity in the loyalty of a client; it was simply a matter of establishing the precedence of their claims upon his

[1] Letters of 29 March '1439' (= 1440?), in ABP E 438.

[2] Letters of 12 Sept. 1425, in ABP E 432.

[3] Below, p. 67, document 8.

[4] Similar renewal of *alliance* was made by Jean de Lamothe seigneur de Castelnau de Mesmes (letters of 11 July 1436), Gaillard de Durfort seigneur de Duras (letters of 17 Aug. 1436), Guirault Avarcha señor de Gavin and his three sons (letters of 18 Aug. 1436), Jean Roger de Comminges vicomte de Couserans (letters of 4 Jan. 1438, in ABP E 438), Jean Dacx seigneur de 'Brutalhs' (letters of 13 Oct. 1438, in ABP E 322), Nompar seigneur de Caumont (letters of 21 May 1439, in ABP E 438); Etienne de Vignolles *dit* La Hire (letters of 4 March 1441, in ABP E 439).

[5] Pierre de Louvain, for instance, promised to serve for the term of his life both Gaston IV de Foix and his heir (letters of 13 Nov. 1438, in ABP E 438).

[6] Referred to (without date) in letters of Gaillard de Durfort of 17 Sept. 1414, in ABP E 425; dated 26 Aug. 1394 in those of Bertrand de Montferrand's proctors and of Jean I de Foix, both of 19 Apr. 1415, in ABP E 427; dated 26 Aug. 1393 in letters of Jean I de Foix of 26 Aug. 1429, in ABP E 434.

[7] Letters of 17 Sept. 1414, in ABP E 425, of 17 Aug. 1436 and of 28 March '1439' (= 1440?), in ABP E 438.

[8] Letters of Bertrand de Montferrand's proctors and of Jean I de Foix, cited above, n. 6.

[9] Its service can be traced through letters of Nompar I de Caumont of 11 May 1394 (below, p. 66, document 6); of Guillaume Ramon II de Caumont of 29 Aug. 1417, in ABP E 427; of Nompar II de Caumont of 30 July and 12 Aug. 1428, in ABP E 434 and of 21 May 1439, in ABP E 438.

affections. In their contracts the *alliés* of the comtes de Foix, like the *alliés* of other magnates, made regular provision for excepting such anterior interests. They could thus quite properly, according to the terms of their contracts, serve against their new lord; or they could contract particularly to stand neutral in any conflict between him and another to whom they owed an older loyalty. Pes seigneur de Puyloaut, for instance, excepted from his *alliance* with Jean I de Foix in 1431 the king of England, duke of Guyenne and the seigneur de Lescun; and he agreed to stand neutral in any conflict between the sire d'Albret and the comte de Foix.[1] If loyalties overlapped at least some attempt was made formally to arrange for the settlement of discord between them.

Multiple loyalty, of course, posed its problems; but, paradoxically, some of these arrangements again display the tenacity of previous agreements. Jean Ferran seigneur de Mauvezin and his sons, Amanieu de Lana and the seigneur de Xaintrailles were amongst the thirty-odd 'adherens, companhons et servidors' in the Bordelais and the Bazadais of Charles I d'Albret and his mother in 1407.[2] Amanieu de Lana seigneur de Causiede became the *allié* of Jean I de Foix in May 1422, Bernard Ferran seigneur de Mauvezin the *allié* of Jean I a month later and Jean seigneur de Xaintrailles the *allié* of Jean I in September 1426.[3] All were careful to except Charles II d'Albret from their *alliances*. In these cases at least a relationship had withstood a death on one or both sides and had survived nearly twenty years. And in the opposite direction, as it were, Nompar II de Caumont was careful to except Jean I de Foix in his *alliance* with Charles II in January 1428.[4] He may not even have been Jean I's *allié*: Guillaume Ramon II de Caumont his father had become the servant of Jean I in 1417 but Nompar's *alliance* with him was not made until July and August 1428; and it was renewed with Gaston IV in 1439.[5] We should perhaps be careful of underestimating the amount of stability of relationship which these contracts reflected in the south-west.

Doubtless one would be rash to assert the complete irrefrangibility of contracts of *alliance*. But a large number of them were made freely; self-interest, at least at the time of their making, must have been consulted; the conflicting pull of major and minor interests could be accommodated; and those made between magnates and local *seigneurs* in the areas in which their

[1] Letters of 14 June 1431, in ABP E 435.

[2] 'Trève accordée par le sénéchal de Guyenne aux seigneurs du Bordelais et du Bazadais, qui tiennent le parti du seigneur d'Albret (22 avril 1407),' *AHG*, vi (1864), 220.

[3] Letters of 29 May and of 19 June 1422, in ABP E 432; of 14 Sept. 1426, in ABP E 434.

[4] Letters of 12 Jan. 1428, in ABP E 62.

[5] Letters cited above, p. 51, n. 9. He had, admittedly, been 'norri' by Jean I and had entrusted his lands to him before his departure on pilgrimage to Jerusalem in 1419 (Brit. Mus., Egerton MS. 890, fo. 8r; printed by le marquis de La Grange, *Voyaige d'oultremer ou Jhérusalem par le seigneur de Caumont l'an MCCCCXVIII* (Paris, 1858), p. 9).

influence was greatest had *prima facie* a chance of survival. It was with such local *seigneurs* that the majority of the Foix *alliances* was made. The *alliés* mustered at Morlaas in 1376 had come from Bigorre, from the Basque coast and Navarre, from the *prévôté* of Saint-Sever, from the Carcassès, from the Agenais, from Astarac, from L'Isle-Jourdain, from the Bordelais, from the Toulousain and from the Lauragais[1]; and this firmly eclectic habit of mind remained characteristic of the comtes de Foix. Their clients were chosen for their usefulness and without regard for the wavering frontier of sovereignty.

Those members, for instance, of the houses of Montferrand,[2] Durfort[3] and Caumont[4] who were, according to the surviving contracts, the most loyal *alliés* of the comtes from Gaston III to Gaston IV were at the same time amongst the main props of the English régime in Guyenne to the very end.[5] Gaillard III de Durfort seigneur de Duras who mustered at Morlaas in 1376[6] was seneschal of Aquitaine for the English between 1399 and 1415.[7] Gaillard IV de Durfort his son who contracted with Jean I in 1414 and with Gaston IV in 1436[8] was *prévôt* of Bayonne from 1423,[9] *sénéchal* of the Landes for the English in 1434.[10] Nompar I de Caumont, the *allié* of Mathieu de Castelbon in 1394,[11] was *sénéchal* of the Agenais for the English in 1399.[12] Bertrand II seigneur de Montferrand, baron of the duchy of Aquitaine,[13] the *allié* of Gaston Fébus and of Archambaud de Grailly,[14] was *sénéchal* of the Landes in 1401[15]; and François de Montferrand seigneur d'Uza and de Belin, his younger son, who contracted with Gaston IV in 1440,[16] was *sénéchal* of the Landes two years later.[17] He and Jeannot his son

---

[1] 'Rôles de l'armée,' *AHG*, xii. 167–73.

[2] Seigneurs de Montferrand [Gironde, ar. Bordeaux, c. Carbon-Blanc, com. Bassens]; A. Communay, *Essai généalogique sur les Montferrand de Guyenne* (Bordeaux, 1889), pp. xvi–xlix.

[3] Seigneurs de Duras [L. & G., ar. Marmande, ch.-l. c.] and Blanquefort [Gironde, ar. Bordeaux, ch.-l. c.]; J. Faure, *Précis historique sur la famille de Durfort-Duras* (Marmande, 1858), pp. 31–47.

[4] Seigneurs de Caumont [L. & G., ar. Marmande, c. Mas-d'Agenais].

[5] R. Boutruche, *La Crise d'une société: paysans et seigneurs du Bordelais pendant la guerre de Cent ans* (Paris, 1947), pp. 79–80.

[6] 'Rôles de l'armée,' *AHG*, xii. 170.

[7] Indenture of appointment, 23 Dec. 1399 (PRO E 101/68/6/148); E. M. J. G. Dupont-Ferrier, *Gallia regia* (Paris, 1942–61), nos. 13451, 13453.

[8] Letters cited above, p. 51, n. 7.

[9] T. Carte, *Catalogue des rolles gascons, normans et françois* (1743), i. 205; *Foedera* ..., ed. T. Rymer (The Hague, 1740), IV. iv. 94 (hereafter referred to as Rymer).

[10] Dupont-Ferrier, no. 13863.

[11] Below, p. 66, document 6.

[12] Carte, i. 182; indenture of appointment, 18 Feb. 1400 (PRO E 101/69/2/302).

[13] Carte, i. 192.

[14] 'Rôles de l'armée,' *AHG*, xii. 171; letters cited above, p. 51, n. 6.

[15] Dupont-Ferrier, no. 13859.

[16] [Uza, Landes, ar. Dax, c. Castets; Belin, Gironde, ar. Bordeaux, ch.-l. c.]. Letters of 29 March '1439' (= 1440?), in ABP E 438.

[17] Dupont-Ferrier, no. 13865.

who shared his *alliance* were, with Gaillard IV de Durfort, amongst the comparatively few to suffer in the final débâcle of 1453.[1] But it was not only the great in Guyenne who sought the patronage of the comte de Foix: Pes de Puyloaut,[2] whose forebear had mustered at Morlaas in 1376 and whose *seigneurie* in the Landes was turned into a barony in 1448[3]; Sampson de Montbrun,[4] *bailli* of Bazas in 1423,[5] *castellan* of Gamarde in 1430–8,[6] are two of the better-known of a group of minor *seigneurs* from the far west who were *alliés* of the comtes from the reign of Gaston Fébus on.[7]

A list precisely similar of loyal adherents of France is easily drawn up. Jean de Bonnay, *sénéchal* of Toulouse from 1414 until he died in office in 1439, captain general in Guyenne in 1425,[8] became the *allié* of Jean I in 1426.[9] Naudonet de Lustrac, the *allié* of Jean I in 1432,[10] was captain in the period 1428–57 of a number of places in the south-west, *sénéchal* of the Agenais and Gascony for Charles VII in 1435–42, in 1437 an *écuyer de l'écurie du roi*.[11] Bernard Ferran seigneur de Mauvezin, *chevalier chambellan*

---

[1] Jeannot de Montferrand probably died in England ('Enquête sur les seigneurs de Fronsac (18 juin 1483)', *AHG*, xiii (1871–2), 89). The names of some 40 emigré nobles are known (A. Peyrègne, 'Les émigrés gascons en Angleterre (1453–1485)', *Annales du Midi*, lxvi (1954), 115).

[2] Letters of 14 June 1431, in ABP E 435.

[3] 'Rôles de l'armée,' *AHG*, xii. 169; Carte, i. 232.

[4] Letters of 12 Oct. 1438, in ABP E 438; described as 'de Gosse [Landes, ar. Dax, c. Montfort-en-Chalosse] en la senescaucie de las Lanes'.

[5] Carte, i. 204.

[6] Gamarde-les-Bains, Landes, ar. Dax, c. Montfort-en-Chalosse; Carte, i. 211, 216, 218.

[7] 'Rôles de l'armée,' *AHG*, xii. 168–72; letters of Bertrand de Lamothe seigneur de Bruch [L. & G., ar. Nérac, c. Lavardac] et de Clermont [Clermont-Dessous, L. & G., ar. Agen, c. Port-Ste.-Marie] of 19 Nov. 1380, ABP E 304 fo. 30r–v; of Guillaume Arnaud de Lamothe seigneur de Roquetaillade [Gironde, ar. & c. Langon, com. Mazères] of 18 Sept. 1398, in ABP E 416 and 2 Aug. 1422, in ABP E 432; of Jean de Lamothe seigneur de Castelnau de Mesmes [Gironde, ar. Bazas, c. Captieux, com. St.-Michel de Castelnau] et de Noaillan [Gironde, ar. Langon, c. Villandraut] of 26 May 1421, in ABP E 429 and 11 July 1436, in ABP E 438; of Arnaud Guillaume seigneur de Poyanne [Landes, ar. Dax, c. Montfort-en-Chalosse] of 15 March 1424, in ABP E 432; of Jean seigneur de Xaintrailles [L. & G., ar. Nérac, c. Lavardac] of 14 Sept. 1426, in ABP E 434; of Jean Dacx seigneur de 'Brutalhs en la senescaucie de las Lanes' of 22 Jan. 1432, in ABP E 435 and of 13 Oct. 1438, in ABP E 322; of François seigneur de Grammont [in Navarre], de Mussidan [Dordogne, ar. Périgueux, ch.-l. c.] et de Blaye [Gironde, ch.-l. ar.] of 3 Nov. 1434, in ABP E 437 and 24 July 1436, in ABP E 438; of Pes seigneur de St.-Martin-de-Seignanx [Landes, ar. Dax, ch.-l. c.] and of Guillaume Arnaud seigneur de 'Bedorede et deu Poey en Goosse' [Gousse, Landes, ar. Dax, c. Montfort-en-Chalosse] of 12 Oct. 1438, of Guixarnaut vicomte de 'Hurens en la senescaucie de las Lanes' of 13 Oct. 1438, in ABP E 438.

[8] Dupont-Ferrier, nos. 21412, 13423[t], 13798.

[9] Letters of 25 Oct. 1426, in ABP E 434.

[10] Letters of 1 Aug. 1432, in ABP E 435. For Naudonet de Lustrac see P. Laplagne-Barris, 'Naudonnet de Lustrac', *Revue de Gascogne*, xviii (1877), 297–311; G. Tholin, 'Notes sur deux seigneurs de Lustrac', *ibid.*, pp. 494–7.

[11] Dupont-Ferrier, nos. 31, 250, 367, 410, 18858.

of Charles VII,[1] *allié* of Jean I in 1422,[2] was *sénéchal* of the Bazadais for the French in 1425[1] and the grantee in the same year of the *seigneurie* of Clermont-Dessous, confiscated forty years earlier from Bertrand de Lamothe seigneur de Bruch and de Clermont, in 1380 the *allié* of Gaston Fébus and now on the English side.[3] The affinity of the comtes de Foix was above the struggles of French and English, though its individual members might not be.

But if they did their duty as well as enhancing the military strength of the comtes de Foix they carried the comtes' political influence westward into the Landes and the Bordelais, northward to the Garonne and beyond into Quercy and Périgord,[4] eastward into the plain of Languedoc,[5] even over the mountains into Spain.[6] But it was not only with such useful local figures[7]

---

[1] [Mauvezin, Gers, ar. Condom, ch.-l. c.]. Dupont-Ferrier, no. 2894 *bis*.

[2] Letters of 19 June 1422, in ABP E 432.

[3] *AHG*, viii (1866), 236; for Bertrand de Lamothe see above, p. 54, n. 7.

[4] Bertrand de 'Sent Artemie' [on 2 Jan.], Jean de 'Chombile' and Guillaume d'Orgueil [T. & G., ar. Montauban, c. Grisolles] [on 12 March], squires of Quercy, made *alliances* with Gaston Fébus in 1389 (letters in ABP E 412); Gaston de Gontaud seigneur de Biron en Périgord [Dordogne, ar. Bergerac, c. Monpazier] with Jean I on 17 Dec. 1421 (letters in ABP E 429); Bertrand Despratz seigneur de Montpezat-de-Quercy [T. & G., ar. Montauban, ch.-l. c.] on 30 Sept. 1424, Marques de Gordon seigneur de 'La Bercantiere en Quercij' on 12 Feb. 1425, Jean seigneur de Puy-cornet [T. & G., ar. Montauban, c. Molières] on 19 Apr. 1425 (letters in ABP E 432); Aymerigon seigneur d'Estissac en Périgord [Dordogne, ar. Périgueux, c. Neuvic] on 12 Sept. 1425 (letters *ibid.*) and with Gaston IV on 7 July 1439 (below, p. 67, document 8); Mondot de Brusac 'du pays de Pierregorc' with Gaston IV on 12 Feb. 1439 (letters in ABP E 438).

[5] 'Rôles de l'armée', *AHG*, xii. 172–3; Jeanne de Voisins made an *alliance* with Jean I on 5 Sept. 1418 as guardian of her son Philippe de Lévis seigneur de Mirepoix [Ariège, ar. Pamiers, ch.-l. c.] and de Lagarde [Ariège, ar. Pamiers, c. Mirepoix] (letters in ABP E 428); Jean de Brueres seigneur de Chalabre [Aude, ar. Limoux, ch.-l. c.] on 23 July 1427 (letters in ABP E 434); Jean vicomte d'Uzès [Gard, ar. Nîmes, ch.-l. c.] on 27 Aug. 1431 (letters in ABP E 435). From the Toulousain: Ramon Caparas seigneur de 'Molijs en Tholsaa' (letters of 28 Oct. 1432, *ibid.*) and Jacques Ysalguier seigneur de Fourquevaux [H.-G., ar. Toulouse, c. Montgiscard; see P. Wolff, 'Les Ysalguier de Toulouse', *Mélanges d'histoire sociale*, i (1942), 35–58] (letters of 18 May 1436, in ABP E 438).

[6] Bernard Aubert of the diocese of Elne [P.-O., ar. Perpignan] in Roussillon made an *alliance* with Jean I on 2 Sept. 1431 (letters in ABP E 435); 'Guiralt Auarca senhor de la honor de Gauin' and his three sons on 6 Sept. 1434 (letters in ABP E 437) and with Gaston IV on 18 Aug. 1436 (letters in ABP E 438); Galceran VI Galceran de Pinos (see J. Serra Vilaro, *Baronies de Pinos i Mataplana* (Barcelona, 1930–50), i. 229–43) on 8 Oct. 1444 (letters in ABP E 439).

[7] *Alliances* with even more local nobles were common; with those of Astarac, for instance ('Rôles de l'armée,' *AHG*, xii. 170–1); *alliances* of Jean seigneur de 'La Mazere en Estarac' (of 19 Oct. 1380, ABP E 304 fo. 28r); of 'Brunoo de Montelhs dEstarac' (of 7 Jan. 1381, *ibid.* fo. 33r); of Beaumont d'Astarac (letters of 4 March 1412, in ABP E 424); of Jean bâtard d'Astarac (of 20 Apr. 1415, noted on the dorse of his brother Beaumont's letters); of Jean 'par la gracie de Diu' comte d'Astarac (letters of 18 June 1423, in ABP E 432, of 22 July 1428 and of 28 March '1428' [= 1429?], in ABP E 434 and of 13 May 1431, in ABP E 435); of Jean d'Astarac

that contracts of *alliance* were made. So national a pair of heroes as Poton de Xaintrailles[1] and 'Esteben de Binholes dijt La Hire de la terre dAuribag'[2] might have their local connexions but the notorious Pierre de Louvain of Velay[3] or the even more notorious Rodrigo de Villandrando[4] hardly had; and such servants around the dauphin Louis as Amaury seigneur d'Estissac[5] and Jean de Daillon seigneur de Fontaines[6] clearly belonged to another world. Their duty primarily was, as their contracts stipulated, the maintenance of the comte de Foix 'en la bonne grace & amour du roy mon souverain seigneur et de mondit sr. le daulphin'.[7] As well as the civil servants and the *routiers*, the courtiers were brought into the affinity.[8] In the same way Olivier de Clisson contracted with Louis d'Orléans in 1397.[9] But the grander courtiers like the rising Pierre de Brézé in 1445 contracted with the magnates on equal terms.[10]

With the contract between equals one enters perhaps fully into that other world of high and at times even international politics. Such arrangements are notorious enough and, apart from providing a useful comparison with the

---

seigneur de 'Montclaa' (letters of 3 Jan. 1438, in ABP E 438); and with nobles of Couserans (*alliances* of Ramon Roger de Comminges vicomte de Couserans (letters of 11 Sept. 1398, in ABP E 416); of Arnaud Roger de Comminges, his brother (below, p. 183, document 7); of Jean Roger de Comminges seigneur de 'Tarride', his son (letters of 15 Dec. 1413, in ABP E 425) and as vicomte de Couserans, seigneur de 'Tarride' (letters of 4 Jan. 1438, in ABP E 438)). Bernard bâtard de Comminges made an *alliance* with Jean I comte de Foix on 20 May 1420 (letters in ABP E 429); Ramon de Comminges and Ramon At seigneur du Fauga [H.-G., ar. & c. Muret] 'caualer en Comenge' *alliances* with him on 18 May 1422 (letters in ABP E 432).

[1] L. & G., ar. Nérac, c. Lavardac; letters of 14 Sept. 1426, in ABP E 434.

[2] Auribat, Landes, ar. Dax, c. Montfort-en-Chalosse; letters of 22 Sept. 1425, in ABP E 432 and of 4 March 1441, in ABP E 439 (printed in *Histoire de Gaston IV, comte de Foix, par Guillaume Leseur*, ed. H. Courteault (SHF, Paris, 1893–6), ii. 291–2).

[3] Letters of 13 Nov. 1438, in ABP E 438. For Pierre de Louvain see P. Champion, *Guillaume de Flavy* (Bibliothèque du xv⁰ siècle, i, Paris, 1906), pp. 92–111.

[4] Letters of 9 Apr. 1439, in ABP E 438 (printed by J. Quicherat, *Rodrigue de Villandrando* (Paris, 1879), pp. 319–20).

[5] Letters of 12 Sept. 1425, in ABP E 432 and below, p. 67, document 8. For Aymerigon d'Estissac see *Lettres de Louis XI*, ed. E. Charavay and others (SHF, Paris, 1883–1909), i. 365–7; Dupont-Ferrier, no. 17600.

[6] Letters of 22 Apr. 1444, in ABP E 439. For Jean de Daillon see *Lettres de Louis XI*, iv. 94–8.

[7] Below, p. 67, document 8. Jean de Daillon promised the cardinal and the comte de Foix 'a eulx et a chacun deulx porchassier aveq mondit sr. le dauphin et autrement tout le bien et honneur que je pourray et les entretenir en sa bonne amour et grace a tout ma possibilite' (letters cited above, n. 6).

[8] Other 'courtier' *alliés* who contracted in this way were Pierre comte de Beaufort vicomte de Turenne (letters of 2 Oct. 1426, in ABP E 434) and John Stuart, constable of the Scottish army in France (letters of 26 Jan. 1427, *ibid.*).

[9] Letters of 18 Oct. 1397, AN K 57ᴬ, no. 9[1]. Louis d'Orléans' counter-letters of 28 Oct. 1397 are *ibid.*, no. 9².

[10] Letters of 18 May 1445, in ABP E 440 (printed by Courteault in *Histoire de Gaston IV*, ii. 308–9. The word omitted on p. 309 line 5 is 'meure').

contracts between unequals, are clearly irrelevant to our discussion of French patronage and clientage in the later middle ages. So far we have seen that the 'contract of retinue' did exist and we have seen something of its nature and use. But it was not the only means by which a lord could attempt to secure service beyond that which might be provided by an older feudal nexus.

The English administration in Guyenne,[1] for instance, and in all probability the Valois dukes of Burgundy seem to have avoided the *alliance*.[2] The military indenture, the contract for a limited period of military service, was certainly used in Guyenne: a number of *seigneurs* from the Bordelais, the Agenais and the Landes, for instance, who mustered at Morlaas for Gaston Fébus in August 1376 served the next summer by indenture with the English.[3] But when the English administration felt the need to reinforce the insecure loyalty of Gascons it seems to have done so with grants of office and with pensions[4]; and these seem again to have been the principal means by which Philippe le Hardi and Jean sans Peur attempted to attract their supporters.[5]

Apart, perhaps, from seats on the council in Guyenne, the offices disbursed to *seigneurs* by the English administration were, though lucrative, primarily local. A French magnate had, as well as these, all the honours of a not inconsiderable court with which to woo his servants. Louis seigneur de Montjoye was retained the *conseiller* and *chambellan* of Louis d'Orléans as well as taking a *fief-rente* from him in 1404[6]; Jean de La Baume became his *allié* when he became Louis' *chambellan* and took from him the collar of his Order in 1405.[7] In 1355 Pierre I duc de Bourbon retained Guillaume de Bourbon 'de nostre hostel et maisnage' in a letter the terms of which are

[1] The only contract at all comparable which has so far come to light seems to be that in which Jean seigneur de Grammont promised 'bona fe & fideutat' to Henry IV on 24 Sept. 1409, on marrying the heiress of Mussidan and Blaye ('Chartularium Henrici V et Henrici VI regum Angliae', BN ms. latin 9134, fo. 66v, printed *AHG*, xvi (1878), 161).

[2] Though one or two of the Burgundian contracts cited by B.-A. Pocquet du Haut Jussé, 'Les pensionnaires fieffés des ducs de Bourgogne de 1352 à 1419', *Mémoires de la Société pour l'histoire du droit et des institutions des anciens pays bourguignons, comtois et romands*, viii (1942), 146, seem to me remarkably like *alliances*.

[3] 'Rôles de l'armée,' *AHG*, xii. 168, 170–2. Indentures of the seigneurs de Duras, de Rauzan [Gironde, ar. Libourne, c. Pujols], 31 May 1377; de Lesparre, de Doazit [Landes, ar. Dax, c. Mugron], 1 June 1377; de Montferrand, de Langoiran [Gironde, ar. Bordeaux, c. Cadillac], 2 June 1377; d'Ornon et d'Audenge [Gironde, ar. Bordeaux], the captal de Buch, 3 June 1377 (PRO E 101/181/4/11, 9, 4, 14, 1, 12, 10, 7); payment for service (counter-roll of Richard Rotour constable of Bordeaux, PRO E 101/181/3 m. 1r–m. 2r). The short-term contract was, of course, known to the comtes de Foix (see, for instance, those made in the period 1391–7, in ABP E 415).

[4] Boutruche, pp. 350–3.

[5] Pocquet, *ubi supra*, pp. 127–50.

[6] Letters of 18 Aug. 1404, AN K 57[A], no. 9[24].

[7] Letters of 17 March 1405, *ibid.*, no. 9[26]. 'Henricus de Rothemberch miles, Barolis curie magister', also became a *chambellan* and member of the Order of Louis d'Orléans as well as his *allié* on 20 Feb. 1405 (*ibid.*, no. 9[25]).

rather similar to those of an English indenture.[1] A glance at the nominal roll of the household say of Jean duc de Berry provides one with ample evidence of the attraction into it of 'hommes de la haute noblesse originaires, soit des pays donnés au duc en apanage, soit d'autres régions'[2]; and similar evidence, though perhaps not so overwhelmingly, would be provided by that of the household of any magnate worth the name. Waleran de Luxembourg and Edouard de Pont had both, for instance, been retained of the household of Philippe le Hardi duc de Bourgogne six years before they made, a few months after Philippe's death in 1404, their contracts with Louis d'Orléans; and Waleran de Luxembourg was to become a member of Jean sans Peur's council two years later.[3]

The purpose of such retaining was only too clearly political; but it was not only local magnates who might be so retained. Those who carried out the central administration of a great estate, those whose duty it was to guide it through the thickets of interminable lawsuits, the civil servants and the lawyers too had their place in the account-books. Any magnate worth the name had his chancellor, his secretaries, his treasurers, his councillors, even his *maîtres des requêtes*[4]; he had his advocates and *procureurs* in every court from Paris to Rome.[5] Jean I Juvenel was one of the *conseillers* in the *Parlement* of Paris of Louis d'Orléans and of Valentine Visconti duchesse d'Orléans after his death[6]; his son Jean II Juvenal des Ursins (though he protested later he had served no man but the king)[7] the *conseiller* in the *Parlement* of Poitiers in the fourteen-twenties of their son Charles.[8] Feed, too, might be men useful eventually in more subtle ways: Jean Petit, the author of the notorious defence of Jean sans Peur's murder in 1407 of Louis d'Orléans, was retained Jean's *conseiller* at 100 *livres tournois* a year in 1406.[9] A Jean de Terre-Vermeille, who it is not inconceivable was the author of the treatise *Contra rebelles suorum regum*[10] of about 1420, took an eight-*livre*

---

[1] Below, p. 68., document 9. For later Bourbon contracts see below, p. 60, n. 6.

[2] R. Lacour, *Le Gouvernement de l'apanage de Jean duc de Berry 1360–1416* (Paris, 1934), p. 144. The nominal roll of the household occupies pp. vii–xiv of Annexe II.

[3] Pocquet, *ubi supra*, p. 146.

[4] Lacour, pp. 158–74; Annexe II, pp. xiv–xviii.

[5] Pocquet, *ubi supra*, pp. 140–4. An advocate or proctor was of course retained by many people; it is difficult to give such retaining much political content.

[6] Warrant by Valentine duchesse d'Orléans for payment of pensions to Jean I Juvenel and Guillaume Cousinot, 28 Feb. 1408, BN Pièces originales 1593, doss. Juvenel, no. 4.

[7] '... Mon souverain seigneur, jay este tousjours a vous et non a aultre, sans fleschir, ne oncques de seigneur particulier, quelquil soit; ne eulx don ne proffit, ne requis a avoir': Jean Juvenal des Ursins, 'Verba mea auribus percipe, Domine', BN ms. fr. 2701, fo. 86ra.

[8] Warrant by Charles duc d'Orléans for payment of pensions to 'Jehan Jouvenel le jeune, advocat' and others, 15 Aug. 1422, BN Pièces originales 1593, doss. Juvenel, no. 9.

[9] Pocquet, *ubi supra*, p. 147.

[10] *Joannes de Terra Rubea contra rebelles suorum regum*, ed. J. Bonaud (Lyon, 1526).

pension from Bernard VII d'Armagnac in 1407–8[1]; it would be pleasant to think he was Armagnac in more senses than one.

Pensions and offices seem to have gone together: the majority of pensions given by the first two Valois dukes of Burgundy, like many of those given by the Crown,[2] were effectively subventions to the wages of officers. A survey made by the officials of the *Chambre des comptes* of Dijon in February 1397 of the pensions then being paid by Philippe le Hardi does not reveal many that could possibly not have been so given[3]; and the scanty financial material that survives for the administration of the comtes d'Armagnac[4] gives much the same impression. The casual annuity,[5] though not the casual gift, seems possibly more difficult to find in later medieval France than in later medieval England.

But the balance is redressed by the abundance in France of those spectacular but hopeful means of collecting members of an affinity: the chivalric Order. The *Pomme d'or*,[6] the *Ecu d'or*,[7] the *Ecu vert à la dame blanche*,[8] the *Fer de prisonnier*,[9] the *Porc-épic*,[10] the *Dragon*,[11] the *Croissant*,[12] the *Hermine*,[13] the *Toison d'or*,[14] all at some time in the later fourteenth and fifteenth centuries adorned various parts of the persons of those whom magnates wished to attract. Some of these Orders lasted longer than others:

---

[1] Account of Jean de Castres, receiver of Creissels and Roquefeuil, 1407–8, fo. 25r, in ATG A 172.

[2] See, for instance, a list of some 700 pensioners of Louis XI, BN ms. fr. 2900, fos. 7r–16v. I hope eventually to publish a full analysis of this text.

[3] BN ms. fr. 4603.

[4] Primarily local accounts, in ATG A. It is possible, of course, that pensions were paid out of a central receipt.

[5] A number appear to have been given by Louis I duc d'Anjou king of Sicily in 1382–3 (*Journal of Jean le Fèvre*, ed. H. Moranvillé, i (Paris, 1887), pp. 35–46 *passim*); but it is difficult to be certain that these were not nominally attached to offices, as a number given at the same time were explicitly.

[6] A. Jacotin, *Preuves de la maison de Polignac* (Paris, 1898–1906), ii. 172–3; A. Bossuat, 'Un ordre de chevalerie auvergnat; l'ordre de la Pomme d'or', *Bulletin historique et scientifique de l'Auvergne*, lxiv (1944), 83–98.

[7] *La Chronique du bon duc Loys de Bourbon*, ed. A. M. Chazaud (SHF, Paris, 1876), pp. 8–15; P. Dumont, 'L'ordre de l'Ecu d'or', *Bulletin de la Société d'émulation du Bourbonnais*, xxvi (1923), 46–9.

[8] *Le Livre des faicts du bon messire Jean le Maingre, dit Boucicaut*, ed. J. F. Michaud and J. J. F. Poujoulat (Nouvelle collection des mémoires, ii, Paris, 1857), pp. 255b–257b.

[9] Douët d'Arcq, pp. 370–4. For a challenge by this group which seems to indicate that Douët's text should be antedated see the article cited below, n. 11.

[10] A. Favyn, *Le Théâtre d'honneur* (Paris, 1620), i. 730 ff.

[11] 'Une devise de chevalerie inconnue, créée par un comte de Foix? Le *Dragon*,' *Annales du Midi*, lxxvi (1964), 77–84. See above, 28-35.

[12] *Oeuvres complètes du roi René*, ed. T. de Quatrebarbes (Angers, 1844–6), i. 51–75.

[13] Guillaume de St.-André, *Histoire de Jean IV*, ed. dom H. Morice, in *Mémoires pour servir de preuves à l'histoire ecclésiastique et civile de Bretagne* (Paris, 1742–6), ii, cols. 356–7.

[14] *Chronique de Jean Le Fèvre*, ed. F. Morand (SHF, Paris, 1876–81), ii. 210–54.

the comte de Foix's Order of the *Dragon* is unknown save for its statutes, the Burgundian Order of the *Toison d'or* endured for centuries. How much stability they might give to their members' relationship with their lord seems doubtful[1]; though undoubtedly they were seen as the most scintillating proof of a person's adherence to a particular magnate.[2] Equally fragile, perhaps, as fragile indeed as the contract between equals of which it was in fact only a variant, was the agreement of brotherhood in arms for noble as opposed to businesslike purposes. Thomas duke of Clarence in a letter written in his own hand (in creditable French) promised Charles d'Orléans in 1412 'destre vray & bon parent, freer, compaygnon darmes & amy'[3]; Charles comte d'Eu promised him much the same in 1413[4] and Pierre de Brézé obliged himself to Gaston IV de Foix in 1445 'ainsi et tant comme la ung frere adoptif et darmes se puet obliger de droit a laultre'.[5] But this, it may be argued, hardly added much to their *alliances*.

As far as the more formal methods of creating a relationship were concerned, though the feudal contract in the later middle ages seems to have had more validity in France, the pattern of 'non-feudalism' emerges much as in England in the later middle ages: of the nucleus of the affinity in the familiars, the officers, the courtiers around a magnate, who might or might not have entered into their relationship with him by formal contract; and of the outer circle of the *alliés* in the country and the *alliés* in the court, bound to the magnate by their *alliances*. More shadowy are the simple pensioners, though they certainly existed; and more shadowy still the simple hangers-on and well-wishers. There are no Paston Letters for France; this intimate world in its more private actions is forever closed to us. Its activity and its size were probably at their greatest when magnates felt most nearly the need for support: as in England when, in the reigns of incompetent kings, it was every man for himself. In Gascony it was every man for himself perhaps rather more persistently than elsewhere. It may have been this that accounts for the proliferation of the Foix *alliances*; more likely, perhaps, it is the chance of survival. But when stress hit them other magnates turned to this convenient means of gaining support[6]; even, for instance, the dauphin Louis in

---

[1] Bossuat, *ubi supra*, p. 96.

[2] François de Surienne, for instance, in Jean Juvenal des Ursins' eyes was 'tenant le parti des Anglois, portant lordre du roy dAngleterre, son conseillier et chambellan' ('Verba mea auribus percipe, Domine', BN ms. fr. 2701, fo. 92rb).

[3] Letters of 14 Nov. 1412, AN K 57[B], no. 29; printed by Douët d'Arcq, p. 359.

[4] Letters of 27 July 1413, AN K 57[A], no. 1[7].

[5] Letters of 18 May 1445, in ABP E 440; printed by Courteault in *Histoire de Gaston IV*, pp. 308–9.

[6] Jean I duc de Bourbon, for instance, sent the seigneurs de La Fayette and de La Forest contracting with *seigneurs* in Auvergne in 1413 (letters in AN P 1355[2], cote 90; P 1358[1], cotes 500–1, 512; P 1358[2], cotes 528, 562[1 and 2], 583, 588[1] and [2], 592; P 1374[1], cote 2314. The *alliance* of Pons de Langeac *sénéchal* of Auvergne, of 5 June 1413 (AN P 1355[2], cote 90) is printed in *Spicilium Brivatense: Recueil de documents historiques relatifs au Brivadois et à l'Auvergne*, ed. A. Chassaing (Paris, 1886), pp. 491–2. For the incident in general see A. Leguai, *Les Ducs de Bourbon pendant la crise monarchique du xv⁰ siècle* (Paris, 1962), pp. 74–7. An *alliance* of

1452.[1] But to attempt a geography of the *alliance*, or even a chronology of it, would be a risky business.

The political effects of such a patronage system seem again to have been much the same as in England. M. Perroy has adumbrated the results of the conflicting claims of members of different seigneurial administrations to public place[2]: a magnate had his duties as well as his privileges of service. But what seems to be utterly lacking is much public comment upon the system. The giving of livery[3] certainly occurred in France; the construction of affinities was clear enough. The mechanism of complaint was less free-working in France than in England; but no representative institution seems to have complained about household or *alliés*. Perhaps the evils that their more riotous members might do paled before those done by more regular soldiery, enemy, friendly or free. And the abuse of maintenance like that of livery seems, if it existed, to have passed unnoticed. No *ordonnance* of a king of France seems to have dealt with either. The royal council held by the duc de Guienne ordered the breaking of certain magnate *alliances* in 1412[4]: and the great military *ordonnance* of 1439, which forbade private companies,[5] might, if any notice had been taken of it, have been interpreted as forbidding the military provisions of an *alliance*; but they, too, seem never to have been attacked direct. The seneschals of Aquitaine and of the Landes were ordered on 21 March 1433 to prevent any of the subjects of the king of England's accepting fees or wages from the comtes de Foix and d'Armagnac, or from allying themselves with them by oaths or *alliance*, as long as they remained on the French side.[6] This did not stop François seigneur de Grammont, de Mussidan and de Blaye from making an *alliance* with Jean I comte de Foix in November 1434[7] nor a number of other Gascons with his

Guillaume de Chalençon bishop of Le Puy, Armand vicomte de Polignac and Louis de Chalençon seigneur de Beaumont with Charles comte de Clermont, made on 23 June 1428, survives in AN P 1373[1], cote 2199; printed by Jacotin, ii. 258. An *alliance* of Rodrigo de Villandrando with the comte de Beaufort vicomte de Turenne of 27 Jan. 1433 survives in AN K 63, no. 22; printed by Quicherat, p. 244.

[1] *Alliance* of the prince of Piedmont with the dauphin Louis, 13 March 1452, *Lettres de Louis XI*, i. 227–8.

[2] Perroy, *ante*, xx. 184–5.

[3] C. Enlart, *Manuel d' archéologie française*, iii, *Le Costume* (Paris, 1916), pp. 401–9. On 17 Oct. 1409 Jean de Montagu was executed 'vestu de sa livrée, d'une houppe-lande de blanc et de rouge, et chapperon de mesmes, une chauce rouge et l'autre blanche' (*Journal d'un bourgeois de Paris 1405–1449*, ed. A. Tuetey (Soc. de. l'hist. de Paris, 1881), p. 6). The bourgeois of Rouen about 1424 were not at liberty to wear 'la livrée ou devise d'aucun seigneur ou autre qui s'en plaingne' (*Rouen au temps de Jeanne d'Arc et pendant l'occupation anglaise (1419–1449)*, ed. P. Le Cacheux (Soc. de l'hist. de Normandie, Rouen, 1931), p. 60). In the 1430s and 1440s Charles duc d'Orléans authorized a large number of persons to wear his 'order' (BN ms. Clairambault 1241, pp. 693–711).

[4] Letters of 22 Aug. 1412, AN K 57[B], no. 20.

[5] Du Fresne de Beaucourt, iii. 402–9.

[6] Rymer, IV. iv. 192.

[7] Letters of 3 Nov. 1434, in ABP E 437.

son later.[1] If they fell into desuetude after about 1450[2] was it because they were no longer needed rather than because they were forbidden ? But how did magnates get their support in the reign of Louis XI, which was for them no less a time of stress than those of Charles VI and Charles VII ? The *alliance* between equals survived[3]; and perhaps some day some contracts between lord and man will come to light. Or had they become unfashionable and a different basis of relationship arisen ?

But if this article has succeeded only in indicating the place of the *alliance* in the more domestic politics of later medieval France it will have served its purpose. There was a non-feudal contract for life service in later fourteenth- and fifteenth-century France and it played much the same part in bolstering up the relationship of lord and servant as it played in England. Its origins were less abrupt than in England, more obfuscated by that most decayed of feudal forms, the money fee for term of life; but it can undoubtedly be distinguished from it. Such a distinction was made by the chancery clerks of the ducs d'Orléans; such a distinction was clearly apparent to those who drew up the roll for the muster at Morlaas of the army of Gaston Fébus comte de Foix in 1376. For some hundred years (though this figure must be tentative) the *alliance* seemed to *seigneurs* in France their most hopeful means of securing service beyond that provided by their tenure. There was, essentially very little difference between it and the *fief-rente* for term of life; that difference subsisted in the absence of homage in the *alliance*, the absence of subjection. One was a companion, an ally, a supporter, even a servant of one's lord: one was not his subject, nor his vassal. It is perhaps this avoidance of an idea that provides the most fascinating, if not the most important, result of an excursion into the formal structure of political society in later medieval France.

APPENDIX [4]

I

(*Endorsed:*) Lomage monsr. de St. Pol. (*9 July 1404*)

Nous Waleran de Lucembourc conte de Liney & de Saint Pol faisons savoir a tous presens & avenir que nous, considerans le devoir en quoy nous sommes

[1] See above, p. 51, notes 4, 7, 9, p. 53 n. 16, p. 54 notes 4 and 7.

[2] The latest *alliance* known to me, apart from that made by the dauphin Louis in 1452 (see above, p. 61, n. 1), was made by Gaillard IV de Durfort with Charles II d'Albret on 13 Dec. 1451 (letters in ABP E 65; printed in *AHG*, viii (1866), 296–7 from a copy).

[3] *Alliance* between the princes of the *Bien public* and Charles d'Anjou comte du Maine, 3 Sept. 1465 (*Ordonnances des rois de France*, xvi, ed. C. E. de Pastoret (Paris, 1814), p. 387 n. b); cf. *Documents historiques inédits*, ed. J. J. Champollion-Figeac (Documents inédits sur l'histoire de France, ii, Paris, 1843), pp. 384–5.

[4] In printing these documents modern practice has been followed in the use of capital letters and in punctuation (except in the use of accents and of the apostrophe). In the documents in French modern practice has also been followed in the use of the letters *i* and *j*, *c* and *t*, *u* and *v*. In the documents in Gascon the letters *i* and *j*, *v*, *b* and *u* have been reproduced as they appear in the manuscript.

tenus damer, honnorer & servir mon tresredoubte seigneur, monseigneur le duc
dOrliens. . ., tant a cause de prochainnete de lignage quil a au roy mon souverain
seigneur, de qui il est frere germain et par consequent le plus prochain de la
couronne apres messeigneurs ses enfans, comme par le lignage en quoy nous lui
povons appartenir; et aussi pour lez biens, honneurs et amours que esperons
trouver en lui a noz affaires & besoignes touchans & regardans nostre honneur &
estat, et que aujourdui il nous a de sa grace & liberale voulente ordonne prenre &
avoir des deniers de ses finances la somme de six mil livres tournois de pension
doresenavant chacun an par la main de son tresorier general: de nostre certaine
science & propre mouvement sommes aujourdui devenu & devenons son homme &
serviteur et lui avons fait foy & hommage. Et avecques ce, pour le grant desir &
affection que nous avons a mondit seigneur dOrliens, lui avons promis & promettons par ces presentes par la foy & serement de nostre corps servir, aidier
& adherer envers & contre tous ceulx qui pueent vivre ne morir, exceptez le roy
mon souverain seigneur et monseigneur le daulphin son ainsne filz et messrs. les
ducz de Berry & de Bar, desquelz nous tenons les contez de Liney & de Saint Pol
(toutesfoiz nous nentendons ne ne voulons qui soit entendu lexception que nous
faisons a nozdiz seigneurs de Berry & de Bar que en desservant noz fiez en gardant
leur seigneurie dont nozdiz fiez sont tenuz & non autrement); et que le bien &
honneur de mondit seigneur dOrliens nous garderons & son dommage escheverons
de tout nostre povoir; et sil avenoit que aucuns se voulsissent efforcier de porter
deshonneur ou dommage a mondit seigneur dOrliens de nostre povoir y resisterons
en le lui mandant & faisant savoir hastivement; se conseil nous demande bon &
loyal nous lui donrrons, & se le sien nous revelle nous[1] le celerons. En tesmoing de
ce nous avons fait seeller ces lettres du seau de noz armes, le ixe jour de juillet lan de
grace mil quatrecens & quatre.

Par monseigneur le conte.   Vasseur.

[Parchment, sealed on a tag. AN K 56[A] no. 8.]

2

Alliance *of Jean I comte de Foix and Jean bâtard d'Orléans, comte de Périgord,
14 January 1434.*

Nous Jehan bastart dOrliens conte de Pierregorc savoir faisons a touz qui ces
presentes verront que, comme vraye amour et unite soyent sur toutes choses
plaisans a Dieu et perfection de bien, attendans aussi le grant bien qui par le
moyen de bonne amistance et concorde entre nous et honnoure seigneur, messire
Jehan conte de Foix et de Bigorre nostre parrin, puent venir au roy nostre
souverain seigneur, a son royaume et subgez, que de tout nostre cuer amons et
desirons a lonneur de Dieu et au bien du roy nostredit souverain seigneur, de ses
royaume & seigneurie: de nostre certaine science & agreable voulente avons
aujourduy pour et par ces presentes faisons avec mondit sr. de Foix et parrin
bonne, ferme, aimable et loyalle amistance, ligue et confederation, a durer a touz
les temps de noz vies, a lencontre de toutes personnes du monde de quelque estat
ou condition quilz soyent, exceptez monsr. le duc dOrliens et monsr. le conte
dAngolesme, a qui je suis frere, ou cas toutesfois que la chose les toucheroyt en

---

[1] There is an erasure at this point in the MS.

leur propre chief, fait et querelle, autrement non; et avons jure & promis, promettons et jurons a Dieu nostre createur sur les Sans Evangiles & vraye Croix pour ce par nous touchez et par les foiz & serementz de nostres corps & sur nostre honneur & loyaulte que de ce jour en avant nous serons a mondit sr. de Foix et parrin bon, parfait et loyal parent, ami et allie, et aurons ses amis pour amis et ses ennemis pour ennemis, sauves les personnes dessus exceptees. Item jurons comme davant que nous ayderons, conseillerons, conforterons, & soccourrons[1] nostredit parrin de nostre personne, gens et biens et par toutes autres voyes et manieres a nous possibles en tout ce quil aura a faire de nous et quant requis en serons, soit pour noz propres guerres ou afferes, se aucunes nous en seurviennent, & autrement. Item que nous garderons en toutes choses le bien, honneur, estatz, droiz, preheminenses, offices de mondit sr. & parrin que pour le temps present thient et pour le temps advenir pourroyt tenir, ses libertez, noblesses, prerrogatives & prouffit; et contre ceulx qui les vouldroyent empescher, diminuer ou mettre en autre subgection en quelque maniere que ce feust et y contresterons, resisterons et les deffendrons, ayderons & secourrons de tout nostre povoir. Item jurons come dessus que le bien, honneur, utilite, prouffit et bien advenir dessa personne et son estat nous vouldrons, pourchasserons, procurerons et garderons et le deshonneur, mal, peril et dommaige dessa personne nous escheverons & destourberons et de tout nostre povoir y obvierons et contresterons; et sil advenoit, que Dieu ne vueille, que aucun ou aucuns de quelque estat ou condition quilz soyent les tractaissent, procurassent ou pourchassassent, incontinent quil sera venu a nostre cognoissance le plus trestost & certainement que poussible nous sera en adviserons et le ferons savoir a mondit sr. de Foix & parrin. Item que se de cy en avant faisons ou fermons aucunes alliances, ligues ou confederations avecques aucun seigneur ou autre de quelque estat quil soit, serons tenu de excepter et excepterons mondit sr. et parrin. Item nosdit Jehan bastart avons promis & jure, promettons & jurons derechief sur les seremens dessusdits et sur peine destre reputez faulx & perjures et soubz obligation de touz noz biens presens et advenir tenir, garder et complir et faire toutes les choses dessusdictes et chacune dicelles, sans contradiction, dissimulation, dilation ou excusation aucune et sans fiction, fraude ou mal engin quelzconques; et non venir au contraire directement ou indirectement, publiquement ou occultement, pour quelconque cause ou raison que ce soit, et soubz lobligation davant dicte. En tesmoing de toutes les choses dessusdictes & chacune dicelles nous avons fait seeler ces presentes du seel a noz armes et signees de nostre propre main, a Bourges en Berry le xiiij[e] jour de janvier lan de grace mil quatrecentz trente troys.

[*signed:*] J. b[as]tart dOrleans.

[Parchment, sealed on a tag. ABP E 437, unnumbered.]

3

Alliance *of Guillaume Sans seigneur de Pommiers with Bernard Ezi II sire d'Albret, 13 May 1358.*

Conoguda causa sia que lo dicmenge apres la festa de Sent Nicholau destiu, so es assaber lo tretzen jorn deu mes de may en lan de nostressenhor mil CCC sinquanta & huyt, regnand Edward rey dAncglaterra & duc de Guiayna, Amaneu

---

[1] MS. 'soccourrons'.

archibesque de Bordeu, en la presencia de min notari public & deus testimonis deius escruitz, lo noble & poderos barou & senhor mossen Guilhem Santz, cauoy, senhr. de Pomers, estant en la cappera Sent Greguori deus Carmes, apperada de la La, disso que vertat era que lo noble & excellent senhor mossen Bern. Edz senhr. de Lebrit laue feyt saenarreyre grans bens & grans plasers, per losquaus ed lera tengut totz temps seruir & adiudar; per que lodeyt senhr. mossen Guilhem Santz juret sobre lautar & sobre lo messau & sobre la Crot que ed sera ab lodeyt senher de Lebrit & ab son primier filh hereter de lostau de Lebrit, tant cum lodeyt senhr. mossen Guilhem Santz viura, & ladiudera de guerra encontra totz los homes deu mon, exceptat contra lo rey dAncglaterra. Deuquau segrament & causas dessusdeytas, lodeyt senhr. mossen Bern. Edz requero a min notari deius escruitz que lenffessi carta o cartas tantas cum mesters len seren, lasquaus jo las autreyey affar de mon offici. En testimoniatge de lasquaus causas & a maior fermetat daqueras lo medis senhr. de Pomers meto & pauset son propri saget en pendent; loquau saget mes o no mes, pausat o no pausat en aquesta present carta, la medissa carta escongua & demore en sa entegra & ferma valor, ayssi & artant be cum si lodeyt saget y ppende & y apparisse. Acta fuerunt hec 'Burdegale' in dicta cappella die, anno, mense & regnantibus quibus supra. Testes sunt lo noble home mossen Ramon de Farguas, cavoy, senhr. de Monteton, los sains et hondratz senhors mossen Guilhem de Cunhous, archidiaque de Vasatz, fray Guilhem Bern. de Laclaustra, comand-ayre de Roquabruna de lordre de Jerusalem, mestre Raynaud deus Claus, bachaler en decretz, mossen Menaud Deguaus, prestre et rector de las Clotas, fray Pey Guiot deu combent deus Frayres Menutz de Bordeu et Pey de Poyana donzet, et io Ayquem deu Poyau, clerc, notari public deu duguat de Guiaynes, qui cesta carta audi, recebuy, escriby e mon senhau acostumat y ppausey.

[Parchment, sealed on a tag, seal gone. ABP E 37, unnumbered.]

4

Alliance *of Bertrand seigneur de Montagut en Agenais with Jean I comte d'Armagnac,
26 July 1370.*

Acordat es entre nos, Johan per la grace de Diu comte dArmanhac, de Fezensac e darRodes, bescomte de Lomanha et dAutuillar, e mi, Bertran senhe de Montagut en Agennes, las causas que senseguen.

Primieramant que jo, senhe de Montagut auantdit, prometi et juri aus Sans Euuangelis de Diu de seruir bien e leyalment lodit mossr. lo comte dArmanhac encontra totas personas ab qui pogos auer a far per guerra o autrament, exeptat lo rey de Fransa nostre sr. o lo duc de Guyaine o comte dAgennes o mos oncles germas o mos cosis germas.

E nos, comte dArmanhac dessusdit, recebem lodit senhr. de Montagut en nostre companho e li prometem que si per aquesta causa auguna persona lo faze o faze far guerra nos laiudaram o lo defeneram cum nostre propri e especiau com-panhon, e li daram per si aperalha iij^C franx daur, deusquaus li faram pagar la meytat presentment e lautra meytat a la Totz Sens.

En testimoni daquestas presentas conuenesas nos auem pausatz nostres propris sagetz en las presens, feyt fo asso a Moissac lo xxvj jorn de jul, lan mil CCC septanta.

[Parchment, sealed on two tags. ABP E 243, unnumbered.]

5

Reference to the alliance *of Gaillard de Lamothe with Gaston III Fébus comte de Foix, 11 December 1375.*

... e volo que ladicte carte de submissiou sie trencade & anullade, ab aixi empero que lodijt mossr. Galhard aqui medixs se fo companhoo & alliat deudijt mossr. de Foixs; el prometo & sobliga, tocan sa maa dextre[1] en la maa deudijt mossr. de Foixs e baisan en sa boque, sus la fee de son cors & en pene deste faus e maubat caualer,[2] que dassi auant eg seruira audijt mossr. de Foixs dauant & contra totz los autres senhors deu mon, exceptat soos dretz senhors deusquaus es subiet & terre thient aujorndeoey. E de las causes dessusdictes losdijtz mossr. de Foixs dune part, e mossr. Galhard de La Mote dautre, requerun & volon sengles cartes de vne tenor. Feit so en lo casteg de Pau lo xj jorn de Decembr. lan m CCC lxxv. Testes son desso los nobles barou mossr. P. de La Mote, senhor de Roquetalhade, mossr. Pelegri Daute, cavalers, Siotes de Sent Arromaa, donzel e jo, B. de Luntz, etc. que la carte retengu.

[Register of the notary-general of Béarn, ABP E 302 fo. 124 r–v.]

6

Alliance of Nompar seigneur de Caumont with Mathieu comte de Foix, 11 May 1394.

Mathiu per la gracie de Diu comte de Foixs vescomte de Bearn, de Castelbou, de Marsan & de Gauardan, a totz & sengles qui las presentz lettres veyran fem saber que per so que Nopar senher de Caumont ses feyt nostre seruidor[3] & alliat nos lauem promes & jurat de aiudar & valer aixi cum hom deu far a son bou alliat & aiudador, contre totz los homis deu mon qui mal lo volossen far, perso que ses feyt de nostre part exceptatz nostres dretz & naturaus senhors. E jo, Nopar soberdijt, ey promes & jurat sus los Santz Euangelis de Diu toquatz de ma propre man dextre & sus pene de estre faus & maubat de aiudar & valer audijt mossr. de Foixs, de ma propre persona, de mon poder & de tote ma terre, e far guerre de madijte terre en fore en totes partz ou lodijt mossr. de Foixs me requerira, contre totz los homis deu mon exceptat mon sobiran senhor. En testimoni desso hauem feytes far ij[es] lettres de vne forme & tenor, sagerades deu sagel de nos, Mathiu comte soberdijt, & deu sagel de mossr. Br. dAydie en abscence deu sagel de mi, Nopar senhor de Caumont, a Ortes lo xj jorn de may lan mil CCCxC iiij. R.[4]

Et jo, Nopar soberdijt, prometi de hauer trames audijt mossr. de Foixs de la data de las presentz en sinc sepmanes semblant lettre que aquest es, sagerade de mon propri sagel & que lodijt mossr. me reda aqueste.

Desseus lodijt jorn la present lettre fo sagerade aixi cum ere estat promes per mossr. de Caumont de son propri sagel.

[Parchment, sealed on a tongue, seal gone. ABP E 415, unnumbered.]

[1] 'A la' crossed out.
[2] A new hand begins.
[3] 'Seruidor' repeated and crossed out.
[4] 'Registrata'?

7

Alliance of Arnaud Roger de Comminges with Jean I comte de Foix, 15 November 1413.

Sapien totz qui las presens lettres beyran que jo, Arnaud Rodger de Comenge, caualer, cossiran et estan jmfformat de la attinenci de linhadge, amor et amistance que monsenhors los bescomtes de Coserans mon pay, qui Diu absolue, et mossr. lo bescomte de Coserans mon fray, qui a present es, et totz los nostres antiquementz an agut et an de present ab los senhors comtes de Foixs et los trops plasers et honors quen an recebut, bolen continuar en aquere jo, soberdijt Arnaud Rodger, lo jorn de la present date me suy feyt et fas per tenor de las presens companhs, aliad et baledor de bos, trop naud et poderoos senhor mossr. Johan per la gracie de Diu comte de Foixs, et bos ey promes et jurat sus ma bone fe cum a leyau caualer, et sus los quoate Santz Euangelis de Diu toquatz de ma maa, que bos sere bou, fideu et leyau baledor et aliad; et totes hores que besonh bos sara et men requeriratz bos ajudare et soccorrere de ma persone ab tot lomes de gens darmes que poyre, contre totes las persones deu mon exceptat lo rey de France mon souuerain senhor, mossr. de Guiayne son primier filh, mossr. lo duc de Borgonhe, lodiit mossr. lo bescomte mon fray, sons jmffans et mossr. lo comte dEstarac; et no sere en loc ou a bostre persone nj a re deu bostre sie feyt mal, deshonor nj dampnadge, abantz ac euitare a mon poder. Et la soberdijte liance ey feyt tant per las rasons soberdiites et per so que lodijt mossr. lo comte me a promes et autreyat baler, soccorrer et ajudar en mas necessitatz, quant aixj ben per cent lb. que me a autreyat balhar de rende cascun an, cum apar lo tot plus larguement per sas lettres. Et en testimonj dasso lou ey balhat la present lettre signade de ma maa et sagerade de mon saget, a Maseres, lo xv jorns de nouembre, lan mil iiij^C et tredze.

[*signed:*] Arnaud Rodger

[Parchment, sealed on a tag. ABP E 425, unnumbered.]

8

Alliance of Aymerigon seigneur d'Estissac with Gaston IV comte de Foix, 7 July 1439.

Sachent touz que comme je, Aymerigon seigneur dEstissac en Pierregorc chevalier, pour la bonne et grant affection que jay eu le temps passe a feu hault & puissant seigneur monsr. Jehan de bonne memoire conte de Foix et de Bigorre et a son hostel eusse fait avec lui certaines alliances plus a plain contenues es lettres par moy sur ce faictes, signees de ma main et seellees de mon seel,[1] et depuis ledit monsr. Jehan conte de Foix et de Bigorre soit alle de vie a trespassement; voulant ensuir la bonne voulente et affection que je avoye a lui et a son hostel, le jour de la date de ces presentes de mon bon gre et certaine science me suis fayt et par la teneur de ces presentes fais allie, serviteur et valledeur de vous, hault & puissant seigneur Gaston conte de Foix et de Bigorre et vous ay promis et jure, promect & jure, sur les Sains Evangiles de Dieu et sur la foy et serement de mon corps et sur mon honneur que doresenavant et par tout le temps de ma vie a vous et a vostre hostel seray bon & loyal allie, serviteur et valledeur. Vostre personne & vostre honneur garderay et deffendray et vostre bien pourchasseray, vostre mal, des-honneur & dommaige escheveray, empescheray et destourberay de tout mon povoir et savoir; et saucune chose au contraire en venoit a ma cognoissance in-

[1] Letters of 12 Sept. 1425, in ABP E 432.

continent et le plus tost que je pourray vous en advertiray et le vous feray savoir par lettre ou messaige. Et avec ce se aucun ou aucuns vous faisoient ou vouloient faire guerre ou debat vous secourray et ayderay de toute ma puissance et avec touz ceulx qui pour moy vouldroyent faire, et se besoing est de mes lieux et places en hors leur feray guerre et en yceulx pour icelle faire recevray de voz gens, se envoyer en y voulez, en faisant toutesfoiz par vous la despense sur ce necessere, toutes et quantesfoiz que besoing en aurez et par vous en seray requis, envers touz et contre touz qui puissent vivre et mourir, exceptez le roy de France mon souverain seigneur, monsr. le daulphin de Viennoys son filz et monsr. le duc dOrleans. Lesquelles choses ay faictes, promises et jurees pour toute ma vie, comme dit est, tant de mon bon gre comme aussi pour ce que vous mavez promis & jure destre mon bon et vray seigneur et ami et me secourir et aydier, se besoing me faisoit, ainsi quil est plus a plain contenu en voz lettres patentes signees de vostre main et seellees de vostre seel; et aussi que mavez donne cinq cens moutons dor pour une foiz et promis trois cens moutons de pension annuelle tant pour ce que dit est que aussi pour vous entretenir tousjours de mon povoir en la bonne grace & amour du roy mon souverain seigneur et de mondit sr. le daulphin. En tesmoing de ce jay signe ces presentes de ma main et seelees de mon seel. Faictes a Thoulouse le vij^e jour de juillet lan mil CCCC trente & neuf, presens messeigneurs le conte de Comminge, les evesques dAyre et de Tarbe, le sire de Vilar, seneschal de Beaucaire, le sr. de Gamasche et messr. Trestant dAure.

[*signed:*] Estissac

[Parchment, sealed on a tongue, seal gone. ABP E 438, unnumbered.]

9

Pierre I duc de Bourbon retains Guillaume de Bourbon chevalier of his household, 18 January 1355.

Pierres duc de Bourbonn. conte de Clermont & de La Marche Chamberier de France savoir faisons que nous avons retenu & retenons nostre ame et feal chevalier messr. Guillaume de Bourbon de nostre hostel & maisnage, pour estre a nous devant tous autres & venir a nostre service toutes fois que mestier en aurons & nous le manderons. Et parmi ce nous lui avons donne & donnons par ces presentes tant comme il vivra chascun an six vins livres tournois, a prendre sur nostre tresor de Bourbonn. jusques que ailleurs len aions assigne; et avecques ce le devons deffraier toutes foiz quil sera avecques nous pour nostre service, cestassavoir a quatre chevaux, et lui devons rendre venues & retours toutes fois que mande sera, comme dit est, et aussi le devons monter pour sa personne, cestassavoir pour la guerre & pour le tournay. Mandons a nostredit tresorier que doresenavant lui paie & delivre ladicte somme aus termes acoustumes, sanz autre mandement atendre; et nous voulons que tout ce que paie & delivre lui aura pour ceste cause lui soit alloue en ses comptes. Donnees a Avignon le xviij^e jour de jenvier lan de grace mil CCC cinquante et quatre.

[*endorsed, inter alia:*] Ces lettres son hemies,[1] rendues & adnullees en la Chambre par certain acort fait avecques messr. Guillaume de Borbon, lequel est enregistrez en la Chambre.

[Parchment, sealed on a tag. AN P 1363^1 cote 1224.]

[1] I am not certain of the reading of this word.

OF BRETON ALLIANCES AND OTHER MATTERS

It appears to be accepted that a form of political contract which can be termed non-feudal existed in later medieval France, and that its emergence can be traced back to the last quarter of the fourteenth century. In about 1389 Philippe de Mézières could put into the mouth of 'la Riche Precieuse, Verite la royne' a detailed commentary upon 'l'aliance publique et, il se doit dire, secrete de tes serviteurs roiaulx, grans princes royaulx et autres du royaume de Gaule' in her interminable discourse to Charles VI in his guise of 'jeune Moyse couronne'.[1] She was quite clear about the nature of the contract: indeed, she might have had an example of the letters giving the terms of such an *alliance* before her.[2] A great lord, she explained, would say to a royal officer well-in with the king:

Beaux amis, pour ta grant vaillance, pour ta vertu, ou pour aucune legiere acointance nouvellement trouvee, et principaument affin que tu me teignes en la grace et amour de mon seigneur le roy, et que je soie souvent garniz et enformez par toy des voulentez et commandemens de mon seigneur le roy, je te donne v^c, mil ou ii^m frans tant comme tu vivras; et se bien me serviras, plusgrant chose je te donray. Mais quoy je veuil que tu soies mon frere espicial et mon alie et te donne ma devise, et que tu me faces serement d'estre avecques moy en tout et par tout, contre tous ceulx du royaume, voire excepte mon seigneur le roy; et que mon bien et mon honneur tu garderas et me feras savoir tout ce qui me pourra touchier, ou bien ou mal, par les lectres secretes ou par loyal messaige, ou par un tel signet.

Nothing could be clearer than that; and nothing, in Mézières's view, could be worse than the effect of the system upon 'gouvernement moral'.

1. *Le Songe du Vieil Pelerin*, ed. G. W. Coopland (2 vols., Cambridge, 1969), ii. 350–5. The remaining quotations from Philippe de Mézières are taken from this section of the *Songe* (§264).
2. See the letters printed in P. S. Lewis, 'Decayed and Non-Feudalism in Later Medieval France', *B.I.H.R.* xxxvii (1964), 183–4 (document 8) and those cited there, p. 172, no. 7. See above 67–8, and 56.

Comment, if comparatively private, was not lacking; some fifty-five years later Jean Juvenal des Ursins could again complain about the evils of clientage.[3] Nor, when Mézières wrote, was the system, in a general sense, new: it can be detected in the political society of the reign of Philipe VI,[4] though we know nothing of the way in which the relationships between lord and client were created. But Mézières's commentary upon the *alliance* is valuable not only for its views upon the organization of patronage and its effects: it shows also, as we shall see, that the distinction in his mind between feudal and non-feudal forms was arguably a clear one. But he saw, too, that there might in a sense be an overlap: royal officers who held land of the great lords could do them 'homage et serement' for that land, but should not be bound by 'autre aliance particuliere, car ilz scevent tout ce qu'ilz doyvent fere ou servir aux seigneuries ou aux seigneurs pour le dit homage'. Mézières repeated the point: royal servants could inherit land held of the princes, or the princes could give them land for life or hereditarily for past or future service; 'en cestui cas', he thought, 'il est bien raison qu'ilz en facent le serement et homage, tel qu'il appartient au seigneur du fief, et non pas autre aliance expresse qui n'appartient pas au fief et que un simple homme ne feroit qui ne seroit pas serviteur ou officier royal'.

How is one to disentangle this last statement? To keep a lord in royal 'grace et amour', to inform a lord of the king's 'voulentez et commandemens', were clearly beyond the capacity of someone not a royal officer. But other elements in the contract which Mézières sketched out were equally clearly not beyond the capacity of the simple man: wearing the lord's livery badge—a practice admittedly all too obscure at present, as far as later medieval France, as opposed to later medieval England, is concerned; swearing to be with the lord against all men except the king; pursuing the lord's 'bien et . . . honneur' and informing him of things concerning him. All these were familiar enough, indeed, from the obligations that one might expect to find in some of the oaths linked with homage in the phrase 'homage et serement'[5] in a relationship that was 'feudal'. But if a royal officer was in fact in a feudal relationship

3. P. S. Lewis, *Later Medieval France: The Polity* (London, 1968), p. 129.
4. R. Cazelles, *La Société politique et la crise de la royauté sous Philippe de Valois* (Paris, 1958), pp. 267–9.
5. See, for instance, the terms of the oath sworn by the sire de Curton when he did homage to Gaston III Fébus, comte de Foix, in February 1382 (P. Tucoo-Chala, *Gaston Fébus et la vicomté de Béarn, 1343–1391* (Bordeaux, 1960), pp. 361–2 (pièce xix)). This text is typical of a number to be found in the registers of the notary-general of Béarn, Arch. Dép. Pyrénées-Atlantiques, E 302 and 304.

with his would-be patron, would not the patron already derive from the 'serement et homage, tel qu'il appartient au seigneur du fief', the advantages made perhaps only more explicit by the specific duties imposed upon his vassal, now his *allié* as well, in the contract of *alliance?* Or does Mézières really mean to say that the whole of the new contract of *alliance*, one made on top of the contract of vassalage, creates somehow a different relationship from the original homage and oath of fidelity done to the lord upon entry into the fief, despite the fact that some of the stipulations may have been the same in both fealty and contract of *alliance?* In short, did this new, non-feudal contract, despite the similarity of wording, create a new and particular relationship for the *allié* on top of the relationship of vassalage?

Given the nature of the contract of *alliance* which Mézières sketched out, it is difficult to avoid the belief that he thought a vassal could also be an *allié*, and that were he not discussing the particular case of the royal officer who entered into an *alliance* with a great lord, his view would be clearer. The similarity between the obligations of 'vassals' and '*alliés*' has been pointed out; and it has been argued that the distinction between the two seems to turn finally upon whether homage was done or not, a distinction perhaps lacking a difference, but one which, in doing so, provided a smooth crossing from the 'feudal' into the 'non-feudal' world.[6] Can one now argue that the crossing was even smoother: that one can find an even more transitional situation than that offered by the two contracts made in 1404 with Louis, duke of Orléans, in one of which Waleran de Luxembourg, comte de Ligny and Saint-Pol, took a money fee and became Louis's vassal, and in the other of which Édouard de Bar, marquis de Pont, took a pension for the same amount and became Louis's *allié*—each contracting otherwise to perform the same services?[7] Could an *alliance* indeed reinforce vassalage, the two relationships existing simultaneously between lord and man?

Here, perhaps, one should turn to the *Trésor des Chartes des ducs de Bretagne*. It seems clear that the *alliance* was known in Brittany as elsewhere. It can be found expressed in an unequivocal form, for instance, in contracts made with Duke John V by Georges de La Trémoïlle in February 1431 and February 1434,[8] by William Stuart, James Rovan,

---

6. Lewis, 'Decayed and Non-Feudalism', p. 44.   7. Ibid., p. 43.

8. Letters of 22 February 1431, Arch. Dép. Loire-Atlantique, E 181, no. 8 and of 1 February 1434, ibid., E 144 no. 9; reproduced below, Appendix, document 1. Documents from this archive are henceforward cited by series, file, and document indication alone.

and John Stuart in April of that year,[9] by perhaps a different William Stuart in September 1436,[10] and by Jean, seigneur de Bueil, in June 1439.[11] It is perhaps unnecessary to expand upon them; some have been printed, two in the Appendix to this article. Rather more equivocal, perhaps, are the documents in which men with Breton names became, apparently, the *alliés* of Duke John IV. In July 1371 Eon Le Moine, chevalier, made his relationship with John IV known in a letter patent remarkable only for its brevity;[12] in October of the same year Rolland de Kergorlé did the same in a slightly longer document.[13] John IV had 'retained' Eon Le Moine 'des siens et de sa retenue', and Rolland de Kergorlé 'un de ses escuiers et gentilx hommes'; there is no breath of vassalage. Nor is there in the contract made in March 1380 by Raoul de Kersaliou in which, recognizing that John IV 'm'a ordiené pour mes gages et pension la somme de doux centz livres par an affin de le servir', he promised to perform the usual duties, with the topical addition of 'pourchacer la delivrance de son duché de Bretaigne',[14] a service we shall encounter again.

But more often, however, in the surviving documents in the ducal archive at Nantes, there is some reference, explicit or implicit, to a 'feudal' relationship with a duke of Brittany. In August 1387, in the court of Vannes, Jean de Poulglou, chevalier, recognized that he was 'de sa nativité dou duché de Bretaigne et de sa droite nature comme vroy home estre tenu voloir le bien et honnour' of John IV 'et estre son subgiet et home feal'.[15] Some contractors, like Rolland, vicomte de Coatmen, described themselves as 'homme lige' of John IV;[16] some, like Jean de Kerenlouët, recognized that the duke was their 'prochain seigneur lige'.[17] In other documents—as, for instance, the contract of

9. Letters of 21 April 1434, E 144, no. 6.
10. Letters of 27 September 1436, E 144, no. 7; reproduced below, Appendix, document 2. The signature of 'G. Stuart' is different from that of 'Guillaume Stuart' on E 144, no. 6, which is unsealed.
11. Letters of 16 June 1439, E 147, no. 8; printed in Jean de Bueil, *Le Jouvencel*, ed. L. Lecestre and C. Favre (2 vols., Paris, 1887–9), ii. 319–20, and see i, p. lxxxj, n. 2. Further *lettres d'alliance* with dukes of Brittany are those of Archambaud de Périgord of 12 March 1393, E 181, no. 14; Jean de Rochechouart, seigneur d'Aspremont, of 13 September 1424, E 181, no. 15; Charles d'Anjou, comte de Mortain, of 13 September 1436, E 179, no. 8; and Jean de Blanchefort of 5 Feburary 1440, B.N., MS. 22332, fo. 222.
12. Letters of 30 July 1371, E 142, no. 16.
13. Letters of 14 October 1371, E 142, no. 20.
14. Letters of 8 March 1380, E 143, no. 3; reproduced below, Appendix, document 3.
15. Letters of 9 August 1387, E 143, no. 19.
16. Letters of 1371, E 142, no. 18. 17. Letters of 1371, E 142, no. 19.

Prigent Le Moine made in April 1380[18]—a 'feudal' element appears to be detectable in the phrases 'mon tres souverain seigneur monseigneur monsr. Jehan duc de Bretaigne', 'estre avecques mondit seignour le duc bon, vroy et loial servant et obboissant' (or, in other documents, 'subgit'),[19] and 'plus proche a lui que a nuls autres', a tag which appears to be associated closely with homage in Brittany.[20]

Equally remarkable, if less common, are those documents in which the phraseology of the 'non-feudal' world appears alongside that of the 'feudal'. In a number for the reign of John IV the concept of retainer appears. In February 1371 Even Chesnel, chevalier, confessed that it had pleased the duke 'me retenir avoucques luy de son conseil et des chevaliers de son ostel';[21] in May 1372 Jean du Juch, chevalier, too, was 'retenu' by Jean IV 'a un de ses chevaliers';[22] in 1379 Brient de Châteaubriant, chevalier, seigneur de Beaufort[23] and Raoullet, seigneur de Coëtquen;[24] in 1380 Jean Raguenel, chevalier, vicomte de Dinan,[25] and Prigent Le Moine;[26] in 1382 Alain Tivarlen;[27] and in 1398 Eustache de La Houssaie, chevalier,[28] each recognized that the duke 'me avoir retenu avecques lui'.[29] In the contracts of Prigent Le Moine and of Eustache de La Houssaie there is mention of a 'pension'. In two or three cases a man refers to himself as an *allié* of John IV: ' . . . confesse estre alié . . . et par ces presentes lettres me ralie' was the formula used by Rolland, vicomte de Coatmen, for instance, in his letters of March 1380.[30]

Probably a month earlier than Rolland de Coatmen, Silvestre de La

18. Letters of 3 April 1380, E 143, no. 6.
19. See, for instance, the letters of Brient de Châteaubriant, chevalier, seigneur de Beaufort, of 29 December 1379, E 142, no. 14.
20. See, for instance, the evidence given in an inquiry into the taking of homage in Brittany on 24 March 1392, E 142, no. 34, printed in Morice, *Preuves*, ii. 595–7; and see the letters of Eustache de La Houssaie of 20 January 1398, cited below, p. 128. But cf., also, the letters of Thibaud du Perrier of 22 February 1391, reproduced below, Appendix, document 5.
21. Letters of 22 February 1371, E 142, no. 13.
22. Letters of 4 May 1372, E 142, no. 27.
23. Letters of 29 December 1379, E 142, no. 14.
24. Letters of 29 December 1379, E 142, no. 15.
25. Letters of 8 January 1380, E 143, no. 7.
26. Letters of 3 April 1380, E 143, no. 6.
27. Letters of 11 October 1382, E 143, no. 9.
28. Letters of 20 January 1398, E 143, no. 32.
29. The term 'retenu . . . de noz genz et de nostre ostel' can be found again in the ducal letters of 10 September 1369 retaining Eustache de La Houssaie and granting him a *fief-rente*, E 154, no. 9. (I am grateful to Dr. M. C. E. Jones for this reference.)
30. Letters of 1 March 1380, E 143, no. 2.

Feuillée, chevalier, used almost an identical wording in his contract with John IV, like Raoul de Kersaliou, 'a la conqueste, pourchaz et recouvrement de sa duchié de Bretaingne'.[31] But in another, longer, document Silvestre de La Feuillée promised 'loyalment a mon tres redoubté seigneur lige monsr. Jehan duc de Bretaigne, conte de Montfort, que tout le cours de ma vie je li seray vray et loial soubgeit lige'.[32] This contract, made some twelve years earlier,[33] did not preclude the shorter contract, nor the inclusion in it of some of the more common general stipulations. But other examples of multiple contracting are not hard to find;[34] nor, indeed, are two examples of a contract with Duke John V by men who had contracted with John IV. On 22 November 1406 Rolland, vicomte de Coatmen,[35] and Raoul de Kersaliou sealed almost identical documents, in which the latter's obligation, apparently 'non-feudal' in 1380, was now, in its recognition of an anterior 'serement de feaulté' seemingly containing the phrase 'prouche a lui que a nul autre', apparently 'feudal'.[36]

But such recognition of, as it were, two layers of contract, one containing an oath of fidelity and the other a seemingly separate obligation, helps, one may argue, to make the matter clearer. In February 1391 Thibaud du Perrier 'sire de Querpignac en l'evesché de Saintes' acknowledged '[je] cognois et confesse par la teneur de ces lettres que combien que j'ey fait fay et homage a mon souverain seigneur [John IV] . . . comme son subgit et feal, que ce noiantmains je me suis alié

---

31. Letters of 8 February '⟨   ⟩9', E 142, no. 12; events would seem to indicate a date of 1379 o.s. rather than 1369 o.s. as given on the modern dossier of this document. Raoul de Kersaliou's contract is cited above, p. 125, and reproduced below, Appendix, document 3.

32. Letters of 5 March 1368, E 142, no. 7.

33. The date is admittedly barely decipherable; but the letters of Girard, sire de Retz, of 20 February 1368, E 142, no. 9, are an almost precise word for word parallel with E 142, no. 7.

34. By Jean, vicomte de Rohan: letters of 21 February 1372, E 142, no. 26, and of 13 April 1381, E 143, no. 5. (The reference to Olivier de Clisson in this document would appear to indicate a date of 1381 rather than 1380. Easter 1380 fell on 25 March, Easter 1381 on 14 April. Another document which falls between the two dates, the letters of Prigent Le Moine of 3 April, E 143, no. 6, I have, in the absence of other indication, assigned to 1380. But the reader should perhaps be warned.) By Geoffroy, sire de Quintin: letters of 11 August 1385, E 143, no. 12, and of 3 January 1389, E 143, no. 16; and by Jean Tournemine, seigneur de La Hunaudaie: letters of 26 January 1386, E 143, no. 13, and of 16 August 1389, E 143, no. 14. The reasons for the multiple letters are sometimes clear—Jean Tournemine, for instance, was going off on pilgrimage to Jerusalem—but the general contract was repeated.

35. Letters of 22 November 1406, E 144, no. 2.

36. Letters of 22 November 1406, E 144, no. 1; reproduced below, Appendix, document 4.

avecques lui a touzjours mes; et par ces presentes li ay promis et juré par la foy et serement de mon corps' to carry out the obligations stipulated, to John IV, to his duchess, Joan of Navarre, and to his heir, the comte de Montfort.[37] In April 1389 Alain du Perrier announced that

comme de raison touz et chascun les habitanz et demoranz ou duché de Bretaingne soient tenuz servir et oboir a mon souverain seigneur [John IV] . . . et plus pres a lui que a nul autre, ce noiantmains je par superhabundant fais savoir que je en esgart et consideracion aus grans biens, honneurs et profitz que mondit seigneur m'a fait, de ma liberale, pure et franche volanté et sens nul pourforcement, combien que paravant ces hores j'ey fait certaines promesses, aliances et confederacions avecques mondit seigneur, ce nonobstant en les confermant et ratiffiant je me alie presentement pour moy, mes heritiers et sucesseurs par la teneur de ces lettres [with John IV and the heirs of his body] . . . a touzjours mes, et li promais et jure par la foy et serement de mon corps et en leauté de chevalerie estre son bon, vroy et loial alié, subget, servant, aidant et oboissant

and also that of Joan of Navarre during her marriage to the duke and of the heirs of his body.[38]

Here the layers become triple: or, rather, the second layer divides itself into two. But the simple bifurcation finds adequate support in other documents. In 1386 the contract of Jean Tournemine, seigneur de La Hunaudaie, had also been made 'par superhabondant';[39] in 1398 Eustache de La Houssaie, having been, as we have seen, retained, swore 'en oultre le serment de fealté et hommaige lige que . . . [j'] ay fait', to John IV 'proche a lui que a nul autre senz nul en excepter'.[40] A number of contracts between 1388 and 1399 introduced the phrase 'combien que ge soye homme lige . . . ';[41] in 1397 Jean, vicomte de Dinan, and his associates, having recognized their 'feudal' relationship with the duke, continued 'toutesfoiz pour le grant desir que nous avons de plus aquerir et deservir sa bonne graice et seignourie . . . ';[42] and in the same way the contracts of Raoul de Kersaliou and Rolland, vicomte de Coatmen, with John V in 1406 continued 'que encores je promois et m'oblige . . . '.[43]

37. Letters of 22 February 1391, E 143, no. 23; reproduced below, Appendix, document 5.
38. Letters of 28 April 1389, E 143, no. 21.
39. Letters of 26 January 1386, E 143, no. 13.
40. Letters of 20 January 1398, E 143, no. 32.
41. Letters of Pierre de Tournemine, chevalier, of 8 April 1388, E 143, no. 15; of Guillaume, seigneur de Montauban, of 5 March 1389, E 143, no. 20; of Raoul, sire de Coëtquen, and others, of 11 November 1397, E 143, no. 31; of Bertrand, seigneur de Matignon, of 19 August 1399, E 143, no. 28.
42. Letters of 7 November 1397, E 143, no. 26.
43. Letters of 22 November 1406, E 144, nos. 1 and 2.

Finally, nearly three-quarters of a century later, in their contracts made in June and September 1475, Françoise de Dinan, comtesse de Laval, and Jean de Laval, sire de La Roche, used, amongst a great deal of grand verbiage, the old formula 'combien que par droit et raison naturelle . . . nous soions tenuz et obligez . . . et encores est nostre intencion de y perseverer . . . mais ce neantmoins . . . nous lui promectons d'abondant . . .' in obliging themselves to Duke Francis II.[44]

If one compares this with, say, the document issued by Pierre de Lesnerac in May 1371, in which he confessed 'que ge suy devenu homme de foy' of John IV 'et que ge li ay fait fay et ligence a cause de doux centz livres de rante . . . le temps de ma vie'[45]—a document recognizing the acceptance of a *fief-rente*—the anteriority of the homage and the oath of fealty to the oath of the contract recorded in the other documents which we have discussed is emphasized. In apparently only one document of this group is it necessary to imagine a fairly close connection between homage-and-fealty and another obligation. In September 1398 Jean Le Barbu, chevalier, announced that John IV had given him the lands, rents, and heritages of a number of defunct persons, and other rents and heritages in the bishopric of Léon, at present held by Tanguy de Kermaon, for which property held directly of the duke he had done him 'foy et homage'. 'Et par ce ait voulu', Jean Le Barbu continued, 'que je en jouisse tantost et incontinent amprés le decés dudit monsr. Tangui senz aucun debat ne impechement selon la teneur des lectres de mondit seigneur a moy sur ce baillees j'ay parmi ce promis et juré et par ces lectres promais et jure' a second obligation.'[46] But this situation must be regarded as exceptional. It seems safe to argue that normally the contract enshrined in our documents represents a secondary contract imposed upon an anterior 'feudal' contract: a secondary contract which would, were it not for that anterior contract, bear more purely the marks of a 'non-feudal' *alliance*: indeed, an *alliance* superimposed upon a contract of vassalage. And if this is so of the documents which give evidence of such bifurcation, it is arguably so of those that do not. In

44. Letters of 17 June and of 23 September 1475, E 147, nos. 11 and 13. It is not my intention to discuss here the documents recording the oaths taken by captains of Breton places on taking office; but one may point out that in a number of these, too, a 'bifurcation' takes place: the captaincy oath is taken 'en oultre' liegeancy. See, for instance, the oath of Jean de Juch of 6 November 1406, E 134, no. 15. Cf., also, the contract of Jean de Bueil cited above, p. 72, n. 11: the oath of *alliance* is taken on top of the *chambellan*'s oath.

45. Letters of 15 May 1371, E 142, no. 5.

46. Letters of 1 September 1398, E 143, no. 27.

this respect, all the documents of this kind from the *Trésor des Chartes de Bretagne* could be classed as Breton *alliances*; in this sense, as much 'non-feudal' documents as that rare life-indenture exchanged between John IV and Thomas 'Aldroiche', an Englishman, on 14 May 1363.[47]

As such the Breton documents compare well with those late medieval French letters of *alliance* that have so far been disinterred.[48] With one interesting exception, which will be discussed later, the documents range in time from that life-indenture of 1363 to the contract of Jean de Laval, sire de La Roche, in 1475.[49] The bulk of them derives from the reign of John IV;[50] a much smaller number coming from that of John V, two in 1406, one in 1422, the rest in the period 1434–9.[51] Two contracts[52] derive from the reign of Duke Peter II; two[53] from that of Francis II. The normal form[54] was a letter patent under a single name, though contracts made by small groups were not infrequent[55] and in 1437 contracts were made with the Breton nobility in mass groups.[56] Not infrequently,

47. E 142, no. 4; reproduced below, Appendix, document 6.

48. A few contracts have come to my attention to add to those cited in 'Decayed and Non-Feudalism'. Professor Philippe Contamine was good enough to bring to my notice the *lettres d'alliance* of Guillaume, seigneur de Marville, contracting with Renaud VI de Pons, of 9 October 1376, printed by J. Chavanon, 'Renaud VI de Pons', *Archives historiques de la Saintonge et de l'Aunis*, xxxi (1902), 91–92 (pièce xii); and Dr. M. G. A. Vale those of Guy de La Roche, seigneur de Montendre, contracting with Jean de Bretagne, comte de Penthièvre, disguised as comte de Périgord, of 30 October 1440, in Arch. Dép. Pyrénées-Atlantiques, E 643 (I have not been able to see this document). The contract of François, sire de Rieux, with Alain IX, vicomte de Rohan, of 19 February 1443, survives in Bibliothèque Municipale de Nantes, MS. 1693, no. 10. A contract between the seigneur de Mussidan and Charles d'Artois was referred to in litigation before the *Parlement* of Paris on 26 June 1385 (A.N., X^{1A} 1472, fos. 292–3: see P. Anselme, *Histoire généalogique et chronologique de la maison royale de France* (9 vols., Paris, 1726–33), i. 387).

49. Excluding those cited above, pp. 171-2, nn. 8–14 and n. 47 above, they are to be found in E 142–7. There are post-medieval copies of some of these contracts in B.N., MS. fr. 2709, fos. 182–222^V; MS. fr. 22339, fos. 83,157; MS. fr. 22340, fo. 130; MS. fr. 22362, fos. 20, 27–50.

50. Numbers by years, including renewals: 1368, 2; 1371, 5; 1372, 8; 1379, 7; 1380, 5; 1381, 3; 1382, 2; 1385, 1; 1386, 1; 1387, 2; 1388, 1; 1389, 4; 1391, 1; 1392, 1; 1393, 2; 1395, 1; 1397, 2; 1398, 2; 1399, 1.

51. Numbers by years: 1434, 1; 1436, 2; 1437, 4 (as well as the oaths taken *en masse*; see below and n. 56).

52. Of 1453 and 1455, both, admittedly, barely within the category we are discussing.

53. Both of 1475.

54. Contracts were recognized before the court of Vannes by Jean de Poulglou, chevalier (letters of 9 August 1387, E 143, no. 19) and of Nantes by Jean Tournemine, seigneur de La Hunaudaie (letters of 16 August 1389, E 143, no. 14). An indenture of 1363 is cited above.

55. See, for example, the letters of Jean, vicomte de Dinan, and his associates, of 7 November 1397, E 143, no. 26.

56. The surviving documents are in E 144–7.

too, as we have seen, the preamble to the document includes a recognition of vassality, occasionally a recognition of alliance or retainer;[57] occasionally there is a 'grand' preamble.[58] The commonest oaths were upon the body and upon the Gospels, sometimes regarded as associated, sometimes as not;[59] other oaths, when they appear, are primarily in reinforcement of one or both of these.[60] Frequently a contractor's property is obliged for non-fulfilment of the contract;[61] frequently, he accepts the penalty of diffamation.[62] The obligations of the contract include a larger or smaller number of elements from the common litany: the contractor promises to be a duke's good subject (or some synonym) or good servant (or some synonym), or both, more or less long-windedly, against all persons, normally without exception,[63] not infrequently *plus proche à lui*, occasionally to live and die with him.[64] Sometimes, too, the promise to hold to a duke's party appears;[65] not infrequently, the promise to help him preserve his rights,[66] particularly, in the spirng of 1380, as we have seen, to help him recover his duchy.

57. I have omitted from those cited above the contract of 'Franscico de Lescasses' of 9 October 1391 (E 143, no. 24), which seems to have a particularly military flavour.

58. See, for example, the letters of Jean, sire de Malestroit, of 20 April 1387, E 143, no. 18.

59. They seem to be regarded as associated in, for instance, the contracts of Rolland de Kersaliou of 28 May 1380 (E 143, no. 4) and of Prigent Le Moine of 3 April 1380 (E 143, no. 6), as separate in, for instance, the contract of Pierre de Tournemine of 8 April 1388 (E 143, no. 15) and, particularly clearly, in that of Guillaume, seigneur de Montauban, of 5 March 1389 (E 143, no. 20).

60. A number of oaths, particularly in the 1370s, were sworn additionally upon God (see, for instance, the letters of Even Chesnel of 22 February 1371, E 142, no. 13); some, particularly in the 1380s and 1390s, upon some chivalric concept (see, for instance, the letters of Alain du Perrier of 28 April 1389, cited above, p. 128). Thomas Pean, écuyer, swore additionally upon the head of St. Guillaume de Saint-Brieuc (letters of 18 May 1393, E 143, no. 25) but he was outdone by Jean, vicomte de Rohan, who swore to Francis II in 1484 on the *Corpus Christi*, the true Cross, the relics of St. Hervé, St. Sebastien 'et autres plusieurs saintes Reliques' (letters of 4 September 1484, printed by Morice, *Preuves*, iii. 439–40; I have not included this document, which came from Blain, in the tally for Francis II's reign: it does not appear to survive in the *cartons Biʒuel* in the Bibliothèque Municipale de Nantes). An oath upon God alone was taken, for instance, by Jean de Juch (letters of 4 May 1372, E 142, no. 27); upon the honour and estate of his person by René de Retz, sire de La Suze (letters of 24 August 1436, E 144, no. 5). No particular oath is mentioned in the contracts of Girard, sire de Retz, of 20 February (E 142, no. 9) and of Silvestre de La Feuillée of 5 March 1368 (E 142, no. 7).

61. See below, Appendix, documents 4 and 5.

62. See below, Appendix, document 4.

63. For an example of such exceptions see below, Appendix, document 2.

64. See, for instance, the letters of Brient de Châteaubriant, seigneur de Beaufort, of 29 December 1379, E 142, no. 14.

65. See below, Appendix, documents 4 and 5.

66. See, for example, the letters of Brient de Châteaubriant of 29 December 1379, E 142, no. 14.

Pursuing a duke's good and eschewing his damage appear fairly commonly;[67] less common, is the obligation to obey a duke's summons.[68] Informing one's lord of matters detrimental to him is a frequent stipulation;[69] other miscellaneous obligations also appear.[70] In a number of contracts the obligation is extended to a duke's heirs,[71] and in some in 1383–99, to his duchess as well.[72] That the contract is for life is e͏ ͏ ͏ icit in a large number of cases[73] and presumably implicit in the others. In some cases recourse against the contract is explicitly renounced.[74] The documents are normally sealed, sometimes by the seals of persons other than the contractors in the absence of their own,[75] sometimes by those seals in reinforcement of the contractors'.[76] Not infrequently the document is signed as well;[77] and other forms of attestation also appear.[78]

Evidence of the counter-obligation of a duke to his subject, servant, or *allié* in the Breton material, unlike that derived from Foix-Béarn,[79] is admittedly much rarer. In 1475 Françoise de Dinan stated in her contract with Francis II that

il a pleu a mondit seigneur de sa grace nous promectre et asseurer par ses lectres patentes que de ce il nous a baillees nous estre bon et leal seigneur et prince, garder, preserver et deffendre a son pouoir par touz moiens licites et raisonnables la personne, bien et estat de nous et de noz terres et seigneuries vers et contre toutes

67. See, for instance, the letters of Silvestre de La Feuillée of 5 March 1368, E 142, no. 7.
68. See below, Appendix, document 5.
69. See the letters of Silvestre de La Feuillée of 5 March 1368, E 142, no. 7.
70. See, for instance, those cited below, p. 80, and in the Appendix, document 5.
71. Ibid.   72. Ibid.   73. Ibid.
74. See the letters of Brient de Châteaubriant, seigneur de Beaufort, of 29 December 1379, E 142, no. 14.
75. See, for instance, the letters of Even Chesnel of 22 February 1371, E 142, no. 13.
76. See the letters of Thomas Pean of 18 May 1393, E 143, no. 25.
77. See, for instance, the letters of Françoise de Dinan, comtesse de Laval, of 17 June 1475, E 147, no. 11.
78. The letters of René de Retz of 24 August (E 144, no. 5) and of André de Laval of 25 August 1436 (E 144, no. 10) are signed only, with additional signatures. The letters of Bertrand de Dinan, seigneur de Châteaubriant, and Jacques de Dinan, seigneur de Montafilant, of 8 October 1437 (E 144, no. 13) are signed in the absence of their seals; Bertrand de Dinan not knowing how to write, Pierre de L'Hôpital signed for him. Occasionally there is the attestation of a tabellion: see, for instance, the letters of Jean Tournemine, seigneur de La Hunaudaie, of 26 January 1386, E 143, no. 13. That a proper seal was regarded as important may be seen from the letters of Jean, vicomte de Rohan, and his associates, of 11 April 1381 (E 143, no. 33) and of Bertrand and Jacques de Dinan, cited above. Documents in which a *constat* is given to interlineations or erasures (as in the letters of Alain de Malestroit of 22 May 1392 (E 143, no. 17) and of Hervé de Voluyre of 22 June 1395 (E 143, no. 30)) again emphasize the evidentiary aspect of these letters.
79. Lewis, 'Decayed and Non-Feudalism', p. 162. See above p. 46.

personnes qui mal, grief, ennuy ou domaige nous vouldroient faire ou porter en quelque maniere que ce soit.[80]

The letters of Raoul, sire de Montfort and de Lohéac, and others, of 28 November 1393 included sworn counter-promises of the same kind by John IV and by Joan of Navarre, who sealed the document as well.[81] In a very few cases, as we have seen, a pension was given; but in the main the nature of the contractor's interest is passed over in silence.

One must, of course, take into account the possibility that some of these obligations were, in fact, imposed upon a contractor because of some dereliction of duty or as a pledge of good behaviour. Hervé de Voluyre, chevalier, seigneur du Pont, a liege man and subject of John IV for the fees and lands he held in the duchy of Brittany, had failed to appear for military service and had had his Breton property confiscated; his contract was made in June 1395 when the duke released them to him.[82] Jean de Poulglou and his father had committed 'plusours granz cas de quoy peussent estre pugniz ou reprins a plusours fins, lesquelx mondit seigneur de sa graice lour a debonairement passez' before he made his contract in August 1387—a contract which contained particularly severe penal terms and which seems something like acceptance of a suspended sentence.[83] The contract made by a repentant Jean, vicomte de Rohan, returning to the fold in the autumn of 1484, has again the nature of a submission rather than a free contract.[84] One might well imagine that promises such as those not to leave the duchy without the duke's permission,[85] or not to make 'confederacion, alliance ne ligue a personne quelxconques de son pais ne d'ailleurs senz son assentement de quelconques matiere que ce puist estre',[86] have an overtone of constraint for good behaviour. Again, the emphasis placed upon obligation of goods[87] does seem to underline the penal aspect of these documents;

80. Letters of 17 June 1475, E 147, no. 11.
81. E 143, no. 29. John V's letters of 2 November 1437 (see below, pp. 83-4) in fact again recorded a counter-promise (Morice, *Preuves*, ii. 1315).
82. Letters of 22 June 1395, E 143, no. 30.
83. Letters of 9 August 1387, E 143, no. 19.
84. Letters of Francis II of 4 September 1484 (Morice, *Preuves*, iii. 439–40.)
85. See, for instance, the letters of Silvestre de La Feuillée of 5 March 1368, E 142, no. 7.
86. See, for instance, the letters of Jean, sire de Malestroit, of 20 April 1387, E 143, no. 18.
87. Obligation of goods is otherwise rare in the contracts known to me. It can be found, however, in those of Guillaume de Marville with Renaud VI de Pons of 9 October 1376, cited above, p. 77, n. 48; of Archaumbaud de Grailly, comte de Foix, and his two sons, the future Jean I de Foix and Gaston, captal de Buch, with Louis, duke of Orléans, of 4 April 1401; of Humbert, seigneur de Villars, with Louis II, duke of Bourbon,

and in one case, that of Rolland, vicomte de Coatmen, in 1406, a contractor agreed specifically to pay 5,000 *livres* 's'il avenoit que nous feissons du contraire, que Dieu ne vueille', as well as to incur the other penalties specified.[88]

There is perhaps no more than an echo here of the kind of pledge taken on both sides of the Channel in the early thirteenth century;[89] but it does serve to remind us, too, that the sort of contract we have been discussing might be thought to have had a respectable ancestry. In May 1241, for instance, Olivier de Termes made a contract at Pontoise in which he recognized that he had sworn on the Gospels faithfully to serve Louis IX against all men who could live and die, never to leave his service, never to join in confederation with his enemies but to make war against them, and finally to protect his men and lands and to warn them of danger to them.[90] But without an investigation of the circumstances of the making of each of these earlier 'fidelities' one cannot be certain of the status of such documents. On 14 June 1270, for instance, Geoffroy de Lanvaux, chevalier, issued letters patent in which he announced, very simply, 'que nous avons juré sur les saints Evangiles servir le Comte de Bretagne byans & loyaument à nostre poer, & li bailler mes lettres saellées'.[91] There is no breath here of a 'feudal' terminology. La Borderie, who discussed the tribulations of the Lanvaux family, seems to have assumed that Geoffroy swore fidelity to Count Jean *le roux* in 1270 because his elderly father Alain had ceded his lordship to him;[92] but Geoffroy seems already to have been co-seigneur of Lanvaux with Alain since at least 1267.[93] What, then, is one to make of his letters?

There would thus seem to be some room for doubt. An apparent emphasis on penalty clauses, and the general absence of ducal counter-obligation in our documents—the Foix letters of *alliance*, as we have seen, generally recorded a counter-promise to the *allié* by the count—

---

of 18 August 1402; of Jeanne de Voisins, dame de Mirepoix and de Lagarde, as guardian of Philippe de Lévis-Mirepoix her son, with Jean I de Foix, of 5 September 1418; and of Nompar II de Caumont with Gaston IV de Foix of 21 May 1439 (Lewis, 'Decayed and Non-Feudalism', p. 166, n. 4; see above, p. 50, n. 4).

88. Letters of 22 November 1406, E 144, no. 2.

89. J. C. Holt, *Magna Carta* (Cambridge, 1969), p. 85.

90. *Layettes du Trésor des Chartes*, ed. A. Teulet and others (5 vols., Paris, 1863–1909), ii. 449, no. 2914.

91. Morice, *Preuves*, i. 1021.

92. L. A. Le Moyne de La Borderie, *Histoire de Bretagne* (6 vols., Rennes and Paris, 1896–1914), iii. 345–6.

93. Morice, *Preuves*, i. 1007.

might seem to place the emphasis upon submission rather than recruitment. But the general obligation of a lord—'aid, help, succor and support', which Lord Hastings in England promised Henry Willoughby, esquire, in 1478[94]—was the same in the 'non-feudal' as in the 'feudal' contract; there was little need for a Breton duke, already in a 'feudal' relationship, albeit perhaps a precarious one, with the persons with whom he was contracting, specifically to state his own duty to them— though on occasion, as we have seen, he did so. The existence of documents much earlier than the later fourteenth century, of the same general purpose as the documents we have been primarily discussing, might seem to cast doubt upon the status we have given them. But perhaps the doubt should turn the other way: if these earlier acts of fidelity were made separately from an act of homage and fealty, then one must ask what their precise purpose within the system was.[95]

Perhaps, as in other matters, we should indeed concentrate upon purpose, rather than precedent. A Montfort duke of Brittany, perhaps more than most, had a need to acquire support. Like other lords, he might find it amongst the members of his household,[96] or the members of his Order. After the second treaty of Guérande in 1381 John IV, according to Guillaume de Saint-André

> . . . fist assembler les prélaz,
> Abbez et clercs de touz estats,
> Barons, chevaliers, escuiers,
> Qui lors portoint nouveaulx coliers
> De moult bel port, de belle guise,
> Et estoint nouvelle devise
> De doux jolez bruniz et beaux,
> Couplez ensemble de doux fermaulx

94. Indenture of 28 February 1478 (W. H. Dunham, Jr., 'Lord Hastings' Indentured Retainers, 1461–1483', *Transactions of the Connecticut Academy of Arts and Sciences*, xxxix (1955), 129).

95. One may take, for instance, the letters of Hervé IV de Léon making his peace with Jean *le roux* in September 1260 (*Layettes*, iii. 550–1, no. 4637; for the circumstances, La Borderie, *Histoire de Bretagne*, iii. 343–4) as presumably recording the equivalent (but without mention here of homage) of the *hommage de paix* referred to very briefly by R. Boutruche, *Seigneurie et féodalité* (2 vols., Paris, 1959–70), ii. 160–1. (For another possible 'purpose' of such documents, see F. L. Ganshof, *Feudalism*, trans. P. Grierson (London, 1964), p. 80.) For the comparatively rare instances of a 'vassalitic' relationship apparently created 'by a simple oath of fealty, without any homage being required', see Ganshof, *Feudalism*, pp. 79–80; Boutruche, *Seigneurie*, ii. 156–7; but see also R. Boutruche, *Une Société provinciale en lutte contre le régime féodal. L'Alleu en Bordelais et en Bazadais du xie au xviiie siècle* (Rodez, 1947), p. 56, no. 3.

96. See, for instance, the obligations of Jean de Vendôme, chevalier, vicomte de Chartres, on becoming John V's *chambellan* on 19 April 1441, E 181, no. 9.

Et au dessouz estoit l'ermine
En figure et en coleur fine;
En deux cédules avoit escript:
A MA VIE, comme j'ay dit;
L'un molt est blanc et l'autre noir,
Il est certain, tien le pour voir.[97]

The creation of what became a highly eclectic company[98] at such a significant time should not need comment. The *alliance* between equals —again a time-hallowed practice, of which examples can be found in the south-west as far back as about 1174[99]—was of course to be found in Brittany.[100] The *alliance* between unequals was likewise to be found there. If a duke wanted to be recognized as 'vray duc de Bretaigne',[101] or needed support in the 'conqueste, pourchaz et recouvrement' of his duchy of Brittany,[102] or support 'par especial' against Olivier de Clisson;[103] or if he needed assistance against Jean de Penthièvre, seigneur de L'Aigle,[104] his *funeste* mother, Marguerite de Clisson, and the whole *cohue* of the 'aliez et bienveillans de la maison de Bluys',[105] or even imagined the need for support against his own cooks or at least against those shadowy figures behind them in Anjou and elsewhere whom his spies had warned him had 'machiné la mort, prinse, mal, ennuy, ou domage de nostre personne, cell. de nos enffans et freres, ou division de nostre seignourie';[106] in circumstances such as these, what

97. *C'est Le Libvre du bon Jehan, duc de Bretaigne*, ed. E. Charrière, *Chronique de Bertrand du Guesclin par Cuvelier* (Documents inédits sur l'histoire de France) (2 vols., Paris, 1839), ii. 544–5, lines 3766–79.

98. See, for instance, G. A. Lobineau, *Histoire de Bretagne* (2 vols., Paris, 1707), ii, *Preuves*, 628–9; Morice, *Preuves*, ii. 1394–5.

99. See, for instance, the letters of Raymond V, comte de Toulouse, contracting with Bernard-Aton VI, vicomte de Narbonne, *c*. 1174, and Bernard-Aton's counter-letters, *Layettes*, i. 107–8, nos. 254–5.

100. See, for instance, the letters of Bertrand du Guesclin and Olivier de Clisson of 24 October 1380, Morice, *Preuves*, i. 1642–3.

101. See, for example, the letters of Rolland, vicomte de Coatmen, of 1371, E 142, no. 18.

102. See the letters of Silvestre de La Feuillée of 8 February 1380, E 142, no. 12.

103. Letters of Jean, vicomte de Rohan, of 13 April 1381, E 143, no. 5.

104. Letters of Jean de Bueil of 16 June 1439, cited above, p. 125, n. 11.

105. Ibid.; cf. the letters of Jean Harpenden, seigneur de Belleville and de Montagu, establishing a protection treaty with John V, of 10 August 1433 (E 181, no. 19) and of 6 August 1438 (E 144, no. 14); similar letters to the first were issued by Jean de Belleville, seigneur de Mirabeau, again on 10 August 1433 (E 181, no. 20). Cf. also the contracts of Jean de Rochechouart of 13 September 1424 (E 181, no. 15) and of Jean de Blanchefort of 5 February 1440 (B.N., MS. fr. 22332, fo. 222).

106. Bibliothèque Municipale de Nantes, MS. 1691, no. 19; printed in Morice, *Preuves*, ii. 1314. For the 'conspiration des cuisiniers' of 1437, see La Borderie, *Histoire de Bretagne*, iv. 247.

was a duke to do? He could appeal for assistance outside his duchy, as indeed John V did against Jean de Penthièvre and Margot de Clisson in retaining Jean de Bueil in 1439.[107] But in general it was to their own subjects that the dukes of Brittany turned, as John V in 1437 turned to Alain IX, vicomte de Rohan, and his associates 'ausquelx ayons fait declerer et exposer ce que en avons peu jucques a savoir et descurir' of the machination in Anjou, 'lesquelx acertanez desd. auterissemens et tres deplessans de lad. deslealle machinacion nous ayent promis et juré et baillé leurs sellez de nous servir en celle matere'.[108] The Breton dukes do not seem to have regarded—understandably, perhaps, in the circumstances—the 'feudal' nexus as strong enough, at least in those cases in which they seem to have felt a supplementary oath and a legal contract as necessary to reinforce it: hence our documents. The purpose of these contracts is clear enough. The form which they took, derived from the circumstances in which they were made, might appear 'feudal'. But arguably it is yet another illustration of that shadowy world in which 'feudal' and 'non-feudal' met. Contracts which established a *fief-rente* without a *rente* belonged, according to M. Sczaniecki, 'déjà à une nouvelle époque où l'on ne se soucie plus du droit et du vrai sens des institutions féodales'.[109] It is not, in our case, the use of a 'feudal' form for a purpose arguably 'non-feudal'; it is an attempt to use arguably a now essentially 'non-feudal' form to reinforce a decayed 'feudal' situation.

Perhaps we should forget about form as well as precedent. Did the Breton contracts ensure the fulfilment of their purpose? This, perhaps, is a question for the historian of the late medieval Breton nobility. In his letters of May 1380 Rolland de Kersaliou, chevalier, was prepared to promise 'que toutes autres lettres et promesses que j'ai fait paravant ces houres contraires de cestes, qu'ils soient anullees et mis hors de nulle value';[110] and in April 1381 Jean, vicomte de Rohan, too, made his promise 'non obstant autres sermanz quiconques que nous aions fait a

107. Letters of Jean de Bueil of 16 June 1439, cited above, p. 72, n. 11.

108. Bibliothèque Municipale de Nantes, MS. 1691, no. 19; printed in Morice, *Preuves*, ii. 1314. This document, one of the *Titres de Blain*, represents John V's counter-letters to those issued by Alain de Rohan, of 19 October 1437, E 144, no. 12. These letters, like those of Bertrand de Dinan, seigneur de Châteaubriant, and Jacques de Dinan, seigneur de Montafilant, of 8 October (E 144, no. 13), Jean de Beaumanoir, seigneur du Bois de La Motte, Jean de Beaumanoir and Guillaume de Beaumanoir of 26 October (E 144, no. 11) and Guy, comte de Laval, and Louis de Laval, sire de Châtillon, of 12 November (E 147, no. 12) took the form of the mass contracts of 1437.

109. M. Sczaniecki, *Essai sur les fiefs-rentes* (Paris, 1946), p. 164.

110. Letters of 28 May 1380, E 143, no. 4.

quiconques persomes'.[111] The views of Jean I de Rohan's great-grandson, Jean II, vicomte de Rohan, on the question of loyalty in the second half of the following century might have been interesting. But if this question must remain open it is still possible to add an element towards the answer concerning that of the enforcement of such political contracts—in this case in English Gascony; an element which illustrates, too, the attitude of English law to the life-indenture. K. B. McFarlane at one stage seems almost to have doubted whether such a contract could be enforced in the courts.[112] Later he was able to cite such a case in which, towards the end of Henry IV's reign, Sir Ivo Fitzwarin and Ralph Brit alleged before justices on circuit in the West Country that the other was responsible for the breach of the terms of their life-indenture.[113] It would be out of place here to go fully into the ensuing litigation;[114] but rather earlier than this, Gilibert, called *Petit* de Pellegrue, chevalier, brought an action before the king against Guillaume-Amanieu de Madaillan, chevalier, sire de Lesparre and de Rauzan.[115] His case was that Florimond, sire de Lesparre, Guillaume-Amanieu's uncle and predecessor, had retained him for life at an annuity of 100 francs, and had confirmed this in his will; but Guillaume-Amanieu had refused to pay him, and the arrears over three years amounted to 600 francs (Pellegrue was including the fringe benefits of the contract). Guillaume-Amanieu's case was that Pellegrue had lost his pension because of some delict committed towards him and for other reasons. Henry IV, or his advisers, seem to have felt rather in a quandary: Pellegrue had been an old

111. Letters of 13 April 1381, E 143, no. 5.

112. 'A first impression is that we must not accept the apparent finality of the phrase "for life" in the indentures at its face value. In the early days of the system some of the contracts had a sanctions clause for breach of the engagement; but after the middle of the fourteenth century this clause disappears. What is more so far no evidence of any attempt to enforce a contract in the courts has been published' (K. B. McFarlane, ' "Bastard Feudalism" ', *B.I.H.R.* xx (1945), 173).

113. K. B. McFarlane, *The Nobility of Later Medieval England* (Oxford, 1973), pp. 105–6.

114. I hope to do so elsewhere. McFarlane appears to have relied on an incomplete copy of the initial action, B.L., Add. Roll 74138. (I am grateful to Mr. James Campbell for this information.) A full record of this action, on Monday, 24 February 1411 before the royal justices William Hankford and William Skrene at Dorchester, can be found on the relevant assize roll, P.R.O., Just. Itin. 1/1519, m. 30.

115. Letters of Henry IV, of 12 July 1401, recording the settlement between the parties, Gascon Roll 2 Henry IV, P.R.O., C.61/108, m. 3. The document was printed in *Lettres de rois, reines et autres personnages des cours de France et d'Angleterre*, ed. J. J. Champollion-Figeac (Documents inédits sur l'histoire de France) (2 vols., Paris, 1839–47), ii. 310–11; but the transcription contains enough minor faults to justify printing it again below, Appendix, document 7.

pensioner of John of Gaunt in Gascony—Henry IV was to retain him for life and confirm his annuity on 19 July 1401[116]—yet the sire de Lesparre, especially one who was to depart from England with seventy 'familiares' and twenty-two sailors in his own barge,[117] could not be overlooked. A tactful compromise was reached. Guillaume-Amanieu was to pay Pellegrue 500 francs at Michaelmas the following year; Pellegrue was then to abandon all claim on Guillaume-Amanieu de Madaillan and his heirs and surrender to him the indenture received from Florimond de Lesparre. Pellegrue may have been more concerned with his pension and his arrears than with the joys of serving a sire de Lesparre; but at least his contract was thought to be legally binding.

Appendix

1. *Letters of Georges de La Trémoille, 1 February 1434*

Sachent touz que je, George seigneur de La Tremoille, de Sully et de Craon, en faveur du mariage nagayres accordé par mon tres redoubté seigneur le duc de Bretaigne et mon tres chier et honnoré sr. et cousin le conte de Laval, de madamoyselle Yolant de Laval, aysnee fille dudit monsr. le conte de Laval et de Jehan de La Tremoille mon filz, considerant que mondit sr. le duc me veult ayder et secourir comme a son parent et serviteur en mes afferes, je, pour lesdictes causes et pour les grans honneurs, biens et pleisirs que je espere que mondit sr. le duc me face en temps advenir, ay promis et prometz par ces presentes en bonne foy a mondit tres redoubté seigneur le duc de Bretaigne de luy estre bon, vray et leal serviteur, porter et soustenir ses faitz, estat et honneur, et le servir, conseiller et conforter en ses afferes, le ayder et garder et deffandre sa personne, messrs. ses enffens, biens, villes, chasteaux, forteresses, terres et seignouries a tout mon pouoir toutes foiz que besoign en aura, contre touz ceulx qui invader, assaillir ou grever le vouldroient, en sa personne, messrs. ses enffens, villes, forteresses, terres et seignouries dessusdictes; et luy reveleray ce que je scauray que on vouldra faire ou pourchasser ou prejudice, ennuy et domage de luy et de ses choses dessusdictes; et ainsi l'ay promis en tiltre de bonne foy sanz fraude, barat ne malengin le tenir a mondit sr., messrs. ses enffens et messrs. d'Estampes et de Laval, desquelx mondit sr. le duc se tient fort de le leur fayre tenir paraillement. Et en tesmoign et a plus grant fermecté desdictes choses j'ay signé ces presentes de ma main et fait seeller de mon seel. Fait a Nantes le premier jour de fevrier l'an mil iiij° trante et troys.

[*signed:*] George de La Tremoylle

[*Parchment, seal applied. Arch. Dép. Loire-Atlantique, E 144, no. 9.*]

116. Gascon Roll 2 Henry IV, P.R.O., C.61/108, m. 7.
117. Licence for the passage of Guillaume-Amanieu, seigneur de Lesparre and de Rauzan, to Aquitaine with this company, 12 June 1401, ibid., m. 15.

2. *Letters of William Stuart, 27 September 1436*

Je, Guillaume Stuart escuier, natiff du pais d'Escoce, cappitaine des gens d'armes et de trait dudit pais estanz en France, promet et m'oblige par la foy et serment de mon corps et sur mon honneur estre bon, vroy et loyal serviteur tant que vivroy a tres hault et puissant prince et mon tres redoubté seigneur monseigneur le duc de Bretaigne et a son aisné filz, et les servir a mon poair vers touz et contre touz qui peuent vivre et mourir, sanz riens en excepter sauff le roy d'Escoce mon souverain seigneur et la personne du roy de France seulement, et empescher celx qui vouldroint faire ou pourchacer ennuy ou domage a mondit seigneur de Bretaigne ou a sondit aisné filz, leurs pais, subgiz, terres ou seigneuries en aucune maniere, et s'aucune chose venoit a ma cognoessance qui fust prejudiciable a eulx ou a l'un d'eulx, leursd. pais, subgiz, terres ou seigneuries, le leur reveler ou faire savoir a mon lige poair, et generalment vouloir et procurer le bien et empescher le mal et domage de mondit seigneur de Bretaigne et de sondit aisné filz et de leursd. pais, subgiz, terres et seigneuries, et tout ce tenir, fournir et acomplir sanz jamais encontre venir ne y commettre ne obmettre, et tout sanz fraude, barat ne malengin. Et en tesm. de ce j'ay signé ces presentes de ma main et seellees du seau de mes armes, le xxvij^me jour de septembre l'an mil quatre cens trante seix.

> [*signed:*] G. Stuart

> [*Paper, seal applied. Arch. Dép. Loire-Atlantique, E 144, no. 7.*]

3. *Letters of Raoul de Kersaliou, 8 March 1380*

Sachent touz que je, Raoul de Kaersaliou, faz savoir que comme mon tres redobté et puissant signeur monsigneur monsr. Jehan duc de Bretaigne, conte de Montfort et de Richemont, m'a ordiené pour mes gages et pension la somme de doux centz livres par an affin de le servir, dont je li ay juré et promis, jure aux sainctes Euvangiles de Dieu touchees et promet par mon serement et en bone foy et foy d'armes et de gentilece, que je le serviray bien et loiaument a mon pouoir contre et vers toutes persomes de quelque estat qu'ils soient qui pueent mourir et vivre, a pourchacer la delivrance de son duché de Bretaigne et de toutes ses autres terres et heritaiges quelque part qu'ils soient; et en cas que je puisse sentir ou apparcevoir aucune mauvestié, domage ou traison envers mondit signeur je suy tenu a les li reveler affin de y pourvoir de remede. Et ce je promet et jure en la maniere dessusdicte tenir et acomplir bien et loyalment, sur poine d'estre repputé faux, parjure et desloyal en toutes courz et devant toutes persomes et juges qui soient ou puissent estre, ou cas que je feroie le contraire. Doné soubz le saell monsr. Jehan Kazvallen a ma priere et requeste le viij^e jour de marz l'an mill trois cenz sextante deiz et neuff.

> [*Parchment, sealed on a tongue. Arch. Dép. Loire-Atlantique, E 143, no. 3.*]

4. *Letters of Raoul de Kersaliou, 22 November 1406*

Je, Raoul de Kaersaliou, cognois et suy confessant que comme feal de monseignour le duc ly dois et ay juré par le serement de feaulté a vouloir et procurer son prouffit et son domage eschiver, le servir, ly oboir, le guarantir et deffandre a mon lige pouoir vers touz et contre touz, prouche a lui que a nul autre, que encores je promois et m'oblige faire a mondit seigneur les choses desurdictes sanz nulle faintise, estre o lui et tenir son parti vers touz et contre touz qui peuent vivre et morir a mon lige pouoir, a paine d'estre reputé faux et parjure vers mondit seigneur et encourir les autres paines qui en tel cas appartient; et quant a ce je m'oblige avecques touz et chascun mes biens meblés et heritages presentz et avenir, et ce jure et promois par mon sere-ment ainssin le tenir sanz aler encontre. En tesmoign desquelles choses en ay baillé a mondit seignour ces presentes seellees de mon propre seell le xxij^me jour de novem-bre l'an mil quatrecenz et seix.

[*Parchment, sealed on a tongue. Arch. Dép. Loire-Atlantique, E 144, no. 1.*]

5. *Letters of Thibaud du Perrier, 22 February 1391*

Sachent touz qui ces lettres verront et orront que je, Thebaud Perier sire de Quer-pignac en l'evesché de Saintes, cognois et confesse par la teneur de ces lettres que combien que j'ey fait fay et homage a mon souverain seigneur monseigneur Jehan duc de Bretaingne, comte de Richemont, comme son subgit et feal, que ce noiant-mains je me suis alié avecques lui a touzjours mes; et par ces presentes li ay promis et juré par la foy et serement de mon corps de tenir son parti et de vivre et morir pour sa querelle et de madamme Jahanne de Navarre sa compaigne, de monseigneur le comte de Montfort son filz et de touz leurs enffanz qui essirent d'eulx ensamble vers touz et contre touz ceulx qui peuent vivre et morir, sens fraude ne malengin et sens nulli excepter, et plus pres a lui que a nul autre, et de li aider et venir a ses com-mandemens toutes foiz qu'il lui plera me mander et que il ait a faire de moy; et que[118] le chastel de Plaineseve que je tiens a present sera au commandement de mondit seigneur et de ceulx qui tendront son parti; et que de tout mon pouoir, tant de corps, de biens, de forteresces que j'ey a present et pourré avoir et conquester ou temps futur par quelconque maniere que ce pourra estre, et touz ceulx que je pourré induyre et amener, serons et tendrons la partie de mondit seigneur ainsi que dit est. Et ces choses et chascune d'elles promais et jure par le serment de mon corps tenir fermes et estables de point en point sens jamés venir encontre par moy ne par autres, et quant ad ce je me oblige a mondit seigneur corps et biens presens et advenir par ces presentes seellees de mon seel. Donné a mon ostel de Cropignac le xxij^e jour de fevrier l'an mil iij^c iiij^xx et dez.

[*Parchment, sealed on a tongue. Arch. Dép. Loire-Atlantique, E 143, no. 23.*]

6. *Indenture of Jean IV, duke of Brittany, and Thomas 'Aldroiche', 14 May 1363*

Ceste endenteure faite parentre tres noble seigneur monsr. Jehan duc de Bretaigne, conte de Montfort et vicote de Lymoges d'une part, et Thoumas Aldroiche d'autre part, tesmoigne que ledit Thoumas est demoré et demorra toute sa vie o ledit duc pour le servir bien et loiaument vers toutes manieres de gienz, fors contre le roy 'd'Engleterre' et sauff sa ligence vers luy, ⟨ ⟩renent dudit duc chascun an quatre

118. me *crossed out.*

cenz escuz et boche a court, lesqueulx quatre cenz escuz ledit duc li a assignez un⟨   ⟩ner sur la renczon de la paroisse de Rex durant la guerre; et si ladicte renczon monte plus par an que ladicte somme led⟨   ⟩s est tenu et obligé de rendre le sourplus audit duc, et si mains vaut ladicte renczon ledit duc est tenu de le ⟨   ⟩lours ladicte somme, et en temps de paez ledit duc li assignera ou paiera ladicte somme chascun an ou il porra estre bon⟨   ⟩e. Et tendra ledit Thoumas par guerre deux archiers pour servir ledit duc a telx gaiges comme sera accordé entre ⟨   ⟩ parties. Et ou cas que ledit Thoumas voudroit faire voyage oultre mer ou autres pelerinaiges, ou aler en Engleterre ⟨   ⟩ ou deux pour ses propres afaires par temps de treves ou de paez, il porra avoir du duc son congé, lesqueu-⟨   ⟩uz ledit Thoumas sera tenu de retorner a faire sondit service. Et ce tenir et acomplir bien et loiaument o⟨   ⟩ctes parties en bonne foy l'un vers l'autre sanz venir encontre. Donné et fait souz les seaux desdictes part⟨   ⟩geablement le xiiij^e jour de may l'an de grace mil CCC soi⟨   ⟩ et troys.

[*Parchment, sealed on two tongues, one seal gone. Arch. Dép. Loire-Atlantique, E 142, no. 4.*]

7. *Letters of Henry IV, king of England, 12 July 1401*

[*In left margin:*] Pur Gilibert Pelegrue, chivaler, de concordia per R. confirmata.

Le Roy a touz ceux qui cestes presentez letres verront, saluz. Come debat & desacord fust par davant nous entre Gilibert autrement appellé Petit de Pelegrue, chivaler, demandant, d'une part, e Guillem Amaniu de Madelhain, chivaler, sire de Lesparra & de Rousan, d'autra part, sur ce que ledit Gilibert demandoit audit sire de Lesparra que come Florimont jadiz sire de Lesparra, predecessor dedit Guillem Amaniu sire de Lesparra, l'eust donné a terme de vie cent francs de rende chescun an & boche en cort a soy & a troys varletz & fen & avena pour quatre chevaus, moyan letre seellee de son. propre seel, lequiel don. en son. testament l'avoit confermé; e ledit Guillem Amaniu sire de Lesparra qui en present est l'ayt contredit de li paier ledit don., dont l'estoit dehu, a ce q'il disoit, le arreradgez pour le terme de trois ans, lesquiels estimoyt a deux centz francs pour an, et sur ce nous suppliest ledit Gilibert que li vousissoms fere compliment de justice. E ledit Guillem Amaniu sire de Lesparra se deffendist que ne l'estoyt en non. tenuz de compleir sa domande pour ascuns trespas que disoit que lidit Gilibert avoit comis vert li, pour lesquiels il avoit pardu sa pension., & pour autres chouses q'il allegoit davant nous, dezquiels chouses nous avoms ehy conysense. Nientmant nous, voulens nurrir pes & concorde entre noz foialx liges & subgiz, pour especial entre ledit Guillem Amaniu sire de Lesparra & ledit Gilibert, lesquiels nous tenoms & pansoms qu'ils soient loyals & prodomes & vailans, si les avoms acordé pour voloir & assent de ambes dues les parties pour la manier que s'ensuyt: c'est assavoir que ledit Guillem Amaniu sire de Lesparra ait a paier audit Gilibert de Pelegrue pour tout que li puet demander a causa de la annuauté surdite le somme de sinq centz francs diutz le terme de seinte Michel qui vient en un an, e ledit Gilibert de Pelegrue, receu ledit paiemant, que ait a quipta audit sire de Lesparra & a ses heirs tout quant que li porroit demander a cause des chouses surdites, e que le soit tenu de rende la obligacion. & ententure qu'il a dudit Florimont jadiz sire de Lesparra, & que d'assi en avant ils soyent bons amiz; lequel nostre apuntament & acort ambedeux les parties si ont approé & loé & chescuin s'en est tenu pour contente, & promys chescun en droyt soy par davant nous de tenir ledit nostre [acort] & apuntament sens venir encountre. Si donoms en mandement a toutz noz officiers & ministres de nostre duché de Guyenne qui en present sont o par temps avenir seront, que en le cas que lesdites parties o aucune d'icelles fussent refusans o contradisans a tenir les chouses surdites, qu'ils les constreinhent a tenir pour les voies & remedies que de droit o de custume du paiis se darra fere. En tesmoignance de quelle chose a ycèstes noz presentes letres nous avons fait mettre nostre graunt seal. Don. a Farnham le xij jour de juyllet l'an du grace mill. quatre centz primer & de nostre regne second.

Per litteram ipsius Regis de signeto.

[*Gascon Roll 2 Henry IV*, *P.R.O.*, *C 61/108, m. 3.*]

7

THE PENSIONERS OF LOUIS XI

At the Estates general of 1484 the question of Crown pensions naturally exercised the delegates a great deal. 'Qu'il plaise,' they requested, 'à messeigneurs qui prennent les pensions, eulx contenter de la revenue de leurs seigneur[ie]s, sans prendre aucunes pensions ne deniers extraordinaires: au moins se aucunes en ont, qu'elles soient raisonnables, modereez et supportables, ou regard aux afflictions et misères du povre peuple; car icelles pensions et deniers ne se prennent pas sur le demeine du roy, aussi n'y pourroit-il fournir, mais se prennent toutes sur le tiers estat: et n'y a si povre laboureur qui ne contribue à payer lesdictes pensions; donc est advenu souvent que le povre laboureur est mort de fain et ses enfans, car la sub[s]tance de laquelle il devoit vivre estoit prinse pour lesdictes pensions. Et n'est point a doubter que au payement d'icelles y a aucunes fois telle pièce de monnoye qui est partie de la bourse d'ung laboureur, duquel les povres enfans mendient aux huys de ceulx qui ont lesdictes pensions; et souvent les chiens sont nourris du pain acheté des deniers du povre laboureur, dont il devoit vivre.'[1] This line of argument is all too familiar. The attitude of the Chancellor of France, Guillaume de Rochefort, was suitably bland. 'Pensionum etiam benemeritis donandarum non est novus mos. Qui enim in rempublicam utilitatem notabilem attulerunt, aut qui, post actam venerabiliter aetatem, laborant inopia, aut qui principi, ob virtutem vel alias, merito grati sunt, consuevit regia magnificentia hos certis pensionibus, secundum eorum qualitatem moderandis, donare et eis, velut munere, gratificari.' But he was prepared to let the Estates have some details: 'cras,' he promised, 'huc ad vos venient financiarum homines, qui vobis omnia exhibeant. Verum de pensionum quantitate, nec forsan vobis haec res ad nimium onus, et minime necessarium videatur, statuit rex vobis tantum nomina pensiones petentium, non summas exhiberi, quatenus super his consilium plenum, et difinitionem capiatis.'[2] On 21 February 1484 six *généraux des finances* and six *trésoriers* presented the financial summary. The sixth and last section on the expenditure side concerned the pensions,

[1] J. Masselin, *Journal des Etats généraux de France tenus à Tours en 1484*, ed. A. Bernier [Documents inédits sur l'histoire de France] (Paris, 1835), p. 676. The reader will realise that references hereafter are kept to a bare minimum.

[2] *Ibid.*, p. 336.

'ubi fere erant nongenti scripti pensionem expectantes, et inter eos feminae repertae. Tantum autem petentium nomina scripta fuerunt, nulla summa addita, sicut hesterno die nobis fuerat a cancellario praedictum'.[3] Guillaume de Rochefort and the 'government' side were probably wise, but their caution was not enough for Jean Masselin, the 'journalist' of the assembly, as its spokesman.

'Ad pensionum statum venio, cujus non nos summae terruerunt, quod in eo minime sunt appositae, sed petentium numerus, qui adeo tensus et debito grandior est, ut si singuli conscripti modicam etiam pensionem accipiant, totos plebis loculos exhaurire necesse sit,' he complained. 'Credunt domini legati nullum pensione dignum esse, qui non aliquod officium reipublicae impendit, et maximam horum parte rejiciendam; numerus summaque proxime ad Caroli tempus in his teneatur.' The appeal to the golden age of the last-but-one king was a pretty hallowed one, but at least a trickle of realism was allowed to dampen Masselin's social fervour: 'quod si non putassent aliquibus esse permolestum, rogassent profecto etiam has pensiones ad tempus cessare, quousque contrita plebs a suis miseriis paululum respirasset'.[4] Guillaume de Rochefort knew how to deal with this one: realism was followed up. 'Reor etiam multos pensionibus donandos, quoniam rex quandiu minor est, omnes sibi benevolos facere, et nullum contristare debet. Quonam certe pacto creditis plurimos aequanimiter ferre pensionibus omnino privari, nec eis vel exiguam concedere, qui nuper maximas capiebant? Id profecto fieri nequit, sed muneribus et beneficiis, in fide et officio eos continere oportet. Vultis et in hoc Carolum septimum imitari, quasi rex in aetate Carolo par sit. Carolus siquidem per se et proprio consilio rempublicam administrabat. Hic autem ob aetatem id facere non potest, sed eum aliena ope uti, manibus non propriis multa gerere, totumque regni ministerium suis credere fidelibus necesse est.'[5]

Earlier on, the bishop of Le Mans, speaking to the Estates on behalf of the princes, suspected that many of the deputies too, 'forsan volent sibi pensiones continuari, et quasdam de novo creari, quae res Ludovici regis diebus maxime subditos gravavit'.[6] But the reign of Louis XI was too easy a whipping-boy. Complaint against the Crown pension was an old theme. It was, inevitably, touched on by Jean Juvenal des Ursins. 'Helas, povres aides,' he wrote in 1445, 'alez vous au fait de la guerre! Mes les estas et penssions des seigneurs du sanc de France et officiers, voire qui ne sont point es frontieres ne ne font ung exploit de guerre; je ne sçay dont vient cecy que il fault qu'i les ayent; ilz sont parens du roy, *ergo* il fault qu'ilz ayent ce que de quoy le roy doit faire guerre a ses ennemis. Il n'y a maintenant celluy qui ne veuille avoir pension, soit connestable,

[3] *Ibid.*, p. 348.
[4] *Ibid.*, p. 378.
[5] *Ibid.*, p. 386.
[6] *Ibid.*, pp. 80–82.

mareschaulx, seneschaux, baillis, cappitaines particuliers, oultre ses gaiges ordinaires. *Deberent esse contenti stipendiis eorum ordinariis.* Se chascun seigneur en son pais vouloit prendre les aides en ses terres et avoir penssions le roy n'auroit riens de demourant.'[7]

The Crown pension was, then, a problem. But rather than begin at the beginning it might be more profitable to stay jumped in the middle, as it were, at the end of Louis XI's reign when, according to Philippe de Luxembourg, they gravely burdened the subject. But first, perhaps, a rapid aperçu of the size of the burden. In February 1470, when Guyenne was in the hands of his brother Charles as an apanage, Louis' net income came, in figures rounded off to the nearest thousand, to some 1,854,000 *livres*. The pensions of the princes of the blood came to 326,000 *livres*, the pensions of the members of the order of St.-Michel and of courtiers to 221,000 and other miscellaneous pensions and gifts to 94,000: 35% of that net income.[8] Well might the 'people' complain. But how did the system work? And who, in fact, profited by it?.

In order to understand this an excursion is first necessary into the workings of the French royal financial system. The difficulties of this need not be rehearsed, but at least the exploration can be made as enlivening as possible. First of all it seems clear, perhaps surprisingly, that the king's final word in the politics of finance was paramount. If cutting someone's pension meant potential trouble then the system would have to wear not doing so. In 1470, for instance, the receipt could not stand the expenditure: 'et pour ce, sire', wrote Louis' financial officers rather desperately, 'que desdictes parties il en y a pluseurs que savons bien que avez a cueur et voulez qu'elles soient appoinctees . . . et impossible nous seroit de y toucher ne prandre conclusion sans savoir . . . vostre bon plaisir'.[9] From the few high-financial-policy documents that survive one derives the impression of constant deficit and reference back on the part of the civil servants: without the king's decision 'nous n'y oserions toucher pour ce que on a fait des retranchemens sur grans personnaiges, dont ne savons se serez content'.[10] At another time, having boldly 'fait des retranchemens sur plusieurs personnes sans y espargner aucun' and cut the deficit sharply they still thought 'sire, il est neccessaire que voiez les parties retranchees car peut estre qu'il y en a a quoy vous ne vouldriés point qu'on touchast'.[11]

The king himself, then – however much under informal influence – ultimately decided. In order to help him in his decision – or in order to

---

[7] *Ecrits politiques de Jean Juvénal des Ursins*, ed. P. S. Lewis [Société de l'Histoire de France], i (Paris, 1978), 533.

[8] B[ibliothèque] N[ationale], ms. fr. 20485, fo 89[r-v].

[9] *Ibid.*, fo 89[v].

[10] *Documents relatifs à l'administration financière en France de Charles VII à François 1er*, ed. G. Jacqueton [Collection de textes pour servir a l'étude et à l'enseignement de l'histoire] (Paris, 1891), p. 101.

[11] BN, ms. fr. 20490, fo 39[r].

provide the data for his decision – he and the 'Mess[rs.] de ses finances font chacun an ung estat général de toutes les finances tant ordinaires que extraordinaires'.[12] This appears to have been a comparatively succinct document of which only one example survives, though two other documents echo others: all these documents surviving, significantly, amongst the Bourré papers.[13] In this survey a pensioner would have found himself *couché*, as the term went, in the tenth item: 'les autres parties de pensions tant du temps passé que de nouvelles par vous [*sc.* the king] ordonnees . . .'[14] This, as it were, half-sheet of paper went to the king, deficit and all, 'ainsi que pourrez veoir . . . par l'estat et declaracion des parties particulieres que avons [wrote the *gens des finances* in 1470] baillé à Mons[r.] du Plessys [Bourré] pour vous monstrer'.[15]

At this point things become a little unclear: but probably – though this is guesswork – what Bourré bore off to the king at Amboise represented the next stage in the process. 'Après que ledit estat général est fait, signé et arresté, le département en est fait par mesdits S[rs.] des finances en [confusingly] divers estatz généraulx',[16] those of – here it is necessary to get down to the structure. The resources of the crown divided crudely into two categories: the 'ordinary' and the 'extraordinary'. Crudely again, the first included demesne revenues, the second taxation revenues. Two teams of *gens des finances*, essentially, ran the system. On the demesne side they were the *trésoriers* of France – the four as it were 'original' *trésoriers* of Languedoil, Languedoc, Normandy and Outre-Seine, with other receipts added on from peripheral areas which had come in through acquisition – notably Burgundy – and one – Dauphiné – never part of the kingdom though accounting through it. Each *trésorier* had his *état*, 'et a chacun des receveurs généraulx de Languedoil, Languedoc, Normandie, Oultre-Seyne, Picardie et Bourgongne [this is a text of the early years of Francois Ier's reign] chacun son estat. Lesquelz quatre estatz du dommaine servent au changeur du Trésor, qui est receveur général dudit dommaine, pour lever les descharges [we shall come to these documents in a moment] de son office des parties emploiées esdits quatre estatz'.[17]

One group of officers, then, for the finances of the demesne. Another group of officers for the 'extraordinary' finances, whose areas coincided roughly with those of the *trésoriers*: the *généraux*. At the end of Louis XI's reign these numbered five: Languedoc, Languedoil, Outre-Seine, Normandy, Picardy.[18] It is probably now simplest to take the pensioner

---

[12] Jacqueton, *op. cit.*, p.243.

[13] See above, nn. 8-11.

[14] BN, ms. fr. 20485, fo 89[v].

[15] *Ibid.*

[16] Jacqueton, *op. cit.*, pp. 243-44. One might suggest BN, ms. fr. 2911, fos 8[r]-9[r] as an example.

[17] Jacqueton, *op. cit.*, p. 244.

[18] G. Dupont-Ferrier, *Etudes sur les institutions financières de la France à la fin du Moyen âge*, i, *Les Elections et leur personnel* (Paris, 1930), p. 57.

through this, the 'extraordinary' side of the finances. To return to the formulary of the beginning of Francois Ier's reign. 'Ainsi qu'il est cy-dessus dit et déclaré, de l'estat général en sont faitz plusiers de particuliers qui sont nommez estats généraulx, c'est assavoir quatre pour le dommaine, dont cy-devant est faicte mencion, et les autres pour chacun des receveurs généraulx en la manière qui s'ensuit: Estat fait par le roy nostre sire de ses finances de la charge et générallité de Languedoil pour une année . . .'[19] The revenue having been estimated, the expenditure was calculated: 'il est a noter que en la despense dudit estat sont couchées et escriptes toutes les parties que le roy veult et entend estre payées, passées, et allouées sur les deniers de la recepte dudit estat . . . Item, pensions et entretenemens . . . Item, y est . . . couché ung article pour les cas inoppinez en ladite charge, dont sont levez acquitz et mandemens patens après la closture dudit estat'.[20] One's pension could therefore be 'couchée' in the 'chapter' of 'pensions et entretenemens': 'en ce chappitre sont couchées les pensions ordonnées par le roy aux princes et S^{rs} du sang et autres personnages ausquelz le roy donne et ordonne pensions par son estat général';[21] it could be assigned during a financial year by a *mandat* ratified by the *généraux*. And it could also be disguised, as it were, as a gift of the revenue of a *grénier*, which appeared in the *estat général* of a receiver general under 'Dons, récompenses et bienffaiz'.[22] But, for reasons which become clear later, one's pension, or part of one's pension, was further assigned upon a particular receiver below the level of a receiver general of a *généralité*.

Take, for instance, the complaint of Jean d'Arly *vidame* of Amiens to the Chancellor of France on 9 June 1465. 'J'estoie', he wrote, 'hier alé en la ville d'Amiens, contendant à parler à vous à cause de ma pension, pource que Jaques de Filescamps [receiver of Amiens] avoit dit a mes gens, paravant que j'eusse laditte pension, qu'il feroit merveilles pour moy, si maditte pension estoit assignée sur luy; et mesmes avoit dit à mon chappelain et à mon recepveur de Larbroye qu'il aloit à Dourlens et qu'il feroit merveilles de faire paiement pour moy; mais c'estoit à fin que on presist la descharge à sa volenté et qu'il me péust de petits morsiaulx, qui ne me feroit point de proffict . . .'[23] Pitfalls lay ahead for the prospective pensioner.

But at the moment the principal concern is with the documentation of what, *en principe*, was supposed to happen. Once *couché* upon the *parties* of the relevant *états*, one, or one's agent, drew one's *décharge* – as did Jean d'Arly – on the relevant accountant. It is at this stage that the through-the-looking-glass – though very understandable – world of French later

[19] Jacqueton, *op. cit.*, p. 258.
[20] *Ibid.*, pp. 259-60.
[21] *Ibid.*, p. 266.
[22] *Ibid.*, see below.
[23] *Documents historiques inédits*, ed. J. J. Champollion Figeac, [Documents inédits . . .], ii (Paris, 1843), 290.

medieval royal finance begins to become apparent. The aim was to avoid the movement of actual cash about the country. 'Pour soullager de peine lesdites recepveurs généraulx et changeur et évicter coustz pour le roy, quant le roy ordonne quelque somme tant à pension que don ou pour bailler ausdits officiers, ilz ont accoustumé de leur bailler une descharge qui monte la somme, levée sur ung recepveur particulier par le nom de celluy à qui elle sera ordonnée, dont ledit recepveur général fera recepte et depuis despence ainsi que s'il avoit receu l'argent et puis payé.'[24]

So the pensioner – or his agent – drew his *décharge* on – on the 'extraordinary' side of the finances – a particular receiver. The *décharge* – this is where the looking-glass world comes in – was a pre-emptive receipt on that particular receiver *via* a receiver general issued by the triumvirate of the *généralité* – *the général*, the receiver-general, and the controller-general.[25] The controller-general should not sign 'qu'il n'ayt cédulle que l'on nomme escroue' from the receiver-general. The pensioner – or his agent – had at this stage to give a quittance to the receiver general for *décharge*,[26] which he, or his agent, then presented to the local accountant. It was at this stage only that the cash – *en principe* – changed hands. But was the cash there? Pretty frequently, it seems, it was not. *Surchargé*, what could a local receiver do? He could pay a part of what was assigned on him, demanding a *cédule* from the pensioner that he would repay that part when the whole *décharge* could in fact be payable;[27] or the pension would have to be postponed to another year.[28]

On top of this the king could, faced with the half-sheet-of-paper *état-général* – in which pensions seem always to have been the most obviously vulnerable – the financial officers having told him that 'ce present estat est trop chargé': more from taxes, or 'd'autant seront recullées aucunes parties de pensions et dons sur les finances de l'année advenir . . .'[29] – decide to cut peoples' pensions. Such general retrenchements occurred. That they could be avoided is equally clear.[30] One played the system. Some people were perhaps better equipped than others to do so.

Some aberrations from this scheme should perhaps be noted. Whilst on the *extraordinaire* side of things one did not, as a pensioner, give a receipt to the receiver from whom one actually drew the cash – the 'pre-emptive' receipt from the *généralité* was enough – it was, in a sense, his evidence of your receipt – on the 'ordinary' side things may have been different – as they were on the question, for instance, of the gift of the revenues of a *grénier*, tantamount to a pension. 'C'est assavoir' (to return to the *Vestige des finances*) 'le roy faict aucunes fois don du revenu d'un grenier aux

[24] Jacqueton, *op. cit.,* p. 202.
[25] *Ibid.,* p. 201.
[26] *Ibid.,* p. 249.
[27] BN p[ièces] o[riginales] 1292 [doss.] Gaucourt 29110 [no] 84.
[28] BN po 1208 du Fou en Bretagne 27199/6.
[29] Jacqueton, *op. cit.,* p. 260.
[30] BN po 1173 Foix 26709/95.

seigneurs de son sang ou autres à l'avoir et prendre par leurs simples quictances par les mains des grenetiers; et, en ce cas, en vertu dudit don, le grenetier doit apporter les lettres originalles ou copie d'icelles s'il est dit par ledit don, avec les quictances, pour luy allouer le revenu dudit grenier . . .'.[31] And one can find, too, examples of quittances to local receivers on the 'ordinaire' side – to *vicomtes* in Normandy, to treasurers in Languedoc.[32] But the aim of the whole, apparently paradoxical, but logical and fined-down system is clear: 'Nota que ung receveur général ne doit payer aucune parties en deniers contans s'il n'y a mandemant exprés du roy pour ce faire, mais il doibt payer les parties assignez sur luy en descharges qui en sont levez sur les grenetiers et receveurs d'aydes et tailles de la charge, desquelz lesdictes parties doivent faire le recouvrement à leurs despens, pour obvier aux fraitz qui seroient s'il en estoit fait par le receveur général et que lesdictes parties fussent payées en deniers contans par luy'.[33]

The pensioner may have received his pension; but the accounting process was not over for the accountant.[34] He – or his proctor – drew up his account in duplicate, and appeared with it in the *Chambre des comptes*, bearing as well the counter-roll of the controller-general and the supporting documents. On the expenditure side the auditor had to examine *inter alia* the documents authorising payment and those recording the fact of payment. As far as receipts general were concerned the authority was a warrant roll for expenditure signed by the king and ratified by the *trésoriers* or *généraux*, presented with the accounts.[35] For particular receivers the authority was the accountant's 'état de prévision' drawn up by those officers or the *décharges* issued by them, accompanied by the controller's *écroue*. Evidence of payment was provided by the quittances. The accounts having been verified and closed, the duplicate account remained with the accountant and the rest of the *paperasserie* went into the archives.

This brief account of the auditing procedure cannot but be a very crude one – as, indeed, the account of the stages leading up to it has been. But both help, perhaps, to make clear the nature of the surviving documents for the disentangling of the French Crown pension system at the end of Louis XI's reign. There is no need to expand here upon the vicissitudes of the *Chambre des comptes* archives, or to appeal for the commiseration of those who have worked upon the débris in the *Quittances et pièces divèrses* and the *Pièces originales*. Enough, perhaps, to say that the situation – as in other areas – is not entirely hopeless.

For the last ten years of Louis' reign, for instance, some seven warrant rolls survive, for the two *généralités* of Languedoc and Normandy. The accounting terms differ from one to the other, but they cover for

---

[31] Jacqueton, *op. cit.*, p. 233. Examples abound.
[32] BN mss. fr. 20390 [nos] 45, 46; 26094/1239, 1272.
[33] Jacqueton, *op. cit.*, p. 241.
[34] H. Jassemin, *La Chambre des comptes de Paris au xve siècle (Paris, 1933)*, pp. 106ff.
[35] *Ibid.*, pp. 118-19.

Languedoc the periods 1476–79 and 1481–82, and for Normandy 1474 and 1482–83.[36] They are supported by the usual miscellaneous flutter of financial *pièces justificatives*. But, most useful of all, they help to illuminate a surviving list apparently of all the Crown beneficiaries, a 'roole des pensionnaires' to which a later hand has added encouragingly 'soubs Louis xie', some seven hundred-odd names on long, narrow strips of paper.[37] The names can be broken down fairly easily into the eight accounting areas of Languedoil, Normandy, Languedoc and Outre-Seine, Guienne, Burgundy, Picardy and Dauphiné. *Prima facie* the list is the answer to an historian's prayer. Controlled against the warrant rolls and other material the list can be seen to have been derived from the (largely missing) warrant rolls for 1480–81,[38] and indeed to include, errors and omissions excepted, the names of all those receiving Crown pensions in that year.

The neatest evidence for that dating comes as one might expect from a fragment of a warrant roll for that year which is not missing. Jean Lalemant became receiver-general of Normandy on 22 June 1481, and his account for the last six months of the year survives.[39] René d'Alençon comte du Perche had been arrested in the middle of August, suspected of intelligence with the enemy.[40] He had long been a Crown pensioner at 12,000 livres tournois a year, two-thirds of which was on Languedoc and one-third on Normandy.[41] On our list of pensions he appears on Normandy for 8,000, and his name appears on Languedoc as well, but is crossed out.[42] He was on the *estat* for Normandy for 1481; but Lalemant paid 3,208l. 6s. 8d. of the sum assigned to him to the up-and-coming young François de Pontbriant as a gift over and above his other wages, pensions and gifts – François appears on our list for 1,000 livres on Languedoil.[43] This would seem pretty conclusive as far as the terminal date of the material from which it was drawn up is concerned. It seems equally clear that that material cannot be dated 1478–79 or earlier: in 1476–79 Guillaume Keraudy had 400 livres on Languedoc, in 1481–82 Briant de Châteaubriant has 400 on that account – 'au lieu de' Guillaume Keraudy, as he does on our list – and as he did in 1480–81.[44] The year 1479–

[36] BN mss. fr. 23264/2-20, 37-54, 23265/1-19, n. a fr. 4419; fr. 23264/23-34, 23266/4-17, 18-36.

[37] BN ms. fr. 2900, fos 7[r]-16[v]; roughly 110 × 300 mm (¼ (taken down it) of the normal French later medieval sheet); watermark Briquet type 1038-41 (Troyes 1461-73 etc.); as far as the physical evidence goes, slips taken from a pile rejecting those with the half-watermark on the right-hand side?

[38] Dupont-Ferrier, *op. cit.*, p. 279.

[39] BN ms. fr. 20683/52-56.

[40] *Lettres de Louis XI*, ed. J. Vaesen & E. Charavay [Société de l'Histoire de France], ix (Paris, 1905), 68-72.

[41] BN mss. fr. 20373/17, 14, 15; 23264/25; 26096/1506; 23264/16, 49; 23265/15, 26097/1776.

[42] BN ms. fr. 2900, fos 10[r], 12[v].

[43] BN mss. fr. 20683/55, 2900 fo 7[r].

[44] BN mss. fr. 23264/13, 47, 23265/13; n. a. fr. 4419/[1], fr. 2900, fo 12[r], po 698 de Châteaubriant 16206/4.

80 seems ruled out by the seigneur de Baudricourt. He appears on the list three times, each time without a figure given and crossed out, on Normandy, Outre-Seine and Burgundy. Under the last he is styled governor of Burgundy,[45] which he did not become until 16 March 1481.[46] He was paid 3233l. 6s. 8d for his pension of 6,000 livres tournois per annum, for six months and fourteen days beginning on the seventeenth by Michel Teinturier, the treasurer-receiver-general of Languedoc on 20 March.[47] An awkward case, had he simply slipped through our compilers' list for Languedoc? A number of objections might be raised: but a reasonable case would seem to be made out for its being compiled from the 1480–81 material. And, perhaps, a final example. 'Michel de Gournaiz', Louis XI wrote to François de Genas general of Languedoc on 23 May 1481, 'de la ville de Metz . . . a acoustumé d'avoir pension XII^c livres oultre Seine. Il a esté mis en vostre charge ceste année': and, indeed, he appears on our list under Languedoc for 1,200, and again on the warrant roll for 1481–82, with quittances to match.[48] So yet again we are led back to 1480–81.

Nothing would seem, from the controlling material, to rule out that year.[49] And if, for the Languedoc part of our list, one marks those names which appear on it and the warrant roll for 1478–79 'A', those which appear on it and the warrant rolls for 1478–79 and 1481–82 'B', and those which appear on it and the warrant roll for 1481–82 'C', then the names in 'A', 'B' and 'C' succeed each other in gratifying order, with a little block of 'C' a third of the way through 'B' to prove the rule. The names in the warrant rolls and in the list are, of course, with a few exceptions in the same order. Everything fits. But one should not, of course, see the list, as based on the warrant rolls for 1480–81, drawn up until some time after the end of that accounting year. If some rolls were warranted the following year – for Languedoc, for instance, de Neve's for 1476–77 on 25 February 1478, for 1478–79 on 10 February 1480, Bayart's for 1484–85 on 4 October 1486 – de Neve's roll for 1477–78 was not warranted until the same time as that for the succeeding year, on 10 February 1480, and for Normandy things were worse: Lalemant's rolls for 1483 and 1482 were not warranted until 6 February 1485, and Raguier's roll for 1474 was not warranted until 24 November 1478.[50] Could it have been possible that by superhuman effort the warrant rolls for all eight accounting areas for 1480–81 were ready by the end of 1483, for a list to be derived from them to provide the basis for the list presented to

[45] BN ms. fr. 2900, fos 10^v, 13^v, 15^r.

[46] G. Dupont-Ferrier, *Gallia regia*, i (Paris, 1942), no 4100.

[47] BN po 222 de Baudricourt 5001/9. For 1481-82 see BN mss. n. a. fr. 4419/[3], fr. 26098/1990.

[48] Vaesen, *op. cit.*, p. 41; BN mss. fr. 2900, fo 13^r, n. a. fr. 4419-[3], po 1377 Gournay 31110/6, 7.

[49] A retrenchment roll for Languedoil for 1480-81 survives [BN, ms. fr. 2906, fos 8^{r}ff]. Discrepancies between certain of its figures and those in fr. 2900 are not inexplicable; and certain eccentric correlations are remarkable.

[50] BN mss. fr. 23264/20, 23265/19, 23266/46, 23264/54; 23266/36, 17; 23264/34.

the Estates general on 21 February 1484? This might seem to be carrying the doctrine of everything fits a bit too far – but it's a tempting thought.[51]

But perhaps we should start upon our analysis of the pensioners,[52] and begin, perhaps, with the more esoteric groups singled out for comment. The *feminae repertae* in 1484: over a dozen are there in force, headed (socially) by Marguerite d'Anjou, queen of England; mesdames de Bourbon, Beaujeu, Orléans, Navarre, Jeanne de Brezé dame de Chabannais wife of the vidame of Chartres, Jeanne de Malestroit widow of Tanguy Duchâtel, Jacqueline de La Rivière, 'damme d'onneur de la royne';[53] Prudence de Chastellade and Grace d'Archeles turn out to be *écuyers d'écurie*,[54] but there is always Ysabeau, widow of Pic Farragut from Rousillon, with a pension of 200 livres for the upkeep of herself and her children in 1476–79; by 1481–82 she is dead, and Pic's son Fortevent Farragut is getting the two hundred.[55] The *baillis* and *sénéchaux* remarked upon by Jean Juvenal des Ursins: almost to a man they are on the list, fifty-odd of them. *Cappitaines particuliers*: a spot check on Rouen and Toulouse, and Vermandois, produces a few names, too few to generalise upon; but it may be that the 'captains of particular places' did not as a rule get pensions. Nor, it seems, did the upper financial officers, on the whole; nor those notorious 'bishops of King Louis'. A search through a hundred and sixty-odd names produces a mere handful of pensioners.[56] The benefice was presumably enough. But, as with the Farragut family, we may console ourselves with the contemplation of the 1,000 livres pension of Anthoine Joliz esq., captain of 'la grant nef du roy nostredit seigneur nommee *La Grant Espagnolle*', the 500 livres of Nicolas Scotz, 'hoste de *La Tour Percé* de Lyon', and (in the following year) the 1,000 livres of Jean Baucher seigneur de Pontereau, *conseiller* and *chambellan*, the *roy d'Yvetot* himself.[57]

Seven hundred and fifty-odd names, let alone the round about 900 guessed at in 1484, is naturally a daunting prospect. The two hundred and fifty-odd for Normandy and Languedoc are more manageable. But even here analysis must at the moment be provisional. Too little is known of a majority of those who, paradoxically, may have provided the most

---

[51] The roll referred to above, n. 39, was warranted on 16 February 1483. I am, of course, aware that the list may have been based on other than the warrant rolls: in the absence of the *état* and receiver-general rolls, I have accepted the evidence of those surviving. The later copies of the receiver-general accounts in mss. fr. 32511 and 20685 provide only corroboration; as does other evidence more recently to hand.

[52] Information given without reference hereafter may be assumed to derive from BN ms. fr. 2900, fos 7^r-16^v.

[53] BN ms. n. a. fr. 4419/[5], [3], [4].

[54] *Ibid.*, [4].

[55] BN mss. fr. 23264/10, 44, 23265/10, n. a. fr. 4419/[3].

[56] Louis d'Amboise bishop of Albi, Pierre cardinal de Foix, Jean d'Amboise bishop of Maillezais; possibly the bishops of Avranches, Besançon, Poitiers, Narbonne and Toul.

[57] BN mss. fr. 23266/12, n. a. fr. 4419/[2], [4].

important cadre of the kingdom: the 'courtiers', disguised here with court office, ubiquitous *conseillers chambellans* and *écuiers d'écurie* as well as greater household officers, whose real significance may be identified in their actions in the informal politics of the kingdom: the agents, the go-betweens, the fixers. Really to get to know this group is therefore really to get to know the politics of the period: here prosopography turns into a study of action.

But to carry out that prosopography is of course another matter. Beyond the bare bones contained in the controlling material for Normandy and for Languedoc so far utilised, beyond the bare bones of the material for some of the pensioners in, say, Dupont-Ferrier's *Gallia regia*, or in Lapeyre and Scheurer's *Notaires et secrétaires*, or in the footnotes to Vaesen, one is at a loss to know precisely the value, in the year 1480–81, of a particular character in the list to the government. Much more work needs to be done: but in the end a dynamic picture of politics in action in the last years of Louis' reign may emerge.

From this question of immediate value in one particular accounting year may be the solution to the question of the variable size of the pensions overall. Why, precisely, was someone worth what? At the top end of the scale – 20,000 écus for Pierre de Beaujeu, for instance, one is out in the blue of princely politics. But even in the area in which the bulk of pensions fall variation can be great: M. d'Argenton at 6,000, M. du Bouchage, M. du Lude are well-known court figures; but placing those lower down the scale, in the great clumps of those receiving, for instance, 1,200 livres, or 600, 500, 400, or 330 (200 écus), the question of, as it were, pensionable status becomes interesting. Some court offices might seem to assimilate a fixed pension – but even here variation can set in. One must know the people.

One must, as it were, get to know them in their own homes; and one must know much more about their place and actual function in politics at their level. At the moment one has only a few clues for the well-known people – and even their political position and actions can seem at times cloudy. But when one has got an overall picture of this political society in action, will it seem as sinister – will the pensions system seem as sinister as it did to the deputies of 1484? The very large pensions of the very great apart, did pensions seem shocking because they were informal rewards for those who ran an informal political system? Due wage for due performance of clear office, like a benefice for the due performance of ecclesiastical office, was one thing; shadowy payments for shadowy function another, and the clandestine will always produce 'opposition' cries for 'open government'. These were obscure payments to comparatively obscure men, who were the lifeblood of the political system, a political system which, possibly like all political systems, could only run by services 'parallel' to open, but far more inflexible, entrenched or vested ones. All the clamour for open-ness makes one suspect – or indeed hope for – a fiendishly clever, effective non-existent system of politics: but this, alas, may only be in the heated imagination. Exposed, the clandestine becomes much more humdrum.

Thus one should not, perhaps, be surprised if there appears to have been no wicked plot, no subversion, no – except perhaps at the highest level, and except in particular cases – political operation of a patronage system. The Crown pensioners were not men bought: they were men rewarded informally for carrying out the informal – and most vital – actions of government. They did not represent a Crown 'affinity', nor a burrowing into the affinity of others – no crowds of Bretons on the list; they were para-civil servants, carrying out the para-administrative work successive waves of administration had become in turn too inflexible to cope with, and as successive waves of administration were probably to become in their turn.

This, it would seem, is what a prosopography taken as far as the material will allow will probably discern. It will also reveal – because it will be dealing with human individuals – the individual, human and potentially ludicrous side of it all. But the ludicrous could in turn have a political significance. Retrenchment might naturally be keenly felt: was it used to keep people in order, the stick aspect, as opposed to the carrot, of patronage? The great could be deprived of their pensions for political displeasure: Nevers in 1463, Charles d'Armagnac vicomte de Creissels in 1468,[58] Perche in 1481. But mere accident might put a pension in jeopardy. A pension – Guillaume Cousinot's for instance, in 1467 – might be cut simply by 'les gens des finances pour la grande multitude qui y estoit'.[59] General retrenchments were of course not unknown; less formal obstacles could fall in the way of the pensioner. In 1483 François de Genas général of Languedoc cut Guinot de Lauzières' pension in half, telling him Louis XI had done it, which, Louis complained, he had not.[60] Aggrieved, the pensioners turned to the king – 'Mons[r.] de Narbonne', Louis wrote to Genas a year earlier, 'm'a escript qu'il ne peust rien avoir de sa pension, dont il est appoincté sur vous. Vous savez qu'il est maulvais mesnagier et qu'il despend beaucoup: je vous prie que le faictes payer de ce qu'il est appoincté sur vous, et luy faictes le mieulx que vous pourrez'.[61] This was mild: the full weight of Louis' formal displeasure could fall on Genas too, as in the Lauzières case, for instance, or in that of a far greater person, René d'Anjou, who in 1479 suffered apparently from the same kind of red-tape obstruction from the general of Languedoc.[62] It was not only the comparatively little man, like the Queen's secretary Jean de Lessau in 1476, who needed royal protection from the civil service.[63] A weather eye had to be kept open for the interests of the politically sensitive;

[58] P. S. Lewis, *Later Medieval France: the Polity* (London, 1968), p. 222.
[59] Vaesen, *op. cit.,* iii (Paris, 1887), 136.
[60] *Ibid.,* x (Paris, 1908), 109.
[61] *Ibid.,* ix. 268.
[62] *Ibid.,* viii (Paris, 1903), 30-32, 34-35.
[63] *Ibid.,* vi (Paris, 1898), 64-65.

but retrenchment could fall pretty even-handedly, at least in principle. In 1478, in order to raise the wherewithal to buy René off from passing Anjou, Provence and Bar on to René II of Lorraine, Genas was ordered to retrench 'sur toutes penssions, au sol pour la livre'[64] – 5% – and the retrenchment roll for Languedoil for 1480–81[65] – the year of our pensions list – shows fairly even-handed dealing over the social scale at least. Madame d'Orléans was cut – even though Louis had promised her son she should not be [66] – M. d'Angoulême, M. de Nevers; Yvon du Fou, Guiot Pot, Josselin Dubois, Jacques Coictier the doctor, great and small from Queen Margaret of England (1,400 of 6,000 livres cut) to a Jean Le Mareschal (20 of his 140). Those who do not appear on that roll may have been those with a particular value to Louis XI that year; even-handedness may have been less politically than socially; but the impression remains that Louis did not think it that unusual a thing to do simply to convert to his own uses the pension of Louis d'Amboise bishop of Albi because he had overspent on a vow to Saint James of Compostella in 1481.[67] Amongst those not paid by certain Norman receivers in the same year because they were over-charged were, as well as our old friend Anthoine Joliz the sea-captain Pierre de Beaujeu, François de Laval comte de Montfort, the bastard of Burgundy Baudouyn and the bastard of Bourbon admiral of France and his colleague the marshal of France André de Laval seigneur de Lohéac.[68] So uncertain then did these pensions seem, so vulnerable to the first imbalance in the accounts; one wonders if here, too, they may in the end seem not quite as significant as they did to the virtuous deputies of 1484.

In 1480–80 – and these figures can be only approximate – the total cost of pensions was about 950,000 livres tournois. Of this half went to sixty-odd names out of 760: 50% of the money to 8% of the people, the smallest of whose pension was 4,000 livres. 75% of the money pushed the figure up to 27%, the smallest pension now 1,200 livres. The remaining three-quarters of the pensioners shared a quarter of the pension cake. Both rumour of the size of the great pensions to the grandees, and the number of pensioners altogether, might take the virtuous complainants' fancy; but they could not have it taken both ways.

Behind the formal reasons for the grant of a pension lay the details of a long workaday reality. Jean du Fou, premier échanson, received his pension of 1,900 livres tournois from Louis XI in the autumn of 1461 'pour consideracion des grans, loables et recommandables services que . . . [il] nous a fais par cy devant par longtemps tant a l'entour de nous en sond. office et en noz plus grans affaires que autrement en plusieurs manieres fait chascun jour et esperons que encores plus face ou temps advenir, et les

[64] *Ibid.*, vii (Paris, 1900), 158.
[65] BN, ms. fr. 2900, fos 8rff.
[66] Vaesen, *op. cit.*, viii. 316-17.
[67] *Ibid.*, ix. 37-38.
[68] BN, ms. fr. 20683/54.

grans paines, travaulx, missions et despenses qu'il a eues et soustenues a ceste cause, voulans aucunement l'en remunerer . . . et afin qu'il se puisse doresenavant mieulx et plus honnorablement entretenir en nostredit service . . . '.[69] Upkeep of a pensioner in royal service was a stock phrase: but the clause before recalls the 'many a shrewd journey'[70] suffered by administrators over the Channel: there is rather more here than mere form.

The career of a Georges de La Trémoille seigneur de Craon – down for 6,000 livres tournois in 1480–81 – described by Philippe Contamine gives one of the example of the higher-pensioned 'courtier'.[71] His colleague on embassy in the 1470's, Guillaume de Cerisay, was much more than greffier in the Parlement of Paris or mayor of Angers, at 400 livres.[72] Or amongst the myriad 600 livres pensioners take Jean de Garguesalle, premier écuyer du corps, who replaced Michel Jouvenal des Ursins as bailli of Troyes during Michel's 'disgrace' in 1461–65, and who may have died early in 1480–81 – and hence is crossed off our list.[73] Or at 800 livres Etienne de Poisieu, *dit* Le Poullailler, sometime king's panter, bailli of Mantes, nephew and successor of Aymar de Poisieu, *dit* Capdorat, bailli of Mantes, who had died in 1477.[74] Or the many more of whom we know even less . . . 'S'il est vrai' – and here I quote Philippe Contamine, 'qu'au sein du personnel gouvernmental de Louis XI certaines figures sont bien connues, d'autres sont demeurées dans l'ombre, au point qe leurs biographies se reduisent à des notices rapides et suspectes'.[75] This was the case of Craon: this is the case of so many others of those who were stood up in 1484 to be counted. Did they deserve that fate – a fate, according to Philippe de Luxembourg bishop of Le Mans, rendered perhaps less than wholehearted by the pensioners amongst those who exposed them as a part of the political wickedness of the *ancien régime*? Crown pensions were not new in Louis' reign, very far from new; and they were to survive Louis' reign, very long after it.

---

[69] BN po 1208 du Fou en Bretagne 27199/2.

[70] *Paston Letters and Papers*, ed. N. Davis, i (Oxford, 1971), 158.

[71] P. Contamine, 'Un Serviteur de Louis XI dans sa lutte contre Charles le Téméraire: Georges de La Trémoille, sire de Craon (vers 1437-1481)', *Annu. – B. Soc. Hist. France* (1976-77), pp. 63-80.

[72] A. Lapeyre & R. Scheurer, *Les Notaires et secrétaires du roi sous les règnes de Louis XI, Charles VIII et Louis XII (1461-1515)* [Documents inédits . . .], i (Paris, 1978), no 136.

[73] Dupont-Ferrier, *Gallia regia*, vi (Paris, 1961), no. 22529. He was apparently still alive in March 1480: Vaesen, *op. cit.*, viii. 165.

[74] Dupont-Ferrier, *Gallia regia*, iv (Paris, 1954), no. 14872.

[75] Contamine, *op. cit.*, p. 63.

8

THE FAILURE OF THE FRENCH MEDIEVAL
ESTATES

THE FAILURE OF THE FRENCH TO DEVELOP AN ADEQUATE SYSTEM OF representation in the later middle ages has long been seen as an essential element in the making of the *Ancien Régime*.[1] Already in the fifteenth century Englishmen were cheerfully aware of the advantages of the English Parliament. The king of England, wrote Sir John Fortescue, "may not rule his people by other laws than such as they assent to. And therefore he may set upon them no impositions without their own assent".[2] It was clear to Fortescue that this assent was given in full Parliament;[3] and it is implicit in his writing that the sanction against a king who fails to observe the rules of a *dominium politicum et regale* was rebellion. However fearful he may have been that the "laws of the English" might be replaced by an intemperate ruler with the civil laws under which the French were ruled, he was assured that the political development of England had given her an inestimable advantage.

The civil laws, Fortescue thought, were not necessarily any worse as laws than the English laws; but they did allow a ruler to act arbitrarily.[4] There was no barrier, however frail, to prevent this; no mean between submission and rebellion. The causes of this unhappy situation were by no means simple. It was not because of greater strength that the French king had been able to act arbitrarily in the first place: he was weaker, indeed, than the English king, since he did not dare tax his nobles "for fear of rebellion".[5] The French courtier Philippe de Commynes agreed with Fortescue; he admired the English system and thought Parliament, indeed, increased the king's power by giving him a great deal of money for his wars.[6] Nor, on a more theoretical plane, was he any better off for being an arbitrary ruler. Since, Fortescue maintained, "the power to sin is no power", the king of England by acting virtuously towards his subjects was stronger than the king of France;[7] and Commynes thought that the English king's summoning his Estates was "a thing very just and holy".[8]

And in the same way as the question of summoning assemblies was not a matter of relative strengths, so it was not a simple matter of good rulers under restraint and bad rulers without it. It is significant that, if they agreed about the nature of the virtuous ruler, Fortescue and Commynes disagreed about the nature of the virtuous subject.

Fortescue thought the number of robberies with violence in England was a signal sign of virtue;[9] Commynes thought that if a king should say "my subjects are indeed so good and loyal that they refuse me nothing I ask of them; I am more feared and obeyed and served than any prince on earth by subjects who bear all evils and all harshnesses more patiently and their grudges less", this would be "great praise to him and the very truth".[10]   Fortescue agreed with him in this at least: he thought the commons of France too spineless to rebel.[11] Behind Commynes' quietism lay a theory of the relationship of king and subject less radical than was that of England since at least the mid-thirteenth century; the views of the English legist Bracton contrast with those of the French legist Beaumanoir[12] in the same way as the views of Fortescue contrast with those of his French contemporary Jean Juvenal des Ursins.[13]   And behind both quietism and theory lay a similar contrast of hard political and social fact.   In the nature of that contrast lay naturally the reasons for the failure of the French to develop a political system in which law was a balance (however delicate) between the prince's pleasure and the subjects' consent.

Some facts are clear.   In England in principle consent to legislation and taxation was given in a single assembly for the whole kingdom, at which the whole community of the realm was represented; and on the whole English kings respected the principle.   In France a single assembly was a rarity.   There was instead a multiplicity of general and regional Estates.[14]   They can be put into two broad groups.   The first contains the general or central assemblies, which met under royal control.   The largest common meetings were of the Estates of Languedoil and of the Estates of Languedoc.[15]   The importance of both fluctuated.   They were active from the reign of Philippe IV (1285-1314); they went into eclipse with the latter years of Charles V (1364-80) and for forty years were summoned rarely. Both revived in the early 1420s; both suffered a second eclipse by 1440.   For the general assembly of Languedoil this decline was permanent.   The Estates of Languedoc entered a long period of firm tutelage.   The second group of assemblies — the regional or local Estates[16]— met some under royal control and some under that of the greater princes.   Their fortunes varied.   Of those under royal control, some were active only within the peak periods of the activity of the general assemblies; others survived them briefly; others again, like those of Languedoc, survived them permanently but found their initiative strictly limited.

Not only was there not a single assembly; but the system of

representation[17] was unformed. Admittedly towns chose representatives as in England; religious houses sent their deputies; but prelates
and nobles were until the later fifteenth century selected, like the
English peers (but unlike the English gentry), on the whole by the
ruler, more or less in accordance with what became a fairly fixed
convention. Representation proper of the nobility in a general
assembly did not appear until 1484;[18] representation of the nobility
in a regional assembly seems to have been confined to Normandy in
the fifteenth century,[19] where it presumably appeared because the
country was twenty years under English rule. In 1484 an apparently
efficient system of representation of regions, which had its
precedents,[20] was evolved; but equally apparent in the fourteenth and
fifteenth centuries was a dislike of any representative system.
However a deputy was chosen, a feeling that he could not fully
represent his constituents seems to have remained. Town deputies
were too often sent only to "hear and report"; nobles and towns
claimed that, if they were not present, their consent had not been
given.[21] As late as 1455 and even in Brittany where a regional
assembly flourished, witnesses to an enquiry into the duke's royal
rights felt it necessary to emphasise that what was decided by the
Breton *Parlement* was carried out "by all the *pays* in general without
any difference".[22]

The development of ideas of representation in late medieval France
is still a very obscure matter; but so, beyond in many cases a bare
institutional outline, is most of the history of late medieval French
assemblies. The general Estates have been very little studied. More
work has been done on the regional assemblies: for those of
Normandy, Béarn, Velay, the Vivarais, the Dauphiné, Burgundy and
Artois, and of central France under Charles VII (1422-61), at least,
there are adequate "constitutional" monographs.[23] With one recent
exception[24] there is no kind of general study. There is a shortage of
easily worked material; and it is partly this which has led to the
emphasis placed on legal, institutional and constitutional matters.
It is hard enough to compile a list of sessions of an assembly, let
alone a list of the people who attended them. The men who *were*
the institutions have therefore been utterly neglected; and it is
inevitably only in terms of them, their aims and interests and
personalities, that a real explanation could be given of the development
of the assemblies. Yet they could work only within a broader
framework of ideas and events; and though the enormous and
multiple complexity of the problem of representative assemblies in
France has produced a stalemate and though, since those assemblies

in fact failed, it might be argued that they should be left in decent obscurity, there is some point in enquiring into the general reasons for the weakness of the French Estates. The vices of those which failed point out the virtues of those which succeeded; and apart from the intrinsic interest of the problem to late medieval French history — indeed, to French history *toute courte* — an enquiry into the reasons for that failure illuminates some of the reasons for the apparent success of the English Parliament in the period.

The nature of medieval representative institutions in Europe in general has, of course, been much discussed; theoretical conflict has been acute.[25]   Essentially they were supposed to be a rather formal means of communication between a ruler and his subjects about matters of interest to them all.   Some of their historians emphasise the need of the ruler to consult his subjects; others the need of the subjects to consult the ruler.   Both needs probably existed everywhere in varying proportions.   Both "sides", therefore, could have an interest in an assembly.   Patently there were important subjects who could communicate with the ruler less formally, though in so far as the formal means of communication had become custom they might still attend the assembly.   But custom — or law — was not, of course, immutable: a new kind of formal communication might usurp the old, as in Flanders;[26] informal communication, under certain circumstances, might oust formal communication altogether. It is clearly a mistake to be at all rigid in one's views about late medieval representative institutions: they were what men made them, and no formal pattern can be imposed on them.   The question remains, why, in France, did the need for formal communication weaken?

What were the views and needs of the rulers?   The initiative in creating assemblies was, in France, clearly with them; and clearly they could at times find the idea distasteful.[27]   "Above all things be sure that no great assemblies of nobles or of *communes* take place in your kingdom", wrote one of his advisers to Charles VI (1380-1422) in 1408, "but take all questions and discords which have arisen and will arise into your own hands and, as king and sovereign, leave them to reason and justice".[28]   In 1442 Charles VII is alleged to have said that to deal with those who thought to "govern the kingdom through the three estates", "he would leave aside all other business to attack them and would treat them like the English his ancient enemies";[29] and Jean Juvenal des Ursins' account of his behaviour to the Estates of Languedoil at Orleans in 1439 seems to show at least that Charles preferred not to get too closely involved with an assembly.[30]   In 1484 some of the old servants of Louis XI (1461-83) thought "it is *lèse majesté* to talk of assembling Estates; it is to diminish the power of the crown".[31]   The greater nobles — like the duke of Berry and the duke of Burgundy — could at times seem to have much the same attitude towards the regional assemblies in their own territories.[32]

But the Estates could also at times be useful to a king or prince; and he could in fact urge their members to assemble.   Usually this occurred when he was under pressure from outside and needed to avoid what trouble his subjects might cause him.   The question of taxation naturally agitated them most. The idea of the necessity of consent was a hallowed one;[33] and an assembly could, by accepting the responsibility for a tax, allow a ruler to avoid local difficulties. At some times and in some places it might be impossible for him to be able to raise it without prior consent.   He might be led even to hand over the administration of a tax to an assembly: a number of regional Estates at various times took over in part or in whole the business of the assessment, collection and audit of the taxes they had voted and as such they might become entrenched as valuable parts of a ruler's financial administration.   An assembly could give more purely political support; it could act possibly as an agent of political unification; it could be a symbol of prestige and a mark of rank.   The necessity of a ruler's doing justice was as hallowed as the necessity of his getting consent to taxation.   An assembly could assist in the process of government by bringing up matters to be dealt with; it could ratify treaties and partitions of the kingdom; and it could act as a sovereign court.

This last reason for a ruler's summoning an assembly was possibly in some ways the most cogent.   But in France only one assembly — the *Parlement* of Brittany — acted as a sovereign law-court:[34] that statute law, made and broken only in Parliament, the foundation, in Sir John Fortescue's view, of English law and English liberty, could never develop in the vast majority of the French assemblies because they were not competent to develop it.   All the other reasons possibly could be more easily avoided by a ruler who felt himself free enough from external pressure to ignore the pressure from within.   The ratifying powers of the Estates could be overlooked;[35] general assemblies were too intermittent to develop precise functions in this or in any other matter; and however much rulers conscious of their duty of dispensing justice declared that they longed to hear the *doléances* of their subjects, Jean Juvenal des Ursins in 1439 and deputies to the Estates-general in 1484 at least clearly felt that the government thought their complaints were a bore.[36]   As a mark of rank an assembly was useful only to a seigneur on the make,[37] not to a king prestigious enough; and if Philippe le Bon (1419-67) might[38] (or might not)[39] dream of an Estates-general of Burgundy as a coagulating force amongst his disparate dominions, there is little evidence that any king of France felt the same.   Political support,[40] again, was possibly less valuable to a king than to princes involved in a succession dispute or with the king himself.   Though some assemblies had acquired considerable rights over the administration of taxation, little administrative chaos was caused in the areas in which they were withdrawn:[41] more was caused in Normandy when the Norman estates recovered them in the 1460s.[42]   And even the clamour for consent could be ignored.   If a number of princes never felt free enough to do this, on a high tide of victory a king of France could take his taxes in many places arbitrarily, and there was little trouble in the country.

Despite theories and laws to the contrary, rulers would abandon assemblies if they wanted to when the pressures which forced them to consult weakened.   How far were their subjects prepared to try to thwart them in this?   How great was the pressure from assemblies from within, which might maintain the institutions in balance against the ruler?   Certainly they seemed popular enough.   From Artois to Gascony, from Normandy to the Dauphiné and from Brittany to Languedoc in guises more or less familiar, the doctrine that what touched all should be approved by all was at one time or another proclaimed.[43]   Reformers dinned the virtues of assemblies into the ears of the government;[44] some politicians, with more or less hypocrisy, adopted them as a party policy.   The chronicler Pierre Cochon thought in 1405 that the duke of Burgundy "wanted the kingdom to be governed by the three estates as it used to be"[45] and the constable Richmond's interest in Estates was apparent in 1425 and 1428.[46]   They were praised by satirists.[47]   The rights of provinces to their estates were enshrined in charters and privileges[48] and were dear to the hearts of at least some of their inhabitants.[49] Yet there was in practice a real reluctance to form assemblies.

Nobody very much except the government in time of need and possibly some propagandists seems to have wanted a general assembly of the whole kingdom.   In the first twenty years of Charles VII's reign — in the depths of a war against Burgundians and English — six attempts were made to get such a meeting; only one was successful, after four or five prorogations, at Chinon in the autumn of 1428.[50] The story had been much the same for the fourteenth century;[51] and the only Estates-general which met in Louis XI's reign begged, "because they could not easily assemble", not to be summoned again.[52] And hardly anyone but the government wanted a large general assembly either of Languedoil or of Languedoc.[53] The meridional assembly had lost the western *pays* during the English occupation of the 1360s; it was reduced effectually to the level of a regional Estates of the *sénéchaussées* of Toulouse, Carcassonne and Beaucaire, and some peripheral regions;[54] as such it was vital enough. The general assembly of Languedoil suffered from much the same incapacity as that of the kingdom.[55] Though Tours warned its deputies, summoned to a meeting at Issoudun in 1426, that they should see that "a single region alone does not, without the . . . three Estates of the other regions, do anything it cannot do" and though in 1435 its representatives, arriving too late for a general assembly at Poitiers, refused to grant a tax without a further general meeting,[56] such feeling seems to have been more often lacking. The government found some difficulty in getting deputies to come;[57] and when they did come they refused to think in general, as opposed to regional, terms. As in the fourteenth century their quota of taxation had still to be granted and possibly modified by local assemblies;[58] local assemblies still granted taxes not apparently authorised by a general assembly.[59] There was very little opposition when Charles VII allowed the Estates of Languedoil to slip into abeyance; as little as there had been when Charles V did so, or the government of Charles VI.

A current of provincial feeling runs, in fact, through every French general assembly from the beginning to the great Estates-general of 1484. It was expressed succinctly by the deputies of Rouergue to the general assembly of Chinon in 1428. Languedoc as a whole might complain consistently against being summoned outside the province;[60] but the Rouergueois went further. "They did not want", they said, "anything to do with or to participate in a general assembly of the kingdom, of Languedoc and Languedoil, because they were not accustomed to be in assemblies with them; but the *pays* of Rouergue was accustomed to have an assembly of its own".[61] "Provincial particularism", in fact, is an obvious *prima facie* cause of so little regret for lost freedom. Admittedly there were some obvious mechanical difficulties in the formation of large assemblies. France was a large country. It was costly to send deputies to a central assembly: the total expenses of the deputies of 1484 were assessed at fifty thousand *livres* and some deputies at least received substantial sums of money.[62] But on other occasions towns were prepared to send their representatives long distances on urban business;[63] if they had thought the expense of an assembly worth-while they would have paid it. Payment of the other orders was a recent thing in 1484;[64] but again, had nobles and clergy thought an assembly profitable, if only for the sake of prestige or entertainment, they would have put up with its cost. An assembly of the whole kingdom was necessarily large; but both in 1356 and in 1484 a perfectly workable *ad hoc* committee system overcame this difficulty.[65] The north could not understand the language of the south; the dauphin could not read a letter written in the romance of Rouergue in 1443 and neither could his secretary.[66] But some southerners at least could certainly understand the ordinary French of the north. On no grounds therefore was the size and linguistic variety of France an insuperable difficulty. Endemic warfare was possibly a greater one. "Englishmen made such war in France, that the three Estates dared not come together", wrote Sir John Fortescue; and very many harassed Frenchmen might have agreed with him.[67] At least the insecurity of the roads was a useful excuse for avoiding attendance at an assembly. Yet still, for other reasons more dear to them, Frenchmen were were prepared to risk the perils of encountering soldiery.[68] The mechanical difficulties could be overcome.

But unlike England, France was a country in which the king had only recently in the early fourteenth century extended a precarious authority over domains from the beginning divided by those geographical, ethnographical and linguistic barriers. Regional economy, law, custom, politics and sentiment had had time to harden under regional rulers effectively independent of the crown. Such independence was still reflected in the fact that no representative sat in a medieval general Estates, for instance, from Béarn or Britanny; representatives from Guyenne sat for the first time in 1468, representatives from Burgundy and from the Dauphiné for the first time only in the Estates-general of 1484.[69] The structure of politics was essentially a regional one. In England centuries of social development had made possible a "community of the shire" and a "community of the realm", however aristocratic these may have been. There were no "provinces" interposed between a unit too small for independent political feeling and the whole kingdom. Such unity seems to have been possible only in England; even Edward I, the Father of English Parliaments, could not beget a central assembly for Wales or for Ireland.[70] It was little wonder Philippe IV, the Father of the French Estates, was unable to do so in his kingdom. To this extent, at least, England by the fifteenth century was the country of "liberty", because her governments had been strong; and France, the country of "servitude", because her kings had been weak.[71]

Yet more local feeling than that of the region as a whole could again weaken a regional assembly. If the fifteenth-century Estates of Languedoc succeeded in stifling the particularist impulses of the local assemblies of its *sénéchaussées* and of the outer areas,[72] it was not so elsewhere. When, at the Estates of Dax in English Guyenne in 1420, the deputies from the Landes insisted on deliberating apart, the representatives of the Bordelais were furious: they thought quite reasonably that "the matter is and was of very bad example, and the reason why that parliament came to no good and due conclusion".[73] Some regional assemblies were popular enough and their deputies even clamoured to attend;[74] but others — especially in regions longest under royal control — appeared wraithlike and faded quickly away. Inertia was at some time or another apparent in even the most fully developed assemblies. Even in Brittany, in Burgundy and in Artois it was necessary at least once to threaten fines for non-attendance;[75] and in areas in which proctors were allowed or in which absenteeism was disregarded the level of vitality of the assembly cannot at times have been high.[76] At a session of the Estates of Bas-Limousin in 1419 six members of the Estates consented to a tax for themselves and for twenty-five other people for whom they were proctors.[77] The circumstances of this meeting were exceptional; but the tendency may well have been general. There were apparently efficient assemblies; given the state of the evidence it is impossible to be more than tentative; but it seems clear, if only from the evidence of those that failed utterly, that in many areas the interest which might drive their members into assemblies was not enough to make them clamour for their lost Estates, or that their influence was not enough to make their clamour heard.

But who were the members of the late medieval French assemblies? The exact composition of almost all the Estates is, because of the same lack of evidence, impossible to establish. Lists of members even of the Burgundian assembly have to be compiled from records of payments made to notaries for writing out the letters of convocation and to messengers for delivering them.[78] Even if one can ascertain roughly the names of the people who ought to have attended any particular session, one can by no means be certain that they actually did so. Nor, having discovered their names, does one at the moment know very much about them. One is therefore forced to generalize. Most regional assemblies were more or less aristocratic; one — that of Languedoc — was dominated by the bourgeoisie;[79] none was dominated by the clergy or the peasantry.   The nobles of the regional assemblies were naturally on the whole of upper rank in their locality; and it was also upper local nobility, the middling nobility of the kingdom as a whole, who formed the bulk of the noble order at a general assembly.[80]   The princes of the blood and the greater magnates had their place physically in an assembly[81] and politically apart.   Many of the most important nobles relied on crown patronage for up to half their income by the reign of Charles VI:[82] their dealings with the king had long outgrown an assembly.   They, and possibly some nobles less important, could, from the beginning, give their consent to the taxation of their subjects individually to the crown.[83] In the same sense as the English Parliament was the thing of the shire knights, so the majority of the French Estates were the thing of the *moyenne noblesse*.

How far did the assemblies serve their interests ?   The protection of regional liberties and privileges might well be of importance to them as to the other two orders; there were private liberties which were more important privately but the common protection of general privilege might become a shibboleth; local pride might provide a kind of inertia which carried an assembly along. But clearly a nobility exempt, as the French nobility (as long as it lived nobly in the practice of arms) was almost completely exempt, from taxation[84] lacked one of the greater spurs towards protecting parliamentary liberties.   Unlike the nobility and gentry of England, whose kings had been strong enough to extract taxation from them, the nobility of France were without the strongest motive for resistance to their rulers.   Their interest lay only in the protection of their subjects, the taxpayers.   The knight Philippe de Poitiers, deputy for the *bailliage* of Troyes in 1484, argued that the nobility and clergy were more active in their defence than the bourgeoisie who claimed to represent the *tiers-état;* he made the obvious point that it was from their peasantry that the clergy and the nobility derived all their living and that it was in their own interest to resist the taxation of the people.[85]   But even if this had been true[86] it was a different thing to be prodded into resistance as it were by remote control.   Nor does the nobility of France seem generally to have been stirred to delight in national administration by practice in it locally.   A number of offices in local administration, royal and seigneurial, was open to the local nobility; but the majority of these was to a large degree shared by clergy and bourgeoisie.   Length of service in office was considerable: there was hardly a rapid turn-over of jobs; and the English proliferation of minor commissions seems to have been unknown in France.[87]   The duty of attending a law-court was confined to the Bretons.   A sense of responsibility must have been all that remained to stir many of the nobility into attending an assembly.

And did more private interests contradict their public duty? Clientage was admittedly very much in the air in the Estates-general of 1484;[88] and Commynes said that the *seigneurs* of France consented to arbitrary taxation "for certain pensions which were promised them for the money taken on their lands".[89]   The *quid pro quo* for consent had been employed since the early fourteenth century;[90] and there was certainly enough in the relationship of nobles and superiors (kings or princes) to provide a basis for a quiet understanding.   But evidence for interference with the choice of members is inconclusive, even when, in 1484, they were all elected;[91] and the "management" of the Estates-general seems to have broken down over the question of taxation: more deep-rooted loyalties put the deputies of 1484 at each others' throats in defence of the region they represented.   In this, at least, duty triumphed.   Was there indeed a line beyond which "interest" could not go?   The Burgundian estates had a reputation for independence in the fifteenth century and the session of July 1448 is regarded as one in which they were, on a matter allegedly of principle, more intransigent than usual.[92]   The duke was particularly anxious to influence this meeting.   The fifteen members of the nobility, the most important order, might seem at a cursory glance amenable to persuasion.   More or less closely inter-related (though this might at times bring more discord than harmony), they included the husband of an illegitimate daughter of Burgundy; nine of them had at one time or another been ducal councillors, officers or courtiers; at least two of them were heavily in debt.   Yet the duke failed to get things all his own way.   That the claims of patronage existed is certain; but one must clearly be careful in generalizations based upon them.

The bourgeoisie allegedly had greater interest in attending an assembly than that which came from a mere sense of responsibility. The question of the administration of taxation ostensibly affected them most nearly, though the privilege again could become possibly a matter of local pride equally protected by the other orders.   And members of the bourgeoisie, too, as Philippe de Poitiers was careful to point out, could become exempt from taxation.[93]   Royal creditors anxious for repayment and urban oligarchs anxious for the support of royal officers in suppressing the lower classes[94] were hardly likely to raise too many difficulties for a ruler.   There were many interests which a town might have to discuss with the government; but was it necessary to discuss them in an assembly?   Backstairs representations and bargaining with their ruler were a perpetual theme throughout the period in towns which varied in status from that of Lyon to that of Millau.[95]   The private arrangement remained the most profitable possibly on both sides; the use of the strict mandate to bind deputies only to "hear and report" was the prolegomenon to direct negotiation and the destruction of a representative assembly.   It was something of a triumph for Charles VII to have persuaded the urban deputies to the Estates of Languedoil in 1421-39 to come with full powers.[96]

Reluctance to attend an assembly which one might regard simply as a convenient device for extracting taxation with little offered in return, (which was what at least some Norman deputies thought of regional assemblies in 1484)[97] might reinforce this kind of particularism. There were pains, as well as constitutional pleasures, in Estates too much under pressure.   At some assemblies royal or seigneurial officers were present and clearly influenced the discussion;[98] in 1484 the president of the Estates was controlled by the government and there were government men amongst the members as well as partisans of the conflicting parties.   Every kind of pressure, according to Masselin, was put on the independent deputies to submit; and eventually they did so.   But there were even more open forms of coercion of a reluctant assembly.   It could be kept in session or threatened with a further meeting under troublesome conditions with a personal summons for its members.[99]   In the last resort the Estates could be bypassed and commissioners sent to make "particular demands" of groups of taxpayers directly.[100]   Direct negotiation, too, had its painful side.   In 1462 the Millavois were threatened with a fine of "a hundred marks of silver and with the seizure and sale of our goods and with the arrest of our persons and on top of that with the penalty of being rebels and disobedient to the king our lord" if they did not accede to such a demand.[101]   Under such circumstances the delaying tactics of deputies — even the wholesale bribery of royal officers by which the Estates of Rouergue attempted in 1462 to avoid taxation[102]— may perhaps be seen more sympathetically.

Yet some assemblies did survive.   At the death of Louis XI there were still Estates under royal control in Normandy, Rouergue, Languedoc, the Dauphiné, Provence and Burgundy; under seigneurial control in Brittany, south-west France, the viscounty of Turenne, the Bourbonnais, the Beaujolais and elsewhere.   By 1484 it had become accepted — at times with envy — that these areas had assemblies.[103] Although some of them showed a tendency towards the development of fragmentary Estates,[104] so destructive elsewhere, many felt a sentimental attachment to and pride in their full Estates.[105] As far as their social structure was concerned they had little in common to mark them out from other areas.[106] Nor had they common ground in the possession of administrative functions marginally useful to the government: if Languedoc, for instance, had retained some administration of taxation, Normandy had tried it again under Louis XI and seems to have abandoned its rights.[107] Nor did their secret lie in the absence of a *mandat imperatif* or in a refusal to allow proctors.[108] Their common characteristic lay rather in the fact that all had for longer than the rest of France enjoyed a greater or less degree of independent political life. Amongst areas whose assemblies were summoned by the king, Provence, Burgundy and Artois were very recently under royal control; the Dauphiné was not finally amalgamated into the kingdom until 1457; the Normans, always more independent than others, had in the matter of assemblies found encouragement under the English occupation; the meridionals were furthest from the centre — though the Estates of Languedoc were threatened with extinction in 1442.[109] Guyenne, which might have been expected to be a member of this group, had never had an effective assembly under English rule.[110] In the other areas the regional feeling which had destroyed the national assemblies, had preserved by its very strength their local assemblies.

As far as those Estates which survived under seigneurial control were concerned the problem was possibly simpler. Not only were regional *seigneurs* weaker *vis-à-vis* their country neighbours — it needed perhaps the exceptional toughness of Gaston Fébus to take taxes arbitrarily in Béarn in the later fourteenth century[111] — but the members of the assembly might have a considerable interest in uniting with the ruler in a common defence of the *pays*. This happened not only, say, in Brittany or fifteenth-century Béarn;[112] it also happened in Turenne. There in 1477 the Estates subvented the viscount's defence of the exemption of the viscounty from royal taxation; and when Louis XI's commissioners appear to have tried to object on the ground that the subvention had not been taken with the consent of the assembly, it was little wonder that the Estates in 1486 could be persuaded to declare, at least, that "they never knew that" the viscount "had ever taken any tax in the viscounty without the consent of the members of the Estates".[113] Here there was a clear political *raison d'être* for an assembly.

And clearly this factor of external pressure had been paramount in the creation of the assemblies which had existed and which no longer survived. They were summoned by the king when he needed political support to raise money in time of war and possible or actual rebellion; when that political need vanished so did the assemblies, both general and local. Some, like those of Auvergne or of Limousin, may have gone with some regret; and if the Estates of Auvergne lost their right to grant royal taxes they continued in existence in order to grant them to the duke of Bourbon.[111]   Here the flame might almost have been permanent. Elsewhere its artificial flicker was all too easily extinguished; easily, too, rekindled for *ad hoc* sessions under royal initiative. The initiative had always been the king's; but regions and their assemblies could have taken advantage of it. That they did not was perhaps their own fault. It seems simply to have been that assemblies were not of interest to them. Without fuel there could be no fire.

Where there was fuel, the fire burned—however much damped down. Assemblies were conscious of the identity of the *pays*, of the unity of its orders. When, in Artois in 1467, the *tiers-état* held out and an attempt was made to make the decision of the first and second orders binding on the third, the assembly declared that "if all the estates were not united together and in common agreement, nothing should be done"; and the government had to give in.[115]   There was the same sort of attitude in the Dauphiné in 1391.[116]   The obvious attempts were made to play off order against order elsewhere:[117] but they do not seem to have been important. More important, possibly — though admittedly it was made in defence of the payment of clergy and nobility as well as of bourgeoisie by the *bailliage* they represented — was the declaration of the unity of the orders made by Philippe de Poitiers in 1484. As well as the hierarchic conception of society there did exist others which implied a greater unity.[118]   Such views, coupled with a strong sense of regional identity and, in some cases, with political purpose, were sufficient to keep the flicker alight. Even in the Estates which did survive it was a precarious matter; but then it was a precarious matter in all assemblies, since the political *conjoncture* on which they depended might be far from stable. No assembly could be guaranteed permanent life; but a respectable history might provide an impetus to carry the Estates, as in England in the late fifteenth and early sixteenth centuries, over an awkward period. The same kind of impetus was found in the French regional assemblies which survived. Elsewhere, and in the kingdom as a whole, it did not exist.

In place of a sentimental attachment to assemblies, and out of the last trials of the country in the Hundred Years' War, came a sentimental attachment to a strong ruler. The readiness of Frenchmen to submit was extolled not only by Commynes but also by Chancellor Rochefort in the Estates-general of 1484. If Sir John Fortescue could complain of French lack of rebelliousness, Guillaume de Rochefort could allege that the English had had twenty-six changes of dynasty since the foundation of their monarchy. "No-one", he added, "no-one will descry such faithlessness amongst the French, such stigmata of crime".[119] Almost the same thing was said by a spokesman of the assembly itself, Jean de Rély; and the formidable Masselin, too, echoed Commynes in his plea that the government should not oppress a people so willing to support it body and soul.[120] In place of the checks to such oppression imposed by Parliament and eventually by revolt, Commynes, like Jean Juvenal des Ursins before and Claude de Seyssel afterwards, offered principally the inner bridle of conscience.[121] "Is it then", he asked, "over such subjects that the king should claim the privilege of being able to take as he pleases, who give to him so liberally? Would it not be more just towards God and the world to take taxes by consent than by uncontrolled will?".[122] More just indeed; but over subjects indeed "so good and loyal" why should a king bother?

NOTES

[1] A. de Tocqueville, *L'Ancien Régime et la Révolution*, ed. J. Mayer, i (Paris, 1952), p. 160.

[2] Sir J. Fortescue, *The Governance of England*, ed. C. Plummer, (Oxford, 1885), p. 109.

[3] Sir J. Fortescue, *De Laudibus Legum Anglie*, ed. S. Chrimes, (Cambridge, 1942), p. 40. The arguments of R. Hinton, "English Constitutional Theories from Sir John Fortescue to Sir John Eliot", *Eng. Hist. Rev.*, lxxv (1960), pp. 410-18, on Fortescue's political ideas seem to me acceptable.

[4] *De Laudibus*, p. 90. [5] *Governance*, p. 114.

[6] P. de Commynes, *Mémoires*, ed. J. Calmette & G. Durville, ii (Paris, 1925), p. 8. Cf. V. Bourilly, "Les Idées politiques de Commines", *Rev. d'hist. moderne et contemporaine*, i (1899), pp. 107 ff.

[7] Sir J. Fortescue, *De Natura Legis Naturae*, *Works*, ed. T. Clermont, (London, 1869), pp. 87-88; *De Laudibus*, p. 90.

[8] Commynes, *op. cit.*, ii. p. 8. [9] *Governance*, pp. 141-42.

[10] Commynes, *op. cit.*, ii. pp. 218-19. [11] *Ibid.*, pp. 114, 141-42.

[12] S. Miller, "The Position of the King in Bracton and Beaumanoir", *Speculum*, xxxi (1956), pp. 263-96.

[13] F. Maton, *La Souveraineté dans Jean II Juvénal des Ursins*, (Paris, 1917), pp. 116-23. Jean Juvenal des Ursins' views were perhaps rather harder than Maton supposed [see, e.g., passages in the treatise *Verba mea auribus percipe, domine*, Bibl. nat., MS. francais 2701, fos. 98^{r}a and 101^{v}b-102^{r}a], but though he produced a number of standard quotations on the right of resistance and the punishment of a tyrant [*ibid.*, fos. 89^{v}a-90^{r}b, e.g.] it seems clear that he himself will allow no sanction on earth against a king except his own conscience.

[14] For their nomenclature see S. Dupont-Ferrier, *Etudes sur les institutions financières de la France à la fin du Moyen âge*, ii, *Les Finances extraordinaires et leur mécanisme*, (Paris, 1932), pp. 24, 27-28, whose rules I follow.

[15] For their general history see G. Picot, *Hist. des Etats-généraux*, 2nd edn., (Paris, 1888), i; P. Dognon, *Les Institutions politiques et administratives du pays de Languedoc du XIIIe siècle aux guerres de Réligion*, (Toulouse, 1895), pp. 195-325.

[16] For these in general see H. Prentout, "Les Etats provinciaux en France", *Bull. of the Internat. Comm. of Hist. Sciences*, i [v], (1928), pp. 632-47.

[17] J. Cadart, *Le Régime électoral des Etats-généraux de 1789 et ses origines 1302-1614*, (Paris, 1952), is not very helpful; some information on the fifteenth century may be found in J. Major, *The Deputies to the Estates General in Renaissance France*, (Wisconsin, 1960). For a recent discussion of a crucial question in relation to representation — the readiness of groups to be represented — see F. Cheyette, "Procurations by Large-Scale Communities in Fourteenth-Century France", *Speculum*, xxxvii (1962), pp. 18-31.

[18] P. Viollet, "Elections des députés aux Etats-généraux réunis à Tours en 1468 et en 1484", *Bibl. de l'Ecole des chartes*, 6. ii (1866), pp. 22-58.

[19] H. Prentout, *Les Etats provinciaux de Normandie*, (Mémoires de l'Académie nationale de Caen, nouv. sér., i-iii, 1925-27), ii. pp. 58-59, corrected by Miss B. Rowe, "The Estates of Normandy under the Duke of Bedford, 1422-35", *Eng. Hist. Rev.*, xlvi (1931), p. 560. In Vivarais and Gévaudan a rota system for attendance at the general meetings of the estates of Languedoc of the nobility was eventually established [A. Le Sourd, *Essai sur les Etats de Vivarais*, (Paris, 1926), pp. 71-73]. For a few other examples of "representation" of the nobility see P. Viollet, *Hist. des Institutions politiques et administratives de la France*, iii (Paris, 1903), pp. 187, 190. But even in Normandy the system of direct summons was not wholly destroyed: see *Letters and Papers illustrative of the Wars of the English in France during the Reign of Henry the Sixth*, ed. J. Stevenson, (Rolls Series, 1864), ii. Pt. 1, pp. 343-46.

[20] Viollet, *Institutions politiques*, iii. pp. 187 ff.; A. Thomas, "Le Midi et les Etats-généraux sous Charles VII", *Annales du Midi*, i (1889), pp. 292-315, iv (1892), pp. 1-16; J. Major, *Representative Institutions in Renaissance France, 1421-1559*, (Wisconsin, 1960), pp. 66-68.

[21] Viollet, *Institutions politiques*, iii. pp. 198-99; J. Marion, "Rapport adressé au roi, sur les doléances du clergé, aux Etats-généraux de 1413", *Bibl. de l'Ecole des chartes*, 2. i [6] (1844), p. 284; R. Lacour, *Le Gouvernement de l'apanage de Jean duc de Berry 1360-1416*, (Paris, 1934), pp. 380-81; *Documents sur la ville de Millau*, ed. J. Artières, (Archives historiques du Rouergue, vii, 1930), p. 300.

[22] H. Morice, *Mém. pour servir de preuves à l'hist. ecclesiastique et civile de Bretagne*, ii (Paris, 1744), col. 1654.

[23] Prentout, *op. cit.*; L. Cadier, *Les Etats de Béarn depuis leurs origines jusqu'au commencement du XVI siècle*, (Paris, 1888); E. Delcambre, *Les Etats du Velay des origines à 1642*, (St-Etienne, 1938); Le Sourd, *op. cit.*; A. Dussert, *Les Etats du Dauphiné aux XIVe et XVe siècles*, (Grenoble, 1915) [or Bulletin de l'Académie delphinale, 5. viii (1914)], *Les Etats du Dauphiné de la guerre de Cent ans aux guerres de Réligion*, (Grenoble, 1923) [or Bulletin cit., 5. xiii. 2 (1922)]; J. Billioud, *Les Etats de Bourgogne aux XIVe et XVe siècles*, (Mémoires de l'Académie de Dijon, 5. iv, 1922); C. Hirschauer, *Les Etats*

d'Artois de leurs origines à l'occupation francaise, 2 vols., (Paris, 1923); A. Thomas, *Les Etats provinciaux de la France centrale sous Charles VII*, 2 vols., (Paris, 1879).

²⁴ Major, *Representative Institutions.*

²⁵ H. Cam *et al.*, "Recent Work and Present Views on the Origins and Development of Representative Assemblies", (Comitato Internazionále di Scienze Storiche. X Congresso Internazionale di Scienze Storiche, Roma ... 1955), *Relazioni*, i. pp. 3-15, 21-27.

²⁶ J. Dhont, " 'Ordres ou puissances': l'exemple des Etats de Flandre", *Annales (Econ. Soc. Civil.)*, v (1950), pp. 289-305.

²⁷ Mr. Major's views on the attitude of Charles VII to the Estates [*Representative Institutions*, pp. 21-49] (which appeared after this paper was originally written) are rather less harsh than mine.

²⁸ *Les Demandes faites par le roi Charles VI ... avec les résponses de Pierre Salmon*, ed. G. Crapelet, (Paris, 1833), p. 101.

²⁹ E. de Monstrelet, *Chroniques*, ed. L. Douët d'Arcq, [Soc. de l'hist. de France], vi (Paris, 1862), pp. 49-50.

³⁰ G. du Fresne de Beaucourt, *Hist. de Charles VII*, iii (Paris, 1885), pp. 136-37.   ³¹ Commynes, *op. cit.*, ii. p. 219.

³² Lacour, *op. cit.*, pp. 383-85; Billioud, *op. cit.*, pp. 331-36; Hirschauer, *op. cit.*, i. pp. 204-13.   ³³ Cam *et al.*, "Recent Work", *op. cit.*, pp. 15-18.

³⁴ The actual work was done from the last years of the fourteenth century by a special judicial commission nominated by the duke. Too close a connection with the ducal council was avoided and until 1492, despite attacks, it kept its rights as a final court: see B. Pocquet du Haut-Jussé, "Les Faux Etats de Bretagne de 1315 et les premiers Etats de Bretagne", *Bibl. de l'Ecole des chartes*, lxxxvi (1925), pp. 400 ff.; "Le Conseil du duc en Bretagne d'après ses procès-verbaux (1459-1463)", *ibid.*, cxvi (1958), pp. 144, 157-62, 165. J. de la Martinière, "La Ville de Vannes siège du Parlement de Bretagne (1425-1554)", *Annales de Bretagne*, xxxv (1921-23), pp. 69-79, "Le Parlement sous les rois de France" (1), *ibid.*, xxxvi (1924-25), p. 270, (3), *ibid.*, xxxix (1930-31), pp. 209-18. The *Parlement* of Brittany is the only assembly in France which clearly emerged, like the English Parliament, out of the *curia* of its ruler.

³⁵ The argument of J. Garillot, *Les Etats-généraux de 1439. Etude de la coutume constitutionelle au XV siècle*, (Nancy, 1943), pp. 53-61 that such ratification had become a *loi fondamentale* is unconvincing. The failure of the Estates to ratify the grant of Normandy to Charles of France was not brought up by Louis XI as an excuse for its withdrawal from him at the Estates-general of 1468 [*Procès-verbal* of the Estates-general of 1468 enregistered at Rodez, Arch. départ. de l'Aveyron, BB 3, fos. 59ʳ-60ʳ].

³⁶ Beaucourt, *op. cit.*, iii. pp. 136-37; J. Masselin, *Journal des Etats généraux de France ... en 1484*, ed. A. Bernier, [Documents inédites sur l'hist. de France], (Paris, 1835), p. 640.

³⁷ Cf. the documents printed by R. Fage, *Les Etats de la vicomté de Turenne* (Paris, 1894), ii. pp. 50-51 and by Morice, *op. cit.*, iii. cols. 367-70.

³⁸ Billioud, *op. cit.*, pp. 351-53.

³⁹ H. Koenigsberger, "The States General of the Netherlands before the Revolt", *Etudes presentées à la commission internationale pour l'hist. des assemblées d'Etats*, xviii (Louvain, 1958), pp. 144-45.

⁴⁰ Cadier, *op. cit.*, pp. 176 ff., 371; Hirschauer, *op. cit.*, i. pp. 26-28; A. Rebillon, *Les Etats de Bretagne de 1661 à 1789*, (Paris, 1932), p. 21; cf. E. Duvernoy, *Les Etats-généraux des duchés de Lorraine et de Bar jusqu'à ... 1559*, (Paris, 1904), pp. 122 ff., 145-48, 189-91.

⁴¹ Thomas, *Les Etats provinciaux*, i. pp. 88ff., 164 ff.

⁴² R. Gandilhon, *Politique économique de Louis XI*, (Rennes, 1940), pp. 282-84.

⁴³ Hirschauer, *op. cit.*, i. p. 204 n. 6; *Livre des Bouillons*, (Archives municipales de Bordeaux, i, 1867), pp. 174-75, 263; *Registres de la Jurade, 1414-16, 1420-22*,

(*ibid.*, iv. 1883), p. 382; A. Artonne, *Le Mouvement de* 1314 *et les chartes provinciales de* 1315, (Paris, 1912), pp. 44-45, 105; Prentout, *op. cit.*, i. pp. 94 ff.; Dussert, *Les Etats du Dauphiné de la guerre de Cent ans* . . . , pp. 59-61; Morice, *op. cit.*, ii. cols. 457-58, 1651-68; A. de la Borderie & B. Pocquet, *Hist. de Bretagne*, iv (Rennes, 1906), p. 422; Dognon, *op. cit.*, pp. 246-47. The list could be continued.

⁴⁴ Viollet, *Institutions politiques*, iii. pp. 465-66.

⁴⁵ P. Cochon, *Chronique normande*, ed. C de Beaurepaire, [Soc. de l'hist. de Normandie], (Rouen, 1870), p. 214; cf. Dognon, *op. cit.*, pp. 241-43.

⁴⁶ A. Thomas, "Les Etats généraux sous Charles VII. . . . Etude chronologique d'après des documents inédits", *Cabinet hist.*, 2. ii [24] (1878) [cited hereafter as "Etude"], pp. 160-62, 167-69.

⁴⁷ J. du Clerq, *Mémoires*, ed. J. Buchon, [Choix de chroniques et mém. sur l'hist. de France, x], (Paris, 1838), p. 266 a.

⁴⁸ *Recueil des ordonnances des rois de France de la troisième race*, iii, ed. D. Secousse, (Paris, 1732), pp. 7-8, 682-84; Cadier, *op. cit.*, p. 299; F. Pasquier, "Privilèges et libertés des trois Etats du comté de Foix . . .", *Bulletin hist. et phil.*, 1896, pp. 348-51; cf. n. 43 above.

⁴⁹ *Registres de la Jurade*, p. 382; Beaucourt, *op. cit.*, ii (Paris, 1882), p. 589; A. Thomas, "Les Etats généraux sous Charles VII: notes et documents nouveaux", *Rev. hist.*, xl (1889) [cited hereafter as "Notes"], pp. 69, 82-83.

⁵⁰ Thomas, "Le Midi et les Etats généraux", *Annales du Midi*, iv (1892), p. 18. The prospective meeting of 1433 seems to have been abandoned before any deputies could come [Beaucourt, *op. cit.*, ii. pp. 292, 597].

⁵¹ J. Strayer & C. Taylor, *Studies in Early French Taxation*, (Harvard, 1939), p. 171; M. Jusselin, "Comment la France se préparait à la guerre de Cent ans", *Bibl. de l'Ecole des chartes*, lxxiii (1912), pp. 229-30; J. Viard, "Une Chapitre d'histoire administrative: les ressources extraordinaires de la royauté sous Philippe VI de Valois", *Rev. des questions hist.*, xliv (1888), pp. 167-218; Dognon, *op. cit.*, p. 210.

⁵² C. de Mayer, *Des Etats généraux et autres assemblées nationales*, ix (La Haye — Paris, 1789), p. 222; Procès-verbal . . . enregistered at Rodez, *op. cit.*, fo. 64ᵛ.

⁵³ Mr. Major [*Representative Institutions*, pp. 34-39] attempts to explain why the government of Charles VII should have wanted general assemblies at all. It may be noted that the pattern of abandonment of general meetings (and eventually of regional meetings) followed that of Charles V's reign and indeed of the 1350s. The reasons for the large assemblies were possibly basically more political than anything else; general support was needed to back up an appeal to regional assemblies. But large meetings were also liable to badger the ruler about their grievances; when there was less need for political support even Charles V (so praised for his attention to the Estates by Jean Juvenal des Ursins [Beaucourt, *op. cit.*, iii. pp. 136-37]) seems to have been prepared to abandon meetings potentially as troublesome to him as those of 1355-59 had been.

⁵⁴ Dognon, *op. cit.*, pp. 215-17.

⁵⁵ For the fourteenth century see the works cited n. 51 above; even at its most lively the assembly was hamstrung by the need subsequently to consult regional assemblies and hindered (possibly, admittedly, to its members' advantage) by absenteeism and the *mandat imperatif*: R. Delachenal, *Hist. de Charles V*, i (Paris, 1909), pp. 245 ff.; L. Mirot, *Les Insurrections urbaines au début du règne de Charles VI 1380-83, leurs causes, leurs conséquences*, (Paris, 1905), pp. 28-60, 147 ff.; A. Coville, *Les Cabochiens et l'ordonnance de* 1413, (Paris, 1888), pp. 159-67.

⁵⁶ Beaucourt, *op. cit.*, ii. p. 589; Thomas, "Notes", pp. 82-83.

⁵⁷ Beaucourt, *op. cit.*, ii. pp. 588-89; Thomas, "Etude", pp. 166-67, 205-6, 217-18.

⁵⁸ Thomas, "Etude", pp. 156, 164 n. 3 [but cf. "Notes", pp. 63-65], 205-6;

"Notes", p. 85 n. 2; Beaucourt, *op. cit.*, ii. pp. 581, 600, iii. p. 435; Thomas, *Etats provinciaux*, i. pp. 69-81, 128-34.

⁵⁹ *Registres consulaires de la ville de Lyon*, i, ed. M. Guigue, (Lyon, 1882), pp. 349-52; Thomas, *Etats provinciaux*, pp. 74 ff. In moments of élan, as early as 1429-30, the government seems to have tried to avoid a general assembly and to deal with the local bodies direct [Thomas, "Etude", p. 169; "Notes", pp. 68-71].

⁶⁰ Dognon, *op. cit.*, p. 207; Thomas, "Notes", p. 68; Beaucourt, *op. cit.*, ii. p. 593.

⁶¹ Thomas, "Le Midi et les Etats-généraux", *Annales du Midi*, iv (1892), p. 8.

⁶² Masselin, *op. cit.*, pp. 508-10; R. Bourquelot, "Documents inédits sur les Etats de Tours, 1484", *Mém. de la Soc. royale des antiquaires de France*, nouv. sér., vi (1842), pp. 506-7; Viollet, "Elections", [cited n. 18], pp. 36-37.

⁶³ *Comptes consulaires d'Albi (1359-1360)*, ed. A. Vidal, [Bibliothèque méridionale, 1. v], (Paris-Toulouse, 1900), pp. 20-22; L. Caillet, *Etude sur les relations de la commune de Lyon avec Charles VII et Louis XI*, (Lyon, 1909), p. 30: two examples among many of hazardous journeys to Paris.

⁶⁴ For some earlier examples see Major, *Representative Institutions*, p. 67.

⁶⁵ "Journal des Etats généraux réunis à Paris au mois d'octobre 1356", ed. R. Delachenal, *Rev. hist. de droit francais et étranger*, xxiv (1900), pp. 429 ff.; Masselin, *op. cit.*

⁶⁶ *Documents sur la ville de Millau*, p. 314.

⁶⁷ Fortescue, *Governance*, p. 113; *Chronique des règnes de Jean II et de Charles V*, ed. R. Delachenal, [Soc. de l'hist. de France], i (Paris, 1910), p. 233; Beaucourt, *op. cit.*, ii. p. 591 n. 6; Thomas, "Notes", p. 84; *Registres de la Jurade*, p. 374.

⁶⁸ See above, n. 63.

⁶⁹ Mayer, *op. cit.*, ix. pp. 204-10; Procès-verbal . . . enregistered at Rodez, fos. 50ᵛ-52ʳ, 58ᵛ-60ᵛ; Masselin, *op. cit.*, pp. 10-12.

⁷⁰ J. Strayer & G. Rudisill Jr., "Taxation and Community in Wales and Ireland 1272-1327", *Speculum*, xxix (1954), pp. 410-16.

⁷¹ Strayer & Taylor, *op. cit.*, p. 94.

⁷² Dognon, *op. cit.*, pp. 283-92; Delcambre, *op. cit.*, pp. 122 ff.; Le Sourd, *op. cit.*, pp. 52 ff.   ⁷³ *Registres de la Jurade*, p. 382.

⁷⁴ Thomas, "Notes", pp. 69, 82-83; Billioud, *op. cit.*, p. 337.

⁷⁵ Morice, *op. cit.*, ii. col. 1568; Billioud, *op. cit.*, p. 57; Hirschauer, *op. cit.*, i. p. 53 n. 3.

⁷⁶ Dussert, *Les Etats du Dauphiné aux XIVe et XVe siècles*, p. 295 n. 3.

⁷⁷ Thomas, *Les Etats provinciaux*, ii. pp. 1-12.   ⁷⁸ Billioud, *op. cit.*, pp. 25-26.

⁷⁹ Dognon, *op. cit.*, pp. 217 ff.

⁸⁰ Billioud, *op. cit.*, pp. 35-49, 55-56; Thomas, *Etats provinciaux*, i. pp. 32-34; Fage, *op. cit.*, ii. pp. 52-62; Hirschauer, *op. cit.*, i. p. 40; Masselin, *op. cit.*, pp. 8-35.

⁸¹ Procès-verbal . . . enregistered at Rodez, fos. 50ᵛ-51ᵛ; Mayer, *op. cit.*, ix. pp. 204-10; Masselin, *op. cit.*, pp. 4-6; H. Stein, *Charles de France*, (Paris, 1921), p. 715.

⁸² M. Mollat, "Recherches sur les finances des ducs Valois de Bourgogne", *Rev. hist.*, ccxix (1958), pp. 314-15; H. de Surirey de St-Rémy, *Jean II de Bourbon, duc de Bourbonnais et d'Auvergne, 1426-1488*, (Paris, 1944), pp. 94-97.

⁸³ Strayer & Taylor, *op. cit.*, pp. 68-72; *Choix de pièces inédites relatives au règne de Charles VI*, ed. L. Douët-d'Arcq, [Soc. de l'hist. de France], i (Paris, 1863), p. 80; Dupont-Ferrier, *op. cit.*, pp. 33-36.

⁸⁴ Dupont-Ferrier, *op. cit.*, pp. 175-79; Major, *Representative Institutions*, p. 11.   ⁸⁵ Masselin, *op. cit.*, pp. 498-506.

⁸⁶ For the necessity of other sources of income see R. Boutruche, *La Crise d'une société: Seigneurs et paysans du Bordelais pendant la guerre de Cent ans*, (Paris, 1947), pp. 345-62; I. Guerin, *La Vie rurale en Sologne aux XIVe et*

XVe siècles, (Paris, 1960), pp. 181-89; J. Bartier, *Légistes et gens de finances au XVe siècle*, (Brussels, 1955), pp. 247-70.

[87] G. Dupont-Ferrier, *Les Officiers royaux des bailliages et sénéchaussées*, [Bibl. de l'École des Hautes études, cxlv], (Paris, 1902), pp. 121-22, 133-34, 176, 181-82, 184, 189-90; *Etudes sur les institutions financières de la France à la fin du Moyen âge*, i, *Les Elections et leur personnel*, (Paris, 1930), pp. 70-72, 85 ff., 112, 121; Lacour, *op. cit.*, pp. 158 ff.

[88] Masselin, *op. cit., passim;* cf. Major, *Representative Institutions*, p. 70.

[89] Commynes, *op. cit.*, ii. p. 289.

[90] Strayer & Taylor, *op. cit.*, pp. 47 ff.; *Recueil de documents concernant le Poitou contenus dans les registres de la chancellerie de France*, (Archives hist. du Poitou, xiii, 1883), pp. 137-38, 164-65; *Choix*, ed. Douët, *op. cit.*, i. pp. 110-11, 243-45; Thomas, "Notes", p. 59; Dupont-Ferrier, *Finances extraordinaires*, pp. 33-34.

[91] Viollet, "Elections", *op. cit.*, pp. 22-58; Major, *Representative Institutions*, pp. 69-70.   [92] See below, Excursus, pp. 23-4.

[93] Masselin, *op. cit.*, p. 502. For urban exemption see Dupont-Ferrier, *Finances extraordinaires*, pp. 179-81; for the exemption of bourgeois *qua* royal officers and masters of mints, *ibid.*, pp. 181-85, 186-88; *qua annoblis* (and for royal resistance to it), *ibid.*, pp. 175-79; Gandilhon, *op. cit.*, pp. 114 ff., 450-52; Caillet, *op. cit.*, pp. 269-72.

[94] Gandilhon, *op. cit.*, pp. 161 ff., 285 ff.; Dognon, *op. cit.*, pp. 168-79; P. Wolff, "Les Luttes sociales dans les villes du Midi francais, XIIIe-XVe siècles", *Annales (Econ. Soc. Civil.)*, ii (1947), pp. 449, 452.

[95] Caillet, *op. cit.*, pp. 28-84, 127-31; *Documents sur la ville de Millau, passim*. Cf. also Major, *Representative Institutions*, p. 42. Other instances could easily be found.

[96] For powers demanded see Thomas, "Notes", p. 80; for some evidence of those actually given see C. de Grandmaison, "Nouveaux documents sur les Etats-généraux du XVe siècle", *Bull. de la Soc. archéologique de Touraine*, iv (1877-79), pp. 144-46; *Registres consulaires de . . . Lyon*, p. 301. For the *mandat imperatif* see above, nn. 21, 55.   [97] Masselin, *op. cit.*, pp. 636-38.

[98] Procès-verbal . . . enregistered at Rodez, *op. cit.*, fos. 50ᵛ-61ᵛ; Mayer, *op. cit.*, ix. p. 209; Masselin, *op. cit., passim;* Billioud, *op. cit.*, pp. 52-54, 140.

[99] *Comptes consulaires de . . . Rodez, Cité*, ii. pp. 165-66.

[100] *Comptes des consuls de Montréal-du-Gers*, (3), (*1439-50*), (Archives hist. de la Gironde, xxxii, 1897), p. 53.

[101] *Documents sur la ville de Millau, op. cit.*, p. 359. They held out and appealed to the crown.   [102] *Ibid.*, pp. 366-67.   [103] Masselin, *op. cit.*, pp. 486-89.

[104] Fage, *op. cit.*, i. p. 52; Prentout, *op. cit.*, i. pp. 103-55; Rowe, *op. cit.*, pp. 558-59; Billioud, *op. cit.*, pp. 21-23.

[105] When the government in 1484 demanded deputies to the Estates-general from *bailliages* and *sénéchaussées* rather than from the whole region there was resistance in Burgundy, Provence, the Dauphiné and the Bourbonnais and the government had to give in; but not for long [Viollet, *Institutions politiques*, iii. pp. 94-97].

[106] The bourgeois fervour of Languedoc against taxation may have enhanced the value of an assembly in that not very homogeneous area.

[107] Prentout, *op. cit.*, i. pp. 181-87; Gandilhon, *op. cit.*, pp. 282-84. Some modifications made in Languedoc were also unenthusiastically received [Gandilhon, *op. cit.*, pp. 276-80]. But cf. Masselin, *op. cit.*, pp. 628-34. Burgundy and Provence kept most liberty in the matter of administration of taxation [Billioud, *op. cit.*, pp. 159 ff.; J. Denizet, *Les Etats de Provence depuis l'origine jusqu'a la réunion de la Provence à la France*, (*1481*), Positions des thèses de l'Ecole des chartes, (1920), pp. 12-14]; considerable rights were retained in Béarn and in the Dombes [Cadier, *op. cit.*, pp. 331-47; E. Perroy, "La Fiscalité royale en Beaujolais aux XIVᵉ et XVᵉ siècles", *Moyen Age*,

xxxviii (1928), pp. 32-33]; in Languedoc and in the Dauphiné too much control by the Estates was avoided though Languedoc kept more than most royal Estates [Dognon, *op. cit.*, pp. 275-83, 313-14; Dussert, *Les Etats du Dauphiné aux XIVe et XVe siècles*, pp. 331-32]; Normandy had already lost its considerable rights in Charles VI's reign and too much control over the administration of taxation, unknown in England, was not allowed it under English occupation [Prentout, *op. cit.*, ii. pp. 172-77; Rowe, *op. cit.*, pp. 569-70]; the Estates of the Centre lost all influence in the 1450s [Thomas, *Etats provinciaux*, i. pp. 171-73]. Artois and Brittany never seem to have had any permanent control of the administration of taxation [Hirschauer, *op. cit.*, i. pp. 97 ff.; Morice, *op. cit.*, ii. cols. 457-58, 1651-68].

[108] The *mandat* flourished in Artois and Languedoc [Hirschauer, *op. cit.*, i. p. 45; Dognon, *op. cit.*, pp. 263-65] if not in Burgundy [Billioud, *op. cit.*, p. 340]; proctors were allowed in Artois and in the Dauphiné [Hirschauer, *op. cit.*, i. p. 43; Dussert, *Les Etats du Dauphiné aux XIVe et XVe siècles*, p. 295 n. 3] if not in Béarn [Cadier, *op. cit.*, pp. 242-43] and absenteeism seems to have been common in the latter if not in Brittany [Dussert, *op. cit.*, p. 295 n. 3; acceptable reasons for absence in the Parlement of Britanny are given in its *assiettes*: Morice, *op. cit.*, ii. cols. 1564-71, 1670-75; iii. cols. 1-9].

[109] Dognon, *op. cit.*, p. 247.

[110] Random references to the Estates may be found, for instance, in J. Rouquette, *Le Rouergue sous les Anglais*, (Millau, 1887); D. Brissaud, *Les Anglais en Guyenne*, (Paris, 1875); Boutruche, *op. cit.; Registres de la Jurade*. The evidence cited by Mr. Major [*Representative Institutions*, p. 51 n. 5] seems to me equally random.

[111] P. Tucoo-Chala, *Gaston Fébus et la vicomté de Béarn, 1343-1391*, (Bordeaux, 1960), pp. 135-39; "Les Institutions de la vicomté de Béarn (Xe-XVe siècles)", F. Lot & R. Fawtier, *Hist. des institutions francaises au Moyen age*, i, *Institutions seigneuriales*, (Paris, 1957), pp. 332-34.

[112] Rebillon, *op. cit.*, p. 21; Cadier, *op. cit.*, pp. 176 ff., 371.

[113] Fage, *op. cit.*, ii. pp. 52-62; Fage's handling of these documents seems to me unintelligible.

[114] Thomas, *Etats provinciaux*, i. pp. 169-71; Surirey, *op. cit.*, pp. 83-85.

[115] Hirschauer, *op. cit.*, i. pp. 66-67.

[116] Dussert, *Les Etats du Dauphiné aux XIVe et XVe siècles*, pp. 111 ff., 312.

[117] Lacour, *op. cit.*, p. 384.   [118] Masselin, *op. cit.*, pp. 498-506.

[119] *Ibid.*, p. 38.   [120] *Ibid.*, pp. 252, 440.

[121] J. Juvenal des Ursins, *Verba mea auribus percipe, domine, op. cit.*, pp. 97vb-98vb; C. de Seyssel, *La Monarchie de France*, ed. J. Poujol, (Paris, 1961), pp. 113 ff.   [122] Commynes, *op. cit.*, ii. p. 222.

EXCURSUS

THE ASSEMBLY OF THE THREE ESTATES OF THE DUCHY OF BURGUNDY AT DIJON, 10 JULY 1448.

For the assembly in general see Billioud, *op. cit.*, pp. 54, 140-41. The "matter of principle" was the rectitude of a grant to the duke for the purchase of a *seigneurie* [cf. *ibid.*, pp. 141, 416] — in this case Chateauvillain, which was being sold up by a member of the assembly, the *seigneur* of Thil, in order to pay his brother's ransom [A. Bossuat, "Les Prisonniers de guerre au XVe siècle: la rançon de Guillaume seigneur de Chateauvillain", *Annales de Bourgogne*, xxiii (1951), pp. 7-35]. The nobility had failed to attend an earlier meeting summoned for 11 June. There is evidence of pressure before this abortive assembly [Billioud, *op. cit.*, p. 140]. Letters were sent before the July meeting to the marshal of Burgundy and to nine members of the Estates (the *seigneurs* of Autrey, Mirebeau, Fouvent, Charny, Couches, Thil, Vitteaux, Scey and Sombernon and the count of Joigny) [Archives départementales de la Côte d'Or, B 1706, fos. 112^v-113^r]). A grant was finally made of 5,000 *francs* in place of one demanded of 12,000 *saluts d'or*.

The fifteen members of the Estates summoned to the assembly were much inter-related. Autrey, for instance, was Fouvent's second cousin and heir presumptive [A. Duchesne, *Hist. généalogique de la maison de Vergy*, (Paris, 1625), p. 222]; his first wife's brother was Joigny, Vitteaux was her brother-in-law and Jonvelle was her second cousin [le p. Anselme, *Hist. généalogique . . . de la maison . . . de France*, iv (Paris, 1728), pp. 180, 164 ff.); and his second wife's son was Talmay [G. Dumay, "Guyard . . . et Guillaume [de Pontailler]", *Mém. de la Société bourguignonne d'hist. et de geog.*, xxvii (1912), pp. 442-43]. Scey, Charny and Mirebeau were brothers; Mirebeau's father-in-law was Vitteaux [Anselme, *op. cit.*, viii (Paris, 1733), p. 425]. Thibaut IX de Neufchatel, marshal of Burgundy, was Thil's son-in-law [*ibid.*, viii. p. 428]. Charny married Marie de Bourgogne in November 1447 [Archives départementales du Nord, *Inventaire sommaire, B*, viii. p. 21].

As far as their offices were concerned, from printed sources alone it is clear that Autrey was a *conseiller chambellan* in 1440 [L. de Labarre, *Mém. pour servir à l'hist. de France et de Bourgogne*, (Paris, 1729), ii. pp. 189, 216], Chastellux a *chambellan* in 1436 [*ibid.*, pp. 185, 211] and governor of the Nivernais still in 1445 [H. de Chastellux, *Hist. généalogique de la maison de Chastellux*, (Auxerre, 1869), p. 95]; Jonvelle, one of the first members of the *Toison d'or*, was still *premier chambellan* in 1448 [Labarre, *op. cit.*, p. 205]; Scey was a *conseiller chambellan* in 1430 [*ibid.*, pp. 186, 213], Thil in 1431 [*ibid.*, p. 220], Villers in 1446 [Bartier, *op. cit.*, p. 39]. Fouvent, a member of the *Toison d'or* in 1433, was governor of Burgundy until some time after 1439 [Duchesne, *op. cit.*, pp. 212, 2[14]], Genlis a *conseiller chambellan* in 1433 [Labarre, *op. cit.*, p. 220] and Charny in 1447 [Archives départementales du Nord, B 1994, fo. 140^r]. Couches was to be a *chambellan* by 1450 [Archives départementales de la Côte d'Or, *Inventaire sommaire, B*, i. p. 165] and Mirebeau by 1459 [Billioud, *op. cit.*, pp. 320-21].

Autrey and Mirebeau were much indebted and Chastellux, Joigny and Talmay seem to have been in trouble [Bartier, *op. cit.*, pp. 211, 216, 230-36, 399]. Thil's difficulties were of course the indirect cause of all the fuss; but it seems impossible to tell if, precisely in July 1448, he was more anxious for the duke to buy Chateauvillain or more anxious to stop him.

9

BRETON ESTATES

The representative assemblies of medieval Brittany have been on the whole too much neglected. This is all the more regrettable in that they exhibit a number of traits which differentiate them from the general run of French local assemblies; amongst these their mere survival is not the least. But there is no equivalent of Rebillon[1] for the middle ages. Indeed his introductory chapter on the Breton estates in the fourteenth and fifteenth centuries is probably the best short *aperçu* of the subject in print.[2] When the only work which Miss Cam could have thought of to have cited[3] is Durtelle de Saint-Sauveur's[4] the topic is dark indeed.[5] Admittedly (as in most areas) the documents have not survived the first archivists of the Republic;[6] but a few fragments survive (mainly due to the care of the

---

[1] A. Rebillon, *Les Etats de Bretagne de 1661 à 1789*, (Paris 1932).

[2] *Ibid.*, pp. 15–22.

[3] H. M. Cam, A. Marongiu and G. Stökl, 'Recent Work and present views on the origins and development of representative assemblies', *Comitato Internazionale di Scienze Storiche, X Congresso Internazionale di Scienze Storiche . . . 1955, Relazioni*, i, (Firenze, 1955), 54.

[4] E. Durtelle de Saint-Sauveur, *Histoire de Bretagne des origines à nos jours*, 2 vols., (Paris, 1935).

[5] This paper was originally put together as ancillary to that on 'The Failure of the French Later Medieval Estates'. Little that has appeared since would seem to me to modify the views in it: one might cite J-L Montigny, *Essai sur les institutions du duché de Bretagne à l'époque de Pierre Mauclerc et sur la politique de ce Prince* (Paris, 1961), pp. 35–41; J-P Leguay, *Un reseau urbain au Moyen âge: les villes du duché de Bretagne aux XIVe et XVe siècles* (Paris, 1981); M. Planiol, *Histoire des institutions de la Bretagne*, iii (Mayenne, 1981), pp. 123–62 (the later edition of the *manuscrit*); J-P Leguay and Hervé Martin, *Fastes et malheurs de la Bretagne ducale 1213–1532* (Rennes, 1982); but such modification (and that from later articles by B-A Pocquet du Haut-Jussé) is noted where it occurs. (The invaluable help of Dr. M. C. E. Jones in the presentation of this piece is acknowledged with gratitude.)

[6] *Cf.* the introduction to *Archives de la Loire-Inférieure, Inventaire sommaire de la série B*, (Nantes, 1902), and to *ibid.*, *Répertoire numérique de la série B* (Nantes, 1945).

Benedictine historians Dom Lobineau[7] and Dom Morice[8]) and some attempt can be made from these to discover at least something about the Breton assemblies. And too often the ghost of Thierry broods over the honest enquirer: the brief passages on the Estates in La Borderie and Pocquet's *Histoire de Bretagne*,[9] for instance, as well as containing a number of errors, are far too incubused by the *tiers-état*. Some of these errors have been corrected (and some more perpetrated) by M. Pocquet du Haut-Jussé *fils*.[10] The *Parlement* of Brittany (and to some extent the Estates) has been dealt with by Texier[11] and (more valuably) by La Martinière.[12] Useful facts about the Estates under Jean V (1399-1442) can be derived from the work on his administration by Bellier Dumaine.[13] But the Breton assemblies are still worth study, because, by their deviationism from the general pattern of local Estates in later medieval France, they emphasise the (often neglected) more vital elements in the more normal bodies. For there is no 'general pattern' in these French local assemblies; and in following too closely the appearance of one of their historians have tended too often to neglect the proper springs of their existence.

Too often the 'classic' definition of Estates is still Cadier's: 'Provincial' Estates are still 'la réunion des trois ordres d'une province en assemblée regulièrement constitutée, périodiquement convoquée et possèdant certaines attributions politiques et administratives dont la principale était le vôte de l'impôt'.[14] This definition will not fit the Breton assemblies in the middle ages. The first problem is that of the *tiers état*. The Breton Estates seem undoubtedly to develop from *Parlement*, itself a more or less narrow enlargment of the *curia ducis*.[15] Into *Parlement* the bourgeoisie entered in the fourteenth century; and the main problem is to decide *either* when the *tiers-état* appeared; *or* whether this appearance matters. If one follows the

[7] Dom G-A. Lobineau, *Histoire de Bretagne*, (Paris, 1633); 2 vols. (Paris, 1707).

[8] Dom H. Morice, *Mémoires pour servir de preuves à l'histoire civile et ecclésiastique de Bretagne*, 3 vols., (Paris, 1742–46) (cited as Morice, *Preuves*).

[9] A. De La Borderie and B. Pocquet, *Histoire de Bretagne*, 6 vols., (Rennes, 1896–1914).

[10] B-A. Pocquet du Haut-Jussé, 'Les faux Etats de Bretagne de 1315 et les premiers Etats de Bretagne', *Bibliothèque de l'Ecole des Chartes*, 86, (1925), 388–406.

[11] E. Texier, *Etude sur la Cour ducale et les origines du Parlement de Bretagne*, (Rennes, 1905).

[12] J. De La Martinière, 'Vannes, siège du Parlement de Bretagne', *Annales de Bretagne*, 35, (1921–23), 69–80; 'Le Parlement de Bretagne sous les rois de France', *ibid.*, 36, (1924–25), 270–98; 37, (1926), 102–30; (1930–31), 217–78.

[13] C. Bellier Dumaine, 'L'administration du duche de Bretagne sous le règne de Jean V', *ibid.*, 14, (1898–99), 562–90; 15, (1899– 1900), 162–88, 468–69; 16 (1900–01), 112–229, 246–73, 477–514.

[14] L. Cadier, *Les Etats de Béarn depuis les origines jusqu'au commencement du XVI siècle*, (Paris, 1888),1.

[15] B-A. Pocquet du Haut-Jussé, *op. cit.*, 401; J. De La Martinière, *op. cit.*, *Annales de Bretagne* 39, (1930–31), 208, 215–16; E. Texier, *op. cit.*

Cadier definition it does; if one takes a broader and more sensible view, it does not. Pretty well everyone (except possibly La Martinière[16]) has concentrated on the first point: La Borderie put back the Benedictines' date[17] and Pocquet du Haut-Jussé put back La Borderie's.[18] Despite La Martinière's criticisms[19] the entry of the *tiers-état* seems settled: they appeared during the Succession War (Dinan 1352) but took no really effective part till the reign of Jean V in the early fifteenth century. Only after this does the *term* Estates become used (and then rarely for home consumption[20]). (Previously the term was *Parlement* or *Parlement Général* (apparently interchangeably[21]), whether the *tiers* was in it or not.)

It seems patently ridiculous to have to follow the Cadier definition and allow only three meetings of a Breton assembly between 1364 and 1399 as *Estates*.[22] It is probably wiser not to worry about the *tiers-état* at all. Their entry into the *Parlement* did not change the character of the institution.[23] When they were in they were and when they were not they were not and *sub specie eternitatis* or even of the institution in the fourteenth and fifteenth centuries it does not really matter.

The Breton political assembly therefore remains until the fifteenth century largely 'feudal'. So, for that matter, did the English Parliament. The term is meaningless. The assembly was clerical and aristocratic but it was none the less 'representative' of the political classes of the country. (There *were* important bourgeois in England; there were none (almost even in the fifteenth century) in Brittany.) For its real origin one must go back to the origins of *Parlement* itself.

Little is known about the institution in its early days. Before Pierre Mauclerc (1213–37) vassals or representatives appear not to have been summoned to the duke's court; it consisted entirely of 'officiers, de conseillers fonctionnaires et de quelques seigneurs qui allaient et venaient'.[24] And not until the end of the thirteenth century did 'les sessions de la plus haute juridiction de Bretagne se tiennent au moment de la réunion des États': until then 'la Cour ducale jugeait elle-même sans périod fixe, sans que l'on puisse rattacher ses audiences à un fait quelconque'.[25] But it was

---

[16] *Ibid.*, criticising B-A. Pocquet du Haut-Jussé, *op. cit.*

[17] A. De La Borderie and B. Pocquet, *op. cit.*, 3, 384.

[18] B-A. Pocquet du Haut-Jussé, *op. cit.*

[19] J. De La Martinière, *op. cit., Annales de Bretagne* 39, (1930–31), 208–222 argues that one cannot, from the surviving documents, prove either that the *tiers-état* was or that the *tiers-état* wasn't present in a number of the meetings of the fourteenth century; or, for that matter, that it was or wasn't present at a number of fifteenth-century meetings either.

[20] J. De La Martinière, *op. cit.*, 222

[21] *Ibid.*, 219–22.

[22] Cf. A. Rebillon, *op. cit.*, 16.

[23] J. De La Martinière, *op. cit.*, 208; A. Rebillon, *op. cit.*, 20.

[24] E. Texier, *op. cit.*, 70.

[25] *Ibid.*

from the holding of sessions of the highest justice at the same time as those of a larger administration, 'bien irregulier sans doute, que dèpendront dèsormais les audiences de la Cour judiciaire ducale'. What seems undoubted is that from the end of the thirteenth century on at least the sovereign court of Brittany, the highest appelate jurisdiction, was firmly attached to and derived its authority from the larger *Parlement*. Texier is unable to give many examples of the meeting of this body in the thirteenth and early fourteenth centuries.[26] And it is equally hard to compile an accurate list of sessions of *Parlement* or of the Estates under either name in the fourteenth or fifteenth. The frequency of meetings cannot be determined accurately. Pocquet[27] had a dream of very frequent meetings all attended by members of the *tiers-état*.[28] Meetings appear to have been rather sporadic until 1379; they are fairly frequent from then until 1431; they seem to have been frequent again only between 1451 and 1462; but this may be an erroneous impression.[29] About the composition of the assembly one may have a clearer picture. Any accurate knowledge of this must derive from the few remaining *procès-verbaux*. These survive (in the fourteenth century) for 1384, 1386, 1389, 1395 and 1398 but none contains any useful *assiette* or list of the people present.[30] For the fourteenth century therefore it is impossible to get a clear idea of the composition of the Estates. For the fifteenth one is luckier. Six *procès-verbaux* survive, three in a fragmentary condition (for 1452-54) and three with a more or less complete *assiette* (for 1451, 1455 and 1462).[31] From these figures can be derived (and then, again, fraught with possible inaccuracies). Otherwise one is forced to rely on the random mentions of the Estates' composition in documents not directly concerned with the *assiette*, which are pretty general and unhelpful for both the fourteenth and the fifteenth centuries.

From those figures the following facts appear to emerge. In the first place there was an overwhelming preponderance in the mid-fifteenth century of the first two Orders: in 1451 they marshalled 73 members against 20 from 19 towns; in 1455 100 against 22 from 24; in 1462 109 against a probable 25 from 25. It seems impossible to say from the evidence whether the 1451 figure for the nobility is abnormal (as opposed to those of 1455 and 1462); of if it is why it is. But it seems likely that the 1455 and

---

[26] He mentions only 1288 and 1289 (*ibid.*, 70–71), 1332 and 1334 (*ibid.*, 89). B-A. Pocquet du Haut-Jussé gives, from De La Borderie, early examples of sessions in 1201, 1205, 1240 and 1289 (*op. cit.*, 401 n.1).

[27] A. De La Borderie and B. Pocquet, *op. cit.*, 4, 3.

[28] *Ibid*, 4, 116.

[29] Cf., for instance, the attempt (equally fraught with danger) made by Planiol, *op. cit.*, pp. 132–43.

[30] They are printed in Morice, *Preuves*, 2, 459–65 (1384); 2, 513–15 (1386); 2, 557 (1389); 2, 649–55 (1395); and 2, 686 (1398).

[31] Morice, *Preuves*, 2, 1546–81 (1451); 2, 1615–16 (1452); 2, 1630–31 (1453); 2, 1635 (1454); 2, 1670–75 (1455); and 3, 1–9 (1462).

1462 figures are the more correct. Second, there seems to have been a preponderance of the nobility over the first and third estates combined (except in 1451). Since it is unlikely that these Orders would in fact combine, initiative in the Estates is clearly in the hands of the nobility. Third, there appears a lack of absenteeism and a level of personal attendance probably unusual in France at this period. This was possibly partly caused by such threats as the 60 *livre* fine imposed for instance in 1451; illness and ducal service seem to have been the only valid excuses for absenting one's-self from the assembly.[32] In fact, despite the mid-fifteenth century pretensions of the Nine Ancient Barons,[33] one derives the impression that the nobles of the Breton Estates were of much the same social level as the English knights of the Shire; except that they seem to have been more responsible (or less sorely tried). And in the frequency of their attendance during the periods when meetings of the assembly seem thickest on the ground they must have seemed very like a collection of Parliamentary greybeards of the House of Commons.

The composition of the Breton assembly therefore naturally reflected the social composition of the duchy. Its existence therefore depended on how accurately its functions reflected the needs of Orders and Duke; on how usefully its functions served both. The attributions of the Breton Parliament were complex. The assembly had begun as an enlargment of the *curia ducis*. It had assumed the *curia's* judicial functions, it had accreted administrative functions, which included dealing with the new taxations of the fourteenth century. But as much as it is impossible to compile a full (and accurate) list of the Breton Estates' meetings, still more is it to discover which of them were (if any) purely judicial. The terms *Parlement, Parlement général* and Estates are used so loosely as to be worthless as a guide to what happened in meetings of which all that is known is that they occurred.[34] The Breton Parliament, like the English Parliament, tended to be omnicompetent. Possibly the best definition was given during an enquiry into 'les droits royaux & anciens usages du pays de Bretagne' in 1455, by the extremely elderly Jean de Breil, who said he had known the institution since 1384.[35]

---

[32] For the fine v. Morice, *Preuves*, 2, 1568. It was remitted this time, at the request of the relatives and friends of the absentees. It is possible that so astronomic a fine argued it was imposed very little. The reasons for absence in legitimate cases are given in the *assiettes*.

[33] For these v. A. De La Borderie and B. Pocquet, *op. cit.*, 4, 386–92 and A. De. La Borderie, *Etude historique sur les neuf barons de Bretagne*, (Rennes, 1895).

[34] J. De La Martinière, *op. cit.*, 219–22.

[35] 'Enquestes sur les Droits Royaux & anciens usages du pais de Bretagne', (printed in Morice, *Preuves*, 2, 1651–68), 1654. The first part of this extract has been taken from J. De La Martinière, *op. cit.*, *Annales de Bretagne* 35, (1921–23), 70–71, where it is retranscribed from Bibliothèque Nationale, ms. fr. 22, 333, fo. 143.

Quand besoin est [he said] lesdits princes font convoquer et assembler les prélas, barons et aultres gens représentans les Estaz dudit pays, et, o l'avisement d'iceulx ou de la maire partie, font en leurs parlemens constitucions et etablissements nouveaulx pour le fait, police et gouvernement du pays, tant en fait de justice que autrement, ou aussi font corecions et inteprétacions sur lesdites coustumes à ce que y est estably et ordonné à force de loy et constitucion, et mesmes sont lesdits princes en bonne possession de tennir et faire tennir par le Président et autres gens de conseil en bon nombre commis et desputez par lesdits princes, expédicion des causes d'appel dudit pays, et est ce appellé Parlement de Bretaigne . . . Item dit ce tesmoin que toutes fois que lesdits Estats sont ainsi assemblés convocqués, ce que y a esté deliberé, soit en fait de éligement de finance par foiage, imposte, taille, subside ou autrement, a esté de tout temps executé par tout ledit pays en general sans aucune difference.

Other witnesses to the enquiry said much the same;[36] and their view seems in fact to have been unchanged since Jean de Breil's early days. The first Estates that he attended endorsed a description of themselves in instructions to ambassadors to the King.[37] In these

Le Parlement de Bretagne seult & a acoustumé tenir par tant & si longue espace de temps que memoire d'hommes n'est du contraire, appellez les Prelatz, Barons, & autres des suffisans du pays de Bretagne, qui est & desmonstre fait Royal; & le pays de Bretagne estre gouverné par Coustumes, & loyx d'iceluy pays, sans avoir regard à loyx & coustumes d'autre pays; & toutesfois qu'il en est debat, & que bon semble aux Prince, les Prelatz, Barons, and commun dudit pays, ou chose leur est necessaire, tand du subcide que de autre chose auprofilt dudit pays, le faire, l'en le fait, & pour l'absence d'un ou de deux ne tarde pas, puisque la maire & plus saine partie se y assent & il est advisé par le Prince & son Conseil le faire. Quia quod Principi placuit legis habet vigorem . . . En celuy Parlement sont toutes reformations faites à chacune personne qui s'en vieult doultoir, soit en causes d'appellations, ou autres complaintes contre le Prince; ou de partie vers autre, & les choses qui par le Conseil des Prelats, Barons, & autres sages assistans en celuy Parlement sont baillée par Arrest, executées, sauf à appeller jouxte & selon la forme présupposée . . .

Clearly, in both these descriptions, as in the three surviving 'propositions' by the Chancellor to the Estates (in 1398, 1451 and 1455[38]),

---

[36] Most of the witnesses in the enquiry mentioned taxation; but all in a rather inferior place. This does not seem entirely due to its place in the interrogatory: the emphasis throughout seems to be on *taxes'* being consented to in an essentially political, judicial and administrative assembly. But see below, note (38).

[37] Printed in Morice, *Preuves*, 2, 457–58.

[38] *Ibid.*, 2, 686; 2, 1566–67; 2, 1674.

justice seemed the core of the Breton estates.[39] The old *Parlement*, heir of the *curia*, had developed the attribution of consenting to taxation; but, possibly because of the absence of a large number of directly tax-paying bourgeois and possibly because the nobles (as elsewhere in France), received cuts of the taxes and exemptions,[40] finance did not loom so large in its mind. Justice was, in fact, to remain the primary *raison-d'être* of the Breton Estates until the final seccession of a Court of *Parlement* at the end of the fifteenth century; despite the creation of a smaller and more efficient body within the larger meeting to deal with judicial matters.

This appears to have been forming since the last years of the fourteenth century.[41] A body of civil-servants from the Council seems to have assisted a number of members of the Estates as a kind of judicial committee from the 1390's; thus developed a Council interest in what had been a purely *Parlement* affair. Why, then, if the business of hearing legal matters was in the hands of a small group, did the rest of the nobility and clergy bother to come? Blows were struck at the Estates' judicial function in 1425 and 1456;[42] but neither seems to have done it permanent damage.[43] Nor was François II's attempt in 1485 more successful.[44] Not until 1492 was the Breton court of *Parlement* permanent[45] and then it was at the request of the Estates, who seem still to have kept some contact with it[46] and which

[39] I am aware of the dangers of this argument. It is, I suppose, possible that the right and duty of consenting to taxes was so enshrined in the Breton assembly that little mention was ever made of it; that because the demands of the dukes were moderate there was little opposition on these grounds in the Estates and so little *éclat* for the subject. But nevertheless the impression remains that taxation did not play a large part in the affairs of the Estates. Like the English *curia regis*, the Breton assembly acquired the right of consent; both previously were primarily judicial and administrative bodies. But whereas the need to gain consent to taxation eventually brought a large number of new members (the shire knights and the burgesses) to the English court, it did not do so to the Breton: because they (except for the not very important bourgeois) were already apparently members of the Estates. As a result they took the business of consenting to taxation in their stride. As it was not the prime *raison-d'être* of their being in *Parlement* they were apparently not as concerned with it as they might have been. In any case, the bourgeoisie in France (some of whom paid taxes) were much more concerned with their right to consent than the nobility (who did not). Admittedly the fact that taxes were agreed on in the Estates was in peoples' minds (Morice, *Preuves*, 2, 1651–68); but it does not seem to have occupied a very important place in the replies of the nobles. More importance seems to have been given it by the clerical and bourgeois witnesses: which is what one would expect. But the clerical and bourgeois elements were not the most important in the Estates.

[40] C. Bellier Dumaine, *op. cit.*, *Annales de Bretagne*, 15, (1899–1900), 168.

[41] J. De La Martinière, *op. cit.*, *Annales de Bretagne* 35, (1921–23), 69–70; E. Texier, *op. cit.*, 83–84. Cf. *ibid.*, 39 (1930–1931), 208.

[42] J. De La Martinière, *op. cit.*, 70–75.

[43] *Ibid.*, 71, 78.

[44] *Ibid.*, 78–79; cf. E. Texier, *op. cit.*, 114.

[45] J. De La Martinière, *op. cit.*, *Annales de Bretagne*, 36, (1924–25), 270.

[46] *Ibid.*, 279.

retained a right of remonstrance in judicial matters.[47] In the interim it appears to have kept its rights as a final court;[48] and the Estates seem finally to have eliminated too close a control by the Council;[49] though one should beware, at least in the ducal period, given interchangeability of personnel, of creating too great hostility between Council, *Parlement* and Estates.[50] But in the end it was the Estates which succeeded in maintaining the independence of the Breton *Parlement* under royal control;[51] and indeed, whether the failure of the attempts to create an independent *Parlement* was the result of the hostility of the Estates seems hard to say. The 1425 constitution was made 'par delibération de Parlement',[52] though the 1456 constitution seems to have been made in its judicial continuation.[53] But the 1485 constitution was promulgated in the duke's 'Estatz et grant Conseil'.[54] Had the Estates now recognised 'qu'en fait il leur devenait impossible de remplir les fonctions judiciaires suprèmes, comme précédemment' and consented that 'ces fonctions soient remplies par la "section judiciaire" émanée d'eux' as long as this was, if only indirectly under their control, not too directly under ducal control either?[55] Members of the Estates who did not belong to the court did not come to the Parliament to judge (except possibly in great matters[56]); they came to discuss political and administrative matters (including the administration of justice) because these interested them; they came to grant taxes; they came for prestige reasons. But the regularity of their appearances was occasioned by the judicial necessities of a court with which they had little directly to deal but which they were pleased to think derived its authority solely from the larger body of which they were members. Until the end of the fifteenth century the Breton *political* assembly was inextricably mixed up with the *judicial* assembly; the Breton Estates could not but survive and survive meeting fairly frequently: as frequently, in fact, as *Parlement* had ever done. On the other hand as far as a legislative function is concerned one may have more doubt.

Historians of later medieval Brittany are a little embarrassed by this question; but it would seem that if excuses can be made for its being

---

[47] *Ibid.*, 270–98, *passim*; *Annales de Bretagne*, 37, (1926), 102–30, *passim*.

[48] J. De La Martinière, *op. cit.*, *Annales de Bretagnne* 39, (1930–31), 212, 214.

[49] *Ibid.*, 215.

[50] *Ibid.*, 216–17.

[51] J. De La Martinière, *op. cit.*, *Annales de Bretagne*, 36, (1924–25), 270–98 *passim*; 37, (1926), *passim*; 39, (1930–31), *passim*.

[52] Morice, *Preuves*, 2, 1157; Planiol, *La Très Ancienne Coutume de Bretagne*, (Rennes, 1896), 395, 4–96.

[53] Morice, *Preuves*, 2, 1699–1700; Planiol, *op. cit.*, 429–31.

[54] Morice, *Preuves*, 3, 478–80; Planiol, *op. cit.*, 453–57.

[55] J. De La Martinière, *op. cit.*, *Annales de Bretagne*, 39, (1930–31), 215.

[56] Such as the trial of Gilles de Bretagne in 1446 (Morice *Preuves*, 2, 1404–6). In this case the Estates refused to judge because of the incomplete state of the necessary procedure.

lacking, the equivalent of a statute law, made and broken only in Parliament, did not in the (ultimate) end develop.[57] Perhaps the idea never occurred to anyone. But in Brittany, any more than anywhere else in France, this function did not emerge. Here, at least, the *Parlement* of Brittany was not the Parliament of England.

The administrative and political functions of the Breton assembly were manifold and largely irregular in incidence. The administrative side is fairly clear-cut: the assembly could be interested in any matter brought to it by the duke. The political side is rather more difficult. Occasionally one finds the assembly acting on its own initiative, or at least appearing to do so.[58] At least during the troubles of the Succession War and probably after (the dukes of Brittany rarely had much peace) a certain amount of political independence was almost imposed on the Estates.[59] In 1468, for instance, the Estates sent ambassadors to the duke of Burgundy on rumours of his support of the Penthièvres.[60] Sending of embassies by Estates was not unusual[61] but in this case the Estates seem made to take up a political attitude; and much the same seems true throughout the Succession War. They had to take sides with one wooing claimant or another; they could not either stay out (this would not be their place) or rule without dukes (this would be even less so). It seems therefore that the difficulties of the dukes, as much as allowing the Estates some political power,[62] actually forced them to exercise it.

Support for the duke inside and outside the duchy was as a result a powerful motive in his summoning the Estates. 'Ce qu'il attend d'eux ce n'est souvent qu'un appui moral et proprement politique',[63] Estates were

[57] Planiol, *op. cit.*, iii. 159; Pocquet de Haut-Jussé, 'Le Conseil du duc en Bretagne d'après ses procès verbaux (1459–1463)', *Bibl. Ec. Chartes*, cxvi (1958), 136–69; 'La Genèse du legislatif dans le duché de Bretagne,', *R. hist.*, 4 sèr., xl (1962), 351–72.

[58] In April 1380 they sent a letter protesting their fidelity to the king of France (Morice, *Preuves*, 2, 285; cf. A. De La Borderie and B. Pocquet, *op. cit.*, 4, 58–59). In 1464 the king of France complained to the Estates about the duke of Brittany (*ibid.*, 3, 77–80; cf. A. De La Borderie and B. Pocquet, *op. cit.*, 4, 436). This was unsuccessful; but in 1423 the Estates apparently refused to follow Jean V into an alliance with England as well as with Burgundy (A. De La Borderie and B. Pocquet, *op. cit.*, 4, 217).

[59] Much the same thing seems to have happened in the German principalities, equally prone to an 'endless succession of internal conflicts [and] fratricidal wars'. (F. L. Carsten, *Princes and Parliaments in Germany from the Fifteenth to the Eighteenth Century*, (Oxford, 1959), 426–27.

[60] Morice, *Preuves*, 2, 815–16.

[61] For those of the Burgundian Estates, for instance, v. J. Billioud, *Les Etats de Bourgogne aux XIVe & XVe siècles*, (Dijon, 1922), *passim*; especially *e.g.*, pp. 292–96. In 1431 these Estates, which showed equal independence and good sense, and equal survival power, to those of Brittany, sent much the same kind of embassy to the Dauphin as the Bretons had in 1408. For other, less spectacular, embassies, v. *ibid.*, 263–78.

[62] Cf. A. Rebillon, *op. cit.*, 21.

[63] *Ibid.*; this was clearly the duke's purpose in 1380, 1384 and 1389 (and also clearly in 1352).

summoned to guarantee treaties, to guarantee a marriage, to guarantee the rights of heirs, for any number of reasons for which their support and preparedness to share in the responsibility of rule seemed necessary.[64] The motive of getting support for taxation is in Brittany less clearly marked.

Taxes appear to begin in Brittany under Jean IV (1364–99). A purely noble assembly was the first to consent to a *fouage* in 1365.[65] In the same year a tax on 'entrees & issues' of merchandise was put on without the bourgeois interested's being consulted and in all the four assemblies at which the *tiers-état* can be proved to be members of the Estates no tax was requested in the fourteenth century.[66] The entry of the bourgeoisie into the *Parlement* of Brittany cannot therefore be tied to the need for taxation. In all the fourteenth-century meetings at which they appeared the aim of the duke seems simply to have been to broaden the basis of his political support in the duchy.

Pocquet[67] appears to believe that from Jean IV on the dukes admitted the right of the assembly to consent to taxes. This appears to be an inference from the fact that assemblies *were* asked for taxes. The first clear text (from the ducal side[68]) seems to come from the Estates at Vannes in July 1459: 'congnoissons et confessons à noz diz Etats', said François II 'que nous ne pouvons ne devons lesdiz fouaige et devoir d'impost imposer et lever ne mectre sus et exiger, lever, percevoir ne recevoir sans l'exprès consentement, avisement et octroy de nos diz Etats'.[69] On the other hand François II did himself anticipate the grant by the Estates, though he seems always to have apologised.[70] But although taxes became tolerably permanent from Jean V's reign and although the right of direct vassals to consent was eclipsed by the right of the assembly,[71] although taxes

---

[64] *Ibid.*; cf. A. De La Borderie and B. Pocquet, *op. cit.*, 4, 116, 256 ff., 261–62, 608–09; 5, 28–29.

[65] Morice, *Preuves*, 1, 1604, 1608; cf A. De La Borderie and B. Pocquet, *op. cit.*, 4, 114 and n. 2; A. Rebillon, *op. cit.*, 18.

[66] Cf. A. Rebillon, *op. cit.*, 18–19.

[67] A. De La Borderie and B. Pocquet, *op. cit.*, 4, 3.

[68] A number of witnesses to the enquiry of 1455 (see above, n. 33) implied that the duke asked the assembly for taxes; and so, possibly, did the memoire of 1384 (see above n. 35). That it was its right to be asked is not so clear; but since in any case the documents were concerned with the duke's rights rather than with those of the assembly one is probably safe in inferring from them that the body did consider it ought to be asked about taxes as about 'autre chose au profilt dudit pays.'

[69] A. De La Borderie and B. Pocquet, *op. cit.*, 4, 422; cf. Dom. G-A. Lobineau, *Histoire de Bretagne*, 2 vols (Paris, 1797), 673; Dom C. Taillandier, *Histoire de Bretagne*, 2 vols., (Paris, 1750–56), 2, 72.

[70] A. De La Borderie and B. Pocquet, *op. cit.*, 4, 609.

[71] Letters of non-prejudice were granted in large numbers still under Jean V but they were now only formal. By the end of the ducal period the right of each lord was only an unpractical memory [A. Rebillon, *op. cit.*, 19]. Nb. also the emphasis placed on the binding power of the Estates' grants in both the 1384 memoir and the 1455 enquiry (see above, notes 34 and 36). But is it possible that this is an assertion more than a merely descriptive fact and that people were still resisting the right of the Estates to bind all to taxation?

multiplied and became quasi-permanent it is still difficult to argue that vote of taxes had become the principal function of the Estates or their main *raison-d'être*. Taxes *were* taken by dukes without the consent of the Estates; and until François II meetings of the Estates were irregular, whereas taxes were regular.[72] The matter is as obscure as anything connected with the assembly but it seems that in Brittany the new right of consenting to the new taxation was eclipsed by the old right of giving consent and advice in political and administrative matters and of giving judgement; and the latter were in no way made dependent upon or purchased by the former.[73]

The role which Pocquet assigned to the Breton assembly (especially to an assembly reinforced by the *tiers-état*)[74] is therefore hardly justified. Not all taxes, not all administrative and legal matters were brought to its attention by the duke.[75] Its task was in any case only ratification: the initiative was taken and the work done by the duke and his council. This is clearly brought out in the *procès-verbal* for the Vannes assembly in May 1451.[76] On Thursday 27 May 'le Duc ne comparut point en Parlement pour ce qu'il besongna sur la conclusion d'aucunes necessaires Constitutions pour le bien de son pays, en la compagnie des Sieurs du Sang, Prelats & Barons'. Parliament was not held on Friday because duke, prelates, barons and others of the Estates and Councillors were working all day 'au fait de certaines Constitutions & autres grandes matieres concernantes le bien universal de la chose publicque de ce Duché . . .' The truth seems simply to have been that the support of the Estates was useful to the much-harrassed dukes of the fourteenth and fifteenth centuries. This in fact simply meant that they wished to win over the more influential nobles and churchmen and at times the more influential of the bourgeoisie. As long as the troubles persisted this support was automatically useful to a duke on (with the Penthièvre claim in the air at least) a none too secure throne. With 'consent' in the mind of every theorist such a body could not but automatically be asked to consent to taxes. But this was not the cause of the existence of assemblies: this is rather to be found in the tradition of the *Parlement* and through it of the *curia ducis*; in the necessity for a law-court and for a ruler's obtaining advice.

But none of these causes explains why the assembly should have *continued* to exist. Here we think of those continual 'troubles' and consider 'political backwardness' in Brittany: a tolerably popular assembly was still in the mid-fourteenth century the supreme law-court and remained at least nominally so until the 1490's. The dukes could not get away with it. The nobility (and the clergy) of Brittany was, at least in the mid-fifteenth

---

[72] A. Rebillon, *op. cit.*, 20.

[73] *Ibid.*, 21.

[74] A. De La Borderie and B. Pocquet, *op. cit.*, 4, 3–4.

[75] C. Bellier Dumaine, *op. cit.*, *Annales de Bretagne*, 14, (1898–99), 584 (for Jean V's reign).

[76] Morice, *Preuves*, 2, 1564–81.

century, precedence-ridden.[77] The dukes, from Jean IV on, were intent, attacking to defend, on reinforcing the 'royal' tradition.[78] From 1417 they ruled by the grace of God.[79]The invention of the Nine Ancient Baronies was an attempt both to prove the antiquity of the duchy and to assert its equality with the kingdom of France. King, nobles and clergy, the effective members of the Estates, all suffered, forcibly or not, different forms of *folie de grandeur*. Both sides were agreed about the role of the Estates in their common world-picture; the duke's memoir, 'touchant les Noblesses & Gouvernement du pays de Bretagne par deliberation faite en ce present Parlement . . .' of 1384, and the witnesses' views in the 'Enquestes sur les Droits Royaux & anciens usages du pais de Bretagne' of 1455,[80] both dealing with both the duke's royal rights and the rights of Parlement, show this clearly. The existence of Parlement was very much part of the duke's royal dignity; and in it were its members dignified. In this state of mind no-one wanted to do away with an institution very much the same as it had been in the thirteenth century. A mid-fifteenth century forger could not but think that a grant of 1302 had been made by 'Artur par la grace de Dieu Duc & Prince de Bretaigne soeant en nostre general Parlement o la solempnité de nos trois Estatz'.[81] Than this *cachet* nothing seemed to him more authentic. That the charter he forged was diplomatically outrageous did not bother him at all. So the nobles wanted to come to Estates, especially the more important nobles, lest they lost their precedence and honour as well as for their other motives; and as well as for his other motives the duke wanted them to come, because in the Estates all his royal *grandeur de la terre* was exhibited for the world to see.[82] It was little wonder François II could write in 1480:

Comme à nous de noz droitz Royaulx, souverainetés & noblesses, & non à autre, en notre pays & Duché appartient croyer [various degrees of nobility, to serve the duke] . . . & au bien de la chose publique dont fuimes seigneur, Protecteur & Administrateur, & que de long & ancien temps paravant ces heures l'estat, honneur & magnificence de nostre Seigneurie & Principauté ait esté par nos predecesseurs en aucun temps Rois & par autres temps Ducs & Princes d'icelle traités, regis & gouvernés en ordre & police de neuf Prélats & neuf Barons, oultre les Bannerets, Bacheliers & autres membres des Estats d'icelle nostre Seigneurie . . . [the] Prélats, Barons, Bannerets, Bacheliers, Chevaliers, Escuyers, gens de Chapitre & bonnes villes, & autres nos sujets faisans & representans nosdits Estats . . .[83]

For that was the way things happened *ét Breizh*.

---

[77] Their concern with it is most marked in the *procès-verbaux* for 1451, 1455 and 1462 (see above n. 31).

[78] B-A. Pocquet du Haut Jussé, *op. cit.*, 391 and note 6; cf. both the 1384 memoir and the 1455 enquiry cited below (note 77).

[79] *Ibid.*, 396 and note 3.

[80] Morice, *Preuves*, 2, 456–59 and 2, 1651–68.

[81] *Ibid.*, 1, 1177–78; cf. Pocquet du Haut Jussé, *op. cit.*

[82] V. the *procès-verbaux* cited above, n. 30.

[83] Morice, *Preuves*, 3, 367–70.

10

THE ESTATES OF TOURS[1]

Fonc expliquat per lod. S$^{r.}$ Andrieu Martj cossi el, ensequen la tenor del darrié cosselh tengut sayus, era anat per la present cieutat al cosselh general que lo rey nostre soueyran S$^{or.}$. [fasut *crossed out*] `avia fach´ tenir et adiustar en la vila de Tors; et que de so que el ley avia besonhat de tot en tot in cossi; el ley [avia *crossed out*] se era presentat per la vila d'estavila [en *crossed out*] in cossi, aprés el avia agut son congiet de s'en retornar. El ne portava lo dobble de tot en tot so que ley se era besonhat, loqual dobble avia el fach scrieure et dobbla a m$^{tre.}$ Bernat Cossanna not., que ley era anat per moss. de Panot; et loqual m$^{tre.}$ Bernat ne avia aguda gran pena et trebalh, et per so lod. S$^{en.}$ Andrieu requeria et preguaua al sobred. cosselh que envers lod. Cossanna aguesso et volguesso aver reguart de sadicha pena et treblh. Et per so lo dobble de tot so que lod. S$^{r.}$ Andrieu avia portat deld. cosselh et conclusio d'aquel fonc legit en presencia dels sobreditz per lod. Cossanna.

Item plus fonc expliquat cossi en hotra tot so desus el avia portadas certanas letras reals contenens que tota l'Auta Marcha sos compellida a paguar la despensa que los trameses de Melhau et deldich S$^{or.}$ Andrieu Martj avian fachas en anar ald. cosselh.

Concusio.

A tot so desus lo sobredit cosselh ausit que agio legit per lod. Cossanna lo dobble et conclusio deld. cosselh general tengut a Tors et congiet que avia agut lod. S$^{r.}$ Andrieu Martj et inpetraceo de lasd. letras reals dissero et respondero que lod. S$^{r.}$ Andrieu avia treben besonhat. Et requerian que lo dobble de tot so que lod. Cossanna avia legit se registrés en lo present libre assi que ne fos memoria sayus et que fos registrat per lod. Cossana; et que era be raso que hom argués reguart envers el, et que els ho remetran alsditz cossols de tot en tot que y aguesso requort, et ly taxesson [ra *crossed out*] so que sera rassonable.

[registrar's signature]

Et per so la tenor de tot so desus que ha portat lod. S$^{en.}$ Andrieu se enset.

Verte.

---

[1] The sources for this paper are: (i) 'L'Ordre observé en l'assemblée des Etats généraux de France à Tours, du regne du roi Louis XI, l'an 1467. Par Jean LE PREVOST, secretaire du roi, & greffier esdits états', éd. C. J. de Mayer, *Des Etats généraux* (Paris, 1789), ix. 204–26 from Arch. nat., J. 393, no 13 [hereafter cited (with some hesitation) as Prev.]; (ii) 'Recit des Etats généraux tenus à Tours en l'annee 1468. Tiré des archives de l'hôtel de ville de Rouen . . .', *Documents historiques inédits*, éd. J. J. Champollion-Figeac, iii [Docs. inéd. sur l'hist. de France] (Paris, 1847), pp. 494–98 [hereafter cited as Rou.]; (iii) Arch. dép. Aveyron, Arch. Comm. Rodez, BB3, fos. 50^{v}–66^{r} [hereafter cited as Rod.] (Professor Neithard Bulst of the University of Bielefeld is preparing an edition of this text). The passage below is derived from fo 50^{r} of this.

Very little that is accurate is known about the physical appearance of a general assembly of the three estates of the kingdom of France in the later middle ages. Partly this is because such assemblies were exceedingly rare. But even this rarity could work the other way: the care with which the towns of Millau and Rodez, in the Midi, for instance, preserved the *dobles* of the procès-verbal of the estates of 1468[2] is evidence of an interest taken in these unusual occurences, and some accounts do as a result survive. The actual arrangement of the seating at such a meeting may not seem to have a very great interest today. For the men of the fifteenth century it had a very great interest indeed. 'Quoniam ad conventionem, cujus gesta sub compendio pro viribus narrare decrevi, ordo, dignitas, et apparatus sedentium, ac vocationis modus non nihil videntur pertinere', wrote Jean Masselin at the beginning of his journal of the estates-general of Tours in 1484, 'de his pauca dicere statui';[3] and of the few documents which survive of the doings of the *Parlement* of Brittany three contain elaborate *assiettes* of the assembly and two of these contain nothing more. For the Bretons the seating-plan of the meeting was vitally important. Their consciousness of precedence seems to have been either greater or more vocal than that even of other fifteenth-century Frenchmen, and a Laval was bitterly wounded if he was made to sit below a Rohan.[4] But such sensibility was not confined to Brittany. Having temporarily settled down the magnates of the estates-general of 1468 Guillaume Cousinot, who with the seigneur of Châteauneuf de Dauphiné[5] 'estoit establi pour assigier chacun sellon son estat', was careful to announce 'que null' ce tint a male s'i n'estoient assigiez sellon leur estat maiz le roy n'enetendoit point de lez priver de leurs perminences et parroquetives'; and it had to be decided just where the count of Perche was to sit, as much as it had to be decided over and over again which of the nine barons of Brittany took precedence over the others. On a noble's exact place on a particular bench at a particular moment depended a great deal of his prestige; and precedence, with its more tangible rewards, was one of the things most dear to the noble heart. Their placing was as eagerly watched by others as they watched it themselves: in 1468 it was carefully noted that the bastard of Bourbon, the admiral of France, 'fut au rang' of the other military officers beneath the constable but was 'le dernier assis';[6] and even to the deputies of the towns their place was important. The order in which they were

---

[2] *Documents sur la ville de Millau*, éd. J. Artières [Arch. hist. Rouergue], vii (1938), 745, 847; for the Rodez relation see the preceeding note.

[3] Jean Masselin, *Journal des Etats généraux de France tenus à Tours en 1484*, éd. A. Bernier [Docs. inéd. sur l'hist. de France] (Paris, 1835), [hereafter cited as Mass.], p. 4.

[4] See above, pp. 105f., 127f.

[5] Soffroy Allemand [*Lettres de Louis XI*, éd. J. Vaesen et E. Charavay [Soc. Hist. France], iii (Paris, 1887), 213]; for the remainder of the passage Rod. fos. 52ᵛ, 51ᵛ, Rou. p. 496 and below, pp. 171, 189.

[6] Prev. p. 208.

summoned to sit marked the eminence of the towns which they represented and of this they might be very properly jealous; as a result the bourgeois deputies were summoned 'sellon lour ordre'[7] in what appears to be an on the whole generally accepted but not wholly invariable way.

The actual seats were specially constructed at considerable cost, elaborately covered and to a great extent symbolised in their arrangement late medieval society as much as the three estates in theory represented it. In 1484 Guillaume Cousinot, now in his dotage, had been put in charge of preparing the hall of the archbishop's house at Tours; when it was alleged the cost had been eleven hundred *livres* the unfortunate old man protested that this and another hall originally prepared at Orléans came to no more than five hundred and sixty *livres* altogether;[8] but even so this was quite considerable. All was as elaborately arranged as a stage set; and nothing was more wounding to the deputies of 1484 when the whole structure, seats and all, was stripped of its coverings – 'quo manifeste praetendebatur', wrote Masselin, '. . . quosdam taedio statuum teneri, et eorum velle decisionem eludere'.[9] The outward show was an integral part of the assembly itself; the height of each area of the meeting, each *parquet* was carefully measured in *marches de degrés* by the eye of each beholder; to them the outward appearance of the assembly had a fascinating meaning.

To a certain extent, however, fascinating and however much a part of the very nature of the assembly, its appearance was an end-product rather than a factor: it was a symptom of the nature of society rather than a cause of any change in it. Contemporaries might notice who sat where and who was derogated; but this was of importance only in the political fortunes of the scorned and not in the working or development of the assembly. But such psychology must have affected the actual operation of the meeting. For some brief moment the political society of France was, in microcosm, in a state of intense activity; what deputies thought of each other and of the place of dignity or indignity from which they rose or from which they moved to the 'solita proponentis sede'[10] to speak cannot but have influenced their estimation of each other's views. A deputy from a backwoods borough could not without great ability persuade a meeting that his view was the right one; the order and structure of society were preserved (there was very little that might tend to disrupt it at this level in the later middle ages); the doctrine of *maior et sanior pars* so dear to the medieval mind was put once more into actual physical operation. The deputies from the towns were present in 1468 'faisant & représentant la plus grande & saine partie des bonnes villes & cités en ce royaume';[11] and in the hall of the assembly were gathered the larger and wiser part of every estate of the kingdom.

---

[7] Rod. fo 52^v.
[8] Mass. pp. 376, 382–84.
[9] *Ibid.* p. 308.
[10] *Ibid.* p. 604.
[11] Prev. p. 210.

Perhaps the argument should not be carried too far; both in 1356 and in 1484 a committee system was set up, since, although indubitably wise, the body was far too large for convenient working.[12] In committee a whole new meeting psychology was inevitably established. In 1484 the assembly was divided into six sections, which each developed its own views and clung to them dearly: a completely new pattern was created. But the meetings of 1356 and 1484 were in every way exceptional: resistance to the government was paramount. Most assemblies grumbled but were not openly in revolt. The assembly of 1468 was far from being rebellious: called to endorse Louis XI's policy during the war of the Public Weal its deputies begged, 'pour ce que aisement ilz ne se peulvent pas assembler',[13] not to be summoned again; and they were not. Central assemblies of the whole kingdom were never popular and were on the whole extremely rare; large general meetings of the estates of Languedoil were almost equally disliked and in the fifteenth century at least lasted under twenty years. Many during this period were not as complaisant as that of 1468; but as far as one can see they followed much the same physical pattern of appearance and procedure. The style of the better known meeting of 1468 is therefore not entirely irrelevant to them.

Accounts of medieval French assemblies are pitifully rare. As far as a general meeting is concerned there are three groups of documents. The first, a journal of the general estates of Languedoil at Paris in October 1356 gives no information of the appearance of the meeting. The second group is comprised by three different eye-witness accounts of the estates-general of the kingdom of France at Tours in 1468: a journal perhaps by Jehan le Prevost, the *greffier* of the estates, and relations on the borough registers of Rouen and of Rodez.[14] The third is the great journal of Jean Masselin, with some ancillary documents. Masselin's description of the hall of the archbishop of Tours is quite brief.[15] All the walls of the room and all the seats were covered with tapestry specially for the occasion. At the bottom end of the hall was a wooden platform about four feet high above the floor of the hall, thirty-five feet long, which filled the whole width of the hall except at one end where, in a five-foot space, a stair which also ran along the whole of the front led up to the stage. In the centre of this was the royal throne hung with fleur-de-lis silk; it was led up to by five easy circular steps. On the left of the throne was left a space for four to six people standing: here in order from the throne were the count of Dunois (on a level with the king) and the count of Albret; behind them the count of Foix and the prince of Orange. Lower down, on the stage and to the right of the throne was an armchair, decorated with tapestry and containing the duke of Bourbon. Opposite him, but with its front turned to the left (presumably towards the front of the platform)

---

[12] See above, p. 112.
[13] Rod. fo 64ᵛ; Prev. p. 222.
[14] References are given above, n. 1.
[15] Mass. pp. 5ff.

was another chair, for the chancellor, lower than Bourbon's and nearer the edge of the stage. Behind Bourbon's armchair was a bench on which sat the cardinals of Lyon and of Tours, the seigneurs of Gaure, Vendôme and several others. To the left, near the throne, was a bench placed acrosswise with the dukes of Orléans and of Alençon, the counts of Angoulême, of Beaujeu and of Bresse on it. Leaning on the back of this bench were the count of Tancarville and other magnates. Many other seigneurs were scattered about the body of the platform, standing. On each side of the body of the hall were three rows of benches with a passage down the centre; behind the benches on either side were three further rows of forms. At the bottom of the hall were rows of seats which filled the space entirely to the door, where, at the very end of the hall, there was a bar to restrain the interloper. These last seats were for, on the right, 'proceres, ut aiunt, regii ordines'; on the left, prelates not of the body of the estates. The upper part of the benches was reserved for seneschals, *baillis*, barons, knights, councillors, secretaries, called by name and all mixed up together, and for the prelates and the greatest dignitaries of the estates; the lower part for the ordinary deputies. Below the platform was a place for the *greffiers*.

This is not a very clear picture but it does help to illuminate (as it is itself illuminated by) the appearance of the assembly of 1468. Here perhaps three sets of eyes were busy recording for posterity and a more accurate impression can be derived from them; and the lively interest of the author of the Rodez relation, fascinated by the minor details of pompous ceremony, has provided an equally fascinating memory of what happened almost each minute, round about eight o'clock in the morning on 6 April 1468 in the house of the archbishop at Tours.[16]

'Grandement fasoit bon voir le brau et grand monde qui estoit', he wrote enthusiastically. 'Et a la premiere porte dedonx qui en failhait passer estoient bien environ dix personiaitges de gran facon et appelloient illeq chacun mandez ausdits estaz. Ont premierement fuirent appellez tout a ung mot les gens du sang, les gens du sang. Et aprés fuirent appellez les gens d'esglic., les nobles et gens des bonnes villes sellon lour ordre et l'on introit ou icelle porte et aprés a la porte de la sale pareilhement estoient appellez.' Inside were Cousinot and m. de Châteauneuf, settling everyone down in their seats. 'Et aprés tout le monde intré les portes bien guardees et fermees le roy vint en ladite sale (we know from the Rouen relation that he came in through "ung huys qui estoit ou costé de ladicte chaire [his throne] dudicte hault estage", and from Prevost that this door "répondant en l'hôtel d'une des chanoines de l'église . . . avoit été fait pour la venue du roi") et demoure auecq tous lesdits seigneurs tout debot bien une heure sans soy assoir et parlarent ensemble sur l'assiete des seigneurs qui estoient presens . . . Et

---

[16] Detailed references to passages from the three (comparatively brief) descriptions are now perhaps otiose: they are hereafter given only when confusion might occur.

assis le roy et ledit cardinal et le roy de Secille, le conte de Dampmartin eust la charge d'assoir les autres nobles come avoit esté ordonné par le roy. Et cela fit et avant que le prepoux se fist ledit monsieur de Chastelneuf et maistre Guillaume Cousinot alarent de hors ladite sale & par ung huissier firent crier les deffaulz contre les non compareus et deffailhans.' But those who had appearèd were now settled, and it is probably time to look around this assembly of the three estates general of the kingdom of France.

The hall was 'bien grande et bien notable et tendue de tapisserie'.[17] At its upper end was the same sort of stage as Masselin described in 1484, except that this, and the other *parquets* described later on, was enclosed inside a wooden barrier which, at the door frame, rose 'd'environ la hauteur d'un homme chacun'.[18] There is a certain amount of discrepancy between Prevost and the Rouen relation about this platform. The former said 'auquel parquet convenoit monter trois marches de degré'. The latter wrote 'où l'on montoit à cinq ou six marches de degrés', and its author's *estage* is rather more sophisticated than Masselin's. It seems that it divided into two: the 'hault estage' of the Rouen relation, which was five or six steps up from floor level, and a lower platform which Prevost included in the 'parquet du roi'. This is described only by the Rouen author. 'A deux marches audessoubs dudit hault estage et à trois marches de hault au fons dudit hault estage avoit une allée de dix piés de lé ou environ', and it was in this 'allée' that 'avoit ou parmi ung huis ou yssue'. It seems as if Prevost, for one of possibly several reasons, miscalculated, because in this particular part of the hall the Rouen author (whose place we might eventually identify) was rather a better observer. (It is even possible that from where Prevost was sitting the king's platform was three steps above and from the Rouen author's seat it was five.) So the upper stage was divided into two: a lower area three steps up and ten feet wide, and a higher area two steps up again and probably about the same width.

In the centre of this higher stage was the king's throne. Prevost and the Rouen author agree that this was up two or three steps (Prevost thought 'trois hauts degrés'). Prevost had a better eye for fabrics than his rival: the throne 'étoit couverte d'un velours bleu, semé de fleurs de lys, enlevées d'or, & y avoit ciel & dosseret[19] de même; & étoit le roi vêtu d'une longue robe de damas blanc, broché de fin or de Chypre bien dru, boutonnée devant de boutons d'or, & fourrée de martres sobelines, un petit chapeau noir sur sa tête, & une plume d'or de Chypre'. On either side of the throne were the 'assistants', who 'tenoient chacun un des deux costés de ladicte chaeire':[20] on the right hand side (from the king's point of view) the count of Foix; on the left the count of Eu and according to both Prevost and the Rodez author

[17] Rou. p. 494.
[18] Prev. p. 204.
[19] 'dosseret' from Arch. nat. J. 393 no. 13.
[20] Rou. p. 497. For 'assistant', Rod. fo 50ᵛ.

the count of Nevers as well (it seems likely that the Rouen author left him out by mistake). On the steps of the throne, in front of the count of Foix, was the prince of Piedmont, 'jeune enfant', 'fils du roy de Savoye et de la seur du roy'.[21] Then 'aux deux côtés du roi y avoit deux chaires à dos, loin de la sienne, chacune de sept à huit pieds, l'une à dextre, & l'autre à senestre, toutes deux couvertes de riche drap d'or sur velours cramoisi'[22] (the Rouen author thought they were nine or ten feet away). These chairs seem to have been facing the king; 'en celle de main dextre' was the 'cardinal de Sainte-Susanne, éveque d'Angers, paré d'une grande chappe cardinal'[23] and in the left hand one 'le roi de Jerusalem & de Sicile, duc d'Anjou, vêtu d'une robe de velours cendré, fourrée de martres'.[24] The only other person seated on the upper part of the high platform was the count of Dunois: he was 'derrière le roi de Sicile, . . . assez loin, sur une petite selle', because he 'étoit si goutteux, qu'il le convenoit porter à force de gens'.[25] The Rodez author too, but not the Rouen author, knew that Dunois had gout; and in fact the Rouen author at times from now on conflates the seating arrangements of this grand opening session and the sessions of subsequent days – Dunois is placed elsewhere. The new door by which the king entered the hall was guarded by 'le capitaine & archers de la garde dudit seigneur, & Guerin le Groin'.[26] The door of the whole *parquet*, which was in the middle of the lower part of the platform, presumably at the top rather than bottom of its steps, was guarded by 'les sires de Blot & du Bellay'.[27]

In this lower part, on either side of the door but apparently quite close to it, were two benches which seem to have been formally for the lay and for the clerical peers of France. They had their backs to the barrier of the *parquet* and the rest of the hall and faced the king. In the right hand bench were five of the six clerical peers (Rheims, Laon, Langres, Beauvais, Chalons; Noyon was 'absent pour cause de maladie').[28] On the other side, the Rouen author noted 'n' y avoit nuls des pers séculiers'. Quite who was on it seems disputed. Prevost thought Dammartin, the marshals Lohéac and Boisménart,[29] the *grand-maître des arbaletriers* Torcy and finally the admiral, the bastard of Bourbon. The Rodez author thought on this 'bancq traversant la sale a l'antree du parq estoient assis' Dammartin, Rouault, Torcy, 'le filz de

[21] Prev. p. 206, Rou. p. 496.

[22] Prev. p. 205.

[23] Jean Balue [H. Forgeot, *Jean Balue, Cardinal d'Angers* (1421?–1491) [Bibl. Ec. Hautes Etudes, cvi] (Paris, 1895), pp. 43–44].

[24] Prev. p. 205. For the colour of costume at the court of René d'Anjou see F. Piponnier, *Costume et vie sociale. La Cour d'Anjou XIVe–XVe siècle* (Paris–La Haye, 1970), pp. 188 ff.

[25] Prev. p. 206.

[26] *Ibid*. For Guerin le Groin see G. Dupont–Ferrier, *Gallia regia*, v (Paris, 1958) 360–61, no. 20509.

[27] Prev. p. 206. Hugues de Chauvigny seigneur de Blot, and Jean du Bellay.

[28] Rou. p. 495.

[29] Joachim Rouault.

monsieur de Dunois monsieur de Arcanvila, monsieur Duboys, monsieur de Tarquanvilla, monsieur de Caissol senescal de Poito, monsieur de Crant' and 'monsieur du Montell'.[30] The Rouen author is very confused at this point and does not mention this bench at all, unless it is a mysterious seat which appears in the text to be the bishops' seat in the second *parquet*, occupied possibly after the first session by Dunois, Tancarville and 'autres plusieurs contes, qui pas n'estoient assis et se tenoient hault auprès du hault estage où le roy estoit': they could hardly be in two places unless they were in them on different days. But the Rouen author does mention the lords who were standing scattered about both parts of the king's platform; 'si y avoit', he wrote, 'ès degrés comme l'en descendoit du hault estage plusieurs seigneurs du conseil du roy', and he names Dammartin, La Forêt, Torcy and 'Cursol'.[31]

The Rodez list of those so standing is limited to 'Buell', le mareschal de Loyat' and 'Chastillon son frere'.[32] The marshal Lohéac was sitting on the lay peers' seat according to Prevost but the other two are on his list of standers. Prevost's list includes some of the Rodez author's sitters: Tancarville, Craon, and 'Crussol'. Others are the viscount of Narbonne (the son of the count of Foix), the seigneur of 'Pennebroc' (brother of the king of England, whom nobody else noticed),[33] Longueville, 'Pierre' de Laval, 'L'Aigle'[34] and La Forêt; with 'plusieurs autres en grand nombre'. If the 'lay peers' seat' was really intended for the lay peers of France and although the number of lay peers certainly exceeded six it did not exceed it by as many as four, the bench must have been very crowded if the Rodez author is right; Prevost's version has an air of authority and it should probably be accepted. There were five officers on the lay peers' bench and a heavy scattering of lords all over both parts of the upper *parquet*.

'Le second parquet' was 'pour les seigneurs du sang, connétable, chanceliers & prélats, lequel étoit au milieu de ladite salle, près de celui du roi, & étoit plus long que large, & y convenoit monter une marche de degré'.[35] The Rodez author thought this *parquet* was 'bien grant'. In it were 'deux hauts bancs, parés de riche tapisserie'[36] and all the eye-witnesses were fairly clear about who was sitting on them. 'Ou premier hault blanc, ou costé destre, avoit au boult de hault ung siége ung pou plus hault que ledict banc, et joingnoit d'ung costé au dos de cellui de monseigneur de Rains, ou quel

---

[30] François comte de Longueville, Jean de Bueil, Tancarville, Louis de Crussol, Craon and Carlo da Monteglio, maître d'hôtel of the marquis de Saluces [cf. *Lettres de Louis XI*, x (Paris, 1908), pp. 270–71].

[31] Louis de Beaumont seigneur de La Forêt, Crussol.

[32] Bueil, Lohéac, Louis de Laval seigneur de Châtillon.

[33] Jasper Tudor earl of Pembroke, half-brother of Henry VI of England by Catherine of France.

[34] 'Pierre' in error for Louis de Laval [above n. 32]?; Jean de Penthièvre seigneur de L'Aigle.

[35] Prev. p. 205.

[36] *Ibid.* p. 207.

siége estoit assis monseigneur le connestable, et au plus près en icellui banc estoit monseigneur le chancellier de France, Juvenel . . .' who was 'vetu de robe de velours cramoisi'.[37] Then on the same seat after a four-inch space[38] came some seventeen bishops, named on the whole identically by the Rodez author and Prevost: the Rouen author names half a dozen and says there were some fifteen to seventeen more. On the left hand of the king were six or seven lay lords; they were joined on the second day by Foix, Eu and Nevers (though the Rouen author is rather confusing about this). Somewhere at the upper end of the second *parquet* was a smaller *parquet*, 'ouquel . . . qui estoit petit et ront, avoit deux secrétaires'.[39] Prevost (who, if it were indeed he who wrote the 'relation' ascribed to him, was one of them) gives the impression he was on his own, 'assis sur une selle, & un buffet devant lui'; but the Rodez author backs up his Rouen colleague and says that 'devant monsieur le chancelier avoit une petite table ont estoient assigiez pour escripvre maistres Jehan le Prevost et Anthoine Raynault secretaires du Roy et greffiez ordonnez par lesdits estaz'.[39 bis] At the feet of the occupants of apparently both high benches were other notaries and secretaries of the crown: how they were sitting one can only guess. Perhaps the high benches had steps; to sit on them would be rather more dignified for a royal notary than to sit on the floor. Finally, 'étoient commis à garder l'huisserie dicelui parquet, les sénéchaux de Carcassonne & de Quercy, vêtus de robes longues de velours noir'.[40]

'Le tiers parquet' was occupied by 'les nobles, comtes, barons, gens du conseil du roi, & gens envoyés de par les bonnes villes. Lequel parquet étoit grand & spacieux, & environnoit de trois côtés celui desdits seigneurs du sang.'[41] Prevost is not so good a witness in this area as the Rouen and Rodez authors, who were, after all, presumably sitting in it. The Rouen man is the more circumstantial. 'Es seconds bancs', he wrote, 'derrière lesdis chancellier et prélats, estoient assis monseigneur Guillaume Cousinot . . ., maistre Pierre Doriole . . ., maistre François Hallé . . ., maistre Jehan de Popincourt, maistre Pierre du Reffuge pour le duc d'Orléans, et autres plusieurs qui estoient pour les ducs et contes qui n'avoient peu comparoir. Item, ou second banc après, oudict costé destre, furent assis ceulx de la ville de Paris, et ou banc ensuivant furent assis ceulx de la ville de Rouen, et après

---

[37] Rou. p. 495. The Fouquet portrait of Guillaume Jouvenel is of course well known.

[38] Prev. p. 207.

[39] Rou. p. 495.

[39 bis] For Jean Le Prévost and Antoine Reynault see A. Lapeyre et B. Scheurer, *Les Notaires et secrétaires du roi . . . (1461–1515)* [Docs. inéd. sur l'hist. de France] (Paris, 1978), i, nos. 417, 578.

[40] For sitting, or not sitting, on the floor see Fouquet's equally well known *Lit de justice de Vendôme*. For Pierre de Raymon seigneur de Folmon see Dupont-Ferrier, *Gallia regia*, v. 67–68, no. 18652 and for Arnaud de 'Milglos' *ibid*. (Paris, 1942), pp. 543–44, no. 489 [Prev. p. 208; 'dicelui' from Arch. nat. J. 393 no. 13].

[41] Prev. p. 205.

ceulx de Bordeaulx furent appellées et mis à choix d'estre après ceulx de Paris ou ceulx de Rouen, et choisirent à estre après ceulx de Paris, et après ceulx de Thoulouse furent appellés et furent assis après ceulx de Rouen, et après Thoulouse furent assis ceulx de Tournay, et après ceulx de Bordeaulx furent assis ceulx de Lyon, et ainsy conséqamment appellés et assis tous ceulx de autres bonnes villes'. The Rodez author thought that beside the royal councillors were 'les gens de Paris, de Rouan, de Bourdeauz, de Thole', les gens envoyés par le duc d'Orilhanx, les gens de Tournay, de la basse Normandie, de Lion et plusieurs autres gens des bonnes villes'. Prevost did not admit such bourgeois figures in this section of the third *parquet*: 'les gens du conseil du roi, & ambassadeurs qui s'ensuivent [fourteen names are given: they include Oriole and Cousinot masquerading as 'Monstereul'] . . . & plusieurs autres en grand nombre, tous conseillers du roi notredit seigneur; les chanceliers ou gardes des sceaux du roi de Sicile & du duc d'Orléans, & autres ambassadeurs, tant dudit duc d'Orléans, que du comte d'Angouleme'. Prevost puts the deputies of Paris, Rouen, Bordeaux, Toulouse, Tournai and Lyon firmly in the third section of this *parquet*, at the bottom of the hall; he was probably wrong to do so, though the Rodez and the Rouen authors – or the Rouen author at least – are wrong to hint that very many bourgeois deputies were crowded in with the councillors (the Rouen author does not even mention the third section of the *parquet*: since he was possibly happily seated up against the back of the clerical peers' seat he was not much interested in the fate of lesser deputies).

On the opposite, left-hand side, 'derrière le premier banc où les contes estoient, furent assis les barons en très-grant nombre, [the Rouen author gives three names] . . . et ès autres bancs ensuivant en icellui costé estoient les chevaliers et escuiers en très-grant nombre, tant que ladicte salle et palais estoit presque tout plain'. Prevost gives twenty-nine names[42] '& autres en grand nombre, qui comparurent par procureurs'. It is therefore difficult to say how many nobles actually attended. Prevost – if it was Prevost – was in a good position to know, because the lay deputies had been told, both nobles and bourgeois, to appear before him before the estates began 'ont chacun y alla et ceulx qui se comparrient par procuracion pairent audit Secretaire ung escu'.[43] It would not be surprising, given the political situation, if in fact comparatively few nobles were actually present at the assembly. But it is impossible to penetrate behind the vagueness of 'plusieurs autres' and 'en grand nombre'.[43 bis]

'Au bout d'en-bas dudit parquet, y avoit plusieurs selles & formes, où étoient assises plusieurs notables personnes, tant gens d'église, bourgeois,

---

[42] The twenty-ninth (m. 'de Mailly') is added from J. 393 no. 13.

[43] Rod. fo. 52[r].

[43 bis] But see forthcoming work by Professor Bulst [*cf Medieval Prosopography*, v (1984) 65–79].

nobles, qu'autres, qui illec[44] étoient venus garnis de pouvoir suffisant, faisant et représentant la plus grande & saine partie des bonnes villes & cités en ce royaume, desquelles villes les noms s'ensuivent [Prevost gives sixty-four[45]] . . . & de chacune ville il y avoit un homme d'église & deux laics'. The Rodez author said that 'au bot de la sale en plusieurs banx les gens des bonnes villes et autres envoyés par les prelaz abscens': he and Prevost are pretty well in agreement. And with Prevost at his *greffier's* table with the scorned Antoine Raynault beside him, with the Rouen author tucked away up in a corner by the high seat of the clerical peers of France, behind the deputies from Paris who were behind the notable councillors like Cousinot and Oriole, who were in turn behind the count of St-Pol constable of France and Guillame Jouvenel des Ursins its chancellor, who in turn were almost on top of Prevost and Raynault, and with the deputy from Rodez heaven knows where at the bottom of the hall, Chancellor Jouvenel 'prepousa ou nom du Roy'.[46]

---

[44] 'illec' from J. 393 no. 13.
[45] For 'Rennes' in the printed text substitute 'Reims' from J. 393 no. 13.
[46] Rod. fo. 51ʳ.

11

THE CENTRE, THE PERIPHERY, AND THE PROBLEM
OF POWER DISTRIBUTION IN LATER MEDIEVAL FRANCE

Should one wish to sense the attitudes of the communities of the periphery to the government of the centre in the France of the earlier fifteenth century one might well begin in Beauvais.[1] After the débâcle of the siege of Orléans and the counter-drive to Rheims the much-maligned and well-battered Pierre Cauchon had prudently departed and his place as bishop had been taken by Jean Juvenal des Ursins — but the Jouvenels, thoroughly identified with the Orléans-Armagnac side, were impeccably 'French', and Jean Juvenal was a very proper person to stiffen the wavering Beauvaisis and the wavering frontier.[2] For the next twelve years, until 1444, when Jean Juvenal was transferred to Laon (on 3 April) and the truce of Tours (on 28 May) Beauvais was, sometimes literally, in a state of siege.

The municipal archives of Beauvais were destroyed during the Second World War; but extracts from them were made by Victor Leblond and Pierre Champion.[3] Jean Juvenal himself had a considerable amount to say about the state of the town during his episcopate. Looking back from Laon in 1445 — where he does not seem to have thought things were much better — he reminded his brother Guillaume that five years before he had put together his *Loquar in tribulacione* (I will speak in the anguish of my spirit) — the text is suitably from Job.[4]

> I do not say of course that I should in the least be compared to Job, [he admitted] but still I have suffered much tribulation, adversity and affliction, because I am the spiritual father of the diocese of Beauvais, and I have fine lands and lordships which used to be ploughed and grazed, but the enemy and those who say they are on our side have killed the local people, taken them and deported them, robbed them and tyrannized them, and they have lost all their stock, and the region is waste and desolate, and churches and houses are burned down and collapsed in ruins, and they have murdered the poor people by imprisonment and other

means, and in short I have lost land, stock and my people who are my children, just like Job did.[5]

These groans were not without their echoes in the municipal council meetings, though recorded more soberly and at very much less length. His service in Beauvais certainly marked Jean Juvenal des Ursins.[6] In 1433 he had already sketched out some of the themes with which he was to deal in his *Loquar* seven years later;[7] and in the 1450s as archbishop of Rheims he could remind Charles VII that 'I was twelve or thirteen years in Beauvais, in the front line, and I wrote to you and to the members of your council to have some help sent; and they made me a whole lot of promises, and you wrote to me and so did your councillors, but I never saw or heard about anything ever happening'.[8]

Beauvais, then, was very much on the periphery. According to Jean Juvenal, 'what a frontier is this town of Beauvais . . . Beauvais is one of the best and principal frontiers'.[9] If one turned away from the westward — from the enemy, twenty kilometres away in Gerberoy — and looked southward, towards the centre, what were one's feelings? But what was the centre? For that good Parisian and quondam Parliamentarian Jean Juvenal clearly Paris was the 'ville capital' of the kingdom, and he reproached Charles VII for avoiding it: 'when you come there it seems as if you would rather not be there'. Charles V, on the other hand, 'came there and stayed there and, aided by Wisdom, Prudence, Force and Patience recovered his lordship and put his kingdom back in order, which he would never have done if he had stuck himself away at Amboise'.[10] The attraction of the Loire for Charles VII does not need emphasis. But Gilles le Bouvier also thought that Paris was 'the mistress-city of the kingdom, and the largest, and the king's palace is there in the middle of the town, with the River Seine on either hand'.[11] The idea that Paris was the centre of France was in fact commonplace. But it was an idea that contemporaries could resist, for, with Bernard Guenée, we should talk of institutional centralization and geographic decentralization.[12] The centre of the kingdom was wherever the king, his court or the great departments of state happened to be.

How was the centre regarded from Beauvais? Beauvais, it is clear, felt isolated. There was a time, Jean Juvenal claimed, 'that there was not between the River Oise, the Seine and the Somme a town in the French obedience except this wretched city, which carried the whole burden of the war, and could rely for help neither upon you (i.e. the king) nor anyone else, but only upon themselves'.[13] The taxation that was raised for the war, but which disappeared into private pockets, was one of Jean Juvenal's favourite grievances. Even the taxes paid by the inhabitants of Beauvais, he thought, 'did not go towards the defence of the town but were frittered away by those you had granted them to'.[14] In 1433 he argued that the 'poor lads in the frontiers' did not even get 'a miserable letter-close to encourage them'.[15] The town councillors felt isolated. As was usual in war soldiery cut communications; beleagured towns lived on the occasional newsletter or on hearsay. Jean Juvenal was not the only citizen of Beauvais who was conscious of 'this frontier', of the daily pillaging by the 'French' garrisons of Gerberoy (which was briefly in French hands in 1435-7) and Clermont of the merchants of Beauvais and others victualling the town.[16]

As a result of its geographical isolation as well as of the misdeeds of the soldiery Beauvais was politically alienated. On 9 June 1432 the city council deliberated upon rumours of disaffection. Some people were saying that if Lagny fell to the English Beauvais should abandon Charles VII; they thought that the urban notables had decided to deliver Beauvais to the English. The council decided, for the sake of peace and union, to do nothing. In February 1433 Senlis wrote to Beauvais that the king should be told about 'the wicked and criminal conduct of the king's troops on our side, and how they tyrannize his wretched subjects, whatever status they are, men, women and children, to show him how it is likely to end up, that is with the loss of his lordship and its transfer into alien hands for ever'.[17] The letter might have been written by Jean Juvenal, who gave an oblique reference to the seductive ways of the English in a harangue to the comte d'Eu about 1438,[18] and returned to the argument in his *Loquar in tribulacione* two years later. Things were far better in areas under English control (and here Thomas Basin might have agreed with him);[19] those who had decided to be French (and the Beauvaisis had been English only because 'their last lord and bishop had made this crazy mistake')[20] found that 'their reduction had been the cause of their destruction' and the English rejoiced at it, because it would make them return to the English fold.[21] 'You have already seen', Jean Juvenal warned Charles VII, 'that your English adversary has had a foot in the door and was held to be king; if he comes back, given the oppression which your wretched people suffer, then there is a danger that things might come to a subverting of your lordship, and that you would be a king without a land or a people, or at least you would have very small ones': and this eleven years after the mission of Joan of Arc. There was hardly much moral conviction here: 'if a powerful prince appeared who was determined to see that justice was done, even if he was a Saracen, it is quite possible that like raving witless madmen they would submit to him'.[22]

Thirty years earlier Bordeaux, too, felt isolated, alienated, and fragmented. Cardinal François Hugotion — like Juvenal des Ursins — was concerned about the miseries of the *pays*. In 1406 he bombarded Henry IV of England with letters saying that he had said so much about the *pays* 'that his voice was hoarse with shouting'. He warned that since no help was coming to the 'barbacanas' (the frontiers with the French) the Gascons were much discouraged. It is gravely to be feared that they will decide upon another course of action to their advantage rather than to decide to remain as they are without a remedy'. Furthermore the seigneur de Limeul, 'whom one certainly thought one could trust, has gone French, or so everyone is saying'. Hugotion, like Jean Juvenal, finally adopted a note of elegiac resignation: 'as I have learned by bitter experience, none of my letters does any good, and so it seems that no-one takes any notice of what I say'.[23] Beauvais from Paris is 48 miles; Bordeaux from Southampton is something like 563 miles; and Westminster to Southampton about 75 miles. Although that pious pilgrim William Wey could make the direct crossing from Plymouth to Coruña in four days in 1456, and forty years earlier a letter from the mayor of Bordeaux to the Jurade took ten days to arrive from London,[24] the Bordelais was nevertheless beset by the insecurity of its routes to the centre of power.[25] As the furthest rampart of the old Plantagenet dominions it was remote.

The centre itself could seem remote: in December 1359 the consuls of Albi decided 'that we should send into France or into England, if we cannot get justice done in France, about the vexatious things' which commissioners of the comte de Poitiers, sent at the request of the bishop (of Albi), were bent on doing. The comte de Poitiers, the king's lieutenant in Languedoc, had been at Grenade near Toulouse at the beginning of the month and had already been appealed to there. The mission to England was presumably to the 'sovereign remedy', the captive John II. In the end R. Vidal went to Paris: his mission was successful, but he had to go by water eleven days and at night 'to keep clear of the English, and his horse got catarrh and he sold it in Paris, and so he lost the horse'. He was given five florins compensation.[26] But the constant travelling from the periphery to its capital is too well-known to need comment. The roads of France seem constantly to have been populated with litigants and petitioners wending their more or less uncomfortable way to the court or the central offices, dodging about to avoid the soldiery, their escorts putting up the rate for dangerous passages; some moving pompously as befitted their dignity at a mere twenty-five miles a day; or others like the legendary foot-messenger Malsafava who sprinted the 281 miles from Périgueux to Paris twice in the summer of 1337 at an average of 47 miles a day, and who only laid up for a day before he started back on his second journey.[27] A specialized system of relay horsemen could of course outdo such travellers, but the need for it was exceptional.

The periphery, therefore, did not lack its lines of communication, both moral and physical, with the centre.[28] The history of another frontier town — though its front line, being in the east, was perhaps softer — also bears this out. Lyons could complain about the misdeeds of soldiers. In 1423 its consuls thought that it was 'in the thick of war', but they felt more aggrieved by the effects of taxation. 'Nearly a third of the inhabitants, both rich and poor (the consuls wrote) have left the town and still go off every day, to Savoy where they are not taxed at all, to Dauphiné and Avignon, where they do very well for themselves and almost nothing for the town of Lyons: which *pays* of Savoy and Dauphiné march with the town of Lyons.'[29] The mission of the procureur of Lyons, Rolin de Mâcon, to the peripatetic court of Charles VII in the autumn of 1425 is also instructive.[30]

In November 1424 the *Estates* of Eastern Languedoil at Riom had granted a tax of which the quota of Lyons was 6,400 francs; on 27 November the city had received at Châteaugay a remission of 2,400 francs which was conditional on its making no further requests for one; and from 25 January 1425 the first payment of the tax had been raised in the city. Those who had assignations on the receipt of the receiver of Lyons quickly came forward. On 27 January the officers of the *Parlement* of Poitiers informed the consuls that 400 *livres tournois* as part of their wages were assigned on the tax. In March they informed the consuls that they were assigned on the second payment, and asked them to ensure that their 400 *livres tournois* 'were not converted to other uses'.[31] By June one Colin Jarlot was putting out rather unsuccessful feelers at Bourges: the interest of the Constable de Richemont in the tax was also involved. On 8 June the consuls decided to defer the second payment until 22 July and to send to the king for a further remission (if the journey could be made safely), or otherwise to Yolande of Aragon (the mother-in-law of Charles VII) and Richemont. Possibly about this time the town succeeded in getting a rebate. The news of this was brought by its messenger La Barbe, but otherwise nothing was of avail. The day after the *Parlement* of Poitiers wrote again rather crossly about its 400 *livres tournois*; Richemont had proved inflexible over the raising of his 1000 and on 20 June the bailli of Mâcon and the *sénéchal* of Lyons interned the consuls in the *maison de Roanne*. There they languished until the summer. On 31 July a new and a different tax was ordered to be raised in anticipation of a meeting of the *Estates* of Languedoil at Poitiers in October; Richemont was also assigned on Lyons for this tax. In September the *Parlement* of Poitiers complained to the consuls of Lyons that they had heard that Caqueran, 'the one-eyed' captain of the Milanese contingents in France, and others had been assigned on the Riom tax after it had been granted, and also that they were trying to get themselves paid first.

At this point Rolin de Mâcon set out for the royal court, 'the centre' of the kingdom. On 26 September he wrote from Bourges.[32] He had seen Mâitre Gérard Blanchet, who was the commissioner for Lyonnais of the so-called 'Poitiers' tax, had exchanged compliments with him, and had also got his promise that he would do his best, either on his own or through his friends, to ensure that Lyons was allowed its largest possible rebate. Mâcon told Blanchet everything that he could think of which might be helpful about the woes of Lyons, and particularly about the assignments on the

Riom tax. Having heard Mâcon, Blanchet wrote letters of recommendation on his behalf to the *généraux des aides*, and particularly to Mâitre Jean Châtagnier. The *généraux*, Blanchet thought, were the people with whom to deal because Richemont did not interfere in financial matters, and, in any case, he was then north of the Loire and therefore inaccessible. Mâcon complained that Richemont's receiver in Lyons was putting the consuls under pressure; Blanchet promised to do something about this; and when Mâcon found that some people were starting for Poitiers — 'the roads are so very dangerous' — he hurriedly set off with them. But at Poitiers at the end of September he found that the members of the *Parlement* were absent because the fairs were then taking place. He also found that the royal council had departed with the king, some said to Thouars, some to Saumur. But· he did manage to catch the *généraux* (Châtagnier was particularly welcoming); they said that Mâcon would have to discuss the question of Richemont's assignments with Richemont himself.

Fortunately, the *généraux* were leaving Bourges; because they would enjoy safety Mâcon travelled with them northwards. By 12 October he was back in Poitiers. He had found at Saumur Buffart, a Lyonnais, who had introduced him to Richemont, though not without difficulty because of the crowd around him. Richemont told him that the question of a rebate on the Poitiers tax was not his business, and also that the king or other people could give Lyons any rebate it liked 'as long as he (Richemont) had the total amount which had been assigned to him' on Lyons or elsewhere. Further representations to Richemont and to the Chancellor had been in vain: Richemont, thought Rolin de Mâcon, had probably better be paid. He would see what he could do with humble petitions to the king and the council, and so on. But also at Saumur Rolin de Mâcon had found Théode de Valpergue, a commander under Caqueran, the one-eyed, that nightmare of the *Parlement* of Poitiers in pursuit of its cut of the Riom tax. Some hard bargaining followed, 'through someone' (wrote Rolin de Mâcon) who is well in with both of us, whom I promised a couple of *écus* for his trouble'. 'If you did not pay up soon', Théode had said, 'you would be in danger of paying the lot without the advantage of any favour the king would have given you.' 'Impossible', Mâcon replied, 'given what you had to pay . . ., and I told him . . . that if I were in his place that I would settle for 400 francs. But though I haggled away on this one . . . he would not have anything to do with it, . . . and so I left him like that. I do not know what he will do about it . . .' 'I talked about it afterwards', Mâcon also said, 'to one of our friends from our region, who is over here, and who knows how to deal with things, who told me that things should not be pushed too far for the moment, because soon there are going to be changes. We do not have many friends over here, which is a great pity for us.'

The arrival of Charles VII in Poitiers on 9 October revived Rolin de

Mâcon's melancholy spirits. He at once had a petition drafted for a rebate on the last tax for Richemont and had submitted to the council by a *maître des requêtes*. He returned, saying that the council would not interfere except according to Richemont's wishes. This was, of course, useless. Mâcon asked the *généraux* to tell the Chancellor what Gérard Blanchet had written to them about, but they refused. 'The whole lot of them turned on me', wrote Mâcon plaintively, 'goodness they did, saying that there was not a town in the kingdom on our side which had always been asking for so much in grants from the king, and getting them, and paying less than the town of Lyons . . . Why did not we go to the *élus*', the Chancellor had asked, 'who were better informed than anyone about it, to modify the tax for us as they saw fit?' 'I told him,' Mâcon said rather weakly, 'that all that could have been done had been done, but that they did not want to do anything about it, and so resort had been had to the sovereign remedy.'

Yet another blow was to descend. 'Messeigneurs of *Parlement*', wrote Mâcon, 'are not at all pleased with you, and monsieur the *premier président* told me in the Chancery, and all the other officers, both of *Parlement* and of the *Requêtes*, Charrier (Richemont's secretary) and all the others, that they would do me as much harm as they could and that they would get the 400 francs'. Worse, the Chancellor had said that the La Barbe remission was worthless, because of the proviso on the first Riom remission that it should not have been made. The *Parlement's* 400 francs, thought Mâcon, should probably be paid; but the Chancellor, on the other hand, seems to have said to somebody who was leaving with the messenger carrying the letter Mâcon was engaged in writing that Richemont never had an assignment for 1,000 francs on the Riom tax; and the fine Piedmontese hand of Théode de Valpergue began to show itself on the way back from Saumur. Mâcon seems to have got 300 francs out of Richemont on his own, and La Barbe's remission was not worth a penny: both the king and the council were determined to take it out on the importunate Lyonnais. 'But', Mâcon wrote with a certain amount of relish, 'after a great deal of "fixing" by messire Théode de Valpergue, you have been excused, with an enormous amount of difficulty, about 900 livres. So you will have to pay messire Caqueran, the one-eyed, 1,250 livres, and *Parlement* 400 livres . . . and nothing else can be done . . . I have not been able to have (the letters yet) . . .; but I should have them tomorrow morning, for messire Théode is being very helpful about them and if he was not, I would not get anywhere . . ."I am fed up" he added equally understandably, 'with being stuck over here.' But all was well: letters *Par le Roi, messire Theode de Valpargue present*, providing for all this, and a *non obstant* for the Châteaugay remission, did eventually arrive safely home in Lyons.[33]

Thus, war produced desperation in Beauvais or Bordeaux; lesser and slower evils like taxation produced negotiation — like that of Rolin de

Mâcon. The expert fixers were, of course, active at all times and in all places: but we might look more closely at some who were busy in later medieval France. Mâcon seems hardly to have been successful, Maître Raymond Queu as agent for Saint-Jean-d'Angély some years earlier seems to have been either more lucky or more wily.[34] *Echevin* and sometime *échevin* by rank, before April 1391 he suceeded in obtaining from the government a *grace* of 400 *livres* for repairs in the town and other matters; he also succeeded in having the gift ratified by the *généraux des finances*. His reward was 40 *livres* on the first payment of the 400 and 20 *livres* on the second payment; but 'should he busy himself and do something profitable for the town' (which meant getting the grant verified by the receiver of Saintonge at La Rochelle) he should have the whole 60 at the first go. In June he was off again to the centre 'on the town's business', getting some of Saint-Jean-d'Angély's privileges confirmed, talking to monsieur de Coucy, who was in charge of the *pays*, about billeting, and doing anything else that was useful. In August he was off yet again, to get a further 200 *livres*; and in January 1392 to get a further 600. In May he was perhaps still in Paris; in August he was asked by letter for a report, and told that if he did not send one his expenses would not be paid; but in September he had yet to reply.

On 7 February 1393[35] in the assembly at Saint-Jean-d'Angély Raymond Queu summed up his services to the town. He had spent a 'long time in France waiting upon the king and his noble council'; he had obtained a letter of 1,200 *livres*, another of 400 *livres*, a third of 200 *livres* for repairs, and other things necessary for the town, and also to help pay the *pâtis*, (the local levies for the maintenance of the soldiery), and finally a letter arranging for the *sénéchal* of Saintonge and the mayor of Saint-Jean to oversee the account of the receiver of the *pâtis*. He had brought back 'all these things at his own cost and expense and out of his own purse, including the drawing up of the letters and their sealing, and without being paid by the town or anyone else, or being advanced anything, to have all these things done and paid for, nor for his own expenses, trouble and salary, and he had paid out a great deal, all out of his own pocket, and would like to be paid and rewarded, or otherwise he would suffer grievous loss'. It was agreed he should be paid 200 *livres*; later in February the methods of payment were worked out and in March 1393 the arrangement was confirmed in assembly. But already it had been agreed that Maître Raymond should go back to France for the town, to get its privileges confirmed, to notify the centre of the dolours of the periphery, to get a renewal of the *souchet* (the local tax on wine) and other things necessary for the town's business, and to appear in the *Parlement* of Paris. Sixty *livres* were assigned to him, and 'Raymond Queu shall not be obliged to pay either for the drawing up or for the sealing of what he obtains of the money granted him'. In January 1394 Queu seems again to have been in Paris about the same kind of business.

Thereafter there is silence on the *échevinal* registers of Saint-Jean-d'Angély for over ten years;[36] but early in 1406 Raymond Queu was in Paris getting royal gifts ratified; with a slight sense of *déja vu* we find him going to La Rochelle to fix things with the receiver there. Again in 1408 he got royal letters ratified and reported that 'someone called Colinet, a clerk of the *grand-maître's*, is willing to take on the business of having the letters verified for the sum of 50 francs to be taken from the assignment'. But he appears to have become testy as a result of being frustrated in his negotiations: probably in the spring of the following year he said to Guillaume Barilh's mother that 'your son is a . . . son of a monk', which would hardly have done for 'someone called Colinet's mother'. But worse was to come. In December 1412 and June 1413 he was again in France, tirelessly getting gifts of *aides* for the town, and tiresomely refusing to hand the letters over until he was paid, so that the *échevinage*, which had determined that he should be 'very well and generously satisfied', lost its temper and threatened to proceed against him. At sunset on 24 August 1413 the mayor of Saint-Jean-d'Angély discovered him beating up Papaillon, son of Jean Papaillon, tailor. A shouting match (at least on Raymond Queu's side) was alleged to have taken place, which ended by Mâitre Raymond's remarking that he did not think that the mayor was a good mayor. Condemned by the mayor and *échevins*, he appealed against them, and did not abandon his appeal for three years. Just before then, in the spring of 1416, he made his last journey recorded upon the registers 'to Paris to wait upon the king and his council upon the town's business'.

Hélie de Papassol, notary of Périgueux, is a comparatively wellknown fixer; he was at the centre in the spring and summer of 1337.[37] Already the wiles are familiar: slipping the 'esquire' of Guillaume de Villars, *mâitre des requêtes* of the household, 5 *sous parisis* 'so that he would help us and be favourable to us in our business'; the chief usher of the *Parlement* of Paris the same 'to have his favour in what we have to do in *Parlement*', besides a host of minor presents; dealing with vendors of purloined documents from the other side; and slipping the son of Mâitre Geoffroy Malicorne, a commissioner in one matter, 5 *sous parisis* 'so that he would help us in our affairs and tell us some of the things that had been done in our absence'. Then there was the pursuit of the king to Val-Notre-Dame, to Pont-Sainte-Maxence, Gisors, Bécoisel, Pontoise, Poissy, Compiègne, and the difficulty of getting to see him. On Tuesday 5 August de Papassol 'did not go to Paris because the king went off towards Compiègne, and it was impossible to follow him on foot because of the crowd of people following'. But it was very possible to obtain, as it were, a season ticket for entry into the king's presence. On 21 July Jean Teulier, usher of the royal chamber, was paid 20 *sous parisis* to give Hélie and his coadjutors the entry; 'he promised us that every time we wanted to go in there he would let us in there and that he would help us as much as he could in our affairs'. And already there was the shadow of the great man 'Mossen Ferri de Picquigny, master of the king's household and a most powerful man', who was given 5 pounds of lemons and 5 pounds of sugar on Thursday 7 August at Compiègne at a cost of 35 *sous parisis*. He, in a sense, was the forbear of *'messire* Pierre des Essars, who was master of the king's household (from 1409); and his position was such that no chancellor or president of the *Parlement* would dare cross him'.[38]

The most succinct portrait of the fixer is perhaps to be found in the powers granted to sire Aymeri Seignouret, proctor of Saint-Jean-d'Angély on 30 June 1396:

> that he should have authority to pursue, ask, and request from the king our lord and from his most noble council, all favours and grants, gifts of cash and others whatever and to the profit of the *échevinage*, the town, *châtellenie* and jurisdiction thereof, and each as far as concerns it; to pursue before *nosseigneurs* of the chambre des comptes, nosseigneurs the *généraux élus sur le fait des aides pour la guerre* [the senior officials dealing with the war taxes], and elsewhere where need be, all that which has or shall be given and granted by our said lord

and to give quittances for any proceeds he received.[39] But perhaps more telling still were the moral qualifications proposed for an emissary from Lyons in September 1426: 'an important and knowledgeable man, with sufficient understanding of how to deal with the matter that he is certain not to come back without a favourable reply'. A few years earlier Lyons also advocated that its emissaries be 'men of importance and position, who would not be frightened to talk personally to my lord the dauphin'.[40]

Professor Chevalier has dealt, as far as the *bonnes villes* are concerned, with the *amici in curia*, the 'good "go betweens" from the king's retinue', who in turn might become the king's agents in dealing with the towns. He has also dealt with the question of the administrative machinery for the ratification of the proceeds of their actions.[41] There is thus no need to dwell on these questions, except, perhaps, to reintroduce a familiar face. Maître Gérard Blanchet, already seen in his dual role in dealing with Mâcon and the Lyonnais, came from a Champenois family in favour with Charles V and Charles VI; early a member of the dauphin's party, he was a councillor and *maître des requêtes* of the household from 1422 and ambassador to the duke of Savoy; in the same year he married Isabeau, the sister of Guillaume de Champeaux, bishop of Laon and sister-in-law of the *trésorier-général* Macé Héron. Further embassies and commissions followed; and when he died in 1433 he left a son, Guillaume Blanchet, aged 6, who later became a counsellor in the *Parlement*.[42] But such 'political' intermarriage in the administrative offices is familiar; and Professor Chevalier has recently demonstrated the rise of the Tourangeaux at the court of Louis XI, gloomy though he is about the prospects of writing its history.[43] I shall now move from the 'marchans affaictiez' at court — the phrase is Alain Chartier's, the 'merchants by appointment' who buy other people and sell themselves[44] — to the question of the relationship of the 'centre' with the 'periphery' in a different sense: the relationship of the court with political forces other than the 'bonnes villes'.

Professor Chevalier has already introduced us to a pair of heroes, Guillaume de Varye and Pierre Doriole, the first and second husbands respectively of Charlotte de Bar.[45] Their brother-in-law Denis also merits attention. Denis de Bar was an importunate cleric.[46] Son of a former colleague of Varye and Doriole, he was slipped by Varye (after mis-shots at Maguelone and Lodève) into the bishopric of Saint-Papoul in 1468; in 1471 he coveted Tulle. Guillaume de Varye was dead, so Denis wrote to his new brother-in-law Pierre Doriole, who like Guillaume de Varye had been a *général des finances* since the 1450s, and who was soon to succeed Guillaume Jouvenel des Ursins as chancellor of France, to fix him up with the second diocese.[47] Pierre Doriole set the wheels in motion, but also wrote to Denis de Bar, asking him whether he was certain that he wanted Tulle. He pointed out that Saint-Papoul and the archdiaconate of Narbonne, which de Bar held in plurality with his bishopric, were worth more. 'There's no doubt whatsoever', Denis replied, 'that [Tulle] . . . is the more use to me; because my two benefices bring in an absolute maximum of nine hundred *écus* and I do not think there is a single benefice in the kingdom worth less [than Saint-Papoul] . . . With a great deal of time and trouble I have not been able to get back what it cost me, nor have I been able to help my relations, which is the thing I desire more than anything in the world.' Pierre Doriole had already mobilized Louis XI, who had promised to write to the Pope to translate Denis from Saint-Papoul, to the cardinals, especially the Cardinal of Rouen, and to his proctor in Curia. Two royal orders were necessary, Denis thought: one for the seizure of the temporalities of Tulle, and one to inhibit the chapter from electing. The commissioners to whom the orders were addressed should not only be well-thought of, but the friends of Pierre Doriole. Denis de Bar suggested one of his own. Would Doriole write to the chapter of Tulle, and to those who 'knew' the chapter, 'recommending my person and praising it much more than it is worth?' But when Louis XI wrote in mid-September 1471 to the archbishop of Bourges, the metropolitan of Tulle, it was to tell him that the chapter was plotting to elect, and to warn him not to confirm the election. The two commissioners sent by Louis, Jean Yver, and Bertrand Briçonnet, reported in October to Doriole from Tulle. The chapter was cavilling, they said, about its right of election and the seizure of the temporalities, but Jean de Blanchefort, the king's harbinger, who was a relative of the deceased incumbent, was presenting the real difficulty. He was behaving peculiarly. If he did not interfere, then there would be no election; they had 'heard secretly' that many members of the chapter were prepared to let the Pope provide. The chapter, however, was in fact split and some of its members elected Gérard de Maumont. Nevertheless, the Pope translated Denis de Bar from Saint-Papoul on 20 November 1471; he took possession in March 1472. Yet he may eventually have found the chapter of Tulle too much for him, because in 1495 he returned, despite his earlier scorn for it, to his former diocese. But Saint-Papoul also appears not to have wanted him: and he consoled himself by composing a treatise on judicial astrology, *De astronomicorum professorum ordine epitoma*.

Such were the means whereby a would-be episcopal climber got his way. Not that a local ecclesiastical community lacked the ability to resist pressure from the centre, however doubtful the outcome might be. A case in point is the reaction of the chapter of Notre-Dame to the nomination of Louis de Beaumont, a royal councillor and chamberlain as well as chancellor of the diocese of Paris as bishop of Paris in 1472-3.[48] On the death of Guillaume Chartier on 1 May 1472 Louis XI had, allegedly without Beaumont's knowledge, asked that Beaumont be provided and he was duly preconized on 1 June. That very day a delegation from the chapter arrived — at Saint-Jean-d'Angély — to ask Louis XI for license to elect.[49] As soon as he saw them, Louis said, characteristically, that he knew what they were up to; that the Pragmatic Sanction was not in force, he had submitted to the Pope; that many of the canons were also royal officers, who ought to mind their behaviour; and that the delegation should see the *premier président* of the *Parlement*. On 17 June the chapter decided to postpone the election, fixed for 25 June, to 24 July. On 10 July Louis wrote to the *premier président* that he was 'most happy' about Louis de Beaumont's provision. He also told the *président* to go with Charles de Gaucourt, governor of Paris, and Denis Hesselin, *prévôt des marchands*, and present his bulls to the canons and inform them of 'my will in the matter, which is that they should receive him without contradiction or delay; and that if they do this I will be most mindful of their affairs and those of their church; and also that if they want to be contrary, I shall give them such a "provision" that they will know I am displeased'. On 20 July Louis's emissaries fulfilled the order, and on 24 July the canons refused the provision on grounds of 'conscience'; but for fear of royal wrath, they also did not proceed to an election, though they drew up a line of defence in case Beaumont fulminated: an appeal to the Pope, or to a future council, 'seu illum vel illos, etc.' On 29 July, though a hardy minority still wished to elect, the election was again postponed; and it continued to be postponed, and the provision of Louis de Beaumont to be resisted, throughout the summer and the autumn and into the winter. Resistance began to crumble in the New Year. On 18 January the chapter again decided, since there were so many different opinions and it was getting late, to postpone matters, this time until 20 January. Then after debate, the 'maior et sanior pars' agreed to let de Beaumont in, but under protest. They would not receive him as true bishop of Paris, recognize his title or abandon their right of election, even though they were not at liberty to elect. On 7 February Louis de Beaumont was received as bishop. Though the chapter eventually gave in, it had stood out against the pressures of the 'centre' for eight months and still, in theory, was doing so: indeed, for whatever reasons, Louis de Beaumont was not consecrated until five years later.

Unlike Louis de Beaumont, a son of the seigneur of La Forêt and a 'courtier' in his own right, the chapter of Notre-Dame perhaps lacked friends at court. 'Friends' of whatever rank were as necessary to a great individual as to a 'community'. Professor Rey has shown how at the turn of the fourteenth century the very great found it necessary to have friends in the departments of state.[50] They continued to be necessary; Charles d'Orléans, comte d'Angoulême, in 1477 obtained the gift of the revenues of the *gabelle* and 1,000 francs for the repair of the fortresses in the county of Angoulême by slipping Louis Tindon, the king's secretary, 100 *livres tournois* for having persuaded the king to make the gift, and Tindon's clerk 4 *livres* for having solicited his master to get the warrant for the gift put through.[51] The 'friends' could also do the wooing: Jacques de Filescamps, receiver of Amiens, told the servants of Jean d'Arly that he would do marvels for d'Arly if d'Arly's new pension was on his receipt.[52] Like importunate clerks in search of expectatives *in forma pauperum* (or for that matter bishops in search of better bishoprics), petitioners besieged the king 'while he was getting up, in his closet, at eight o'clock in the morning', after Mass, after his lunch, after his siesta, during his strolls in the fields around Vincennes, after dinner, even at three o'clock after midnight.[53] Even Louis had to give in. Just before Denis de Bar began to badger him about Tulle Louis wrote to Pierre Doriole, saying that 'I have been under heavy pressure from some of monsieur de Guyenne's people to give the *grenetier* of Rheims leave to resign his office . . . to the benefit of his son. And since I was not able to hedge any longer I ordered the letters to be made out; but I want *you* to hedge about sealing them for as long as you can — say that he will have to pay caution money, or that there is something else wrong, as you think fit, so that the letters are *not* sealed. And warn the chancellor and anyone else you think, so that they are not sealed; and do not show this letter to anyone, and burn it at once.'[54]

If more letters of this kind had survived we would be better informed about what kings really wanted. In 1483 one of Louis's emissaries in Rome, when trying to get Jean d'Armagnac translated from Castres, made it clear that 'the prosecution of this case issues from the personal initiative, instance and proper judgement of the king, without favour to another'.[55] Was 'favour to another' regarded by the importunate petitioner operating through his friends those famous *rouages* of administration the real norm? Admittedly there were administrative traps for petitioners. The Constable Richemont obtained the grant of the much-disputed lordship of Parthenay in 1425, supposedly 'by the king in council'; but, as Jean Juvenal des Ursins, as king's advocate, argued a few years later,

> when the king in his council had been told of it all had been amazed: and the king asked Villebresme [the secretary who had signed the donation] what had happened. And then Villebresme said that at the end of a council Richemont had made out his request by a certain clerk; the king had granted it and ordered Villebresme to make out the letters. The king might have said that Villebresme was telling the truth; but none of his council had heard of it, and one can only say that it was importunity and worthless, and such things are revoked every day: the king is powerless to make such alienations, and it is null . . .[56]

But even the *gens du roi*, with their paralysing doctrines of the inalienability of sovereignty, were not the be-all and end-all of life: the administration might be there, but in the end politics might get their own back. The politicians might, admittedly, find the process a bore. When Guillaume Jouvenel des Ursins as chancellor of France in 1470 hedged about sending a case before the great council to commissioners in Berry even Louis XI was reduced to something near bluster: 'I beg you, my good sir, not to be so *rigorous* in my affairs; because I have not been in *yours*. . . . Now send the case back as it should be, and do not let me have to write to you again.'[57] Perhaps Louis XI was not such an effective tyrant as he has been made out to be.

Initiative and counter-initiative, decisions taken and decisions resisted: an analysis of the whole, or of as great a part of the whole as we can get — and much of this subterranean process is inevitably obscure — seems to me to provide the basis for a theory of power distribution as pluralistic as any produced by, for example, a present-day American sociologist.[58] Power is everywhere and nowhere; but still to be seized. Arthur de Richemont and Charles d'Angoulême, Louis de Beaumont and Denis de Bar, Hélie de Papassol, Raymond Queu, Rolin de Mâcon, all were as much a part of the power process as Gérard Blanchet and Théode de Valpergue, Pierre Doriole and Guillaume Jouvenel des Ursins, Louis XI; or Jean Juvenal, or Cardinal Hugotion. One should perhaps commiserate with Beauvais and Bordeaux in their agony, imploring help which could never come and that 'policing of the soldiery' which could come, and came, only with peace.[59] But their sense of isolation was equally a product of the war: under anything like the normal coming and going of agents, either of the centre or of the members of the community, was the pulsing lifeblood of later medieval French politics, as of any politics. One played the system: one did not try to break it if one had any sense. Individual nobles or groups of nobles, it is true, sometimes rebelled about the way in which the system seemed at some particular moment to be stacked against them; but local communities had more wit than to be herded into collective, or representative, institutions to 'control' the centre. They did perfectly well out of backstairs negotiations: as, in the end, did members of the other politically important classes. It was, after all, to everyone's advantage. In 1421 the aediles of Poitiers explained that,

> because the reverend father in God Maître Guillaume de Lucé, bishop of Maillezais, had worked upon Monsieur the regent to give and grant us for the repair of the town the sum of 2,000 *livres tournois* to be taken upon the emoluments of the Poitiers mint, some of us thought it would be a good idea to give him something on the occasion of his ceremonial appearance in the town as bishop, . . . and also because Maître Jean Tudert, dean of Paris, had pursued and advanced the issue of the letters for the gift of 11.000 *livres tournois* and sent them to us;

they also decided to give him something. Guillaume de Lucé got a pipe of pinot, twelve fat capons and wax torches weighing 25 pounds; Jean Tudert 100 *sous* worth of fish.[60] But then perhaps the dean and the bishop dined together.

NOTES

1. V. Leblond, 'Beauvais dans l'angoisse pendant la guerre de Cent Ans', *M. Soc. acad. Oise*, xxvii (1932), 92-361.
2. As Charles VII, who had arranged it all, wrote in recommending Jean Juvenal to the town, his provision 'was and is to us most gratifying and acceptable, since not only the region but the church has been provided with someone completely loyal to us, and both to you and to the region of great advantage, who, both he and his forbears, has served us and ours long and loyally in great and honourable positions and offices' [P.L. Péchenard, *Jean Juvénal des Ursins* (Paris, 1876), p.140, from apparently a later copy then in private hands].
3. Unfortunately with a considerable amount of duplication: Leblond, see above; Champion, Institut de France, MS.5227, fos. 286-317.
4. 'At the time', he recalled, 'I was worried stiff, because in the way in which the war was going and in the way in which it was being run there was neither rhyme nor reason but simply inefficiency and exploitation, and I was in the hottest spot, that is to say at Beauvais, which was simply falling to bits' (B.N. MS.fr.2701, fo.51ᵛa).
5. B.N., MS. fr. 5022, fo. 1ʳ.
6. Jean Juvenal was clear that it was political service: 'you instructed me', he told Charles VII in 1440, 'that I should come over here and carry out your orders, because always, as long as I am alive, I would want to serve you and obey you' [ibid., fo. 5ᵛ].
7. B.N. MS. fr. 5038, fos. 4ʳ ff.
8. B.N. MS. fr. 2701, fo. 89ʳb.
9. B.N. MS. fr. 5022, fos 20ᵛ, 23ᵛ. The sense of 'frontiere' here is clearly that of 'place fortifiée faisant face aux ennemis' [Godefroy, *Lexique*].
10. B.N. MS. fr. 5022, fos. 5ʳ, 14ʳ⁻ᵛ.
11. *Le Livre de la description des pays*, ed. E.T. Hamy [Rec. de voyages et de docs. pour servir à l'hist. de la géog., xxii] (Paris, 1908), pp. 50-51.
12. 'Espace et Etat dans la France du Bas Moyen Age', *Annales*, xxiii (1968), 758.
13. B.N. MS. fr. 5022, fo. 3ᵛ.
14. Ibid., fo.20ᵛ.
15. B.N. MS. fr. 5038, fo. 5ʳ.
16. Leblond, op. cit., pp. 259, 260.
17. Ibid., pp. 210-11, 216-17.
18. B.N. MS. fr. 2701, fo 120ᵇ.
19. B.N. MS. fr. 5022, fos. 3ʳ ff.; T. Basin, *Histoire de Charles VII*, ed. C. Samaran [Classiques de l'histoire de France au Moyen âge, xv] (Paris, 1964), p. 88.
20. B.N. MS. fr. 5022, fo. 3ʳ.
21. Ibid., fos. 3ᵛ, 14ʳ.
22. Ibid., fos. 17ʳ, 25ʳ.
23. Printed in *Registres de la Jurade*, i [Arch. municipales de Bordeaux, iii] (Bordeaux, 1873), pp. 87-93.
24. *The Itineraries of William Wey* . . . ed. B. Bandinel [Roxburghe Club] (London, 1857), pp. 153 ff. *Registres de la Jurade*, ii [Arch. municipales de Bordeaux, iv]] (Bordeaux, 1883), 329-31.
25. See, for instance, *Registres de la Jurade*, i 121.
26. *Comptes consulaires d'Albi (1359-1360)*, ed. A. Vidal [Bibliothèque méridional, I. v] (Paris-Toulouse, 1900), pp. 20-21, 16.

27. A. Higounet-Nadal, 'Le Journal des dépenses d'un notaire de Périgueux en mission à Paris (janvier-septembre 1337)', *A. Midi*, lxxvi (1964), 382-83.

28. From this point Professor Chevalier (above, pp. 111 ff.) and I are, to some extent, arguing in parallel. But although we reach broadly similar conclusions, we do so from very different points of view.

29. L. Caillet, *Etude sur les relations de la commune de Lyon avec Charles VII et Louis XI (1417-1483)* (Lyon-Paris, 1909), p. 331.

30. The background of Mâcon's mission can be reconstructed (rather hazardously) from Caillet, op.cit., pp. 40 ff., corrected and amplified by the documents published pp. 345 ff.

31. Ibid., p. 348.

32. His letters are printed by G. du Fresne de Beaucourt, *Histoire de Charles VII*, iii (Paris, 1885), 501-9.

33. Caillet, op.cit., pp. 353-4.

34. The material for the remainder of this paragraph is derived from *Registres de l'échevinage de Saint-Jean-d'Angély*, ed. D. d'Aussy, i [Arch. hist. Saintonge-Aunis, xxiv] (Paris-Saintes, 1895), pp. 325, 356, 361, 367, 381, 383.

35. The material for this paragraph is derived from ibid., pp. 385-90, 413. (The chronology of the documents there printed needs some disentanglement).

36. The material for what follows is derived from ibid. ii [Arch. hist. Saintonge-Aunis, xxvi] (Paris-Saintes, 1897), pp. 144, 149, 264, 269; iii [Arch. hist. Saintonge-Aunis, xxxii] (Paris-Saintes, 1902), pp. 18, 19, 60, 70-71 (cf. 171), 162-63.

37. What follows is derived from the document printed by A. Higounet-Nadal, op.cit., pp. 387-402.

38. *Choix de pièces inédites relatives au règne de Charles VI*, ed. L. Douet-d'Arcq [S.H.F.], i (Paris, 1863), 378.

39. *Registres de l'échevinage de Saint-Jean-d'Angély*, ii. 11-12.

40. Caillet, op.cit., p. 370; *Registres consulaires de la ville de Lyon*, i, ed. M.C. Guigue (Lyon, 1882), p. 331.

41. Above, pp. 113, 116.

42. A. Thomas, *Les Etats provinciaux de la France centrale sous Charles VII* (Paris, 1879), i. 287-91.

43. *Tours, Ville royale (1356-1520)* (Louvain-Paris, 1975), pp. 481 ff.

44. *Le Curial*, ed. F. Heuckenkamp (Halle, 1899), p. 23.

45. *Tours . . .*, pp. 293 ff. Cf. R. Gandilhon, *Politique économique de Louis XI* (Rennes, 1940), pp. 249-50.

46. On Denis de Bar see E. Baluze, *Historiae Tutelensis libri tres* (Paris, 1717), pp. 225-9, 234-6; *Dict. d'hist. et de geog. ecclésiastiques*, vi (Paris, 1932), col. 539; *Dict. de biog. française*, iv (Paris, 1948), cols. 113-15.

47. The letters upon which the remainder of this paragraph is based are printed by J. Vaesen, *Lettres de Louis XI* [S.H.F.], iv (Paris, 1890), 360-1, 268-71, 361-3.

48. On Louis de Beaumont see *Dict. d'hist. et de géog. ecclésiastiques*, vii (Paris, 1934), cols. 217-20; *Dict. de biog. française*, iv, col. 1150.

49. The remainder of this paragraph is based upon the material printed by Vaesen, op.cit. x (Paris, 1908), 474-87; Louis's letter is printed ibid., pp. 329-31.

50. M. Rey, *Le Domaine du roi et les finances extraordinaires sous Charles VI, 1388-1413* (Paris, 1965), pp. 295-7.

51. B.N. MS. fr. 26096, no. 1642.

52. 'Lettres . . . relatifs à la guerre du Bien public', ed. J. Quicherat, in *Documents historiques inédits*, ed. J.J. Champollion Figeac [Documents inédits sur l'histoire de France], ii (Paris, 1843), 290.

53. P.S. Lewis, *Later Medieval France: The Polity* (London, 1968), p. 123.

54. Vaesen, op.cit. iv. 241.
55. F. Pasquier, *Boffile de Juge* (Albi, 1914), p. 155.
56. Lewis, op.cit., pp. 216-17.
57. Vaesen, op.cit. iv. 176.
58. I have in mind R.A. Dahl and his associates [R.A. Dahl, *Who Governs? Democracy and Power in an American City* (New Haven-London, 1961); N.W. Polsby, *Community and Political Theory* (New Haven-London, 1963)].
59. Cf. P.S. ·Lewis, 'Jean Juvenal des Ursins and the common literary attitude towards tyranny in fifteenth-century France', *Medium Aevum*, xxxiv (1965). **Below 181-2.**
60. M. Rédet, 'Extraits des comptes de dépenses de la ville de Poitiers, aux XIVe et XVe siècles', *M. Soc. Antiq. Ouest*, vii (1840), 388 ff.

12

JEAN JUVENAL DES URSINS AND THE COMMON LITERARY ATTITUDE TOWARDS TYRANNY IN FIFTEENTH-CENTURY FRANCE

'ILZ ont une maniere en Angleterre', wrote a fascinated Jean Juvenal des Ursins in 1444, 'quilz ne tiennent comte de changier leur roy quant bon leur semble, voire de les tuer & faire morir mauvaisement'. Guillaume de Rochefort in 1484 alleged that the English had had twenty-six changes of dynasty since the foundation of their monarchy. A precise list of martyred rulers was given in a piece of Gersonian apocrypha and by Noel de Fribois;[1] and more recent examples came easily to mind.[2] 'En Angleterre ilz ont souvent mis à mort leurs roys', said Jean de Rély, the spokesman for the Estates general of 1484, 'ce que ne fist jamais le bon et loyal peuple de France'.[3] 'Non erit profecto', agreed Guillaume de Rochefort, the chancellor of France, 'qui in fideli Gallorum populo hanc inconstantiam, hanc sceleris notam deprehendat'.[4] The loyalty of the French was indisputable. Louis XI thought approvingly of 'ses bons et loyaux subjects, qui oncques ne refusèrent de luy octroyer ce qu'il leur demandoit';[5] and so did Philippe de Commynes, who admired the more peaceable parts of the English system. If a king should say, Commynes wrote, ' "J'ay les subgectz si très bons et loyaulx qu'ilz ne me reffusent chose que je leur demande et suys plus crainct et obéy et servy de mes subgectz que nul autre prince qui vive sur terre et qui plus patientement endurent tous maulx et toutes ruddesses et à qui moins il souvient de leurs dommaiges passéz" . . . cela luy seroit grant loz et diz la verité'.

A king should not say, ' "J'ay privileige de lever sur mes subgectz ce qu'il me plaist" '. The wishes of the subjects should be consulted. Was it over such a good and loyal community, Commynes asked, 'que le roy doit alleguer privileige de povoir prendre à son plaisir qui si liberallement luy donnent? Ne seroit-il plus juste envers Dieu et le monde le lever

---

[1] 'Two Pieces of Fifteenth-Century Political Iconography. (b) The English Kill Their Kings' *Journal of the Warburg and Courtauld Institutes* ̇ xxvii. Below 189-92. The author of a political treatise on the English claim to the throne of France, written soon after Henry V's occupation of Normandy, and Thomas Basin (*Historiarum Ludovici XI* vii ii ed. J. Quicherat *Histoire des règnes de Charles VII et de Louis XI* (Société de l'histoire de France) (Paris 1855–59) III 138) gave the figure as twenty-two.

[2] An aberrant version of Noel de Fribois' recension, dated about 1500, added 'tous leurs roys presques ont este depuis occiz et jusques a present, ou par la commune, ou par leurs prouches parens' (John Rylands Library MS. fr. 57 f. 95). The theme was developed in a verse 'Epistre envoyée par feu Henry, roy d'Angleterre, à Henry son fils, huytiesme de ce nom, à present regnant oudict royaulme (1512)' ed. A. de Montaiglon *Recueil de poésies françoises des xve et xvie siècles* (Paris 1855–78) III 29 ff.

[3] J. Masselin *Journal des Etats généraux tenus à Tours en 1484* ed. A. Bernier (Documents inédits sur l'histoire de France) (Paris 1835) p. 253.

[4] Ibid. p. 38.

[5] A. Dussert *Les Etats du Dauphiné de la guerre de Cent ans aux guerres de Religion* (Bulletin de l'Académie delphinale 5 XIII ii) (Grenoble 1923) p. 60.

[par octroy] ... que par volunté desordonnée?'[6] The formidable Jean Masselin, journalist of the Estates of Tours, had asked much the same question.[7] But over such subjects why should a king bother? Loyal as they were, they had no sanction against him; if the ruler was a tyrant, they had no remedy except submission and hope and the wrath of God upon the unbridled will. The good subject did not rebel. In this mood the articulate of late fifteenth-century France agreed with those 'commons' who, according to Sir John Fortescue, for 'lakke off harte and cowardisse ... rise not ayen thair souerayn lorde'.[8] But there was more to the genesis of their mood than this; and notions about the king and his relationship with his subjects played only a part (and perhaps mainly an *ex post facto* part) in its creation. But as the expression of that mood they cannot be overlooked. A number of problems of definition within well-established themes faced the writers of the period; the answers they gave define at the same time the political attitude they were prepared to adopt. And since Jean Juvenal des Ursins faced so many of them in his treatises[9] his views provide a framework within which to place those of the generation as a whole.

'Le Roy nostre Sire', it was argued in 1380, 'n'a pas seulement temporalité, mais divinité avec':[10] the idea of the ruler as a *christus* provided the first problem. The unearthly light which hung about the king had been brightened up by the propagandists not entirely without ulterior political motive; the christological tradition of kingship had been reinforced by the Gallican controversy.[11] 'Et est ung roy comme ung vaillant prelat. Car au resgart de vous, mon souverain seigneur, vous nestes pas simplement personne laye mais prelat ecclesiastique, le premier en vostre royaume qui soit aprez le pape, le bras dextre de lesglise', wrote Jean Juvenal des Ursins in the 1450's.[12] This was mild enough: the charismatic qualities attributed to the ruler could go to extremes. In his preface to his translation of St. Augustine's *Civitas dei* Raoul de Presles told Charles V 'Vous avez telle vertu et puissance, qui vous est donnee et attribuee de Dieu, que vous faictes miracles en vostre vie' and Jean de Terre-Vermeille went so far as to say that the king 'est Deus in terris'.[13] The superstitions

[6] *Mémoires* v xix ed. J. Calmette & G. Durville (Les Classiques de l'histoire de France au Moyen âge) (Paris 1924–25) II 218–19, 222.

[7] Op. cit. p. 440.

[8] *The Governance of England* xiii ed. C. Plummer (Oxford 1885) pp. 141–42.

[9] For these see P. L. Péchenard *Jean Juvénal des Ursins, historien de Charles VI, évêque de Beauvais et de Laon, archevêque duc de Rheims* (Paris 1876); F. Maton *La Souveraineté dans Jean II Juvénal des Ursins* (Paris 1917). I have undertaken an edition of them.

[10] M. Bloch *Les Rois thaumaturges* (Paris 1923) p. 212.

[11] Ibid. pp. 134–40, 197 ff.; P. E. Schramm *Der König von Frankreich* (Weimar, 1960) I 236 ff.

[12] Verba mea auribus percipe, Domine, [a treatise on kingship composed before April 1452] Bibliothèque nationale MS. fr. 2701 f. 89.

[13] *Monseigneur saint Augustin de la cite de Dieu* (Abbeville 1486) I sig. a iiiv; *Joannes de Terra rubea contra rebelles suorum regum* [c. 1420] ed. J. Bonaud (Lyon 1526) f. 53v (he added 'id est et locumtenens Dei in terris'). Raoul de Presles' opinion was shared by Etienne de Conty (Bibl. nat. MS. lat. 11730 f. 31v; Bloch op. cit. p. 92 n. 1) and by the French clergy in 1478 (J. Combet *Louis XI et le Saint-Siège* (Paris 1903) p. 258).

of the crown of France, the 'biens et graces a icelle par Dieu donnee comme de la saincte ambole, les floures du lis, louriflan et degueri des escourelles', were eagerly cherished by all Frenchmen, including Jean Juvenal; they appeared almost every time anyone thought about the king.[14] The idea that the *tres-chrétien* crown of France was 'singulierement aornee de grace & prerogative celestielle', was widespread; and it gave content to Jean Juvenal's text *Regem honorificate* in 1433.[15]

Resistance to such grace was naturally sacrilege: this was accepted by Gerson in 1405 as well as by Jean de Terre-Vermeille in 1420.[16] Treason acquired this added stigma: resistance to royal command, it was thought in *Parlement* in 1490, was 'incidere in sacrilegium et in crimen laesae majestatis'.[17] Yet divine right did not presuppose despotism. It could be argued, as Jean Juvenal argued, that the vicariate of God implied a number of duties.[18] Like many mediæval arguments the theory of sacerdotal kingship could be turned inside out.[19] 'Qui igitur ex domo Dei in superbiam erigitur Deum sibi adversarium hostemque constituit?', demanded Nicolas de Clamanges; and Robert Blondel, through St. Louis, warned Charles VII, 'Te souviengne bien que ce tresnoble royaume entre tous les autres est especialement fait et gouverné par ordonnance divine et non pas par dispo[si]cion humaine. Et, quant il plaist a Dieu pour aucune cause latente, il en puet transporter le gouvernment de l'um, quant il n'y est ydoyne, a ung autre qui plus y est prouffitable.'[20]

---

[14] Guillaume Cousinot at the Estates general of 1468 [Relation of the Estates general of 1468 enregistered at Rodez] Archives départmentales de l'Aveyron BB 3 ff. 55ᵛ–56; J. Juvenal des Ursins, Audite celi que loquor [an allegorical discourse on the English claim to France written in 1435] Bibl. nat. MS. fr. 5022 f. 31; Traictie compendieux de la querelle de France contre les Anglois, Bibl. nat. MS. fr. 17512 f. 9ᵛ. Cf. *Le Débat des Hérauts d'armes de France et d'Angleterre* ed. L. Pannier & P. Meyer (Société des anciens textes français) (Paris 1877) pp. 12–13; N. de Fribois, Cest chose profitable, British Museum Add. MS. 13961 ff. 8, 20ᵛ; and for other examples Bloch op. cit. pp. 134 ff., 224 ff.

[15] Mirouer historial abregie de France, Bodleian Library MS. Bodley 968 ff. 1, 201. The idea was accepted by the author of the *Somnium viridarii* i clxxiii ed. M. Goldast *Monarchia s. romani imperii* (Hanover 1612–14), I 129 and by Gerson (*Sermon fait devant le roy Charles sixiesme* [the sermon *Vivat rex* of 1405) (Paris ? 1505) sigs. a iiiᵛ–[a iv]. Jean Juvenal argued that the king should be loved and honoured because he was in some special way beloved of God, who by giving him victory had declared him true king of France (Epistre faicte par Jehan evesque et conte de Beauvays pour envoier aux troix estas qui se devoient tenir a Bloiz, Bibl. nat. MS. fr. 5038 ff. 12ᵛ ff. The text was naturally I Petri ii 17). Jean Juvenal never mentioned Joan of Arc as a proof of divine favour but others of course did: e.g. R. Blondel Des droiz de la couronne de France ed. A. Héron *Oeuvres de R. Blondel* (Société de l'histoire de Normandie) (Rouen 1891–93), I 460.

[16] *Vivat rex.* sigs. a iiiᵛ–[a iv]; Terre-Vermeille op. cit. f. 53ᵛ.

[17] P. Imbart de La Tour *Les Origines de la réforme* 2ᵉ éd. (Melun 1946–) I 39 n. 2.

[18] Loquar in tribulacione spiritus mei [a discourse on the miseries of the kingdom written about 1440] Bibl. nat. MS. fr. 5022 f. 15; A,a,a, nescio loqui quia puer ego sum [a treatise on the office of chancellor written for Guillaume Juvenel des Ursins in 1445] Bibl. nat. MS. fr. 2701 f. 45; Verba mea auribus percipe, Domine, f. 101.

[19] St. Louis, the saint in the family, could also turn upon his descendant. Robert Blondel begged Charles VII 'que les droiz de vostre couronne et vostre peuple françois vueillez songneusement deffendre jouxte et scelon les saintes lois et louables coustumes du bon saint Loys, vostre aieul' [op. cit. p. 470]. The virtues of St. Louis appealed also to Jean Dubois (Bibl. nat. MS. fr. 5743 f. 64; N. Valois 'Conseils et prédictions adressés a Charles VII, en 1445, par un certain Jean Du Bois', Annuaire-Bulletin de la Soc. de l'hist. de France XLVI (1909) 237–38].

[20] N. de Clemangiis opera omnia (Leiden 1613) p. 350; Blondel, op. cit., p. 472 (cf. ibid. p. 461). Texts such as this could be re-inverted to emphasize divine right, as might those of the kind distilled by

Jean Juvenal des Ursins said much the same thing at considerably greater length.[21] 'Dieu paradis aux tirans nye', wrote Jean Meschinot:[22] the wrath of God in heaven, even the wrath of God on earth, were things with which to threaten the prince. But how far was one justified in advancing the hand of God?

A second common theme to which Jean Juvenal subscribed was that of the anthropomorphic conception of society as an explanation of the relationship of ruler and ruled: the idea that the king was the head of a *corpus mysticum* of which the various groups in society were the members.[23] The notion appeared, for instance, in Gerson's sermon *Vivat rex* linked to the idea of the king's, in Gerson's case, three bodies. 'Ung roy', said Gerson, '. . . nest mie personne singuliere mais est unge puissance publicque ordonnee pour le salut de tout le commun, ainsi comme du chief descent, et se espant la vie par tout le corps'.[24] From this notion, too, conclusions could be drawn left and right. Jean de Terre-Vermeille, in the midst of civil war, could use it to argue for almost a Hobbesian degree of obedience by the members of the body politic to the head and single will: rebellion was un-natural.[25] But, again, obligations and threats could be derived from the anthropomorphic idea. If, argued Gerson some years before civil war actually broke out, 'par lenseignement de nature tous les membres en ung vray corps se exposent pour le salut du chief, pareillement doit estre ou corps misticque des vrays subgectz a leur seigneur. Mais dautre part le chief doit adresser & gouverner les autres me[m]bres, autrement ce seroit la destruction;

Noel de Fribois from John of Paris; 'le roy de France... a plain droit de souverainete absolue en tout son roiaume' [Fribois op. cit. f. 75ᵛ; cf. the Mirouer historial abregie f. 219]; cf. Imbart de La Tour op. cit. p. 42. The legists' theme of popular sovereignty, which appealed to the author of the *Somnium viridarii* (I lxxviii ed. Goldast I 84) and Gerson (*Vivat rex* sig. c ii) does not seem to have been popular in the later fifteenth century; its use by Philippe Pot at the Estates general of 1484 was far from disinterested (Masselin op. cit. pp. 138–56; A. Lemaire *Les Lois fondamentales de la monarchie française* (Paris 1907) pp. 63–70; H. Bouchard 'Pour l'histoire des ducs et des Etats bourguignons de 1315 à 1493, vii): Philippe Pot et la démocratie aux Etats généraux de 1484'. *Annales de Bourgogne* XXII (1950) 33–40.) The furthest Jean Juvenal des Ursins would go towards popular sovereignty was to quote (*via* St. Augustine *Civitas Dei* xix xxi) Cicero *de Republica* I xxv (Verba mea auribus percipe, Domine, f. 88ᵛ).

[21] Verba mea auribus percipe, Domine, ff. 86ᵛ ff. Jean Dubois told Charles VII that his predecessors had been told that if they did not remedy 'les deffaulx de leglise... il seroit permis de Dieu quilz seroient ostes hors de leurs seigneuries et dominations par le moyen de leurs subgies, comme a apparu de fait longtemps, parquoy on ne le peut ignorer' (op. cit. ff. 48ᵛ–49; Valois op. cit. p. 217).

[22] *Les Lunettes des princes* (Paris 1505) sig. e iᵛ.

[23] Verba mea auribus percipe, Domine, f. 88. The idea was derived, inevitably, from John of Salisbury (*Policraticus*, v ii ed. C. C. I. Webb (Oxford 1909) I 282–84).

[24] *Vivat rex* sigs. [a vi]ᵛ, c ii. Cf. E. Kantorowicz *The King's Two Bodies* (Princeton 1957) pp. 218–19.

[25] Op. cit. ff. 49ᵛ ff. The same argument against rebellion was used by Meschinot [op. cit. sigs. [piiiᵛ–piv] and by Jean Juvenal des Ursins [see below, p. 113]. The strongly right-wing flavour of Terre-Vermeille's third treatise is well brought out by R. E. Giesey 'The French Estates and the Corpus Mysticum Regni' *Album Helen Maud Cam* I (Etudes présentées à la Commission internationale pour l'histoire des assemblées d'Etats XXIII)(Louvain 1960) pp. 153–71. Terre-Vermeille also argued that a man's duty to his head and lord *qua* subject supervened upon that *qua* vassal (Terre-Vermeille op. cit. f. 56); the same distinction was used to practical effect by Louis XI (B. A. Pocquet du Haut-Jussé 'Une Idée politique de Louis XI: La Sujétion éclipse la vassalité' *Revue historique* XXVI (1961) 383–98) though the idea was of course not new (cf. P. Chaplais 'La Souveraineté du roi de France et le pouvoir législatif en Guyenne au début du xivᵉ siècle' *Le Moyen Age* LXIX (1963) 450–52).

car chief sans corps ne peult durer.'[26] Therefore the ruler has 'natural' obligations to the subjects; if rebellion was un-natural so was tyranny.

> Le prince est gouverneur & chief [wrote Jean Meschinot]
> Des membres du corps pollitique
> Ce seroit bien doulent meschief
> Sil devenoit paralitique
> Ou voulsist tenir voye oblicque
> A lestat pourquoy est fait
> Tout se pert fors que le bien fait.[27]

For Jean Juvenal des Ursins, too, the head had as much need of the body as the body had of the head. 'Vous', he said to the king, 'estes larme de la chose publique, et oncques larme ne destruisist le corps mais le corps bien larme. ... Vous estes aussi le chef de ce corps; et ne seroit ce pas grant tirannye se le chef dune creature humaine destruisoit les cuer, mains et pies? Il fauldroit que le chef perist ...'. This has a true Gersonian ring.[28] But once more we are on the brink of discussing resistance; and had not in England in 1326 the text *Caput meum doleo* been used to preach resistance?[29]

The king and the law provided a further problem. That the king should conserve the laws was pretty generally agreed upon. As Pierre Salmon wrote to Charles VI at the beginning of the century, 'la bonté et vaillance du Roy est considérée quant il garde et fait bien garder ses loys et ordonnances; et apperçoit on là deffault du Roy quant elles ne sont pas bien gardées, et quant le Roy n'a l'ueil et la considération à icelles garder et faire bien garder'.[30] The idea of the immutability of the positive laws was an old one; so was the idea that the king should submit to them. Jean Courtecuisse could be both a common lawyer and an Aristotelian when he argued in 1413 that 'puisque la Loy est une fois mise & elle est raisonnable, le Prince ne la peult, ne doit par raison rompre ne venir à l'encontre; car comme dit Arist. 5 Polit. Les Princes sont seigneurs des choses qui ne sont point determinées par les Loix, mais des Loix non.'[31] Gerson thought the king should obey the law in imitating the submission

---

[26] *Vivat rex* sig. c ii. Subjects' duty to help the head was stressed by Blondel:

> Membres, mectez vous en arroy
> Pour secourir a vostre chief;
> Deffendez vostre noble roy
> Qui est en si tresgrant meschief

(R. Blondel *La Complaincte des bons François, Oeuvres,* op. cit. I 83).

[27] Op. cit. sig. e iiiv.

[28] Verba mea auribus percipe, Domine, f. 98. Jean Juvenal thought highly of *Vivat rex* (*Histoire de Charles VI* ed. D, Godefroy (Paris 1653) p. 177).

[29] IV *Regum* iv 19; *Chronicon Galfridi le Baker* ed. E. Maunde Thompson (Oxford 1889) p. 23.

[30] *Les Demandes faites par le roi Charles VI... avec les réponses de Pierre Salmon* ed. G. A. Crapelet (Paris 1833) p. 32.

[31] *Quaedam Propositio & exhortatio facta in presentia Regis Karoli VI* ed. C. E. du Boulay *Historia Universitatis Parisiensis* (Paris 1665–73) V 88. For the date of this sermon see A. Coville 'Recherches sur Jean Courtecuisse et ses oeuvres oratoires' *Bibliotheque de l'Ecole des chartes* LXV (1904) 506.

of Christ; Jean Meschinot that he should do so in anticipating the chilly equality of the grave:

> Seigneurs pas nestes dautre aloy
> Que le povre peuple commun
> Faictes vous subjetz a la loy
> Car certes vous mourres come ung
> Des plus petis. . . .[32]

Jean Juvenal des Ursins, too, thought that a king, as opposed to a tyrant, submitted to the laws. 'Suppose . . .', he wrote, 'que ... [le prince] soit pardessus les loys; car cest grant chose que destre roy ou prince. Mais est encores plus grant chose de soubzmettre a raison et aux loys le royaume.... Et ne veux pas dire que lempereur ou le roy soit astraint ou subget aux loys, tellement que quant bon luy semble il ne puisse faire le contraire et muer et changer les loys; *nam princeps solutus est legibus*.... Toutevoye il ne le doit point faire sans juste cause ne raisonnable et si se veult et doit soubzmettre aux loys; car aultrement on pourroit dire que ce seroit fait de tirant et non mie de roy.'[33] 'Plusieurs en peut avoir prez des princes qui les induisent a maintenir que tout est licite au prince de faire ce quil veult, et que sa voulente est repute pour loy, *quia quod principi placuit legis habet vigorem*. Helas! Ilz doivent appliquer ceste puissance ad ce que ung vray prince doit faire, tellement que celle voulente ne se puisse appliquer a voulente de tirant.'[34] In this Jean Juvenal anticipated the argument of the *premier Président* of the *Parlement* of Paris in 1527: 'Sçavons bien que vous estes par dessus les loix et que les loix ou ordonnances ne vous peuvent contraindre.... Mais nous entendons dire que vous ne voulez ou ne devez pas vouloir tout ce que vous pouvez, ains seulement ce qui est bon et équitable.'[35] The will of the prince is a true will only when it is good. Otherwise it is a tyrant's will. But what should one do with a tyrant?

Gerson dealt with the problem in *Vivat rex*. Two allegorical figures, Dissimulation and Sedition, were let in to have their say. 'Il fault temporiser, je te dy vray. Il fault dissimuler ...', said Dissimulation. 'Las!', said Sedition, 'ou sont ores les preux et les vaillans champions de la chose publique, qui pour le bien commum contre les tyrans exposoient jadis leurs corps et chevance ...; ont sont telz parsonnages pour delivrer ce royaulme de miserable oppression? A eulx doit estre la voye de faire ce que dit Seneque, que il nest sacrifice tant plaisant a Dieu comme la mort de tyrant.' But, thought Gerson, 'dissimulation fault et tinidite,

---

[32] *Sermo in die circumcisionis Domini, Gersonii opera* ed. E. du Pin (Antwerp 1706) II 61; Meschinot op. cit. sig. e iii[v].

[33] *Verba mea auribus percipe, Domine*, f. 98.

[34] Ibid. f. 102. Jean Juvenal could argue more forcefully in defending Charles VII's *quondam* brother-in-law Richard II that the king's 'seule voulente est reputee pour loy et raison et na juge que Dieu' (Traictie compendieux f. 38[v]).

[35] G. Zeller *Les Institutions de la France au XVIe siècle* (Paris 1948), p. 80.

sedition en temerite, discretion tient le droit chemin royal, sans decliner a destre de dissimulation ou a senestre de sedition'.[36] But in what direction did this right royal road run? In Gerson's case with a rather uneasy course distinctly leftwards. Admittedly he argued that, since all power came from God, resistance was sacrilege, especially against the king of France whose power had especial divine approbation; but he also quoted (and under the stern eye of Discretion), *'vim vi repellere licet'*[37] and he did argue that resistance was legitimate. Subjects should try first to cure the ruler; immediate tyrannicide would be madness; sedition, 'rebellion populaire sans rime et sans raison, elle est pire souvent que tirannie'; care should be taken that the results of resistance are not worse than its causes.[38] 'Si fault a merveille grant discretion, prudence et atrempance a bouter dehors tirannie, pourtant doivent estre oys les saiges philozophes, juristes, legistes, theologiens et aussi gens de tres-bonne prudence naturelle et de tresgrande experience'; and one should be really sure that the tyrant is subverting the whole commonwealth, not just simply indulging in a few tyrannical eccentricities. But on the whole tyrants did seem to come to unpleasant ends; they should take care to use more reason and, like Theopompus, accept a more limited and more durable seigneury.[39]

But very few writers in fifteenth-century France were as firm as Gerson. None dealt with the question of tyrannicide specifically in relation to a sovereign. Jean Petit defended it in his notorious justification of Jean *sans peur's* murder of Louis duke of Orléans in 1407;[40] and after Jean *sans peur's* own demise at Montereau Jean de Terre-Vermeille on the Armagnac side argued (on rather slender grounds) that 'unicuique regnicole licet interficere notorium tyrannum, destructorem rei publice, sicut & quenlibet hostem'. But such a tyrant was only a ruler with a title in Terre-Vermeille's eyes unjust.[41] After the bright revolutionary days of the first decade or so of the century discretion totters miserably rightwards towards dissimulation;[42] the right royal road becomes royal

---

[36] *Vivat rex* sigs. [b vi]–c iᵛ. For Seneca's views see *Hercules furens* ll. 922–24.

[37] *Digest.*, IV, II xii, XLIII xvi i.

[38] Cf. Aquinas, *Summa theologica*, II ii q. 42 a. 2.

[39] *Vivat rex* sigs. c iiᵛ–[c v]ᵛ. Theopompus [Aristotle, *Politics*, v xi 2] also appealed to Nicholas Oresme (*De moneta* xxv ed. C. Johnson (London 1956) p. 45.)

[40] E. de Monstrelet *Chronique* ed. L. Douet d'Arcq (Soc. de l'hist. de France) (Paris 1857–62) I 178–242; A. Coville *Jean Petit: La Question du tyrannicide au commencement du XVᵉ siècle* (Paris 1932) pp. 133–68.

[41] Op. cit. f. 47. Robert Blondel's view was that 'combien que plusieurs aient désiré d'y regenter, toutesvoies la providence divine n'a point encores souffert, ne, s'il lui plaist, ne souffrera ja que aucum tirant intrus y ait esté oing de la saincte huylle du ciel, ne qu'il y ait peu et puisse par force occupper si noble couronne' (*Des droiz de la couronne* p. 472).

[42] In arguing (in reference again, admittedly, to Richard II) that a king should be obeyed Jean Juvenal des Ursins did in fact say that a tyrannical action should be 'dissimulated'; and he advised his brother Guillaume Juvenal des Ursins as chancellor not to behave like their father, whom he thought had been insufficiently flexible, but 'que vous gardez de cuider resister a la voulente de ceulx qui seront a la court, car cela vous feroit baillier le bout et mettre hors; et vault mieulx avoir pacience et dissimuler et estre cause de faire moins de mal, puisque on ne peut pourfiter aultrement que estre trop ferme et perdre son estat' (Traictie compendieux, f. 38ᵛ; A,a,a, nescio loqui quia puer ego sum f. 46ᵛ).

indeed. The king should be left to God was the normal reaction in the fifteenth century to the question of resistance. 'Un prince', wrote Gilbert de Lannoy, '... n'a aultre correction sur luy que la crémeur de Dieu et sa propre conscience'.[43]

> Pren que ung seigneur pire que sarrazin [wrote Jean Meschinot]
> Te griefve fort peuple soir & matin
> Endure le: car cest chose notorie
> Que desraison le conduit & maistrie
> Par folles gens quil croit comme lon crye
> Et heyt tous ceulx dont digne est la memoire.
>   Trop mieulx luy fust user de sapience
> Que soy tenir en telle insipience
> Faisant les cas de quoy tyrant resemble
> Mais la haulte divine precieuse
> Congnoist son faict & voit son inscience
> Et les pechez quen sa povre ame assemble
> Dont il aura enfer pour son butin

and Meschinot could also argue that a bad ruler was a punishment deserved by an *ipso facto* bad people.[44] That tribulation was a divine punishment for sin was a common theme to which Jean Juvenal des Ursins subscribed heavily;[45] but he was not prepared to accept it without some protest.

His normal views[46] on government were outspoken enough to incur the epithet *mécontent* from Charles VII's modern panegyrist.[47] He did not preach resistance; but he quoted, in the usual way, innumerable examples of divine punishment.[48] He threatened the king with the sedi-

---

[43] *Instruction d'un jeune prince* ed. C. Potvin *Oeuvres de G. de Lannoy* (Louvain 1878) p. 360.

[44] Op. cit. [Ballade xix] sig. k iiᵛ; sig. [e iv].

[45] Epistre faicte par Jehan evesque et conte de Beauvays f. 6 ff.; Loquar in tribulacione spiritus mei f. 14ᵛ. Cf. Gerson *Vivat rex* sig. (f ii); *Les Demandes faites par le roi Charles VI...* pp. 17–18.

[46] In the treatise on the chancellor in 1445 he could say 'quelque chose que [le roy]... veuille faire nous le devons endurer et supporter et tenir ferme et estable, voire suppose quil semblast dur et desraisonnable; nam *quod principi* [*placuit*] *legis habet vigorem*' and at the Estates general of 1468 argue that 'il en y eut ung qui en ung conseil dit, "Exiges et tailles hardiment, tout est vostre", qui sont parolles de ung tirant, non digne de estre entendues; toutesvoie non obstant ce que dit est [concerning excessive taxation] je suis tousjours doppinion que devons acomplir mon theume, *quecunque volueris faciemus, obediemus et tibi*' (A,a,a, nescio loqui quia puer ego sum f. 47; La deliberacion faicte a Tours aux trois estas par larcevesque et duc de Reims premier per de France [an account of Jean Juvenal's conduct at the Estates general of Tours] Bibl. nat. MS. fr. 2701 f. 122ᵛ). The text is a conflation of *Josue* i 16 and 17.

[47] G. du Fresne de Beaucourt *Histoire de Charles VII* (Paris 1881–91) III 137.

[48] E.g. *Ecclesiastici* x 8 (Verba mea auribus percipe, Domine, f. 90ᵛ). That most revolutionary of texts, Cicero *de Officiis*, iii vi. 32 was quoted in ibid. f. 90. Some quotations were made with specific appropriateness to the actions of the officers of the king and to the king's condoning their misdeeds by inaction; the text quoted after the accustion made in ibid. f. 102 [see below, p. 180] was, e.g. III *Regum* xx 42. 'Cancellarius Nostre Domine Parisiensis', acting as spokesman for the clergy at an assembly in 1411, appeared to argue ' ...nec reges digne vocari, si exactionibus injustis opprimant populum suum, sed quod eos deposicione dignos possent racionabiliter reputare, in annalibus antiquis possunt de multis legere'. This raised a storm: the chancellor of France and some seigneurs accused him 'dixisse regem posse destitui a suis subditis'; but when his proposition in writing had been seen by canon lawyers ' ᶥictum fuit et in regis presencia quod id exemplariter referebat' (*Chronique du Réligieux de Saint-Denis* ea. L. Bellaguet (Doc. inéd. sur l'hist. de France) (Paris 1839–52) IV 416–18).

tion of the lower orders if conditions were not improved for them.[49] 'Et me doubte encor plus', Jean Juvenal wrote, 'que le peuple mesmes ne se eslieve et contre vous & contre [voz gens] ... et quilz ne facent comme on leur fait'. 'Et Dieu scet que ilz dient de vous, en disant, "Ou est nostre roy?"; et dient aucuns quilz crient a Dieu vengance de vous mesmes'.[50] The example of the subtraction of obedience from the pope at the turn of the last century was one which might be followed in a general subversion.[51] But despite all this Jean Juvenal des Ursins would not preach that moderate withdrawal of obedience for which Gerson argued at the beginning of the fifteenth century and Jacques Almain at the beginning of the sixteenth; and, as we shall see, which Thomas Basin was prepared to justify in the 1470's.[52] As well as the possibility of sedition Jean Juvenal emphasized the obedience of the subjects of the king of France. All these persecutions, he wrote, 'ont este et sont sur nous; et toutevoye nous ne tavons point oublie ne navons envers toy fait aucune chose inique; et avons eu avons, tousjours le cuer a toy. Et toutevoye tu nous as humiliez en affliction, en tribulacon, et tellement que nous ne attendons que lombre de la mort pour nous couvrir, enfouir et mectre en terre ...'.[53] In this elegiac attitude Jean Juvenal des Ursins lined himself up with all those who effectively preached quietism and, like Commynes, thought 'tout bien regardé, nostre seulle esperance doit estre en Dieu'.[54]

Some people, of course, were not prepared to rely on Him. The 'commons' of France had once been seditious enough; though their understandable anger had not led to coherent argument. The duke of Anjou, thought Guillaume the juponnier, 'souspris de vin' in Orléans on 29 December 1384, 'est mort et dampné, et le roy saint Loys aussi, comme les autres. ... Estront, estront de Roy et de Roy; nous n'avons Roy que Dieu; cuides tu qu'ilz aient loyaument ce qu'ilz ont? Ilz me taillent et retaillent, et leur poise qu'ilz ne povent avoir tout le nostre; que a il à faire de moy oster ce que je gaaigne à mon aguille? Je ameroie mieux que le Roy et tous les Roys feussent mors que mon filz eust mal ou petit doy.'[55] However much they may have sympathized with the

---

[49] About 1440 he argued that misgovernment might cause the people to go over to the English, since their administration of occupied France was so much better. [Loquar in tribulacione spiritus mei f. 3ᵛ.]

[50] Ibid. ff. 23, 22. God was naturally on their side: 'car les povres gens sont de par Dieu ordonnez a estre juges de ceulx qui lour font les maulx et ne les saulve point Dieu' (ibid. f. 22). Jean Juvenal also made dark hints of a movement of taxpayers, 'nobles, gens desglise et peuple, qui... se mestroient ensemble', presumably as Estates, to take over the administration of taxation (Verba mea auribus percipe, Domine, f. 97ᵛ).

[51] See below, n. 57.

[52] J. Almain *Libellus de auctoritate ecclesiae, Gersonii opera* I 708; for Thomas Basin's views see below, p. 179.

[53] Loquar in tribulacione spiritus mei f. 11ᵛ.

[54] Op. cit. I xvi ed. Calmette & Durville I 93.

[55] *Choix des pièces inédites relatives au règne de Charles VI* ed. L. Douet d'Arcq (Soc. de l'hist. de France) (Paris 1863–64) I 59.

lower orders in their predicament their effective advocates, the intellectuals, did not sympathize with such natural feelings of anarchy. To a certain extent it was a *trahison des clercs* for the lower orders: but since they were inarticulate it is impossible to say to how great an extent. Despite the reiterated warnings of Jean Juvenal des Ursins about popular sedition the *peuple* in the fifteenth century seems to have been as unwilling to rebel as he (alternatively) and Sir John Fortescue thought; and how many were prepared as a result to believe the superstitions of kingship, as the eighty-year old Jean Batiffol of Bialon in the Massif central, for instance, believed in 1457 that true kings bore as a birthmark the 'enseigne de roy ... la flour de liz' (though this led him to have his doubts about Charles VII); or to hear with happy approbation Charles VII praised in the *Mistère du siège d'Orléans* by the Maid herself, so clearly favoured of God:

> Obayr tous nous devons à celui;
> C'est nostre roy, c'est le bien obay,
> C'est nostre prince et nostre souverain.
> Mal fait seroit de luy avoir failli,
> Et ne devons pas le mectre en obly,
> Que c'est le roy qui est de droit divin?[56]

The nobility, on the other hand, was certainly seditious enough;[57] but it, too, neither produced for itself nor does it seem to have felt it needed others to produce for it intellectual justifications for its actions. In the Praguerie, for instance, the duke of Bourbon's reply to a démarche by the king, far from being a reasoned account of his conduct peppered with a little theoretical justification, was 'plusieurs grandes, oultrageuses et deshonnestes paroles, qui bien seroient longues et deshonnestes pour luy à reciter' and the rebel lords, like everyone else, were quite prepared to state 'qu'ilz ont tousjours tenu et veulent tenir le Roy estre leur naturel et souverain seigneur, et le veulent tousdis honnorer, servir et obeir ainsi que raison est ...; qu'ilz ont tousjours eu vouloir et auront de faire l'obeissance au Roy, comme ses vrays et loyaux parens et

---

[56] A. Thomas 'Le "Signe royal" et le secret de Jeanne d'Arc' *Revue historique* CIII (1910) 280 n. 2; *Le Mistère du siège d'Orléans* ed. F. Guessard & E. de Certain (Doc. inéd. sur l'hist. de France) (Paris 1862) pp. 779–80. Urban proletariats, though mutinous, seem never to have wanted to change fundamentally the systems of town government (cf. B. Chevalier 'La Politique de Louis XI à l'égard des bonnes villes. Le Cas de Tours' *Le Moyen Age* LXX (1964) 479–80).

[57] One of the evils which might ensue from peace, Jean Juvenal des Ursins argued about 1440, was that 'la guerre que vous avez occuppe voz princes et voz barons tellement que a paine auroient ilz loisir de eulx diviser. Se avez paix aux Englois ilz se diviseront et voz subgetz aussi, car ilz y sont assez enclins; par quoy vendront & sourdront guerrez civiles & particulieres, lesquelles seront plus dangereuses & perilleuses que la guerre que avez contre voz ennemis et espoir seroient cause de faire une subverssion generale contre vous et espoir substraction aussi bien que on a fait au pape; et par guerre vous les entretenez pres de vous' (Loquar in tribulacione spiritus mei f. 19). As evidence for the magnates' tendency towards internecine feeling he quoted the recent example of the Praguerie.

subjects'.[58] The participants in the war of the Public Weal came in the beginning with cries of loyalty to the king; the count of Charolais 'diceva venivano per bene et utile del reame, et non per fare guerra ni dispiacere ad questo signore re de Franza'; and the duke of Berry declared that in his confederacy he did not intend 'toucher en aucune maniere à la personne & autorité de mondit Sieur'.[59]

'Mondit Sieur' and his father and grandfather before him were not impressed by such protestations. The spectre of Richard II (and of the duke of Orléans) dangled before them as warning of what people could actually do to 'tyrants',[60] even if they wanted to make no changes in the political system in principle. Louis XI was clear about the causes of magnate revolts. 'La cause principale pourquoy ledit duc de Bourbon, ses adhérans et complices, se sont ainsi eslevez et mis en rébellion à l'encontre du roy', he declared to the three estates of Auvergne in 1465, 'si a esté et est pour ce qu'ilz ont voulu avoir pensions et bienffaiz du roy très excessivement et plus beaucoup qu'ilz n'avoient du temps du roy son père ...'; and he was not so very far wrong.[61] As unprincipled, these revolts produced very little theory; and as unprincipled they received very little intellectual support. Jean Meschinot could argue for a rather crude resistance:

> Roys sont tenus—
> A quel debvoir? Nourrir paisiblement—
> Qui? Leurs subgectz. Sainsi nest? Voysent jus!

but for Jean Juvenal des Ursins revolts such as the war of the Public Weal were 'chose deffendue et prohibee et conmettre crisme de leze majeste' and he was prepared to use arguments similar to Jean de Terre-Vermeille's against such unnatural behaviour.[62] Thomas Basin had taken a more dubious part in the affair; and having burned his boats he could afford to be less inhibited. He saw in the revolt a noble cause betrayed by ignoble behaviour; and some years after the war he justified on not very comprehensive grounds the right of subjects to coerce a tyrant. Given his hatred for Louis XI his views were a model of Gersonian discretion; and however faintly the old Gersonian battle-cry of *vim vi repellere licet* was heard once more in France.[63] But it caught no echo.

[58] M. d'Escouchy *Chronique* ed G. du Fresne de Beaucourt (Soc. de l'hist. de France) (Paris 1863–64), III 11, 20.

[59] *Dépêches des ambassadeurs milanais en France sous Louis XI et François Sforza* ed. B. de Mandrot & C. Samaran (Soc. de l'hist. de France) (Paris 1916–23) III 214; P. de Commynes *Memoires* ed. Lenglet-du Fresnoy (Paris 1747) II (Preuves) p. 439. Cf. the protestation of the duke of Bourbon (ibid. p. 445); the comte du Maine joined the league in September 1465 under such conditions (*Documents historiques inédits* ed. Champollion-Figeac (Doc. inéd. sur l'hist. de France) (Paris 1841–74) II 384).

[60] Escouchy op. cit. III 11; *Les Demandes faites par le roi Charles VI...* pp. 97–100.

[61] *Documents historiques inédits*, op. cit. p. 214. For the pensions and benefits they in fact acquired see Escouchy op. cit. III 82 ff.

[62] Op. cit. (Ballade *Parle plus beau*) sig. n i; Juvenal des Ursins, La deliberation faicte a Tours f. 122.

[63] T. Basin *Histoire de Louis XI* ii iii ed. C. Samaran (Les Classiques de l'hist. de France au Moyen âge) (Paris 1963–   ) I 177 ff.

The articulate members of the late fifteenth-century generation as a whole did not want to resist. For Jean Juvenal des Ursins the only political hope lay in the king: 'il semble a mon peuple', he wrote about 1440, 'que quant on laura remonstre au roy quil y pourvoirra'; and Thomas Basin, too, had once put his faith in presenting a memoire on the evils in the kingdom to Louis XI.[64] Investigation of Jean Juvenal's views on the nature of tyrannical actions in the fifteenth century makes this attitude more comprehensible. Many seemed to him those of a tyranny of inefficiency: of insufficient, rather than of over-much, royal power. *Quare obdormis, Domine?* was a text which came easily into his mouth.[65] The king tacitly allows the misdeeds of others: 'qui peut empescher les maulx a faire & on ne le fait ce nest que donner faveur aux tirannies'.[66] Gerson had seen the same fault in the unfortunate Charles VI: 'toy prince: tu ne faiz mye telz maulx, il est vray; mais tu les seuffres. Avise se Dieu jugera justement contre toy en disant, "Je ne te pugnis mye: mais se les dyables denfer te tourmentent je ne les empescheray point"; cestoit mal pour toy'.[67] 'Oncques tirannies si horribles ne detestables ne furent faictes ou royaume ne que ilz ont este en vostre temps', Jean Juvenal des Ursins wrote to Charles VII in the 1450's, 'et tout sen est ale par dissimulacions, abolissions et remissions'.[68] This group of governmental misdeeds divides conveniently into three.

The first contains those occasioned by taxation. Jean Juvenal was perfectly prepared for people to pay taxes for proper purposes.[69] He objected to arbitrary taxation and threatened Charles VII with the wrath of God for being excessive in his exactions.[70] But his main outbursts were directed against misappropriation of taxation.[71] Over and over again he insisted that taxes taken for the war went into private pockets. 'Helas, povres aides', he wrote in 1445, 'alez vous au fait de la guerre!

---

[64] Loquar in tribulacione spiritus mei f. 13ᵛ; Basin *Apologia* ed., Quicherat op. cit. III 252 ff.

[65] *Psalmorum* xliii 23; Loquar in tribulacione spiritus mei f. 2.

[66] Loquar in tribulacione spiritus mei f. 13ᵛ (quoting Gratian *Decretum* II xxiii q. 3 c. 8).

[67] *Vivat rex* sig. e ivᵛ. Much the same note was struck by Philippe de Villette in 1414 (C. J. Liebman jr. 'Un Sermon de Philippe de Villette abbé de Saint-Denis, pour la levée de l'oriflamme (1414)' *Romania* LXVIII (1944–45) p. 462) and by Jean Dubois (op. cit. f. 52; Valois op. cit. pp. 221–22).

[68] Verba mea auribus percipe, Domine, f. 102.

[69] Epistre faicte par Jehan evesque et conte de Beauvays f. 15; Loquar in tribulacione spiritus mei f. 4ᵛ; Verba mea auribus percipe, Domine, f. 97.

[70] A,a,a, nescio loqui quia puer ego sum f. 54; La deliberation faicte a Tours f. 122ᵛ; Verba mea auribus percipe, Domine, f. 97ᵛ.

[71] Admittedly he was rather old-fashioned in demanding that the king should live off his own (the reforming *Ordonnance cabochienne* of 1413 had allowed the king half the profits of taxation for ordinary expenses) (A,a,a, nescio loqui quia puer ego sum f. 53ᵛ; *L'Ordonnance cabochienne* ed. A. Colville (Collection de textes pour servir à l'étude et à l'enseignement de l'histoire) (Paris 1891) pp. 70–71) but misappropriation of taxation also incurred the wrath of Jean Courtecuisse (A. Coville *Les Cabochiens et l'ordonnance de 1413* (Paris 1888) p. 129) and Gilbert de Lannoy (*Instruction d'un jeune prince*, p. 394). Jean Juvenal was equally indignant about the collapse of the *domaine* revenues; and amongst the reasons he gave for the fall he included grants of land and revenues (A,a,a, nescio loqui quia puer ego sum ff. 52ᵛ–53). At least as far as can be told from the vestiges of evidence that remain (R. Fawtier *Comptes du Trésor* (Paris, 1930) pp. lxv–lxxi) his views were accurate: a possibly increasing practice of local assignment (which might have included some gifts and pensions) (cf. F. Lot & R. Fawtier *Histoire des institutions françaises au Moyen âge* (Paris 1957–) II *Institutions royales* p. 267) might indeed partly explain the fall.

Mes les estas et penssions des seigneurs du sanc de France et officiers ..., je ne scay dont vient cecy que il fault qui les ayent: ilz sont parens du roy, *ergo* il fault quilz ayent ce que de quoy le roy doit faire guerre a ses ennemis. Il ny a maintenant celluy qui ne veuille avoir pension, soit connestable, mareschaulx, seneschaux, baillis, cappitaines particuliers, oultre ses gaiges ordinaires.... Se chacun seigneur en son pais vouloit prendre les aides en ses terres et avoir penssions le roy nauroit riens de demourant.'[72] Misappropriation of taxation, Jean Juvenal thought by the 1450's, was 'souldoyer tous pesches et les deables denfer et faire guerre a Dieu, aux vertus et a ses commandemens'.[73] The question of resumption came into his arguments then and in 1468, as it had into those of the reformers of 1413, of Thomas Basin in 1461 and as it was to come into those of the Estates general of 1484;[74] but the pensions remained.

In 1484 (when the government wanted to grant nine hundred of them) Guillaume de Rochefort's justification of the system was that 'rex quandiu minor est, omnes sibi benevolos facere, et nullum contristare debet. Quonam certe pacto creditis plurimos aequanimiter ferre pensionibus omino privari, nec eis vel exiguam concedere, qui nuper maximas capiebant? Id profecto fieri nequit, sed muneribus et beneficiis, in fide et officio eos continere oportet. Vultis et in hoc Carolum septimum imitari, quasi rex in aetate Carolo par sit. Carolus siquidem per se et proprio consilio rempublicam administrabat. Hic autem ob aetatem id facere non potest, sed eum aliena ope uti, manibus non propriis multa gerere, totumque regni ministerium suis credere fidelibus necesse est.'[75] *Pace* the chancellor his argument could equally well apply to Charles VIII's grandfather, and not only in his early years; and it could also apply to Charles VIII's father.[76] If he could ignore the liberal shibboleths of the fifteenth century, the king of France could not ignore the claims of patronage; and that very weakness contributed to those actions which Jean Juvenal des Ursins came close to stigmatizing as those of a tyrant and not of a king.

The second sub-group of tyrannies were those committed by the *gens-d'armes*. The depradations of the soldiery agitated Jean Juvenal des Ursins very much in 1433–40, as they had agitated Nicholas de Clamanges in 1408 and the reformers in 1413;[77] but by 1444–5 he was prepared to

---

[72] A,a,a, nescio loqui quia puer ego sum f. 54.

[73] Verba mea auribus percipe, Domine, f. 99.

[74] Ibid. f. 116; La deliberacion faicte a Tours f. 123; *Ordonnance cabochienne, passim*; Basin *Apologia* p. 254; Masselin op. cit. p. 676.

[75] Masselin op. cit. p. 386.

[76] See, for instance, the list of pensions about 1450 in Beaucourt op. cit. V 72 n. 5; and the charges on the receipt of the *aides* from the *généralité* of Seine-Yonne in 1465–66 and the account of increased charges in 1466–67 (*Documents historiques inédits*, II 459–70). For the part his pension and other gifts played in a magnate's finances at this time see, e.g. H. de Surirey de St.-Rémy, *Jean II de Bourbon, duc de Bourbonnais et d'Auvergne (1426–88)* (Paris 1944) pp. 94–97.

[77] Epistre faicte par Jehan evesque et conte de Beauvays; Loquar in tribulacione spiritus mei *passim*; J. Gerson *Oeuvres completes* ed. P. Glorieux (Tournai 1960–   ) II 116–23 (a letter of Clamanges); *Ordonnance cabochienne* pp. 172–75.

admit that pillaging had ceased and by the 1450's to say that the soldiery did not now commit misdeeds for fear of the king.[78] In this he agreed with Mathieu d'Escouchy, with Jacques du Clercq and with Georges Chastellain; and even with the author of the hostile *Livre des trahisons de France*.[79] Certainly a considerable collection of letters of abolition for military misdemeanour testifies to pressure on the soldiery in Poitou in 1446.[80] But Thomas Basin could still complain about the soldiery in 1461 and the troubles of Louis XI after 1465 again brought up the question of bringing 'pollice aux gens de guerre'.[81] How many were there like the anonymous figure who, at the beginning of Lent, 1465, was on the road in Berry, 'en habit d'omme de guerre, vestu court d'une jaquete, une grant espée à son col, avecques ung petit manteau et une bougette troussée à son espée et une dague à sa sainture et ung becquet en un exsil en sa main, lequel becquet il avait osté celluy jour à ung marchant de poisson du Blanc en Berry', who took away the shoes of little Denis Duvergier, aged twelve, on his way to the village to fetch oil, in order to make Denis show him the way, and who was eventually killed in a scuffle with a couple of villagers trying to retrieve them?[82] A vaudevire of about 1474 could still complain of the 'si grant pillerye' in Normandy.[83] And the permanent army remained, costly and troublesome. In the 1450's Jean Juvenal des Ursins, like Thomas Basin in 1461, thought that it ought to be abolished on the grounds of expense and general uselessness.[84] It was not that Jean Juvenal saw in it a prop of despotism; he was much more concerned with the fact that the soldiery in leisure gave themselves over to 'tous vices, comme puterie, gourmanderie, jeux de des et avoir chemises deliees'.[85] It was its inefficiency rather than its efficiency and the king's lack of control over it rather than his using it as a ready weapon of oppression that constituted its tyrannies in Jean Juvenal's eyes.

The third sub-group of evils were those committed by the king's servants. Both in the treatise on the office of the chancellor and in that of the 1450's Jean Juvenal des Ursins gave a detailed account of the misdeeds of royal officers. Two examples may suffice to give the flavour of his accusations. 'Que de manieres fait on de recepveurs', he wrote, 'et plusieurs ou il nen fauldroit que [ung seul]. Je ne prens exemple que en ce pais. Il y a le recepveur ordinaire du demaine; le recepveur de la

[78] Traictie compendieux f. 8ᵛ; A,a,a, nescio loqui quia puer ego sum f. 54; Verba mea auribus percipe, Domine, f. 94.

[79] Beaucourt op. cit. IV 395–96.

[80] *Recueil des documents concernant le Poitou contenus dans les registres de la Chancellerie de France* ed. P. Guérin (VIII) *1431–47* (Archives historiques du Poitou XXIX) (Poitiers 1898) pp. 217 ff.

[81] *Apologia* pp. 253–54; (Relation of the Estates general of 1468 enregistered at Rodez) f. 60.

[82] *Recueil des documents concernant le Poitou* (IX) *1465–74* (Arch. hist. du Poitou XXXVIII) (Poitiers 1909) p. 33.

[83] *Recueil de chants historiques français* ed. Le Roux de Lincy (Paris 1841–42) I 378.

[84] Verba mea auribus percipe, Domine, ff. 96–97; Basin *Apologia* pp. 252–55. Jean Juvenal saw the danger of trouble if the *compagnies d'ordonnance* were all let loose unpaid.

[85] Verba mea auribus percipe, Domine, f. 96ᵛ.

prevoste de Laon, qui est le prevost mesmes (et Dieu scet si ou temps passe se le prevost a este recepveur pour faire son plaisir et laisser les heritaiges du roy en desert et a non chaloir). Et puis ung recepveur de confiscacions, mortemains, formariages et aultres; et toutevoye ung tout seul suffiroit et trop mais que il feust bien choisy.'[86] Proliferation of office; plurality of office: innumerable examples could be found to bear Jean Juvenal out, inevitable complaint in 1413 and 1484.[87] 'Je suis cy a Laon', he wrote at the same time; 'ou est le chef du bailliage de Vermendois, qui est, ou deust estre, le plus notable. Mais il ny a de present ne bailli ne lieutenant ne capitaine ne lieutenant ne prevost. Item et pour ce est neccessite que ilz resident; et se ilz sont empeschez que leurs lieutenants ou vicesgerens y soyent residens; et que ilz ne ayent aultre charge ne office daultre que du roy. Nous en avons cy ung bien notable homs mais il ne arreste point en ceste ville; et luy baille on commissions particulieres et si est bailli daultres seigneurs. Et vault bien le bailliage de Vermendois loccuppacion dun homme sans aultre charge; et pareillement de tous les aultres.'[88] And non-residence, especially, in the case of higher officers, on special commissions and the dividing of an officer's interest between king and private lord were again indeed common themes.[89]

But it was not only to such comparatively minor misdeeds that Jean Juvenal des Ursins objected; he disliked the way in which they seemed to be only too ready to create the ruler's tyranny for him. Certainly members of the royal entourage seem to have been ready enough to use 'parolles de ung tirant non digne de estre entendues', to advocate throwing those who complained into the river, or to say ' "Exiges et tailles hardiment, tout est vostre" ', or that ' "peuple tousjours crye et se plaint et tousjours paye" ' or to argue that it was 'cryme de lèze majesté que de parler d'assembler Estatz et que c'est pour diminuer l'auctorité du roy'.[90] Certainly the *gens du roi* in *Parlement* were by the end of the century prepared to take a very high view of sovereignty indeed: in 1491 the king's proctor general denied discussion of 'l'auctorité du roy, c'est sacrilège d'en disputer ...; car l'auctorité du roy est ...

---

[86] A,a,a, nescio loqui quia puer ego sum f. 53.

[87] For receivers alone see G. Dupont-Ferrier *Les Officers royaux des bailliages et sénéchaussées* (Bibliothèque de l'Ecole des hautes études CXLV), (Paris 1902) pp. 171–72; *Etudes sur les institutions financières de la France à la fin du Moyen âge* (Paris 1930–32) I *Les Elections et leur personnel* pp. 117–18, 184–85. For complaint on the two points in general see *Ordonnance cabochienne* pp. 4–6, 34–35, 78–79, 104; Masselin op. cit. pp. 683, 694.

[88] A,a,a, nescio loqui quia puer ego sum f. 55. For the bailli of Vermandois in 1445 (the notorious Jamet du Tillay, councillor and chamberlain of the king, servant of the duke of Orléans, frequent royal commissioner) see G. Dupont-Ferrier *Gallia regia* (Paris 1942–61) VI 123–24.

[89] For baillis and sénéchaux alone see Dupont-Ferrier, *Les Officers royaux des bailliages et sénéchaussées* pp. 90–98 (for commissions, see G. Dupont-Ferrier, 'Le Role des commissaires royaux dans le gouvernement de la France spécialement du XIVe au XVe siècle' *Mélanges Paul Fournier* (Paris 1929) pp. 171–84). For complaint on the two points in general, see *Ordonnance cabochienne* pp. 100–04; Masselin op. cit. pp. 683, 690.

[90] Juvenal des Ursins, La deliberacion faicte a Tours f. 122[v]; Loquar in tribulacione spiritus mei f. 5; A,a,a, nescio loqui quia puer ego sum f. 45; Verba mea auribus percipe, Domine, f. 97[v]; Commynes op. cit. v xix. ed. Calmette & Durville II 219.

plus grande que les advocatz ne le pourroient exprimer et n'est subgecte aux oppinions des docteurs'.[91] This was an end of argument; and by their production in a law-court the words themselves became deeds of civil-service despotism. The *peuple* might suffer from the misdemeanours of minor officials; but it was the magnates, otherwise fairly immune from institutional oppression, who, like the duke of Burgundy and the duke of Bourbon, found their own servants involved in endless quarrels with those of the king over questions of authority and jurisdiction;[92] and the greater clergy (as Jean Juvenal des Ursins knew only too well)[93] who saw the jurisdiction of the church succumb to the lay jurisdiction of royal officers.

The government's lack of knowledge and lack of control of at least part of the working of the civil-service machinery was quite considerable; and internecine warfare between rival sections of the administration was as acute as that between royal servants and seigneurial ones.[94] But some of the onslaughts of those local commandos of despotism do seem to have been 'inspired'.[95] Jean Juvenal des Ursins did not look into the tricky question of initiative; he remained prepared in this matter to regard the king as the victim of his officers. 'En verite', he declared in 1445, 'je scay que le roy a aussi bonne voulente et est aussi vaillant, sage et prudent que fust oncques roy'. He was simply misled. 'Et ne veulx pas dire que soyes tirant; mais yl peut avoir aucunes faultes en vos gens et officiers lesquelles a[s]poir on vous impute', he wrote in the 1450's. 'Et ne veulx pas dire que vous ayez aucune condicion de tirant mais de vray prince et que ce que je recite nest que pour vous advertir que aucunesfoys par mauvais conseil ne enchees en aucunes espesses de tirannies.'[96]   On very few matters was he prepared more openly to attack Charles VII; and even in these he hoped that the king's good sense would prevail.[97]

The most important, perhaps, of these more direct onslaughts concerned the summoning of the Estates. Jean Juvenal's complaint is well known. 'Vos predecesseurs ont accoustume', he told Charles VII, 'quant

---

[91] Imbart de La Tour op. cit. p. 40. Cf. the sentence before the remark of the *premier Président* of the *Parlement* of Paris in 1527, quoted above, p. 108: 'Nous ne voulons révoquer en doute oud isputer de votre puissance. Ce seroit espèce de sacrilège' (Zeller op. cit. pp. 79–80).

[92] Surirey op. cit. pp. 177–97; A. Bossuat *Le Bailliage royale de Montferrand, 1425–1556* (Paris 1957) pp. 39–57; J. Richard 'Enclaves "royales" et limites des provinces: Les Elections bourguignonnes' *Annales de Bourgogne* XX (1948) 89–113.

[93] A,a,a, nescio loqui quia puer ego sum f. 49; Verba mea auribus percipe, Domine, ff. 112ᵛ ff.

[94] G. Dupont-Ferrier 'Ignorances et distractions administratives en France aux XIVᵉ et XVᵉ siècles' *Bibl. de l'Ec. des chartes* C (1939) 145–56; Bossuat op. cit. pp. 59–77.

[95] Richard op. cit. pp. 101 ff.; Surirey op. cit. pp. 177 ff.

[96] A,a,a, nescio loqui quia puer ego sum f. 47; Verba mea auribus percipe, Domine, ff. 90ᵛ 102. Complimentary remarks about Charles VII are littered around Jean Juvenal's treatises.

[97] E.g. (on the question of the charges on the people): 'nest chose si pourfitable au peuple que la voulente du prince en neccessite soit acomplye, et que sa voulente ne soit point contraire a raison et justice. Et croy que aucunement ne le vouldries faire se en esties adverty. Or est il ainsi que de tout le temps de vos predecesseurs et de vous, si non depuis aucun temps en ca, on a aceoustume de appeller les trois estas; et en tant que ne lavez fait ce nest pas selon lusaige ancien' (Verba mea auribus percipe, Domine, f. 98ᵛ).

ilz avoient affaire pour la guerre, ilz faisoient assembler les trois estas, en demandant aux gens desglise, nobles et commum peuple que ilz feussent vers eulx en quelque bonne ville.... Et vous mesmes lavez tousjours fait, jusques ad ce que vous avez veu et congneu que Dieu et fortune (qui est variable) vous avoient aide tellement que vous vous sentiez comme audessus.... Et se on vouloit dire que le roy peut mettre sur son peuple charges ... pour ses neccessites urgentes [another well-worn theme] on peut respondre que ceulx de ce royaume sont frans et en possession et saisine, que sans leur consentement on ne les doit point charger.'[98] The cry for consent to taxation had echoed about France; but it had not been enough.[99] Despite occasional rumblings of protest and such satirist's appeals as

> Prince, quy veult leur donner allégeance?
> A quy? A eux; je vous prie humblement—
> De quoy? Que vous ayez leur règne en remenbrance—
> Quy peut donner bon conseil prestement?
> Quy? Voire quy? Les trois estats de France![100]

the general mood was too clearly that of the deputies of 1468, who begged, 'pour ce que aisement ilz ne se peulvent pas assembler', not to be summoned again.[101] It was not only against the king but against his own compatriots that Jean Juvenal was fighting in vain.

For Sir John Fortescue the salvation of England lay under the English laws of Parliamentary consent to legislation and taxation;[102] and Parliamentary authority for the legitimate coercion of a sovereign was an old argument in England. It was understandable (if ironical) that Jean Juvenal des Ursins should make one of his most open stands upon the Estates; it was his only hope of avoiding utter reliance upon the benevolence of the ruler. What other checks were there? The duty of taking counsel was the most hallowed: 'Que on me die, je vous prie, qui est prince ou roy qui fut onc si saige q[ui] ait presume de son seul sens gouverner son royaulme?', asked Gullaume Fillastre in 1468.[103] 'Le seigneur doit nommie demander conseil seulement mais le croire et le excuter ...', Gerson had thought; 'roy sans prudent conseil est comme le chief en ung corps sans yeulx, sans oreilles sans nez'.[104] But Jean Juvenal des Ursins had nothing to add to the moral clichés of the ages; nor the leaguers of 1465 had hoped to make cover contravention of the

[98] Ibid. f. 97.
[99] 'The Failure of the French Medieval Estates' *Past and Present* XXIII (1962) 8. Above 110.
[100] J. du Clerq *Mémoires* ed. J. A. C. Buchon (Choix de chroniques et mémoires sur l'histoire de France X) (Paris 1838) p. 266. The style of this ballad circulating before the battle of Montlhéry in 1465 is very reminiscent of Jean Meschinot's.
[101] (Relation of the Estates general of 1468 enregistered at Rodez) f. 64ᵛ; C. J. de Mayer *Des Etats généraux et autres assemblées nationales* (Paris 1788–89) IX 222.
[102] *Governance of England* pp. 109 ff.
[103] *La Toison d'or* (Paris 1530) II f. 104.
[104] *Vivat rex* sigs. d iiᵛ, [d iv].

did other possible checks appeal to him. He had nothing to say on the question of royal submission to Parlement as a law-court: a theme used by Gerson and, a century later, by Claude de Seyssel.[105] He did not follow Seyssel in extending a *de facto* right of disobedience to royal commands made in contravention of the fundamental laws: a right which the leaguers of 1465 had hoped to make cover contravention of the enactments of the reforming committee of thirty-six.[106] In the idea of an assembly he made his only practical stand.

And it was, of course, unthinkable that the theoretical powers of the Estates could ever be argued up to the level of those of Parliament. By 1484, after decades of royal tutelage over those that survived, deputies to the Estates general could maintain that 'nec esse statuum consensum per juris rigorem expetendum, nisi in levandis tributis; quod si aliter conceditur, gratia principum est, atque facilitas'.[107] The general Estates had in practice never worked;[108] it was too late to rely on them in theory. Nor was the idea of Parliament sufficient in itself as a political panacea; Sir John Fortescue was terrified that there would be a sweeping away of Parliament and a reception of civil law. The inert force of centuries of Parliamentary existence might carry it over an awkward gap; but in the last analysis ideas were not enough. The only way to prevent a ruler immune to inertia or to argument from doing things one did not want him to do was to stop him from doing so by force, the *voie de fait*. But of the *voie de fait* Jean Juvenal des Ursins (and others) had, by the second half of the fifteenth century, had quite enough. Its use in the civil war had, in the end, only strengthened peace-lovers' affection for strong monarchy:

> Soit doncques cellui noble prince,
> [wrote Robert Blondel of the dauphin Charles [VII]]
> Françoiz, craint et amé de vous.
> O peuples! congnoissiez pour vostre
> Seignieur, le Dalphin noble et sage,
> Car son salut si est le nostre
> Et sa ruine est nostre dommage.[109]

In the aftermath of war, and given a social and political development which had broken the community of the country up in disunity, there was little those who loved peace and moderation could do but submit to the king, to complain about tyrannies which one hoped either were not committed by him or were against his better nature and to cry, with Jean Juvenal des Ursins, 'Je ne vouldroye deprimer vostre puissance mais laugmenter de mon petit povoir'.[110]

[105] *Sermo super processionibus faciendis pro viagio regis Romanorum*, *Opera* II 279; C. de Seyssel *La Monarchie de France* ed. J. Poujol (Paris 1961) pp. 117–18.
[106] Seyssel op. cit. p. 119; Commynes op. cit. ed. Lenglet-du Fresnoy II [Preuves] 514–15.
[107] Masselin op. cit. p. 140.
[108] 'The Failure of the French Medieval Estates' pp. 6–11. Above 108-13.
[109] Blondel *La Complaincte des bons François* p. 82.
[110] Verba mea auribus percipe, Domine, f. 97ᵛ.

The mood of Jean Juvenal des Ursins, like that of others, was thus essentially one of submission. Like theirs, it was formed by the developments of the past, by present events and present influences, by notions and theories accepted because they seemed important and which often seemed most important because they rationalized an existing political situation. Unlike the royal propagandists and the royal servants, men such as Jean Juvenal des Ursins did not preach obedience for interested motives: they preached it disinterestedly because there seemed no alternative to it. In all countries members of other social groups might use more direct methods of getting their way with the government; and direct methods might mean, too, direct subjugation. The articulate moderates seem to have felt in the aftermath of civil war that peace was worth it at any price, rather than the resistance of any group to a ruler incapable of dealing with it. In France royal weakness had paradoxically produced a disunited opposition and the king could afford to accept large assemblies only when it was really convenient to him. There was no safety-valve for moderation; no nucleus around which a moderate 'popular' opposition could form. One had to go in with one side or the other; and in the circumstances it was understandable that the moderates of the late fifteenth-century generation plumped for the king and drew from the political notions current arguments in support of non-resistance. But in doing so their views acted as precursors of a dangerous theory of submission. Jean Golein criticized Raoul de Presles for over-stressing the miraculous in Charles V's touching for the evil; and his reason for doing so might stand as a rebuke *sub specie eternitatis* to all those who, however reluctantly, preached the untouchableness of the lord's anointed. 'L'ay fait', he wrote, 'affin que ceulz qui venront apres ou temps a venir, moins soutilz et moins exercitez en science ou avis que n'est mon devant dit Seigneur, n'i prengnent occasion de vaine gloire ou de soy tenir pour sains et faisans miracles'.[111] If men are told they are gods, this may mean that their successors will behave like it.

---

[111] J. Golein *Traité du Sacre* ed. Bloch op. cit. p. 489.

Legends of Clovis ... Noel de Fribois, *Cest chose profitable ... aux roys ... de scavoir...*, Paris, Arsenal, MS. 3430, fol. 1. *(See p. 190.)*

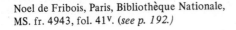

Noel de Fribois, Paris, Bibliothèque Nationale, MS. fr. 4943, fol. 41v. *(see p. 192.)*

Noel de Fribois, Geneva, Bibliothèque publique et universitaire, MS. fr. 83, fol. 49v. (Photo: Arlaud, Geneva) *(see p. 192.)*

13

TWO PIECES OF FIFTEENTH-CENTURY POLITICAL ICONOGRAPHY

(a) *Clovis touches for the King's Evil*

Marc Bloch in 1924 seems to have thought (on the authority of Durrieu and of Henri Martin) it unlikely that any French mediaeval illustration of a king touching for the Evil would come to light.[1] A medallion which survived in a window at Mont-St.-Michel until the mid-nineteenth century is alleged to have done so; but from the description which survives it is impossible to derive a precise idea of the original.[2] A thirteenth-century English miniature on the theme survives in Cambridge.[3] At the same time Marc Bloch was unable to find any literary evidence of the view that Clovis par-

ticipated in the royal miracle before the later sixteenth century. 'A dire vrai', he wrote, 'une seule chose étonne: c'est que ce mythe ait apparu si tard'.[4] Certainly Clovis' part in others of the miracles of the crown of France, in those 'biens et graces' conveniently summarized by Guillaume Cousinot in 1468 'comme de la saincte ambole, les floures du lis, louriflan et degueri des escourelles &c',[5] was invented at a much earlier date.[6]

Arsenal MS. 3430, a copy of Noel de Fribois' first recension of 1459, contains a frontispiece illustrating in six frames various aspects

---

[1] M. Bloch, *Les Rois thaumaturges*, 1924, p. 449.
[2] *Ibid.*, pp. 144–45, 450–51.
[3] Cambridge University Library, MS. Ee. iii. 59,

fol. 21v; reproduced by M. R. James, *La estoire de Seint Aedward le rei*, (Roxburghe Club), 1920.
[4] Bloch, *op. cit.*, p. 357.
[5] Procès-verbal of the Estates general of Tours enregistered at Rodez, Archives départementales de l'Aveyron, BB 3, fols. 55v–56r.
[6] Bloch, *op. cit.*, pp. 225, 230–32, 236.

of the Clovis legends.[7] A group of four of these deals with the origin of the *fleurs-de-lys* and with the descent of the *sainte-ampoule* at Clovis' baptism; an oblong frame at the bottom of the page shows, presumably, the battle of Tolbiac. And, within an architectural encadrement to the right of the page, a prominent miniature displays the king (attended by two figures, both in skull-caps, one in an ermine cope) with his right hand on the left shoulder of the foremost of two kneeling figures. So banal a gesture in so significant a place calls for explanation; and a reasonable explanation seems to be that this miniature represents Clovis touching for the king's Evil. There is, admittedly, no direct evidence of this either in the miniatures or in the text itself. But Clovis' action has some religious significance, since it takes place in an ecclesiastical setting. Clovis touches approximately the seat of the disease (as does Edward the Confessor in the Cambridge manuscript). The kneeling figures in the scene are clearly of the class which might be expected to benefit most from the royal miracle; and, all in all, everything seems to indicate that the miniature shows Clovis performing it.

It may be dated probably to the earlier sixteenth century. But already, probably, a more distinguished artist had illustrated the theme. Mâcon MS. 1, a copy of Raoul de Presles' translation of St. Augustine's *City of God*, contains, on fol. 2r, a very large miniature on the Clovis legends.[8] The king is shown, *inter alia*, emerging from the scene of his baptism. Three figures kneel before him. In the left foreground, on the steps of the church, a man in a short robe looks up at him; his left hand touches his right shoulder. The courtier immediately behind Clovis extends a hand to beckon him up and before the king. Clovis has his left hand upon the right side of the neck of the second kneeling figure (in a long robe), whose hands are joined in prayer and whose eyes turn Heavenward. Clovis' right hand is raised in benediction. A third figure (also in a long robe) kneels in the right foreground; his hands are clasped and he has a pathetic expression on his face.

There can be very little doubt about this miniature. What is surprising is not the inclusion of a king touching for the Evil in an illustration of the royal miracles remarked upon in Raoul de Presles' preface but its absence from the four others that, in different manuscripts of his translation, do so.[9] 'Et ne tiengne vous ne autre que celle consecration soit sans tresgrant, digne et noble mistere', he had informed Charles V on the subject of his unction with the oil of the *sainte-ampoule*; 'car par icelle voz devanciers et vous avez telle vertu et puissance, qui vous est donnee et attribuee de Dieu, que vous faictes miracles en vostre vie, telles si grandes & si appertes que vous garissiez dune treshorrible maladie qui sapelle les escroelles'.[10] But certainly the text of Raoul de Presles gave the illustrator of Mâcon 1 no authority for allowing *Clovis* to participate in the royal miracle. It is possible to argue that he was led on by the reference to the touch in association with the recognized Clovis legends in it to ascribe the power to touch to him; but he was faithful enough to Raoul de Presles on at least two other points. Not only did he omit all reference to the eagle-and-sun symbol, which was never specifically attached to Clovis, but he omitted also any reference to the oriflame. In Raoul de Presles' preface the oriflame legend stars Charlemagne: to detach the oriflame from him would perhaps have needed more deliberate effort, but at least by the time of Robert Blondel and of the author of the *Débat des hérauts d'armes*, some thirty years before the suggested date of the illustration in Mâcon 1, the oriflame legend had figured Clovis.[11] It is surprising, at least, that an artist so avant-garde as to include him in the legend of the touch should have omitted him from one in which his position was apparently more secure.

But the artist of Arsenal 3430 had no authority in the text of Noel de Fribois for his introduction of Clovis into the touching legend either; and it seems equally reasonable to argue that both he and the illustrator of Mâcon 1 had formed their notion of Clovis' participation in the touch for the king's Evil from another source. What this can have been is a matter for conjecture. And it is

---

[7] Bibliothèque de l'Arsenal, MS. 3430, fol. 1r; plate p. 188 above.

[8] Bibliothèque municipale de Mâcon, MS. 1, fol. 2r; reproduced by A. de Laborde, *Les Manuscrits à peintures de la Cité de Dieu de St.-Augustin*, iii, 1909, plate CV.

[9] *Ibid.*, plates XXXII and XLII; ii, pp. 321, 366–67.

[10] R. de Presles, *Saint Augustin de la cité de Dieu*, Abbeville, 1486, i. sig. a iij v.

[11] R. Blondel, *Des Droiz de la couronne de France*, ed. A. Héron, *Oeuvres de R. Blondel*, [Société de l'histoire de Normandie], i, Rouen, 1891, p. 402; *Le Débat des hérauts d'armes de France et d'Angleterre*, ed. L. Pannier and P. Meyer, [Société des anciens textes français], 1877, p. 12.

doubtful even if the period of the general emergence of Clovis into the legend should be dated by his emergence into it in these illustrations. A woodcut, showing the fleurs-de-lys canon (a little abbreviated), the baptism and the descent of the *sainte-ampoule*, appeared in the first printing of the *Mer des histoires* of 1488.[12] It shows close affinities with the illustration in Mâcon 1; but it omits, as well as any reference to the oriflame, any reference to Clovis' touching for the Evil. This cut, and versions of it, remained popular:[13] the notion thus retreated, apparently, from the common iconography of it as it had, apparently, never entered a written text. But at least it had appeared; and it would probably be as wrong to deny that it had not appeared before, or that it would not appear again, as it was rash to deny the existence of a miniature depicting it.

(b) *The English Kill Their Kings*

The regicidal proclivities of the English had a considerable fascination for fifteenth-century Frenchmen. 'Ilz ont une maniere en Angleterre', wrote Jean Juvenal des Ursins in 1444, 'quilz ne tiennent comte de changier leur roy quant bon leur semble, voire de les tuer & faire morir mauvaisement.'[14] The

chancellor of France alleged in 1484 that the English had had twenty-six changes of dynasty since the foundation of their monarchy.[15] The author of a political treatise on the English claim to the throne of France, written soon after Henry V's occupation of Normandy, thought that they 'ne pourroient bien faire a autrui quant ilz traisent et destruissent leurs roys et souverains seigneurs, comme on puet savoir par le roy Richart et par plusieurs autres de leurs roys jusques au nombre de xxij quilz ont desappointez et faulsement traiz et fait morir ou temps passe par leurs faulses et mauvaises traisons'.[16] A precise list of martyred monarchs was given in a piece of Gersonian apocrypha.[17] Although heavily in disguise, they are identifiable as Oswald,[18] Oswin,[19] Elfwin,[20] Egfrid[21] and Osred;[22] with, apparently, Uhtred earl of Northumbria[23] and St. Cnut[24] of Denmark thrown in for good measure and with scant regard for chronology.[25] The theme was taken up by Noel de Fribois:

La seconde chose que les Anglois ont fait dogmatiser et semer est que ilz sont a recommander sur toutes autres nations en vraie subjection & ferme obeissance envers les roys & princes et seigneurs temporelz

---

[12] Editions alleged earlier than this should probably be regarded as ghosts. The identification by Wm. Baynes and Son (*Bibliotheca Selectissima*, 1826, pp. 23–24) of the copy they offered for sale in 1826 as by Jean du Pré, Lyons, 1486, seems to rest upon a misreading of the colophon in the edition of Jean du Pré, Lyons, 1491. The Lyons edition of 1486 once owned by Albert Bentes (*Bibliotheca Bentesiana*, Amsterdam, 1702), part 2, p. 13, no. 113) and the Paris edition of 1485 'avec figura, du nombre 285', listed by Cornelius à Beughem (*Incunabula typographiae*, Amsterdam, 1688, p. 161) remain mysterious.

[13] The first version was used at least in Verard's re-edition of the *Mer des histoires*, Paris [1503?]. A second version (for the relationship of which to the first see A. Claudin, *Histoire de l'imprimerie en France au xve et au xvie siècle*, iii, 1904, p. 497) was used in the Lyons editions of Jean du Pré, 1491, and of Claude d'Avost, 1506; and it reappeared at least in the Paris editions of the French version of Robert Gaguin's *Compendium de origine et gestis Francorum* by Jean Petit, 1532, and Antoine de La Barre, 1536. A third version, copied ineptly from the second, was used at least in the two French versions for Poncet Le Preux and Galiot du Pré, Paris 1514 and Paris 1515; in the edition by Poncet Le Preux, Paris 1516; and in the edition of the *Mer des histoires* for Galiot du Pré, Paris 1517. A direct copy of this block was used at least in the edition of the French version of Gaguin by N. de La Barre, Paris 1527.

[14] J. Juvenal des Ursins, Traictie compendieux de la querelle de France contre les Anglois, Bibliothèque Nationale, MS. fr. 17512, fol. 34v a.

[15] J. Masselin, *Journal des Etats généraux de France tenus a Tours en 1484*, ed. J. Bernier, [Documents inédits sur l'histoire de France], 1835, p. 38.

[16] Apres la destruction de Troye la grant, Bibliothèque Nationale, MS. fr. 5059, fols. 49v–50r.

[17] *Gersonii opera*, iv, ed. E. du Pin, Antwerp, 1706, col. 857; Petri episcopi Cameracensis & S. R. E. Cardinalis (Pierre d'Ailly) Dialogi II de querelis Franciae et Angliae . . . , ed. M. Goldast, *Sibylla Francica* . . . , Oberursel, 1606, ii, p. 40. Du Pin identified his source as MS. St.-Victor 699; now Bibliothèque Nationale MS. fr. 23135. This identification was clearly an error and it seems impossible, for the moment at least, to discover the whereabouts of Du Pin's manuscript. Goldast's original was in his own library. Another copy of the second part of the dialogue (beginning 'Fluxu biennali spacio . . .') is preserved in Bibliothèque Nationale, MS. fr. 5038, fols. 49r–56r; and it is from this manuscript, fols. 54v–55r, that the names in the following notes have been derived.

[18] 'Osuas [642]'; *Venerabilis Baedae historiam ecclesiasticam*. ed. C. Plummer, 1896, i. 145.

[19] 'Offin [651]'; Bede, *op. cit.*, i. 155.

[20] 'Elfinus [679]'; Bede, *op. cit.*, i. 249.

[21] 'Egfrid [695]'; Bede, *op. cit.*, i. 267.

[22] 'Obred [716]'; Bede, *op. cit.*, i. 346.

[23] 'Vitinheres dux regni Nortahumbrorum [648]'. Bede's text is innocent of any reference; the closest seems to be to Uhtred earl of Northumbria, who was murdered in 1016. His name is omitted from Noel de Fribois' list.

[24] 'Kinitum'.

[25] Reference was of course made to Richard II and to St. Thomas of Canterbury.

dicelle nation dAngleterre. Sensuit la confutation & impugnation de ceste assertion :

En lan de lIncarnation Nostreseigneur six cens quarante deux Osualdus roy dAngleterre fut tue par les Anglois.

Item en lan six cens quarante huit Breuil[26] roy dAngleterre fut tue par les Anglois.

Item en lan six cens soixante dix huit Elfredus roy dAngleterre fut tue par les Anglois.

Item en lan six cens quatre vings & quinze Edgarus roy dAngleterre fut occis par les Anglois.

Item en lan sept cens & seize Obred roy dAngleterre fut occis par les Anglois.

Item Karnithius roy de Danemarche & dAngleterre fut par les Anglois occis en leglise cathedral de Ottonie en lisle nommee Pheonne; lequel Karnithius a este par saincte eglise canonize comme martir, et en signe de punition & infame perpetuelle saincte eglise ordonna lors que les prestres dAngleterre porteroient en leurs chasubles quant ilz celebreroient messes une flesche rouge. Et en oultre de leurs perverses meurs & conditions vicieuses et superstitions detestables peut apparoir par le Decret en la premiere partie, appellee les Distinctions, ou chappitre *Si gens Anglorum*;[27] et par autres saincts docteurs de leglise, sicomme Bede venerable, prestre Anglois, Guillaume de Malmesbery, Anglois, Sigibert et Vincent de Beauves, tresnotables historiens. Par les choses ci dessus briefment recitees appert evidenment que les Anglois ont este envers leurs roys faulx, mauvais, desloiaux, et commis crime de felonnie et de lese majeste; et par consequent que ce quilz ont fait dogmatizer &

semer est mensonge evidente et que nul ny doit adjouster foy.[28]

The basic source for the names of the martyred was clearly in both cases Bede's *Historia ecclesiastica*; the story of St. Cnut was easily found in 'Dannorum hystoria'. More obscure is the view, which both treatises shared, that English priests wore an arrow in memory of a crime that their countrymen certainly did not commit. Equally difficult to explain are the discrepancies of nomenclature between the lists of murdered monarchs. Clearly the two texts are related in some way; it is possible that Noel de Fribois' was derived from the pseudo-Gersonian dialogue; it is equally possible that both were derived from a common source.

The illustrator of Bibliothèque Nationale MS. fr. 4943, a copy of Noel de Fribois' second recension of about 1461, took the theme for a miniature on fol. 41v of the manuscript. An identical miniature appears in Bibliothèque Publique et Universitaire de Génève MS. fr. 83, fol. 49v.[29] Prominent in the foreground is a pile of six dead kings of England and one defunct and sainted bishop (St. Thomas of Canterbury). At the head of a military group behind it a soldier sheathes his sword and an ecclesiastic looks down regretfully at the holocaust. In the left foreground six substantial figures—perhaps doctors?—are engaged in lively discussion of the scene. Their agitation is expressive of the disquiet with which the literary in fifteenth-century France claimed they observed the homicidal tendencies of their neighbours. For the English *did* kill their kings; but whether as a result they got better ones than their French contemporaries (except, perhaps, from the point of view of a few principal regicides) is a matter for doubt.

---

[26] Both 'Breuil' and the reason for his supplanting Oswin in Noel de Fribois' list seem impossible to discover.

[27] Gratiani decretum, part i, distinctio lvi, cap. *Si gens Anglorum.*

[28] British Museum, Add. MS. 13961, fols. 6ov–61r.

[29] Plates, p. 189 above.

14

WAR PROPAGANDA AND
HISTORIOGRAPHY IN
FIFTEENTH-CENTURY FRANCE
AND ENGLAND

A T its lowest and most popular, verity concerning the war between England and France in the fifteenth century was slipped into the minds of its recipients by such itinerant *chansonniers* as the one who, according to Louis XI, 'se soit mis a aller par nostre royaume pour chanter et recorder chancons, dictez et records touchant les bonnes novelles et advantures qui nous sont survenues et surviennent chacun jour au bien de nous et de nostre seigneurie';[1] it could be found obfuscated in the mysteries of semi-heraldic prophecy, to which even so respectable a figure as Christine de Pisan in her old age contributed;[2] its sediment settled in commonplace note-taking on both sides of the Channel.[3] In the form of verse it could vary from the Latin epigram[4] to the twenty thousand lines of the *Mistère du siège*

---

[1] B[ibliothèque] N[ationale], MS. fr. 5909. fo. 29^r, printed by C. Samaran, 'Chanteurs ambulants et propagande politique sous Louis XI', *Bibliothèque de l'Ecole des Chartes*, c (1939), p. 233.

[2] *Je, Christine, qui ay plouré*, ed. J. Quicherat, *Procès de condamnation et de réhabilitation de Jeanne d'Arc*, v (S[ociété de l'] H[istoire de] F[rance], 1849), p. 8. A considerable elaboration of this theme may be found, with other prophecies, in the last of a group of treatises addressed to Charles VII about 1445 by his 'povre, petit et ignorant subgiect, Jehan Dubois' (B.N., MS. fr. 5734, fos 58^r–59^r).

[3] For example see L. Delisle, 'Notes de Nicole de Savigny, avocat parisien du xve siècle, sur les exploits de Jeanne d'Arc et sur divers événements de son temps', *Bull. de la Soc. de l'hist. de Paris*, i (1874), pp. 42–44; B[odleian] L[ibrary], Rawlinson MS. B.214, fos 121^{r-v}, 150^r–152^r.

[4] Delisle, *op. cit.*, p. 43; *Political Poems and Songs*, ed. T. Wright, ii (R[olls] S[eries], 1861), pp. 127, 130.

d'Orléans.[1] In the form of prose it naturally had wïder scope: for in prose there could be a literature of political reason, as well as a literature of political sentiment.[2] The authors of a considerable number of treatises[3] sought to convince their readers of the legal and historical truth about the quarrel between England and France. Most of them have never been printed; and the corpus as a whole[4] has never been examined. Yet it serves to illuminate the mentality both of the contestants and of the writers who contributed to it.

The inevitable characteristics of propaganda—the slander of one's opponents and the ridicule of their opinions, the, use of emotional symbols, the claim to wide support and the assertion of inevitable victory—were still to be found in these treatises. The pride and wickedness of the English, who 'puis cent ans en ca ... aient tue et fait mourir plus de Crestiens que toutes autres nations nont fait',[5] and who killed even their kings,[6] were still stressed; 'quant je voiz', wrote Jean de Montreuil about 1411, 'que ilz ne desirent riens tant que gaster et destruire ce royaume, dont Dieu le gart, et que a tous leurs voisins ilz ont guerre mortele, je les ay en tele abhomination et haine que jaime ceulz qui les heent

---

[1] *Le Mistère du siège d'Orléans*, ed. F. Guessard and E. de Certain (Documents inédits sur l'histoire de France, 1862). For other examples see Wright, *op. cit.*, and *Recueil de chants historiques français*, ed. Leroux de Lincy, i (Paris, 1841).

[2] For an example of the latter see A. Chartier, *Le Quadrilogue invectif*, ed. E. Droz (2nd edn, Paris, 1950), pp. 17–19. Verse could be used occasionally for sterner stuff: *e.g.* Wright, *op. cit.*, pp. 131–40; *cf.* below, p. 201, n. 3.

[3] Full reference to these, and to the MSS. in which they are found, is given below, pp. 202-3, nn. 3–6, 1–5, 1–2, pp. 206-7, nn. 4–6, 1–2.

[4] Some of the texts have been discussed by J. M. Potter, 'The Development and Significance of the Salic Law of the French', *Eng. Hist. Rev.*, lii (1937), pp. 235–53; A. Bossuat, 'Les Origines troyennes: leur rôle dans la littérature historique au xve siècle', *Annales de Normandie*, viii (1958), pp. 187–97. A sensitive *aperçu* of the group as a whole (though one innocent of very much reference for its source material) is given by A. Bossuat, 'La littérature de propagande au xve siècle: le mémoire de Jean de Rinel, secrétaire du roi d'Angleterre, contre le duc de Bourgogne (1435)', *Cahiers d'histoire*, i (1956), pp. 131–46.

[5] Jean de Montreuil, *A toute la chevalerie de France* (B[ibliothèque] R[oyale de Belgique], MS. 10306-7), fo. 6^v.

[6] 'Two Pieces of Fifteenth-Century Political Iconography: (b) The English Kill their Kings', *Journal of the Warburg and Courtauld Institutes*, xxvii (1964), pp. 319–20. See above 190-1.

et hez ceulx qui les aiment'.[1] 'Toutesfoiz que je suis en matiere qui touche les Anglois', wrote Noël de Fribois in 1459, 'je ne puis contenir ma plume.'[2] The image of a France 'toute deschevelee, dessiree, dissipee, gastee et desrompue, acompaignee de tribulation, affliction, impatience, murmuration, division et dissimulation de humilite et esperance et delaissement ou oblivion de choses passees et acomplissement de possibilite'[3] was still invoked; the 'bons, vrays François du royaulme' could still be exhorted to think of the fleurs-de-lis.[4] Before the English occupation of Normandy at least Jean de Montreuil was certain that 'naura, se Dieu plaist, creature du plus grant au plus petit qui voulsist souffrir ou consentist jusques a la mort que Angloiz en chief ou comme roy seignorist en France':[5] later writers were perhaps less confident. But others than he could be found who followed him in thinking that after the English 'auront asses tourmente les Francois, ilz seront apres tourmentes et punis, et si demoura France aux Francois'.[6]

But some of the authors were prepared to be sweetly reasonable towards the English. Jean Juvenal des Ursins thought in 1435 that the English princes who had died in the French wars 'estoient taillies en aultre terre que en France de conquester ung monde';[7] Jean de Montreuil wrote about 1411 that 'je vouldroye que les Angloiz feussent tousjours bien aise et quilz ne nous feissent jamaiz mal ne contraire'.[8] A little earlier he had required

'tous ceulx qui ce present traictie liront ou orront, par especial sil vient entre [les] mains daucuns Angloiz, quilz ne dampnent riens jusques a ce quilz aient tresbien tout veu, mesmement que

[1] *A toute la chevalerie de France*, fo. 10ʳ.

[2] *Cest chose profitable* (B[ritish] M[useum], Add. MS. 13961), fo. 58ᵛ.

[3] Jean Juvenal des Ursins, *Audite celi que loquor* (B.N., MS. fr. 5022), fo. 28ʳ.

[4] *Response d'un bon et loyal François au peuple de France de tous estats*, ed. N. de La Barre, *Mémoires pour servir à l'histoire de France et de Bourgogne*, i (Paris, 1729), pp. 315, 321.

[5] *A toute la chevalerie de France*, fo. 6 bisᵛ.

[6] *La Geanologie des roys de France* (B.N., MS. fr. 833), fo. 91ᵛ. The sentiment was attributed by Jean de Montreuil, of whose larger treatise this 'genealogy' is in fact a variant abbreviation, to Richard II ('Precursory text' (B.N., MS. fr. 23281), fo. 12ᵛ).

[7] *Audite celi que loquor*, fo. 57ʳ.

[8] *A toute la chevalerie de France*, fo. 10ʳ.

tout ce que iceulx Angloiz pevent mettre au devant pour eulx ou principal de la besoingne y est argue et oppose et y respondu et solu a nostre loyal povoir et savoir. Et se apres ilz alleguent droiz et dient raisons pour leur partie plus evidantes que celles qui sont cy devant mises pour la nostre, ou produisent plus grant tesmoingnage de verite, que nous ne creons mie, nous, qui sans mettre raison ou sans actentique auctorite ne disons chose quelconque, sommes prestz de tout veoir ou oir courtoisement et doulcement, et respondre, se mestier fait, mais quilz baillent ainsi que nous faisons, par escript; car on ne doit pas ne appartient mie a parler de voulente en si haulte matiere comme celle qui est cy devant ouverte et aucunement traictie.'[1]

The appeal to reason could not be clearer, not, admittedly, so much to the reason of the English as to that of Jean de Montreuil's own compatriots. The purpose of these treatises was above all to instruct: to present the argument against the enemy in a convincing and yet viable form.

The 'grandeur et prolixite' of the sources, thought Noël de Fribois, prevented investigation of the past by members of the nobility, 'obstans la brieste et fragilite de ceste vie humaine et les grans affaires en quoy ilz sont souventesfoiz occupez pour le bien de la chose publique'.[2] Abbreviation was the bait with which the authors of these treatises hoped to attract their audience; their labours were 'pour relever le liseur de tant descriptures veoir et cerchier'[3] and a determination not to bore their readers allowed them ruthlessly to clear out the complicated legal citation that so weighed down the relevant chapters of the *Songe du Verger*.[4] A

---

[1] 'Precursory text', fo. 28ᵛ.

[2] *Cest chose profitable*, fo. 2ʳ.

[3] J. de Montreuil, 'French text' (B.N., MS. fr. 4983), fo. 78ᵛ.

[4] The authors of the treatises do not seem in general to have derived much help from the *Songe*. Jean de Montreuil made frequent reference to 'un autre traictie a part assez plus grant que cest ycy' ('Precursory text', fo. 22ʳ), which may have been the *Songe* but which was possibly more likely to have been the *Memore abrege grossement* (see below, p. 17). The relevant chapters of the *Songe* were copied out for English diplomats (B.M., Cotton MS. Tiberius B.xii, fos 37ʳ–42ʳ; Harley MS. 861, fos 67ʳ–72ʳ; Harley MS. 4763, fos 35ʳ–41ʳ (*Somnium Viridarii*, cap. 186); B[odleian] L[ibrary], Bodley MS. 885, fos. 4ʳ–7ᵛ (*Somnium*, cc. 186–87); B.M., Harley MS. 4763, fos 199ᵛ–209ʳ (*Songe du Verger*, cc. 145–46)).

recital of legal authorities was, thought Jean de Montreuil, 'trop prolixe et obscure a gens laiz, par especial a la chevalerie de ce royaume'.[1] This was perhaps to underestimate not only the chivalry of the kingdom but also its bourgeoisie. In 1453 Jean d'Orléans, count of Angoulême, had a copy of the *Songe* written by 'Guillaume Arbalestier, escripvain, demourant a La Rochelle';[2] a copy of the *Songe* remained in the library at Cognac on the death of his son Charles in 1496.[3] Guillaume Giroult, 'merchant et garde de la monnoye de Tours', seems to have bought a copy of the printed edition of 1492 fairly soon after it was published.[4] Though a fairly brief summary of the facts could find a ready market, the intellectual capacity of the audience of the treatises should not be regarded too lightly.

The market it provided was well catered for. In 1459 Noël de Fribois felt it necessary to defend the brief discussion of the English claim to the throne of France which he had introduced into his historical compendium. 'Saucun disoit que escrire de ceste matiere', he wrote, 'nestoit besoing et que autres en ont autresfoiz escript, response: il est vray que autres en ont autresfois escript, desquelz jay veu les escripz'; but none, he claimed, had dealt with the problem as deftly as he.[5] And the audience was a wide one. If Jean de Montreuil at the beginning of the century was intent upon educating the chivalry of the kingdom,[6] another author in 1471 confessed, 'avant que je procede au principal de [ce] present euvre, je scay et congnois que plusieurs nobles escuiers et gens clercs scevent ce que je veulx descripre. Pour lesquelz mon intention nest pas, mais seulement pour simples gens, ayans nobles couraiges et vertueux, qui ont vouloir de garder et defendre la noble couronne et le royaume de France, afin de y encliner tousjours leurs cueurs et couraiges.'[7] And indeed the appeal of the treatises seems to have been felt at all levels of literate society. Copies of at least some of the texts seem

---

[1] 'Precursory text', fo. 26[r]. The 'devote creature' of Jean Juvenal's vision in *Audite celi que loquor* was conveniently unable to carry the more complex argument of the principal protagonists in her head (fo. 37[r]).

[2] Quittance of 22 May 1453, B.M., Add. Ch. 8121.

[3] Inventory taken in Nov. 1496, B.M., Add. MS. 11538, fo. 2[v].

[4] *Le Songe du Vergier* (Paris, 1492), B.L., Auct.2.Q.4.1., sig. [v vij][r].

[5] *Cest chose profitable*, fo. 58[v].

[6] 'Precursory text', fo. 26[r].

[7] *Pour vraye congnoissance avoir* (B.N., MS. fr. 25159), p. 2.

certainly to have been numerous enough. Most of them were
written in the vernacular; and three of those that were not were
rapidly translated: one, Robert Blondel's *Oratio historialis*, 'pour
l'instruction des François presens et avenir, et mesmement de
ceulx qui point n'entendent latin et qui ne sçavent pas aucunes
gestes passées'.[1] Examples of the treatises[2] remain in all the qualities of fifteenth-century book production from a little way below
the best to the very poorest. Copies of one or another belonged
to Jeanne de France, duchess of Bourbon;[3] to the bibliophile
Jacques d'Armagnac, duke of Nemours, and to the bibliophile
Louis de Bruges, lord of Gruuthuse;[4] to Pons d'Aubenas, lieutenant of the *sénéchal* of Beaucaire and Nîmes,[5] and to an obscure
'Guillaume Dorleans le jeune'.[6]

But the authors of the treatises were intent not only on preach-
ing to the converted, though it may have been the converted who
in fact provided the greater part of their audience. Jean de Montreuil wrote about 1409 both for the loyal chivalry of the kingdom,
'a eulx advertir de la bonne cause quilz ont maintenu et main-
tiennent en ceste partie pour leur souverain seigneur le roy de
France; et mesmement pour ce que nous avons sceu que pluseurs
de la duchie de Guienne par ignorance ont pense les choses estre
toutes autres quelles ne sont et, qui piz est, ont cuidie par erreur
et faulte de bonne information tout le contraire de la verite'.[7] As
well as to encourage the committed the propagandists hoped to
hearten the waverers, to force the facts upon the politically
apathetic and to corrupt the *collaborateurs*.

Though Jean de Montreuil early in the century hoped to convince the English, though he drew up the Latin version of his

---

[1] *Oeuvres de R. Blondel*, ed. A. Héron, i (Soc. de l'hist. de Normandie,
1891), p. 295. For the parallel French and Latin texts of Jean de Montreuil
see below, p. 203, n. 5.

[2] Reference to these is given below, as above, p. 194, n. 3.

[3] *Audite celi que loquor* and *Pourceque pluseurs*, finished at Amboise on
7 Feb. 1470 (B.N., MS. fr. 5056).

[4] Decorated copies of *Pourceque pluseurs* (B.N., MSS nouv. acq. fr.
20962 and fr. 5058).

[5] *Audite celi que loquor* (described as 'commentum et romancium')
written at Nîmes and dated 10 Mar. 1452 (B[ibliothèque] Mun[icipale de]
Troyes, MS. 2380).

[6] A poor copy of *Audite celi que loquor* (B. Mun. Bourges, MS. 242).

[7] 'Precursory text', fo. 26[r].

treatise for foreigners unable to understand French[1] and though another author sought to convince the pope,[2] it was all too clear after the English occupation had begun that it was not only neutrals and the enemy who needed education in the truth. There were, wrote Jean Juvenal des Ursins in 1444, 'plusieurs, tant Anglois que Francois, come lon dit, qui sont aveuglez dentendement et vraye congnoissance'.[3] The attitude of the majority of Frenchmen in the occupied areas was hardly as firm on the question of English rule as the patriots would have liked.

> 'Tous les natifs de Normandie,
> Qui ont vostre party tenu,
> Sont traistres, je n'en doute mie,
> Autant le grand que le menu',[4]

complained an aggrieved loyalist; but it still remained true that some three-quarters of the landowners of areas of western Normandy were prepared at least to accept the government of the English king of France.[5] No amount of patriotic special pleading can obscure the fact that the majority of Frenchmen were, as far as action went, at least apathetic about the identity of their ultimate ruler and even about his nationality. But the problem of persuasion was by no means confined to the inhabitants of the occupied north. Seduction of the inhabitants of Guyenne was a perennial question; and there were those in other areas of France who might choose to doubt the validity of the French king's title to his throne.[6] From the very beginning there had been Frenchmen eager to point out to the king of England the claims he might have

---

[1] 'Latin text' (B.N., MS. lat. 18337), fo. 3ʳ.

[2] *La Geanologie des roys de France*, fos 91ᵛ–92ʳ.

[3] *Traictie compendieux [de la querelle de France contre les Anglois]* (B.N., MS. fr. 17512), fo. 2ʳ.

[4] *Recueil de chants historiques français, op. cit*, p. 326.

[5] A. Dupont, 'Pour ou contre le roi d'Angleterre (les titulaires de fiefs à la date du 2 avril 1426 dans les sergenteries de Saint-Lô, Le Hommet, Sainte-Marie du Mont, La Haye du Puits et Sainte-Mère-Eglise, dépendant de la vicomté de Carentan)', *Bull. de la Soc. des antiquaires de Normandie*, liv (1957–58), pp. 164–66.

[6] For picaresque examples see R. Cazelles, *La Société politique et la crise de la royauté sous Philippe de Valois* (Paris, 1958), p. 204; A. Thomas, 'Le "Signe royal" et le secret de Jeanne d'Arc', *Revue historique*, ciii (1910), p. 280, n. 2.

in France;[1] from Robert d'Artois in the 1330's to Jean, duke of Alençon, in the 1450's there were French princes ready to urge him to descend upon his inheritance. And possibly more dangerous still were those who, for the sake of peace, were prepared to admit some of the English claims: even so loyal a servant as Jean Juvenal des Ursins could waver.[2] That the king of France was in the right, and that his right was worth fighting for, were the convictions that the propagandists hoped to inculcate in their less enthusiastic countrymen.

One should perhaps not underestimate the part which such conviction of right might play in the affirmation or conversion of men wavering between two claims to rectitude. Even so realistic an adviser as Sir John Fastolf could argue in 1435 'that if the king shulde take the . . . offre [to be made at the congress of Arras] in the maner and wise at it is offred hym be his . . . adversaries, that it myght be said, noised and demed in all Christien londis where it shuld be spoken of, that not Here the king nor his noble progenitours had, nor have, no right in the corone of Fraunce, and that all there werres and conquest hath be but usurpation and tirannie'.[3] The whole question of the justice of the war was raised implicitly by the authors; and with it a moral background far wider than that involved in a mere discussion of legal title. The ease with which authors both French, like Jean Juvenal des Ursins,[4] and English, like William Worcester,[5] passed from political to moral exhortation, to an emphasis upon moral rectitude as a predisposing factor for victory, should perhaps warn us that beyond the appeal to reason lay an appeal to a greater Reason which had an implicit hold upon the imagination of their contemporaries. The audience to which they appealed could understand arguments about rights, based upon evidence; but they were also to be moved by arguments about duties, based upon evidence in the end far less easy to controvert or to accept.

'God', thought Fastolf in 1435, 'the sovereine Juge, in the

---

[1] P. Chaplais, 'Un Message de Jean de Fiennes à Edouard II et le projet de démembrement du royaume de France (janvier 1317)', *Revue du Nord*, xliii (1961), pp. 145–48.　　[2] *Traictie compendieux*, fos 41ʳ–43ᵛ.

[3] Lambeth Palace Library, MS. 506, fo. 31ᵛ; *Letters and Papers Illustrative of the Wars of the English in France*, ed. J. Stevenson, ii.2 (R.S., 1864), p. [576].　　[4] For instance in *Audite celi que loquor*, fos 50ᵛ ff.

[5] *The boke of noblesse* (B.M., Royal MS. 18 B.xxii,) fo. 28ᵛ; ed. J. G. Nichols (Roxburghe Club, 1860), p. 56.

pursuyng of their right hath ever gretely eured [King Henry and his predecessors] . . . herebefore, and yeven them many worthy victories; or ellis it shulde be said and demed that the king had no power nor puissaunce to susteyn his right with'.[1] God's rôle in the struggle was considerably debated;[2] but the English seem to have felt before the war turned against them that His verdict was sufficiently obvious. If the English government felt its English or French subjects needed further to be stiffened in their resolve, the bulk of any English propaganda directed towards them has not survived. The government of the duke of Bedford seems to have felt it necessary only to hang in 1423 the true genealogy of Henry VI, king of France and England, accompanied by explanatory verses, in Notre-Dame de Paris and possibly elsewhere.[3] The French government had naturally more anxiety; and it set its more literary-minded civil servants to the task of persuasion. The polemical *pièce d'occasion* had in France a respectable ancestry. The men of letters around Charles V had not, in the pursuit of their master's sanctification, neglected his more mundane problems. Nicole Oresme, according to the author of a *Mirouer historial abregie de France*, was 'lun des clers qui lors feussent dont ledit roy Charles se aida plus en escriptures contre les Anglois et Navarrois, comme experience de ses escriptures le monstre'.[4] Those of the authors of the fifteenth-century treatises who may be identified belonged to the same ambience. Jean de Montreuil, the friend of Gontier and Pierre Col,[5] and Noël de Fribois[6] were

[1] Lambeth Palace Library, MS. 506, fo. 31ᵛ; *Letters and Papers Illustrative of the Wars of the English in France, op. cit.*, p. [576].

[2] For instance by Jean de Montreuil (in a letter printed in *La Cronique martinienne* (Paris, 1502?), fos 267ᵛ–268ᵛ) and by William Worcester (*The boke of noblesse*, fos 21ʳ–22ʳ; ed. Nichols, pp. 41–42).

[3] B. J. H. Rowe, 'Henry VI's Claim to France in Picture and Poem', *The Library*, 4th Ser., xiii (1932–33), pp. 77–88. For other propaganda produced on the English side see below, pp. 14–15.

[4] B.L., Bodley MS. 968, fo. 187ᵛ. According to Noël de Fribois (fo. 70ʳ) Oresme 'parle du droit du roy contre les Anglois' in his translation of Aristotle's *Economics, Ethics* and *Politics* (*cf.* R. Bossuat, 'Nicole Oresme et le "Songe du Verger" ', *Le Moyen Age*, liii (1947), pp. 114–16).

[5] A. Coville, *Gontier et Pierre Col et l'humanisme en France au temps de Charles VI* (Paris, 1934), p. 251; A. Thomas, *De Joannis de Monsterolio vita et operibus* (Paris, 1883), pp. 6–13.

[6] G. Du Fresne de Beaucourt, *Histoire de Charles VII*, vi (Paris, 1891), p. 406.

secrétaires du roi; Robert Blondel, the author of a *Livre des douze perils d'Enfer* as well as more political pieces, was the schoolmaster of François, count of Etampes, and of Charles de France;[1] Jean Juvenal des Ursins, who composed a considerable number of moral-political treatises and a history of Charles VI, based uncomfortably largely on that of the 'Religieux de St-Denis', as well as war propaganda, was a royal *avocat* before he became successively bishop of Beauvais, bishop of Laon and archbishop of Rheims.[2] As propagandists these authors were clearly well qualified.

A number of fashionable prose forms lent themselves more or less uncomfortably to the purposes of polemic. Jean Juvenal des Ursins cast his *Audite celi que loquor*[3] into allegorical form; the author of *Fluxo biennale spacio*[4] employed the dialogue; Noël de Fribois[5] and an earlier writer[6] injected the truth about the

---

[1] *Oeuvres de R. Blondel, op. cit.*, pp. xiv–xxxj, xiij.

[2] P. L. Péchenard, *Jean Juvénal des Ursins, historien de Charles VI, évêque de Beauvais et de Laon, archevêque duc de Reims* (Paris, 1876).

[3] (B.N., MS. fr. 5022), fos 27^r–61^r (lightly corrected and signed in Jean Juvenal's hand; *cf.* B.N., M.S. Dupuy 673, fos 51^r, 56^r). Other fifteenth-century copies survive in B.N., MSS fr. 1128, 2701, 5038, 5056, 6160; Musée Condé, MS. 923; B. Mun. Bourges, MS. 242; B. Mun. Troyes, MS. 2380; B.R., MS. 14785–86. A résumé is given by Péchenard, *op. cit.*, pp. 167–77. The treatise was written in May 1435.

[4] B.N., MS. fr. 5038, fos 49^r–56^r. The treatise was printed in *Gersonii opera*, ed. E. Du Pin, iv (Antwerp, 1706), cols 850–59 (from a St-Victor MS. now untraceable) and in *Sibylla francica . . .; item dialogi duo de querelis Franciae et Angliae et iure successionis utrorumque regum in regno Franciae*, ed. M. Goldast (Oberursel, 1606), pp. 28–43 (from a MS. in Goldast's library). Goldast identified the author as Pierre d'Ailly; if he was correct the text must have been refurbished at least two years after Ailly's death in 1420.

[5] *Cest chose profitable* (B.M., Add. MS. 13961). Other fifteenth-century copies survive in B.N., MSS fr. 1233, 4943, 4949, 5026, 5701, 5705, 10141, 13569; B[ibliothèque de l'] Arsenal, MS. 3430; B. Mun. Bordeaux, MS. 728; Bibliothèque publique et universitaire de Genève, MS. fr. 83; Burgerbibliothek Bern, MS. 560; B[ibliotheca apostolica] V[aticana], MSS Reg. 725 (a fragment), Reg. 829; John Rylands Library, MS. fr. 57. The compendium survives in two versions, the first of which, written in 1459, is less well developed but contains more material than the second, which was put together soon after 1461. The versions do not vary in their treatment of the English claims in France.

[6] *Apres la destruction de Troye la grant*, B.N., MS. fr. 5059, fos. 41^r–55^v. Other fifteenth-century copies survive in B.N., MSS fr. 10139, 19561;

English pretensions into abbreviated chronicles. The expanded genealogy of the line of St Louis provided a more direct approach;[1] and even more direct was the exhortatory epistle used by Jean de Montreuil[2] and by the author of an enraged *Response d'un bon et loyal François au peuple de France de tous estats* evoked by the treaty of Arras in 1419.[3] But apart from *Audite celi que loquor* these were on the whole only minor works. Larger and more important was Robert Blondel's *Oratio historialis*,[4] in which a large recital of past history was employed to prove the infidelity of the English. But the main pattern of French propaganda was to be found in another treatise produced by Jean de Montreuil;[5] in Jean Juvenal's *Traictie compendieux de la querelle*

B[ibliothèque] Ste-Geneviève, MS. 1994; B.M., Harley MS. 4473. A commentary is given by Bossuat, 'Les Origines Troyennes', *op. cit.*, pp. 195–96. The compilation was put together probably about 1419.

[1] *Pour vraye congnoissance avoir* (B.N., MS. fr. 25159), pp. 1–38. Another fifteenth-century copy survives in B.N., MS. fr. 15490. The genealogy was compiled in 1471.

[2] *A toute la chevalerie de France* (B.R., MS. 10306–7), fos 1ʳ–12ʳ. Another fifteenth-century copy survives in B.N., MS. nouv. acq. fr. 12858 (fos 3ʳ–14ᵛ, 50ᵛ–59ᵛ). A Latin version of the text exists with the incipit *Regali ex progenie*, B.N., MS. lat. 13062, fos 157ʳ–164ᵛ; another fifteenth-century copy survives in Biblioteca Riccardiana, MS. 443. The Latin text was printed in *Veterum scriptorum . . . amplissima collectio*, ed. E. Martène and U. Durand, ii (Paris, 1724), cols 1350–61, and in *Deliciae eruditorum*, ed. L. Lami, iii (Florence, 1737), pp. 17–36. In common with those of the French versions of Jean de Montreuil's larger treatise, the MSS of the French version of this text display considerable variation. The Latin and French versions exist as independent essays at the same text; both were written probably about 1411.

[3] Ed. N. de La Barre, *Mémoires pour servir à l'histoire de France et de Bourgogne*, i (Paris, 1729), pp. 315–22.

[4] *Oeuvres de R. Blondel*, ed. A. Héron, i (Soc. de l'hist. de Normandie, 1891), pp. 155–294. This treatise was written in 1449; a French translation was made in 1460 (*ibid.*, pp. 295–486).

[5] Three versions of this treatise may with some difficulty be distinguished: (**I**) the 'Precursory text' (B.N., MS. fr. 23281). Other fifteenth-century copies survive in B.N., MS. nouv. acq. fr. 11198 (fos 32ʳ–40ʳ: fragments which correspond with fos 4ᵛ–5ᵛ, 16ᵛ–17ᵛ, 13ᵛ–14ᵛ, 25ᵛ–26ᵛ, 20ᵛ–21ᵛ, 11ʳ–12ʳ, 23ᵛ–24ᵛ, 24ᵛ–25ᵛ, 28ʳ⁻ᵛ of MS. fr. 23281); MS. nouv. acq. fr. 12858 (garbled with the text of *A toute le chevalerie de France* and with fragments, some variant of material appearing in the text proper: the text reads through in the order fos 59ᵛ–62ᵛ, 28ᵛ–50ᵛ, 14ᵛ–28ᵛ, 62ᵛ, 68ᵛ–69ʳ). (**II**) the 'Latin text' (B.N., MS. lat. 18337), fos 1ᵛ–21ʳ. Another fifteenth-century copy survives in B.N., MS. lat. 10920. (**III**) the 'French text' (B.N., MS. fr. 4983),

de France contre les Anglois,[1] and in an anonymous tract beginning *Pourceque pluseurs*.[2]

The last, for its system and its coherence, clearly deserved its contemporary and its posthumous popularity; but it dealt primarily with the cruces first raised by Jean de Montreuil at the beginning of the century: with the question of the English right to the throne of France, and with the question of the English right with or without sovereignty and *ressort* to various of the French *pays*. The use of the Salic law as a weapon against the English claim to the throne seems to have owed at least its popularity[3] to Jean de

---

fos. 78ʳ–94ᵛ. Another fifteenth-century copy survives in B.V., MS. Reg. 894. This text was printed in *La Cronique martinienne* (Paris, 1502?), fos 254ᵛ–267ʳ. An abbreviation of the latter texts survives in Latin in B.L., Bodley MS. 885, and in French in B.M., Cotton MS. Tiberius B.xii; Harley MSS 861, 4763; with additional later material in B.M., Sloane MS. 960; and in a different and later version in B.N., MS. fr. 833 (printed as *La Genealogie des roys de France depuis sainct Loys jusques à Charles VII et l'extinction du faux droit et musie querelle pretenduʒ sur le royaume de France par les Anglois*, ed. A. Du Chesne, *Les Oeuvres de maistre Alain Chartier* (Paris, 1617), pp. 253–59). Other fragments of material by Jean de Montreuil are to be found in B.N., MS. lat. 18337; B.R., MS. 10306–7; B.V., MS. Reg. 894. The problem of the composition of this treatise is far more complicated than it appeared to Thomas, *op. cit.*, pp. 16–29. Versions of the 'Precursory text' may have been written as early as the later 1390's, refurbished about 1402–3 and added to later. The 'French text' is a reworking, avowedly in the autumn of 1416, of this material; the surviving copies, though close to each other, vary in the degree to which they derive from it directly. The 'Latin text', an independent version close to the 'French text', was written avowedly in 1415.

¹ (B.N., MS. fr. 17512.) Other fifteenth-century copies survive in B.N., MS. fr. 2701; MS. Dupuy 310; B. Arsenal, MS. 3731; the copy in B. Mun. Arras, MS. 740, was destroyed in 1915. A résumé is given by Péchenard, *op. cit.*, pp. 225–36. The treatise was compiled in 1444.

² (B.N., MS. fr. 5056, fos 1ʳ–30ʳ.) Other fifteenth-century copies survive in B.N., MSS fr. 5058, 12788; nouv. acq. fr. 6214, 20962; Bibliothèque Mazarine, MS. 2031; B. Arsenal, MS. 3434; B.R., MSS 9469–70, 12192–94; Österreichische Nationalbibliothek, MS. 3392; B.V., MS. Reg. 1933; Biblioteca reale di Torino, MS. L II 36; B.M., Add MS. 36541. For sixteenth-century printed editions see Potter, *op. cit.*, p. 249, n. 3. The treatise was also printed in *Mantissa codicis juris gentium diplomatici*, ed. G. W. Leibniz (Hanover, 1700), pp. 63–97, and in *Pretensions des Anglois a la couronne de France*, ed. R. Anstruther (Roxburghe Club, 1847). The treatise was written in 1464.

³ For the problem of the origin of the use of the Salic law in the debate between England and France see P. Viollet, 'Comment les femmes ont été exclues, en France, de la succession à la couronne', *Mémoires de l'Académie*

Montreuil.[1] A considerable amount of decoration was added to the theme by the author of *Pourceque pluseurs*; but he, like his predecessors, relied also upon a host of ancillary arguments for the exclusion of the king of England from the crown of France. Custom, reason, civil law, the decision of the peers of France in 1328 and the question of unction provided a barrier against female succession. The view that Queen Isabella could have passed on to her son Edward III a right which she herself never had was derided: 'sont les pont et planche si foibles et pourris', wrote Jean Juvenal, 'quilz ne se pevent soustenir'.[2] The argument that the claim *via* the daughter of Louis X had been passed on to the English was found equally easy to dispose of. The estoppel implicit in the homages done to the king of France by Edward III, in the renunciation of the English title in the treaty of Brétigny, in the negotiations of Richard II with Charles VI, in the acceptance of regency by Henry V, was eagerly revealed. The English claim by the treaty of Troyes was met with an examination of the condition of Charles VI in 1420 and with the assertion that the king of France could not disinherit the dauphin. That the Lancastrians were usurpers, that the Yorkists were usurpers and that the English were all murderers anyway completed the catalogue of the disabilities of the descendants of Edward III.

The English claim to a considerable area of France by inheritance the authors of the treatises countered primarily with a recital of the misdeeds against their sovereign lord for which the English kings of the past had forfeited their rights. The English

---

des Inscriptions et Belles-Lettres, xxxiv.2 (1895), pp. 125–78; R. E. Giesey, 'The Juristic Basis of Dynastic Right to the French Throne', *Transactions of the American Philosophical Society*, New Ser., li (1961), part 5, pp. 17–20.

[1] Two of the surviving MSS of his 'Precursory text' have the words 'in regno' inserted into a version of the Salic clause accompanied by a fully explanatory French gloss, 'qui exclut et forclot femmes de tout en tout de povoir succeder a la couronne de France, comme icelle loy et decret die absolument que femme nait quelconque portion ou royaume' (B.N., MS. fr. 23281, fo. 4ᵛ; MS. nouv. acq. fr. 11198, fo. 32ʳ). The third surviving MS. has a different version of the clause in which the words 'in regno' are omitted but which is followed by an identical gloss, reinforced with the words 'cest a entendre a la couronne de France' (B.N., MS. nouv. acq. fr. 12858, fo. 29ʳ). The 'Latin' and 'French' texts follow the second reading of the Salic law, the 'French text' with the gloss slightly abbreviated (fo. 80ʳ; *La Cronique martinienne, op. cit.*, fo. 257ᵛ), the 'Latin text' without a gloss.

[2] *Traictie compendieux*, fo. 11ʳ.

claim by the treaty of Brétigny they countered with the argument that the English had not fulfilled its provisions and with the paralysing argument that the king of France had no power to alienate his sovereignty. A flat assertion of this the authors reinforced by reference to the coronation oath and to the need for consent; and Jean Juvenal des Ursins borrowed from Jean de Terre-Vermeille the further justification that the king had only an usufruct in his kingdom.[1] Matters topical at the moment each of the treatises was compiled tended to be dealt with naturally at rather disproportionate length: the breaking of the truces in 1449, which long remained a burning question, took up a third of the length of *Pourceque pluseurs*. And a number of authors saw in counter-attack the best means of defence: Jean Juvenal des Ursins especially set himself the task of proving on historical grounds that the true king of England was the king of France;[2] the author of *Pourceque pluseurs* treated the question with rather more diffidence.[3] And in general the treatises confined themselves to a defence of the rights of the king of France within his own kingdom and of his actions in repulsing the English from it.

Treatises written by the English themselves seem to have been considerably fewer. Thomas Walsingham put together his *Ypodigma Neustrie* in 1421 with an avowed purpose much the same as that of Robert Blondel some thirty years later: to warn an innocent king of the immemorial treachery of his enemies.[4] But his work in fact was far less limited than this, as was Tito Livio's *Vita Henrici Quinti*, if Tito Livio ever had a propaganda purpose.[5] In fact English propaganda in a clear form does not seem to have appeared until the war was perhaps a minority cause.[6] In the early

[1] *Audite celi que loquor*, fo. 38ʳ; *Traictie compendieux*, fos 12ᵛ–13ʳ, 32ᵛ–33ʳ; *Joannes de Terra Rubea contra rebelles suorum regum*, ed. J. Bonaud (Lyons, 1526), fo. 15ʳ.

[2] *Audite celi que loquor*, fos 36ʳ–37ʳ; *Traictie compendieux*, fos 33ᵛ–41ʳ.

[3] Fos. 13ʳ, 21ᵛ–22ʳ; ed. Anstruther, pp. 50, 84–86.

[4] Ed. H. T. Riley (R.S., 1876), pp. 3–5. For the dating of the text see *The St Albans Chronicle, 1406–1420*, ed. V. H. Galbraith (Oxford, 1937), p. lx, n. 6.

[5] C. L. Kingsford, *English Historical Literature in the Fifteenth Century* (Oxford, 1913), p. 53.

[6] The commentary by Jean de Rinel, *secrétaire du roi* to Henry VI, written in 1435 against the French view of the treaty of Troyes (B.M., Harley MS. 4763, fos 196ᵛ–199ᵛ; another fifteenth-century copy survives in B.M., Cotton MS. Tiberius B.xii), has the air more of a private official mem-

1450's William Worcester put together his *Boke of noblesse*[1] and a rather random collection of Anglo-French administrative and diplomatic documents[2] in order to encourage Henry VI to war; both were rather clumsily refurbished for Edward IV and the second was finally produced again by Worcester's son for Richard III.[3] Apart from this despairing appeal on behalf of the disinherited there appears to survive only a 'breve tretise . . . compiled for to bringe the people oute of doute that han nat herd of the cronycles and of the lineal descensse unto the crownes of Englande, of Fraunce, of Castel Legions' and unto þe duchie of Normandie sith it was first conquest and made',[4] a glorified genealogy compiled originally in 1461. Otherwise there seems to have been silence from the English side.[5]

William Worcester, like his French colleagues, was intent in a part of his treatise upon a demonstration of the English right in the *pays* of France, of the impropriety of the English king's relinquishing it and of the immemorial infidelities of the French. The English claim and the French defence against it both he and the authors of the French treatises saw as an historical problem. Their material for its elucidation they derived from a number of

orandum than propaganda; of the same kind may have been the 'learned treatise in confutation of the *Salique law*, to prove the right of the kings of England to the crown of France', allegedly written by Thomas Beckington as dean of the Arches (J. Collinson, *The History and Antiquities of the County of Somerset*, iii (Bath, 1791), p. 384), which does not appear to survive. But see Bossuat, 'La littérature de propagande au xve siècle', *op. cit.*

[1] (B.M., Royal MS. 18 B.xxii.) The treatise was printed in *The Boke of Noblesse*, ed. J. G. Nichols (Roxburghe Club, 1860).

[2] Lambeth Palace Library, MS. 506. The collection was printed partially in *Letters and Papers Illustrative of the Wars of the English in France*, ed. J. Stevenson, ii.2 (R.S., 1864), pp. [521]–[607].

[3] K. B. McFarlane, 'William Worcester: A Preliminary Survey', *Studies presented to Sir Hilary Jenkinson*, ed. J. Conway Davies (Oxford, 1957), pp. 210–14.

[4] B.M., Add. MS. 10099, fos 205^r–210^v. Other fifteenth-century copies survive in B.M., Harley MSS 116 and 326.

[5] The eagerness with which copies were made in the early-seventeenth century (B.M., Lansdowne MS. 223; B.L., Bodley MSS 710 and 875; Cambridge University Library, MS. Ee.II.10; Lambeth Palace Library, MS. 713; Canterbury Cathedral Library, MS. C.19; Holkham Hall Library, MS. 683) of a translation of a collection of fifteenth-century diplomatic documents (B.L., Bodley MS. 885) then in the possession of Sir Peter Manwood emphasizes the shortage of material on the English side.

sources. Some of the writers had access to the royal archives.[1] Indeed, Jean Juvenal des Ursins had, he declared, been instructed by Charles VII 'que je me transportasse en vos Chambres des comptes, du Tresor de vos chartres et ailleurs pour veoir les lettres et chartres qui pourroyent estre necessaires a la convention' of 1444.[2] For Jean Juvenal, and Jean de Montreuil and the author of *Pourceque pluseurs*, had a further purpose than that of encouraging the loyalty of their compatriots: they were intent as well upon providing the government and its diplomats with a case to argue against their opponents.

Amongst the authors of the treatises Jean de Montreuil at least had considerable diplomatic experience; and he felt clearly that the grander members of embassies dealing with the English needed instruction. 'Comme les Anglois', he wrote in the preface to the French version of his treatise, addressed to the dauphin Jean in 1416, 'ayent livres les plus beaulx et les plus notables quilz pevent faire de ce quilz demandent en France, lesquelz ilz portent communement avecques eulx quant ilz doivent assembler avec les Francois pour traicter, et scavent par especial les grans seigneurs tout ce quilz cuydent qui face pour eulx, semble que veue la grandeur de ceste matiere, qui est celle du monde qui plus touche le roy, vous et tout le royaulme de France, vous la devez scavoir, pour en parler en lieu et en temps et avoir a cueur pour y pourveoir sur toutes choses'.[3] Certainly the English had had enough practice in collecting together their diplomatic evidences. The rôle of royal archivists as compilers of diplomatic collections after the apparent ending of the office of *custos processuum*[4] in 1339 is an obscure one; but by the reign of Henry V the compilation of such useful manuals as the *Liber recordorum* was once more in full swing.[5] The activity of French royal clerks is far less clear. Collections of diplomatic documents concerning negotiations with the English at least from the treaty of Paris in 1259 to the end

[1] William Worcester, for instance, made effective use of the record of the homages taken in Aquitaine in 1363–64 (*The boke of noblesse*, fos 18^{v}–19^{v}; ed. Nichols, pp. 37–38).

[2] *Traictie compendieux*, fo. 1^{v}.

[3] *La Cronique martinienne, op. cit.*, fo. 255^{r}.

[4] G. P. Cuttino, *English Diplomatic Administration, 1259–1339* (Oxford, 1940), pp. 19–83.

[5] *The Anglo-French Negotiations at Bruges, 1374–1377*, ed. E. Perroy (*Camden Miscellany xix*; Camden Third Series, lxxx, 1952), pp. vii–viii.

of the fourteenth century are not hard to find;[1] and there is some evidence of analysis made before 1400 of the cruces of Anglo-French diplomatic relations.[2] But still Jean Juvenal des Ursins could be called in, in 1444 and again in 1449,[3] to prepare a case for the French diplomats. An official memorandum, apparently of the early years of Charles VIII's reign, proposed that 'beaulx livres a perpetuel memoire pour estre mis tant en la Chambre des comptes que on Tresor des chartes' should be compiled, dealing with the king's rights in a number of other areas as well as with 'la querelle du roy a lencontre du roy Dangleterre'.[4] The three points which it raised had, in fact, already been dealt with in the highly competent treatise *Pourceque pluseurs* in 1464. Either this side of French diplomatic administration was in a perpetual muddle, or it had a perpetual mistrust of work prepared for its predecessors.

But the compilers of such material for the diplomats had, as investigators of the recent or the remote past, clearly an unrivalled opportunity in their access to its documentary sources. That the writers of the French texts based their arguments upon the documents—or at least that they hoped to give this impression—is abundantly clear. But in fact their use of them was strictly limited. Their views on the diplomatic problems of the fourteenth century were necessarily confined to official opinions. In 1390 a very convenient 'Memore abrege grossement de la matiere de la guerre dentre le roy de France et le roy Dangleterre' had been compiled, 'extrait des lettres et instructions sur ce faictes ou temps passe, lesquellez', its author added encouragingly, 'fauldroit veoir qui vouldroit veoir et bien clerement entendre tout le fait, qui ne pourroit pas estre comprins en si peu descripture comme est ceste

---

[1] Such collections survive as B.N., MSS fr. 2699, 15490 (fos 27^r–135^v; fos 43–135 are misbound: they should be read in the order fos 43–66, 123–135, 109–22, 67–108; some leaves are missing); MSS nouv. acq. fr. 6215, 6224; MS. Dupuy 306; B.R., MS. 10306–7.

[2] See below.

[3] According to a contemporary annotator of B. Arsenal, MS. 3731, p. 77, after the taking of Fougères 'charga le roy ledit Je[han] Juvenel des Urssins, lequel a fait ce prese[n]t traictie, de fere aucuns advertissemens pour savoir se il pourroit licitement fere guerre, non obstant les treves; lequel vint a Paris et vit la teneur des treves et envoya au roy environ dix articles pour monstrer clerement que licitement il pourroit fere guerre, se quil a fait, et quil ne devoit actendre a paix'.

[4] B.N., MS. fr. 4054, fos 241^r–243^r.

presente'.[1] To a certain extent the writers of the treatises took his advice: Jean de Montreuil, who was heavily indebted to the *Memore abrege grossement*, also made direct use at least of so well-known an example of its sources as the English *bille* of 1369 and the French reply;[2] and the memorandum itself was regularly found in conjunction with collections of diplomatic documents dealing with events both before and after the turn of the century.[3] To this extent the material for the official view of the diplomatic problems was almost too easily available. The documentary *preuves* of Jean Juvenal's *Traictie compendieux*[4] may have been derived directly from the royal archives; but a number could have been lifted from the repertories. Amongst the three clearly 'official' authors it was the compiler of *Pourceque pluseurs* who, in his discussion of the diplomatic relations between France and England in the five years leading up to 1449, made fullest use of documentary material. For evidence for the more remote past he and the other authors turned to more familiar material: to the chronicles and the abbreviations of the past.

Jean Juvenal's task in 1444, as he reminded Charles VII, was that he should have copies made of the documents relevant to the truce negotiations 'soubz seel auctenthicque et que je queisse toutez aultres choses servans a la matiere; laquelle chose . . . jay faicte', he added, 'ainsin, se cest vostre plaisir, que pourres veoir par ce que dessoubz est escript, ou jay mise ma petite ymagination en accumulant ce que jay trouve es croniquez et histoires anciennes'.[5] Jean de Montreuil seems to have set the fashion for an historical analysis of English rights in the *pays* of France. His description of the descent of Guyenne was based, as he admitted, primarily upon Aimon de Fleury and Guillaume de Nangis;[6] and it, in turn, was found a profitable source by later writers: Jean

---

[1] B.N., MS. nouv. acq. 6215, fos 32ʳ–43ᵛ. Other fifteenth-century copies of the mémoire survive in B.N., MS. fr. 15490; MS. Dupuy 306; B. Arsenal, MS. 2450; B.R., MS. 10306–7. It seems to have been fairly widely circulated: it was known, for instance, at St-Victor (B.N., MS. lat. 14663, fo. 277ʳ).

[2] Readily available in the *Grandes chroniques* (*Chronique des règnes de Jean II et de Charles V*, ed. R. Delachenal, ii (S.H.F., 1916), pp. 76–116).

[3] See above, p. 209, n. 1.

[4] These occupied nearly a half (fos 44ʳ–73ᵛ) of his text.

[5] *Traictie compendieux*, fo. 1ᵛ.

[6] 'French text', *La Cronique martinienne, op. cit.*, fo. 261ᵛ.

Juvenal des Ursins, in particular, borrowed it almost *verbatim*.[1] Guillaume de Nangis remained a principal source:[2] Robert Blondel's narrative was often little more than an envenomed paraphrase of his chronicle. But Blondel, like Jean Juvenal and like the author of *Pourceque pluseurs*,[3] had as well access to a number of other authorities. The comparatively brief narrative of the latter writers was based in fact, like that of William Worcester, upon 'divers cronicles' and 'many other historiall bookis of auctorite';[4] and too extended an analysis of its sources would be otiose. William Worcester's collections[5] alone demonstrate the range of chronicles and historical books major and minor upon which a determined propagandist might draw. Of more importance was the writers' treatment of them.

Each naturally asserted the irrefrangible authority both of his sources and of the analysis he derived from them. Dispute about the existence of the vital phrase in the Salic law gave Jean Juvenal a moment of unease;[6] but he and others could marshal references to copies of the text 'escripte de lettre tresancienne ou ladicte clause estoit et de ce faisoit mention expressement'.[7] Elsewhere he

---

[1] Probably from a copy of the 'Precursory text': *Audite celi que loquor*, fos 41^V–42^r; *Traictie compendieux*, fos 24^V–25^r.

[2] The author of *Apres la destruction de Troye la grant* drew upon his text extensively.

[3] The author of *Pourceque pluseurs* (fos 7^V–8^r; ed. Anstruther, p. 30) seems, for instance, to have derived his story of the bastardy of Philippa of Clarence from one of Sir John Fortescue's tracts on the Yorkist claim (*The Works of Sir John Fortescue*, ed. Lord Clermont (London, 1869), pp. 499, 517; Sir J. Fortescue, *The Governance of England*, ed. C. Plummer (Oxford, 1885), p. 354). In 1468 Fortescue delivered to Guillaume Juvenel des Ursins as chancellor of France 'ung grant memoire declaratif des drois que le roy Edouart pretend a la couronne Dangleterre et apres a la couronne de France, et par lequel, en oultre, il monstre que ledit roy Edouart ne peult aucune chose reclamer es dictes couronnes de France et Dangleterre et quil ny a aucun droit par les moyens quil recite et declaire ou dit memoire; lequel est en forme de livre [et] est devers mons^r le chancellier' (B.N., MS. fr. 6964, fo. 27^r; printed by J. Calmette et G. Périnelle, *Louis XI et l'Angleterre (1461–1483)* (Paris, 1930), p. 303).

[4] *The boke of noblesse*, fo. 11^V; ed. Nichols, p. 24.

[5] B.M., Cotton MS. Julius F.vii; Royal MS. 13 C.i; College of Arms Library, Arundel MS. 48.

[6] Viollet, *op. cit.*, p. 174.

[7] This particular copy was 'a Saint Savin, qui est une abbaye entre Le Blanc et Chauvigny' (*Traictie compendieux*, fo. 3^V). Geoffroy Vassal,

and the other French authors were, like William Worcester, rather careless about giving reference: the minute accuracy of the compiler of *Pour vraye congnoissance avoir* provides a striking contrast.[1] Both Jean Juvenal and the author of *Pourceque pluseurs* were prepared to deal with conflict between one source and another. But further criticism of their evidence was not to be expected of them, any more than it was from Robert Blondel. Cultivated literary men though they were, their treatment of the past was conditioned by their official purpose; their rapid raids upon its sources were made in order to rifle it of evidence with which to confound their enemies and convince their friends. The better of these authors handled their material competently in the manner of the compilers of the innumerable later medieval historical compendia. Their works, like these, were fashionable; but they were far more partisan.

Yet some of them remained popular long after their immediate purpose was served. The best of them, *Pourceque pluseurs,* was much reprinted in the sixteenth century;[2] it and others were much copied in manuscript until at least the eighteenth century.[3] The

---

archbishop of Vienne, drew the attention of Regnaud de Chartres and Christophe d'Harcourt to a copy 'ou monastere ou abbaye de Savigny en Poictou' which they thought to translate for Charles VII; and Gerard Machet knew of a copy in St-Rémy de Reims (Mirouer historial abregie, B.L., Bodley MS. 968, fo. 41[r–v]). Jean de Montreuil ('Precursory text', variant in B.N., MS. nouv. acq. fr. 12858, fo. 64[v]) and the author of *Pour vraye congnoissance avoir* (p. 36), perhaps following him, gave reference to a copy in 'tresanciens livres de Saint Denis'. The annotator of a fragment by Jean de Montreuil had seen 'ycelle loy en un ancien livre' and had discussed it possibly with Jean Chartier at St-Denis (B.R., MS. 10306–7, fo. 12[v]; *cf. Chronique de Richard Lescot*, ed. J. Lemoine (S.H.F., 1896), pp. xiv–xv).

[1] One example from many will perhaps suffice: Charles, count of Valois, he recorded, married as his third wife Mahaut de St-Pol, by whom he had a first-born son, Louis, who died aged seven on 2 Nov. 1328, 'comme il appert ou trente huitiesme feulliet du livre signe *B* estant en la ... Chambre [des comptes] et pareillement ou commancement du ... livre *Noster*. Neantmoins lepitaphe de sa sepulture estant aux Cordeliers a Paris, au pie de la sepulture de ladicte dame Mahault contesse de Valois sa mere, ou il gist, porte quil deceda ledit deuxieme jour de novembre lan mil trois cens vingt neuf, qui est ung an subsequent' (pp. 12–13).

[2] Potter, *op. cit.,* 249, n. 3.

[3] In the sixteenth century, B.N., MSS lat. 10921, fr. 17182; in the seventeenth century, B.N. MSS fr. 7079, 7144, 17969, 19001, 23364, nouv. acq. fr. 7006, Dupuy 105; B. Ste-Geneviève, MS. 794; B. Mun. Charolles,

case which these treatises contained had still to be defended, although the heat had long gone out of the battle. As far as their physical presence was concerned it might have been true that 'il n'est plus mot de ces Engloys couez';[1] but their moral presence remained, even though it became increasingly clearer that France was French and England English. The permanence of victory made valid for the French the 'national sentiment' the propagandists had so long asserted. The struggle between the kings of England and France had always been more than one over inheritance rights, set against a background of legal conflict between a magnate and his sovereign; it was one between two sovereigns and it could never have been settled finally except in terms of a 'national' war. Such a confrontation of the two countries thus conceived as a whole was bound to force men to think in terms of 'French' and 'English', to produce a semblance of 'national sentiment'; and the emotional propagandists hastened to fan the flames of patriotism and xenophobia. Victory made valid the anger and the lies; and victory, too, made valid for the French the case the more cerebral propagandists had produced. In their search for material in the past they emphasized far more than the chroniclers could an historical consciousness of the identity of the two countries. They forced their readers towards an historical perspective of that identity; they reinforced with reason the promptings of sentiment. The fleur-de-lis in the bellies of the French[2] was given a respectable ancestry; and in the quiet of victory the uncommitted in France could contemplate the historical justification for the Valois resistance to the Plantagenets. To this extent at least the more historiographically-minded propagandists contributed towards the formation of national mentalities in the fifteenth century.

MS. 5; B. Mun. Besançon, MS. Chiflet 74; B.M., Add. MS. 30664; in the eighteenth century, B.N., MS. nouv. acq. fr. 741; B.M., Add. MS. 12192, to give only a few examples.

[1] *Olivier Basselin et le Vau de Vire*, ed. A. Gasté (Paris, 1887), p. 105.

[2] 'Les ... Angloiz norent onques se plainement la duchie de Guienne ne la conte de Pontieu', wrote Jean de Montreuil, 'quilz neussent suspecon que les gens et habitans des pays neussent le cuer au roy de France, comme tres-souvent ilz leur reprouchoient, disans que tousjours avoient ilz la fleur de liz ou ventre ...' ('Precursory text', fo. 11ᵛ).

15

SIR JOHN FASTOLF'S LAWSUIT OVER
TITCHWELL 1448-55

WHEN Edmund Paston was at Clifford's Inn in the spring of 1445 he was firmly advised by his mother 'to thynkk onis of the daie of yowre fadris Counseyle to lerne the lawe for he seyde manie tymis that ho so euer schuld dwelle at Paston schulde have nede to Conne defende hymselfe'. In this much-quoted remark as in other opinions her sound and sensible husband, judge William Paston, was far from being original. The advice was at least two centuries old, if not older; the popularity of law-books for their estate managers in the thirteenth century is evidence of how many landlords then took it to heart.[1] A landowner's land was a permanent temptation for his neighbours; such legal knowledge in some degree was therefore vital to ·'m or to his stewards for its defence. More violent action was restricted, ·t wholly extinguished by twelfth-century legislation; but that legislation itself and later enactments provided new, more subtle and probably more certain ways of depriving an honest possessor of his property. And titles to land, complicated from the thirteenth century on by landowners' increasing employment of the entail and the use, gave in the later Middle Ages ample scope for the dexterous at law. Lawsuits on three manors bought on dubious and complicated titles nearly doubled their cost for an over-eager Sir John Fastolf in the middle of the fifteenth century. As Agnes Paston told Edmund her son and as an anonymous versifier told other potential landowners, it was as well to beware.[2]

'Jhesu as thou art heuen kyng', wrote the latter hopefully, 'Sende vs grace to haue knowyng.' For some the prayer was answered; for others it was not. The retired career soldier, Sir John Fastolf, was amongst the unlucky ones. His old age was vexed and his servants' ingenuity much exercised by his lack of knowledge; by his unfortunate habit of buying land for prestige purposes on titles perhaps even more defective than most were in the fifteenth century without a thorough investigation beforehand. Carelessness made his legal title weak; but a weak title was not the only hazard to his property. When his

[1] Dorothea Oschinsky, 'Mediaeval Treatises on Estate Management', *Economic History Review*, 2nd ser., VIII (1955–6), 296–309.

[2] [*The*] P[*aston*] L[*etters, A.D. 1422–1509*], ed. James Gairdner, 6 vols. (1904), II, 72; the versifier is best printed in [K.B.] McFarlane, ['The Investment of] Sir John Fastolf['s Profits of War'], *Transactions of the Royal Historical Society*, 5th ser., VII (1957), 112.

titles came to be challenged, it was not the law alone that was not on Fastolf's side; as he himself knew well, in the Norfolk of his time law went as it was favoured, and favour, too—the patronage of the great—was too often lacking. Against strong opponents under powerful patronage and with a title even as frail or frailer than his own Sir John's struggles were apt to be long ones and the results too often disappointing. Without law, without lordship, only luck remained for Sir John Fastolf. In one affair at least of which we know—that of Titchwell—he was probably luckier than he deserved to be. Its history illustrates extremely well the vexations of a fifteenth-century landowner and the trials of a group of gentleman administrators who managed his estates and ran his affairs. And one member of this group deserves especial notice. William Worcester's knowledge of law may have been small, but his knowledge outside the law was highly eclectic. His tastes ran to astronomy (at least in his early days), to medicine, to geography, to translating Cicero, to the history of Norfolk families and of the war in France. In the formidable literary circle around Sir John Fastolf his was not the least light. His experience of lawsuit business in France and in England sharpened his aptitude for collecting facts and gave him a knowledge and ability which made him the more useful to his employer. Many members of Fastolf's circle, as we shall see, collected pedigrees and archives in the course of their duties; but none save Worcester developed a mania for it and became an historian. His place in the history of the development of historical research has been recognised; and the work involved in the lawsuit over the manor of Titchwell is a good example of the kind of employment which formed his tastes. The interest of the Titchwell affair is therefore double; the complexities of the fifteenth-century lawsuit make clearer the figure of 'the first Englishman to deserve the name of antiquary'.[3]

The manor lies on the north coast of Norfolk, a third of the way from what is now New Hunstanton to Holkham and Wells-next-the-Sea. The property of a cadet branch of the Lovels of Titchmarsh in the thirteenth century, it remained in Lovel hands until the fifteenth. It was then worth some £20 a year.[4] When Sir John Fastolf bought the manor for £400 in 1431 from John Roys, the widower of apparently the last Lovel of Titchwell, Margery, who died without issue in 1424, he was paying a full and normal twenty-years'-purchase price for it.[5] The manor was no bargain. He probably imagined it

---

[3] [K.B.] McFarlane, 'William Worcester[: a Preliminary Survey'], *Studies Presented to Sir Hilary Jenkinson*, ed. J. Conway Davies (Oxford, 1957), 198. Cf. V. H. Galbraith, *Historical Research in Mediaeval England* (The Creighton Lecture in History, 1949 (1951)), 44–5.

[4] Its income in 1433–4 was £19. 7s. 11½d. ([Magdalen College Muniment Room,] F[astolf] P[apers] 9, m. 2). Even as a bad tenancy in 1470 'the whole manor' of Titchwell (possibly including a parcel called 'James' lands' worth £2 a year) could still be farmed for £20 ([Magdalen College Muniment Room,] T[itchwell] 60).

[5] A valor of 1444–5 gives the purchase price (F.P. 69, m. 2). A letter of Fastolf in 1450 mentions a quittance of Roys for the purchase of Titchwell (*P.L.* II, 188). The conveyancing was complicated, but the manor probably left Roys' possession in November 1431 (T. 34).

was held in fee simple; or, if he suspected a more complicated tenure, that any claimants to his title were unlikely to appear. Eager to acquire real estate with his surplus income, Fastolf thought Titchwell was a safe bet. He was mistaken. Some seventeen years after his purchase of the manor, on 30 October 1448, a royal inquisition was taken at Litcham in Norfolk on the status of Margery Roys' lands at her death. Its jurors' verdict challenged Fastolf's title to Titchwell radically. It alleged first that Margery, *née* Lovel, the wife of a Sir Edward Hull, and Agnes her sister, the wife of Thomas Wake esquire, were Margery Roys' heirs under an entail.[6] Fastolf's purchase from Margery Roys' husband was therefore improper. More immediately dangerous was the jurors' statement that Titchwell was held in chief and that Margery Roys had entered into her inheritance without the necessary formalities. For, as a result of this allegation, the manor, as that of a tenant-in-chief deceased, was seized into the king's hand. On 14 December Sir Edward Hull was granted the farm of the manor at the rent of ten marks a year, the net figure at which it had been tactfully undervalued by the inquisition.[7] Sir John Fastolf had been neatly excluded; his title by purchase from John Roys had been shown by the inquisition to be no proper title at all and he had been deprived of Titchwell before he had even had time to recoup the purchase price.

The hero of the Battle of the Herrings was not temperamentally inclined to allow his enemies victory so easily; and he was as loth to lose as he was certainly fain to purchase a fair manor. But he was now nearly seventy and a long sickness was soon to begin. For a number of other people than Sir Edward Hull his lands seemed easy prey and his ability to protect them diminishing. But if his grip on his affairs was loosening, if he was in fact declining into his dotage, like that other elderly soldier John Talbot, earl of Shrewsbury, Fastolf would still come out to fight, however unwisely. He might still be a formidable opponent. But so were his assailants: the people behind the taking of the inquest, the husbands of the alleged co-heiresses, Sir Edward Hull and Thomas Wake. Neither could be called a negligible adversary.

Edward Hull had the advantages of the courtier on his side. He was the child of two careerists in the royal circle, John Hull, king's esquire, and Eleanor, daughter and heir of Sir John Malet of Enmore in Somerset, servant to Queen Joan the consort of Henry IV.[8] Born probably about 1410, he married Margery Lovel some time before 1441.[9] By 1431 he had become a

---

[6] P[ublic] R[ecord] O[ffice,] C 139/131, no. 18. The text of the inquisition misnames Thomas Wake 'John'.

[7] C[alendar of] P[atent] R[olls] 1446-52, 210; C[alendar of] F[ine] R[olls] 1445-52, 105.

[8] John Hull was called king's esquire at least by 1415 (C[alendar of] C[lose] R[olls] 1413-19, 212). His wife was in Queen Joan's service at least by 1417 (C.P.R. 1416-22, 304).

[9] [J. C.] Wedgwood, [*History of Parliament, Biographies 1439-1509* (1936),] 481, gives the date of his birth and 1431 as the date of his marriage, both without authority. The first reference to Margery and Edward Hull together appears to be in November 1441 (C.C.R. 1441-47, 9-10). (Wedgwood's accounts of both Hull and Wake cannot unfortunately be used without the utmost caution.)

'henchman of the queen' and his career in turn at the Court had already begun.[10] By 1438 he was an esquire of the king's body.[11] In this favoured position he acquired pensions and grants; appointments as sheriff of Somerset and Dorset and to commissions in the west country were balanced by missions abroad; to Aquitaine especially.[12] In October 1442 he was ambassador with Thomas Beckington, the king's secretary, and Sir Robert Roos to the count of Armagnac on the delicate matter of Henry VI's marriage proposals to Armagnac's daughters.[13] From the beginning of the year at least he had been temporary 'Gouverneur del office de la Constabularie de Bourdeaux'; in the autumn he was appointed constable by the royal council of Guyenne.[14] The duties of the office were financial; the constable was second in importance only to the seneschal of Guyenne; he was formally appointed by the Crown and accountable only to the Exchequer in England. Hull, as was normal, was authorized to act when necessary by lieutenant; but it seems impossible to tell from his surviving accounts, except in the broadest terms, when he did so. In these records periods of an apparently unusual amount of activity by his principal lieutenant, George Swillington, seem to show he was in England rather more than usual in the period 1447–50; and when Bordeaux was in French hands between June 1451 and October 1452 Hull's duties naturally ceased.[15] But as an active and important royal officer he might be difficult to bring to law; and as the favour of the Crown increased he became the more powerful in attack as well as in defence. At the end of November 1443 he was made one of the feoffees of the duchy of Lancaster, a member of a tight circle of royal intimates.[16] About Christmas 1444 Hull was knighted and at Queen Margaret's coronation in 1445 he acted as a knight of the body.[17] More grants fell into his hands 'as for long service'. By November 1448 he was one of the queen's carvers.[18] It seems to have been he who from his advantageous position in the Court had, probably in the previous spring, planned the attack upon Sir John Fastolf's property.

His wife's brother-in-law, Thomas Wake, was less colourful. The son of Thomas Wake of Blisworth in Northamptonshire and Margaret, daughter of

[10] *Proceedings of the Privy Council*, ed. Harris Nicolas, IV (1835), 77.

[11] *C.P.R. 1436–41*, 232.

[12] *C.P.R. 1436–46*, *C.F.R. 1437–45, passim*; T. Carte, *Catalogue des rolles gascons, normans et françois*, 2 vols. (1743), II, 287; P.R.O. E 101/53/27.

[13] *Official Correspondence of Thomas Bekynton*, ed. G. Williams, 2 vols. (Rolls Series, 1872), II, 177–248.

[14] P.R.O. E 101/193/9, no. 6; E 364/84, m. 1.

[15] Hull's accounts are enrolled for the periods 17 Sept. 1442–Michaelmas 1446 (P.R.O. E 364/84), Michaelmas 1446–24 June 1451 (E 364/91), 20 Oct. 1452–18 July 1453 (E 364/92). Bundles of receipts, etc. remain in P.R.O. E 101/193/9–15. There are two strays in the B[ritish] M[useum] Harleian Charters 42 B 52, 53. George Swillington was a member of the Council of Guyenne and held important crown lands in the duchy (*Archives Historiques du Département de la Gironde*, XVI (Bordeaux, 1878), 281–3, 290, 363).

[16] R. Somerville, *History of the Duchy of Lancaster*, I (1953), 210.

[17] Wedgwood, 482.

[18] *C.P.R. 1446–52*, *C.F.R. 1445–52, passim*; called queen's carver *C.P.R. 1446–52*, 210.

Sir John Philpot, he was born about 1402. His father died before 1425, leaving him heir to the Wake inheritance. Older pedigrees called the younger Thomas 'The Great Wake'; why he deserved the title is not apparent.[19] His was a rather dull life of an influential country gentleman. Probably in 1432 he married Agnes Lovel; the next year he sat in Parliament for Northampton-shire and in 1434–5 was the county's sheriff. He continued to appear in Parliament, to act as sheriff and as justice of the peace in Northamptonshire and Somerset in the 1440's.[20] In the opposition to Sir John Fastolf over the Titchwell affair he was of much less importance than Hull: indeed, to be called 'one Wake' was as much recognition as Fastolf's council often gave him. For Sir Edward Hull, though landless, had more power through his connexions with the Court than the Great Wake of Blisworth. Wake, in fact, was a sleeping partner; it was Hull who carried through the successful assault on property Sir John Fastolf thought safe enough to pay a full market price for.

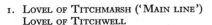

1. LOVEL OF TITCHMARSH ('MAIN LINE')
   LOVEL OF TITCHWELL

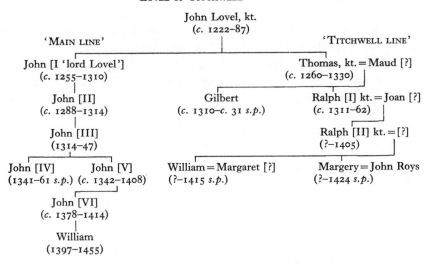

Fastolf had, in fact, not been careful enough. John Roys seems to have been rather a shady land-dealer, and judge William Paston had trouble with him in 1436.[21] The descent and title of the manor Roys sold to Fastolf was far from simple. Perhaps Roys himself knew little about the complications; perhaps he kept quiet about them; perhaps Fastolf had been over-optimistic about their danger. There were in fact two entails in the descent; though both had been interfered with, they were still a hazard, as Fastolf was to discover. In

[19] *Victoria County History of England, Northamptonshire Families*, ed. Oswald Barron (1906), 321.
[20] Ibid.; *C.P.R. 1436–52, C.F.R. 1437–52, passim*; Wedgwood, 913.
[21] *P.L.* II, 41–3. He assisted Fastolf over the purchase of a manor in Gorleston (near Great Yarmouth) in 1433–4 (F.P. 9, m. 5).

1270 Sir John Lovel of Titchmarsh had entailed Titchwell upon his younger son Thomas, who was then a minor, to hold of the Lovel main line with reversion to it.[22] This entail, made apparently without royal licence, was complicated by a further re-entailing in 1341. With the assent of the reversioners, John III 'lord Lovel' of the main line and perhaps his uncle William, a new tail special was created upon Ralph, Thomas Lovel's surviving son, his wife Joan and the heirs male of their bodies; with remainder to their right heirs.[23] Ralph died early in 1362 and Joan Lovel continued in possession under the entail.[24] She died before 1378; her son Ralph succeeded and died, in turn, in 1405.[25] Ralph II had two children, William, who died without issue perhaps at Agincourt, and Margery, who married John Roys and died in 1424.[26] The tail special of 1341 had been complicated but probably (according to the somewhat lax contemporary notions) not broken by enfeoffments apparently to uses of her brother and herself; and the widow of William Lovel, Margaret, had had dower in Titchwell (improperly, at any rate according to later views, as it was entailed land, but in this she was only following the example of her husband's great-grandmother who had had dower there in 1330).[27] Roys entered into possession of Titchwell either ignoring the entails or as a tenant by courtesy; if children were born to him and Margery certainly none survived, but Roys seems to have been secure in his possession of the manor. Though he acted questionably in making a permanent alienation of Titchwell by selling it to Sir John Fastolf, Hull and Wake as claimants under the entails

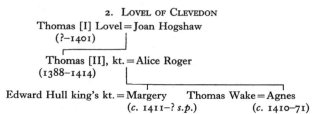

2. Lovel of Clevedon

Thomas [I] Lovel = Joan Hogshaw
(?–1401)

Thomas [II], kt. = Alice Roger
(1388–1414)

Edward Hull king's kt. = Margery   Thomas Wake = Agnes
(c. 1411–? s.p.)   (c. 1410–71)

[22] The original grant is undated (T. 203); the letters of attorney for delivery of seisin are dated 3 June 1270 (T. 174) and so is a notice of the gift to the inhabitants of Titchwell (T. 183).

[23] The grant is dated 3 May (T. 98).

[24] According to his inquisition *post mortem* Ralph died in February 1362 (C[alendar of] Inq[uisitions] P[ost] M[ortem], XI, 276). Joan conveyed her interest to feoffees in June 1363 (T. 66).

[25] Ralph II was in possession by April 1378 (T. 90). No inquisition *post mortem* seems to have been taken after his death; his will, dated June 1405, survives in Norwich Probate Registry, Reg. Harsyk, fo. 325. It was proved in July 1405.

[26] William was alleged to have been killed at Agincourt in a letter to Fastolf from three of his servants written on 12 Jan. 1449 (T. 158). This is now missing; I owe my knowledge of it to [W. D.] Macray['s manuscript catalogue of Magdalen College Muniments], Norfolk, III, 162. William was certainly at Agincourt in the retinue of the duke of Gloucester (Harris Nicolas, *The Battle of Agincourt* (1832), 334); and he was certainly dead by December 1418 (T. 46). The date of Margery's death is given in the 1448 inquisition as 6 Sept. 1424.

[27] The original deeds creating the uses are dated 21 June 1415 (T. 84) and 8 Dec. 1418 (T. 46). Mid-fifteenth century copies of both show that Fastolf's lawyers were interested in them (T. 156, 173). A deed giving Margaret and her second husband an annual rent as dower in Titchwell is dated 20 Sept. 1421 (T. 78); dower was assigned there to Matilda, widow of Thomas Lovel of Titchwell, on 23 Nov. 1330 (*C.C.R. 1330–33*, 393–5).

may have waited until he was dead before they attacked the purchaser; or possibly they may only later have discovered the existence of their claim.

Sir Edward Hull and Thomas Wake effectively asserted by the inquisition of October 1448 that the grandfather of their wives, Thomas Lovel of Milton Clevedon in Somerset, had been a brother of the second Ralph Lovel of Titchwell. He had died leaving his son Thomas II a minor; Thomas II in turn was the father of Margery Hull and Agnes Wake.[28] Under the entail of 1270 they were the remaindermen, as the next kin and heirs of Margery Lovel. This was the statement of their right to Titchwell. Hull based Agnes' and Margery's case on the first entail of 1270 either because his father-in-law, Thomas II Lovel of Clevedon, had in fact pre-deceased William Lovel of Titchwell (though the inquisition, by grossly underestimating the ages of his daughters, had made him long survive him) and he thought they had a weaker claim under the tail special of 1341; or because he or his agents were ignorant of this second entail. If in fact his view of the Lovel pedigree were true—if his wife's grandfather, Thomas I Lovel of Clevedon, were a younger brother of Ralph II Lovel of Titchwell—then Margery and Agnes seem to have had a claim under either entail in late medieval practice, despite all complications, re-entails, uses and dowers.

Hull acted by proceeding by inquisition in a rather roundabout, though perhaps not unusual way. And, apparently in alliance with that powerful and (to Fastolf at least) malignant figure in Norfolk politics of the mid-fifteenth century, John Heydon of Baconsthorpe, he had taken adequate precaution that the inquisition would be returned in his favour, though this, too, might be mere prudence on the part of an honest claimant.[29] According to Fastolf (whose understandable prejudice should be allowed for) some two years later, Thomas Shernborne, the escheator who supposedly took the inquisition, instructed his under-escheator, John Dalling, to 'forge' it; and Dalling, Fastolf said, 'cam to Castre [Fastolf's castle near Yarmouth] and ther seye myn evydence and than made the office therby'.[30] False inquisitions cost Fastolf dear on other manors than Titchwell, and Dalling, according to Fastolf, was something of an expert in making them.[31] Dalling had as an assistant a

---

[28] The date of Thomas I Lovel's birth is unknown; he married first, about 1387, Joan Hogshaw, co-heiress, with her sister Margaret wife of John Bluet, of their brother Edmund (who died in 1388), heir of their father Sir Thomas Hogshaw of Milstead in Kent and their maternal grandfather Sir Edmund Clevedon of Milton Clevedon; second, Eleanor widow of John Huntley of Adbeer in Somerset; and died on 11 Sept. 1401 (P.R.O. C 137/23, no. 34; E 149/79, no. 11). Thomas II was born on 23 April 1388 (C 137/77, no. 24); married by November 1410 Alice daughter of John Roger of Bridport (*C.P.R. 1408–13*, 273); and died on 10 Sept. 1414 (P.R.O. C 138/8, no. 30). His daughters Agnes and Margery were born about 1410 and 1411 (ibid.).

[29] See below, p. 222 For John Heydon see Wedgwood, 452–3; *P.L. passim*.

[30] B.M. Add. MS. 39848, fo. 17 (abstracted *P.L.* II, 233); *P.L.* II, 201–2.

[31] Lawsuits on the three manors of Titchwell, Beighton and Bradwell cost Fastolf £1085 in ten years: F.P. 42 contains details of the expenses. Dalling was alleged to have forged the Bradwell inquisition as well as that of Titchwell (*P.L.* II, 202).

William Willy, to whom, at least by the end of 1449, Hull was to sub-let Titchwell.[32] It was by his labour, two of Fastolf's servants, Thomas Howes and Geoffrey Sparling, informed their master about Christmas 1448, that the 'office' was taken.[33] Seals of jurors seem certainly to have been attached to the document, but whether they really gave a verdict is a dubious matter.

In getting an inquisition to recognize Agnes and Margery's right—even by having the inquisition 'forged'—Hull need only have been adopting the easiest method of securing that right in all honesty. But he could not succeed in getting them full possession of Titchwell. His plan had obviously been twofold: first to get the manor out of Fastolf's possession and into the king's hand by having it declared held in chief; then to sue it out of the king's hand and into the possession of his wife and his sister-in-law by having them declared Margery Roys' heirs under entail. But the most he could get was the under-valued farm. The first stage of his well-planned attack had succeeded; the second had not. For the land was caught in the king's hand by Fastolf's prompt counter-attack.

The inquisition had been returned into Chancery on 5 November; on 22 November Fastolf's feoffees entered a pleading there against it.[34] On 14 December Hull was farmed the manor; on 30 December a yeoman of his and young Willy—presumably William Willy's son—came riding down to Titchwell and gave Fastolf's farmers notice to quit.[35] When Thomas Howes and Geoffrey Sparling wrote to Fastolf after Christmas with the sad news that they had been unable to bribe Dalling, the under-escheator, into giving them a copy of the inquisition they were very much out of touch with affairs, for the pleading of 22 November had recited part of it. But their letter did at least tell Fastolf something of the politics of the matter. Dalling, they said, swore that as soon as the inquisition had been taken John Heydon had sent for him and made him promise to destroy all record of it and never under any circumstance to let Fastolf know its details. Fastolf's servants felt that Dalling had probably had a greater part in the affair than he admitted, but they do not seem to have doubted Heydon's interference.[36]

For such interference there was no remedy; Fastolf knew the impossibility of attacking Heydon, for, as he said, 'the world was allwey set after his Rule'.[37] But his remedy for the taking of the inquisition lay in law in the action of a traverse.[38] By 'traversing'—claiming erroneous—the actual facts of the

---

[32] As farmer under Hull Willy complained to Howes of Fastolf's interference in the manor about this time (T. 208). He is called Hull's deputy in F.P. 42, m. 3.

[33] Howes and Sparling to Fastolf (T. 41).

[34] Filed with P.R.O. C 139/131, no. 18.

[35] T. 41.

[36] Ibid.

[37] *P.L.* II, 137.

[38] Holdsworth, *History of English Law*, IX (1926), 24–6; Staunford, *The King's Prerogative* (1607), fos. 60r–70v; *Statutes of the Realm* (Record Commission Edition), I (1810), 368, 374–5 (Statutes 34 Edw. III c. 14, 36 Edw. III c. 13).

inquisition in Chancery Fastolf could, under statutes of Edward III, get the whole inquisition reviewed and, if he could prove his right, recover the manor. The action was theoretically a simple means of suing the crown, brought into existence by the need to check the misdeeds of fourteenth-century escheators. In the interval between producing good evidence in Chancery and securing a judgment he could be farmed the manor in Chancery. In fact, as we have seen, it was Sir Edward Hull who was farmed Titchwell, either by exercising influence on the Chancery masters or because Fastolf did in fact have very little good evidence for his right as it was challenged by the inquisition. Apparently he had been as careless of that most guarded and precious possession of a late medieval landowner, the 'evidences'—the deeds, the court-rolls, the transcripts of records from Chancery, the materials of long-settled lawsuits, anything in fact which might help to prove his title before a court of law—as he had been of what they might tell him about the complicated descent of the land he had purchased. The evidences seem to have been scattered; and in any case there were problems raised by the inquisition which probably not even the most perfectly kept titles could tell him. Sir John had therefore to discover the truth of the matter elsewhere. As it seemed to him about Christmas 1448, he had to prove, in order to traverse the inquisition, not only that Titchwell was not held in chief—a claim already made in November, together with the perfectly correct denial that Margery was not seized of the manor when she died (it was in fact in the hands of her feoffees)— but also that the true descent of the manor and of the Lovel family was not as the inquisition said; for obviously Sir Edward Hull's attorneys would force Fastolf to deal with this point during the pleadings. The prospect of suing the Crown was always an unpleasant one, and the task was complicated by the fact that his opponent was a powerful king's knight who could if necessary delay Fastolf interminably.

Fastolf's lawyers continued the action in Chancery in January 1449.[39] By the middle of the same month his servants had begun to gather facts. The discovery of the truth of the matter needed considerable research and considerable sifting of the various pieces of evidence such research provided. Neither of these occupations, nor the final production of at least a plausible synthesis for the pleadings, was unusual to the circle of administrators around their much-beleaguered master. He himself seems to have directed them from the beginning in a somewhat confused and muddling way. But one of the first necessities was quite clear: finding out more about the Lovels. In the middle of January a letter to Fastolf from Howes and others mentioned William Lovel killed at Agincourt, the will of the elder Ralph Lovel, whose wife Joan was the widow of Thomas Fastolf and who died in '1361', and the

---

[39] The chronology of the lawsuit depends on F.P. 42, as no pleadings save the initial and final ones seem to survive. Its dating is perhaps rather casual; and there is an inactive year from autumn 1449 to autumn 1450. (No membrane of the manuscript is missing.)

will of the second Ralph, father to William.[40] Soon evidence appeared which allowed him to speculate on possible flaws in the inquisition's argument. He wrote to Howes and his colleagues that by the evidence of the second entail of 1341—a copy of which he now obviously had—William Lovel was the last of the entail, while Hull claimed that Thomas the second Lovel of Clevedon was the last of the male stock.[41] Hull never claimed that Thomas II Lovel should have held under the tail special after William, but Fastolf thought he had; thinking in terms of the 1341 entail rather than of the 1270 entail under which Hull claimed, Fastolf imagined Thomas Lovel could not have existed under it, for if he had he should have held the manor: this was quite true. And William Lovel, Fastolf thought, should, by the entail of 1341, have held the manor in fee simple. If in fact Margery Roys had been a reversioner rather than a re-mainderman this would have been true of her tenure of the manor rather than her brother's, but clearly Fastolf was muddled. Fastolf's cunning, like that of his servant William Worcester, did not know much what the law meant.[42] He admitted almost as much: 'I praye ʒow', he wrote to Howes and the others, 'comon hereof saddely to Grene', who was one of his legal counsellors and paid a fee to deal with such complexities.

Before Green could deal with the matter, Fastolf pointed out more sensibly to them, 'ʒe must have wysely the pedegre from Rauf downward to whom the tayle was nowe to &c and wheder ther were any Thomas shethe that Rauf as they have alegged or nought &c and also that ʒe wele serche the Cort roll sethe Edwardes dayes how many lordes haue be ther for at ther entre the names of the lordes but put in evyry corte roll as the forme is I praye ʒow send me alle the names and in what kynges tyme þei were'. By now Fastolf had searched his own evidences; he had found out from them at least that William Lovel had died without issue and that Margaret his widow, who had married John Fastolf of Olton, had had dower in Titchwell (in another letter he asked Howes why, for this questionable behaviour might presumably cast doubt on the validity of the entails).[43] Margaret's second husband, Fastolf thought, had probably had the chief deeds of the manor to secure the payment of the dower and had probably kept them. It was inefficient of Fastolf to have bought the manor without them in the first place and now Howes was asked to set someone on to tracking them down.

---

[40] Howes, Shipdam and Sparling to Fastolf, 12 Jan. 1449 (T. 158, now missing; Macray, Norfolk, III, 162).

[41] Fastolf to Howes, Cole and Shipdam, undated ([Magdalen College Muniment Room, Adds. 99 (the] L[ovel] P[apers),] 23). T. 14 is Fastolf's copy of the entail; the point he makes here is noted on it.

[42] 'I knew neuere of oyer ne terminer', wrote Worcester to John Paston at one time, 'ne rad neuere patent before ne my maister [Fastolf] knew neuere the condyt of such thyngs; and when he wrote of hys grevonse to hys frendys he commaunded no man to be endyted for he wyst not whate belonged to such thyngs ne the parson [Sir Thomas Howes] neyther but remitted it to hys councell lerned' (*P.L.* III, 105).

[43] Fastolf to Howes, undated (T. 170, now missing; Macray, Norfolk, III, 164).

In February, it seems, the suit had been got under way. Fastolf's lawyers, Ralph Pole, Thomas de la Rue and Nicholas Girlington, received fees and encouraging breakfasts, John Vampage 6s. 8d. for 'expediting' matters; 3d. was spent on wine for Girlington while he discussed the traverse. On 27 January a crowd of lawyers had received fees and 1s. 9d. had been spent in the tavern. Expenses continued into February. A half-mark was paid to William Wayt, the clerk of justice Yelverton of King's Bench, 'for friendship in the matter of Titchwell'. The legal side of the affair seems to have been well in progress.[44]

The research work necessary to produce evidence for the suit continued. Fastolf's servants were as active and as knowledgeable of their sources as later tracers of the descents of medieval manors. They began searches in the royal archives, to find out anything about the Lovels of Titchwell, about the lords of Titchwell and about the status of the manor. In January Thomas Ricolf was paid 8d. for searching 'knight's fees' to find out of whom the manor was held, and the clerk of Thorp of the Exchequer received a half-mark for searching through 'writs of liberation after *diem clausit extremum*' of the Lovels from Edward III and Richard II to the present day. The sum of 2s. 2d. was spent 'apud le Rolles' to find the names of feoffees. In February the clerk of the Tower of London had a fee of 2s. 8d. for a search of inquisitions *post mortem* of the lords of Titchwell. A half-mark was spent in scrutinizing Domesday book (it went to Stoker of the Receipt of the Exchequer), but the clerks keeping the rolls of Chancery had only 11d. for their pains during a search of their charges. Henry Windsor of Chancery went through the inquisitions concerning the manor, with the help of the Chancery clerks. The pleas of the Lovels were hunted for 'ad sciendam geanologiam eorum'.[45] The results, neatly written out, were brought to Fastolf's council. Dusty hours spent *apud le Rolles* were as profitable then as now. Copies of writs and inquisitions and enrolled grants and distant pleadings and recorded knowledge as far back as 1086 piled up in Fastolf's London inn, neatly tied together in bundled files, ready for interpretation. On the back of more complicated documents a neat synopsis was written, to assist the arduous process.[46]

To the files of record material came files of local information. The possibilities of Norfolk do not seem to have required the exercise of the talents of Fastolf's servants as much as those of the west country. It was here that the person about whom it was most important to find out—Thomas I Lovel of Clevedon, the grandfather of Margery Hull and Agnes Wake—had had his chief seat near Bruton in Somerset. It was here that William Worcester, that most remarkable person in the group of Fastolf's administrators, was, in this lawsuit, particularly concerned.

[44] F.P. 42, m. 2.   [45] Ibid.
[46] On the files survive clear and accurate extracts from the Feudal Aids (L.P. 9–11), a copy of the inquisition *post mortem* of Sir Edmund Clevedon, the grandfather of Thomas I Lovel of Clevedon's wife (L.P. 15) and a copy of a writ to the sheriff of Worcester which has endorsed a note of its genealogical content (L.P. 17).

In April or early May 1449 he was sent off to Somerset to find out what he could; but little evidence, unfortunately, survives of his expedition.[47] When he returned to London a friend of his in Bristol, John Crop, carried on his investigation for him and two long letters show how busily he did so.[48] After negotiating (not too successfully) matters on the lawsuit with Sir Nichol of Glastonbury, he went on next day to Wells, where Edmund Waxchandler told him that Sir Thomas Lovel's father was a squire, and had a son died at Bryanston, and Crop should go there and find old John Roger, who would tell him much more than Waxchandler could. Then Crop went on to Clevedon, where a 'stainer' he took with him copied the arms of the lord of Clevedon and his wife, while Crop wrote down the inscription on their tomb. The coat of arms, neatly tricked, survives on the file; but Crop's copy of the inscription unfortunately does not and neither, now, does its original.[49] Crop then returned to Glastonbury and had intended to go by Blandford and Bruton to speak with old John Roger (who was perhaps an uncle of Margery Hull and Agnes Wake). But, he wrote to Worcester hurriedly, he promised to tell him all these matters as soon as he could in another report. Too much time had been taken in this one in writing of Mr Ralph Hoby's delivery to Crop of 'the copye of Wallens de vita & doctrina philosoforum Also the queiere of Oved de vetula de remedio moris de Arte amandi & of the verse vpon Boicius'.

Crop's second letter showed that Glastonbury had proved a blank. Sir Nichol had said that inquisitions were not kept in the abbey longer than six years. Dan Thomas Brabant had made him welcome and inquired of Dan Hugh Forster and the abbot's carver for him concerning Lovel evidences; keeping the matter quiet meant working slowly and after some delay Brabant promised to send anything he found to Crop at Bristol. Crop then went to Wells and from Wells to Frome, where he inquired of aged men. 'One seid me', he wrote, 'that there was a Shere thorsday was xxxvij wynters that the lorde Lovel made a sawte aʒenst Frome and that same lord had ij doughtris that one doughter was weddid to Sir Ric. Stafford and the other doughter was weddid to Sir Iames of Vrmoth. And the yong lord Talbot weddid Sir Iames of Vrmowthis sister but where that lord deyed they couth tel me no redy trouth'.[50] From Frome Crop went to Mells and on the way he met a baker who used to live in Glastonbury who told him there was once a lord called

[47] F.P. 42, m. 2.

[48] L.P. 21, 22.

[49] Four coats of arms of Lovel and one of Clevedon remain amongst the Lovel Papers; for a description of the tomb see *Proceedings of the Somersetshire Archaeological and Natural History Society*, LXXI (1925), 51–2. As Crop said the tomb was a knight's it is presumably that of Thomas II Lovel. (Despite some confusion it seems clear that he was knighted, while his father remained an esquire (P.R.O. C 137/77, no. 24, C 138/8, no. 30).)

[50] A niece of John VI lord Lovel (who died in 1414) married as her second husband Sir Richard Stafford, and her daughter Avice married James Butler 5th earl of Ormond and died in 1456 (G. E. C[ockayne, *The Complete Peerage*, revised and ed. Gibbs, Doubleday, Howard de Walden and White (1910–),] II, 361–2). John Talbot later 2nd earl of Shrewsbury certainly married Elizabeth Butler, the latter's sister, about 1444–5 (G.E.C. XI, 705).

lord Lovel the Rich, who had two daughters, one of whom married Sir Guy Brian, and died at some (unknown) place in Gloucestershire.[51] The well-meaning Crop was as confused as his readers must have been by this time. 'And in euery place where that y laboured for this seid mater', he wrote in perplexity, 'y myght not fynde iij men ne ij men yn one tale but euery man haue dyuers talis and so y wote neuer after whom to wryte the redy trouth'. Wearily Crop promised to try again, to go and see Roger at Bridport, and inquire at Castle Cary, Northbarrow, Southbarrow, Blackford and other places. He probably did; but here our knowledge of this engaging character ends.

As a Bristol man Worcester had local connexions his colleagues lacked. But not all: Henry Filongley, by now probably keeper of the writs of the court of Common Pleas, Fastolf's kinsman and probably his most experienced counsellor, had an acquaintance in Churchill near Axbridge.[52] John Austell was probably nearing fifty and anxious to please; but his reply to Filongley's inquiries was not very helpful.[53]

Right worshipfull & entyer belouyd Soone [he wrote on 14 January 1450],...y haue receyued a lettre of yourys willyng me to sende the pedygre of Sir Thomas Lovell to you. So helpe me God & Holydome y wote nere where hit ys become. Wherfore this ij dayes y shalle make a serche amonge all the evidence that y haue to fynnde hit. And yf y fynnde hit not y shalle ryde to my lady Dynham that was doughter to the worthi lord Lovell in kynge Richardys daye and to haue the informacion of hir and so to sende hit you. And as towchand Sir Thomas Lovell of Clevedon y shalle do enquere and sende you worde.[54]

But in other directions the search was more successful—perhaps too successful. England seemed swarming with Lovels, as John Crop had discovered, and answers to the problem of their genealogy varied considerably. From the beginning red herrings were scattered thickly on the trail. James and Richard Lovel, lords of Castle Cary; a Sir John Lovel of 'Lillington' in Buckingham, who had livelihood in Friday Street, London; a Sir Ralph Lovel who lived in Norfolk, kin of lord Lovel: all confused the issue.[55] One of Worcester's contributions (an interesting list of John V lord Lovel's children) had appended a long catalogue of possible clues which ought to be investigated and of people

[51] Possibly the Guy Brian who died in 1386, leaving a wife Alice, of now unknown parentage (G.E.C. II, 362). Her father could have been John III or John V lord Lovel (G.E.C. VIII, 218–21). It is also possible the baker's memory was no better than the aged men's and he was being confused by the fact that John V lord Lovel's son Robert married Elizabeth granddaughter and co-heiress of Guy lord Brian (ibid. 221).

[52] Margaret Hastings, *The Court of Common Pleas in Fifteenth Century England* (Cornell, 1947), 277; *P.L.* III, 138.

[53] For John Austell see Wedgwood, 30.

[54] L.P. 7. G.E.C. IV, 376 is probably wrong in making Philippa Dinham the daughter of John VI rather than John V lord Lovel.

[55] L.P. 8.

to ask about them.[56] Edson of Kenn, ten miles from Bristol, knew the genea-logy of Thomas Lovel; so did Moorcock of Clopton. A Spencer, who lived at Frampton, between Hook and Dorchester, knew about Robert Lovel esquire who lived at Rampisham a mile from Hook. Some Lovels (a John Lovel esquire of Wincanton, four miles the Shaftesbury side of Mere, for instance) were not kin of lord Lovel. There was a Lovel tomb at Mere. John, lord Lovel of Minster Lovel, Titchmarsh and Elcombe, adopted new arms (on a field *or* three fetterlocks) in 1400. John Lovel, knight, was a relative of lord Lovel, was of 'Lilly' in Buckinghamshire and had issue Roger, who was with the duke of Clarence and had a house in London; Thomas Chamber was his half-brother. William Worcester's delight in miscellaneous detail was only too obvious.

It was not allowed to pull the progress of research too awry. Guessing wildly at putative parents of Thomas I Lovel of Clevedon could lead only to despair; the answer was to be found in working from Thomas himself. When some connexions of his had been verified his stepson, Thomas Huntley, still alive, was questioned by a messenger of Filongley, provided with a list of questions.[57] By this time—probably over a year since their investigations began—Fastolf's servants had developed several precise theories about the parentage of Thomas I.[58] Who could he possibly be, they wondered, if he was not a younger brother of Ralph II Lovel of Titchwell? One of their theories made him the youngest son of the Great Lord Lovel, John V of the main line of Lovels of Titchmarsh and Minster Lovel. A second made him a bastard, again probably of John V lord Lovel. In this matter knowledge of Lovel arms seemed to gain for the Fastolf group increasing importance. Filongley's messenger was instructed to ask Huntley about Thomas I Lovel's will and whether he bore a bend or a baton in his arms; and to inquire of Lady Dinham, of any other old person with possibly a long memory, and round about Bruton. Huntley replied that he would look for a copy of Thomas Lovel's will; that Thomas Lovel bore a bend, not a baton, in his arms; con-fusingly, that he did not know who old Sir Thomas Lovel's father was, but that he did know he himself was a brother of the old lord Lovel (John V, the Great Lord); and he married Bluet's sister or daughter and had issue Ralph who died and Thomas, and Thomas had issue Thomas the last, and Thomas the father was not a bastard. As eager to help as John Austell, he told the Fastolf group much it already knew and also, more usefully, had produced a

---

[56] L.P. 2. Although he identified correctly John (later VI lord Lovel), Ralph, canon of Salisbury and rector of Stanton Harcourt, Thomas (who probably died young), Maud abbess of Romsey, an anonymous Minoress in London, and Philippa lady Dinham, he left out at least the Robert who married Elizabeth Brian and lived at Rampisham, although he mentioned his existence in the same document.

[57] His father John Huntley died in 1376 (*C.F.R. 1369–77*, 376) and he himself, well over eighty, in 1460 (ibid. *1452–61*, 246–7). The list of questions is now L.P. 13.

[58] These appear in their notes and lists of questions, especially L.P. 3, 8 and 13.

third theory for it: that the first Thomas was in some way a son or perhaps nephew of the Great Lord Lovel.[59]

But despite Filongley's methodical approach to the problem, despite all the evidence which poured in (and not a little thanks to its confusion) the theories remained unproven. Fastolf's servants could still only guess at the parentage of Thomas I Lovel. He held no land in his own right. Testimony, correctly, was against their first theory—that he was a son of John V lord Lovel, though Fastolf seems to have stuck doggedly to this view.[60] The hope that he was a bastard seems to have been abandoned, probably as a result of Huntley's testimony. Filongley apparently developed an opinion which modified Huntley's version and made Thomas I the son of a brother of the Great Lord Lovel, also called John.[61] This was perhaps a mistake. It was obviously an attempt to eradicate Huntley's extra Thomas Lovel by removing the eldest one and re-naming him John. No trace of Huntley's extra generation between Thomas I and Thomas II Lovel can be found; but one piece of evidence certainly alleged that Thomas I Lovel was over sixty when he died (though this makes his age at first marriage over forty).[62] If he was over sixty he could possibly have been a younger son of John III lord Lovel who died in 1347, though no one in the Fastolf circle seems to have taken this view. Given the confusion of Huntley's evidence, this was understandable. But it seems the most likely solution to the problem, though this in fact remains as insoluble today as it was in the fifteenth century. The Lovels of Clevedon certainly bore the same arms as those of Titchwell; but there all immediate relationship seems to end. Connexions between the Lovel main line (whose arms, except for a bend difference, were of course the same) and the Clevedon Lovels seem to have been closer. Probably John VI lord Lovel, for instance, and Robert his brother were feoffees with Thomas II of Clevedon, his wife Alice Roger and members of her family in Bryanston in an entail created for Thomas and Alice's heirs in 1410.[63] Any connexion between the Clevedon Lovels and any other Lovel family than that of Titchmarsh may probably be dismissed. Thomas I Lovel of Milton Clevedon may have been a bastard son, or a brother or nephew legitimate or illegitimate of John V lord Lovel (and enough witnesses said he was some kin of him) but that he was the son of

[59] L.P. 12. He followed Filongley's messenger with a letter offering all the help he could (L.P. 16). It seems probable that at some time after this Worcester was sent down to Somerset again to bring him up to London for further interrogation (F.P. 72, m. 8).

[60] L.P. 3 (an opinion marked 'F'). John V lord Lovel did have a son called Thomas, but he was still alive in 1409 (*C.C.R. 1409–13*, 75) and Thomas I Lovel of Clevedon died in 1401. At least one witness pointed out that the former Thomas was irrelevant (L.P. 8).

[61] L.P. 3 (an opinion marked 'HF'); L.P. 1(b), 4. John V's brother, John IV lord Lovel, died at least without legitimate children in 1361.

[62] L.P. 2.

[63] *C.P.R. 1408–13*, 273. Ralph II Lovel of Titchwell and Thomas I Lovel of Clevedon may have been together with John V lord Lovel in Ireland in the 1380's and 1390's (*C.P.R. 1377–81*, 409; ibid. *1391–96*, 486; ibid. *1396–99*, 571); if this was family solidarity it may have given Sir Edward Hull such clues as he had about the Titchwell Lovels.

Ralph I Lovel of Titchwell, as Sir Edward Hull and Thomas Wake claimed, is unlikely. The probability is, in fact, that Hull and Wake were, if not lying, guessing their wives' family history at least as hopefully as Sir John Fastolf was in the opposite direction.

But guessing was little help to Fastolf, for Hull and Wake had a great advantage in the guessing game: the burden of disproving the verdict of the 1448 inquisition was on him and the problem baffled him. The most Fastolf seems to have been able to do was to assert the pedigree of Margery Roys from Thomas Lovel of Titchwell her great-grandfather downwards with a flat denial of the connexion of Thomas I Lovel of Milton Clevedon with this pedigree at all. As much detail as possible was entered to bolster out Margery's genealogy.[64] More Fastolf's servants could not prove. Presumably on this point of the pleading Fastolf's only hope was to make the other side produce more evidence if it could. The Lovel pedigree had therefore proved an insuperable difficulty for him. And the entails of 1270 and 1341 had always been so. Little could be done to contest them. After his first rather wild thoughts on the subject Fastolf seems to have abandoned any attempt at challenging either; he was probably wise. It was a much easier matter to prove that the manor was not held in chief. The very deed creating the first tail general of 1270 was evidence that this was so and there was more besides. The problem had arisen before, and an inquisition taken in 1336 showed that the manor was held of the Lovel main line by Ralph I of Titchwell.[65] But Sir Edward Hull's view neither of the pedigrees nor of the entails could be contested, and Fastolf's case faltered.

The suit dragged on interminably; pleas were put in apparently fruitlessly. In the autumn of 1450 Fastolf planned to take a 'special assize' at least for one of his affairs at that time—that of Hickling—with John Paston; but Paston failed to sue this out, and Fastolf seems to have determined to try traversing the three inquisitions of Titchwell, Beighton and Bradwell again in Hilary term 1451.[66] He seems at the same time to have thought of the possibilities of a suit of conspiracy in the collusive nature of the taking of the 1448 inquisition. Towards the end of 1450 Nicholas Bocking, a servant now apparently retired from his service, was riding about Norfolk trying to persuade the jurors of the 1448 inquisition to 'tell the truth' about the 'false conspiracy' of the forging of that inquisition by Willy and John Dalling.[67] By 11 November Bocking had succeeded: a certificate had been procured and Fastolf's only concern was to get it sealed quickly, 'for taryeng drawyth

---

[64] Drafts for pleadings, undated (T. 198).

[65] *C. Inq. P.M.* VIII, 2–3; *C.C.R. 1333–37*, 563. This inquisition was much copied by Fastolf's servants (T. 1, 140, 194). A note on T. 1 shows that Fastolf thought it important and wondered if his lawyers did too. (He had had it exemplified under the Great Seal on 23 Aug. 1455, during the final proceedings (T. 30).)

[66] *P.L.* II, 199, 168.

[67] F.P. 42, m. 3.

parell', he wrote, 'And it wolle ease myne hert gretely that it may be sped and be a grete evidense to Recuuere my maner ayen'.[68] On 15 November this was done.

The group of jurors attached their seals with Bocking's to a document in which they denied they had ever sealed the inquisition of 1448.[69] With this evidence Fastolf seems to have planned to attack the agents of Sir Edward Hull at the Lynn session of the current Norfolk *oyer and terminer* on 13 January 1451.[70] On 23 November Howes and his colleagues were warned not to forget 'Wyllie &cis for Tychewell enquest forgyng'.[71] His case, Fastolf seems to have thought, would be the stronger if Dalling told the truth too. On 20 December he wondered if the under-escheator could be conveniently kidnapped, taken to Caister 'bethout damage of hys bodye and there to be kept yn hold that he may confesse the trouth of the fals office he forged off my maner of Tychewell'.[72] Fastolf's letters and choice of epithets at this time betray only too clearly that Dalling was, as he said, 'sore at my stomak'; he was insistent that Dalling should be pursued to the utmost and made to confess to the commissioners of *oyer and terminer*.[73] But Dalling escaped the Lynn session and by April 1451 Fastolf was almost beaten.

Item as to Fals Dallyng [he wrote to Howes at Caister] I veele well hys obstinat wille in hys vntrouth. And they it so be ye can not ghete wrytyng nethyr syght of lettres of hym I pray you to wryte vnto my trusty frend Nicholas Bokkyng that as y am credible lerned may meoffe and onle hym moost of onye man in Norffolk so thanne that the seid Bokkyng may take a labour for me at thys tyme to speke wyth Dallyng and entreete hym in hys best maner by all the weyes that he canne to have wrytyng or the lettres that were sent to hym by Sharbourn to forge that office. And y shall reward hym well for hys labour & cost. He qwyt hym full well in the mater certyfyeng by the jure named in the office and so I doubt not but he wolle in thys and ye labour to hym on my behalf.[74]

But the golden-tongued Bocking's best manner did not succeed. Dalling could not be caught; neither could Sir Edward Hull. Fastolf's traverse (if he brought it) seems to have gone no better. The Chancery seems still to have been unmoved by his lawyers; in law and in favour Hull was in too powerful and protected a position. Draft offers of arbitration made probably about this time show Fastolf on thoroughly uncomfortable ground. One maintained that 'forasmoch [as] he ys aged & feble he wold not cause no vexacion ne trouble'.[75] According to the other 'Fastolf knowyth well that [Hull and

---

[68] B.M. Add. MS. 39848, fo. 9 (abstracted *P.L.* II, 188–9).

[69] T. 83.

[70] *P.L.* II, 201.

[71] MS. in the possession of K. B. McFarlane, esq. (abstracted *P.L.* III, 191).

[72] *P.L.* II, 200.

[73] B.M. Add. MS. 39848, fo. 15 (abstracted *P.L.* II, 212). The jurors of the 1448 inquisition were also to certify before the commissioners (ibid. II, 201).

[74] B.M. Add. MS. 39848, fo. 17 (abstracted *P.L.* II, 233).

[75] T. 212.

Wake]...bee men of worshyp and of concience and supposith that they wold desyre no manys goode but that they hafe ryghtfull title vntoo and also that the said Fastolf for hys part woold eschew to put ony man in trouble or vexacion'.[76] Despite the labours of his servants Fastolf was still uncertain of his title, uncertain of the Lovel pedigree, uncertain of his chance in pleading against a king's knight. For his arbitrators Fastolf chose lord Cromwell and lord Beauchamp. The arbitration probably never took place: Hull, like Dalling, had no need to be blandished. In any case he seems to have been left in peace as farmer of Titchwell. A loan of £40 to the Crown to get the farm of the manor out of Hull's hands had failed in its purpose at the end of 1450 and Fastolf was having difficulty in getting this back, too.[77] At last, as at another battle, Fastolf seems to have preferred discretion to valour. In the end he knew how to cut his losses: 'be hardy', he would tell young nobles and soldiers seated at his feet in the old days in France, 'but don't be foolhardy'; and this advice came well from the captain whose troops had lived to fight again after the battle of Patay and who had had his view upheld against a not unnaturally aggrieved commander.[78] Sir John would be hardy but not fool-hardy; if he tended to be rash in the purchasing of manors, if sickness and old age made his temper uncertain, his strategy in lawsuits lack precision and his tactics unsound, they might also lead in the end to caution and weariness with the battle. Aged indeed, sick and much troubled, by the middle of 1451 he seems to have given in. The manor of Titchwell was apparently lost to him for ever.

For Sir Edward Hull, the constable of Bordeaux, commissions, royal favour and grants had continued.[79] In June 1451 he and his mother Eleanor granted a survivorship life-interest they possessed in a royal annuity of fifty marks from the abbot and convent of St Albans to Eton College.[80] The king had already granted his reversion to Eton in 1445. If the Hulls' grant was a *douceur* to the Crown over the Titchwell affair alone, it was an expensive one. In the summer of 1452, having prudently made his will, Hull sailed with Talbot to recover Aquitaine from the French.[81] He never returned home. In May 1453 he was elected a knight of the Garter *in absentia*; but Sir John Fastolf's new colleague was never installed.[82] Two months later Sir Edward

---

[76] T. 19.

[77] F.P. 42, m. 3.

[78] For Fastolf's views see Worcester's note in *The Boke of Noblesse*, ed. J. G. Nichols (Roxburghe Club, 1860), 64–5; for the trouble they caused him see the *Dictionary of National Biography*, VI, 1099–1104, and McFarlane, 'William Worcester', 200.

[79] *C.P.R. 1446–61*, *C.F.R. 1445–52*, *passim*.

[80] *C.P.R. 1446–52*, 429.

[81] His will was made on 26 Aug. ([*The*] *Reg[ister of Thomas*] *Bekynton*, ed. H. C. Maxwell-Lyte and M. C. B. Dawes, Somerset Record Society, 49–50 (1934–5), I, 224); for details of his voyage to Aquitaine see *C.P.R. 1452–61*, 108.

[82] J. Anstis, *The Order of the Garter*, 2 vols. (1724), II, 150–1. He had failed to be elected in 1449 (ibid. 143).

Hull was killed before Castillon, with Talbot and his son the lord Lisle, in the last battle of the Hundred Years War.[83]

Fastolf was swift to take advantage of this unexpected stroke of good fortune. On 14 September he was granted the keeping of Titchwell.[84] Hull had kept him out long enough. It was fortunate for him, too, that Hull had neglected or been still unable to sue the manor out of the king's hand. It would have been much more difficult for Fastolf to extract it from the Lovel co-heiresses if they had in fact been in possession of the property. As it was, he still had to traverse the inquisition of 1448 in order to raise the king's hand; but with Hull safely dead this was apparently an easier matter. Thomas Wake does not seem to have made any move to hinder him, but the affair still took some time. Not until Michaelmas term 1454, apparently, was money being paid out in pleadings, but by 1455 the fictitious action necessary had been planned.[85] Filongley and Jenney, both of Fastolf's council, were first intended as men of straw; but it was Hugh Fenn, another of his servants, who finally was committed Titchwell, at the cost of a twenty pence increment on Fastolf's ten-mark farm, on 12 February.[86] By Michaelmas term 1455 the matter was settled. The case began in Chancery on 15 May, in Easter term. Fastolf traversed the whole inquisition of 1448 and claimed a recovery. The case proceeded, Fenn, as had been planned, defaulted and the Norfolk jury found for Fastolf on all his points. These included now not only a denial that Titch-well was held in chief, but also an outright denial that the original entail by John Lovel of Titchmarsh and Titchwell in 1270 had ever been made. The manor was held by Fastolf directly of William lord Lovel, the chief lord of the fee.[87] The complicated conveyancing during Roys' sale to Fastolf in 1431 allowed him to ignore any connexion his title had with that of the Lovels of Titchwell. If they really had a claim Agnes Wake and her widowed sister were as neatly excluded as Fastolf himself had been by her brother-in-law; and so were the possible reversioners. The genealogical problem, the problem of the entails, were both avoided. In its end as in its beginning the Titchwell affair was not based on right. Fastolf's attempt to discover the truth, by the

---

[83] Wedgwood's emendation of Stow is unwary. *An English Chronicle*, ed. J. S. Davies, Camden Old Series, 64 (1856), is suffering from a misplaced editorial semi-colon on p. 70. Hull's inquisition *post mortem* (P.R.O. C 139/155, no. 41) in fact gives the date of his death fictitiously as 3 Sept. 1453. On his accounts the date is given as 18 July 1453 (P.R.O. E 364/192, m. 1); Hull must have been killed on 17 July or died of his wounds the following day. A writ of *diem clausit* was issued on 28 Oct. (*C.F.R. 1452–61*, 55) and the inquisition was taken on 5 and 7 Nov. On the 10th Bishop Beckington commissioned the collecting of his debts (*Reg. Bekynton*, I, 221). In January Eleanor Hull was granted administration of his will (ibid. 224). An obit was performed for him in Bridgwater that year (*Bridgwater Borough Archives*, ed. T. B. Dilks, IV, Somerset Record Society, LX (1945), 72).

[84] *C.F.R. 1452–61*, 64.

[85] F.P. 42, m. 3.

[86] Draft letters patent for committal of Titchwell to Filongley and Jenney (T. 207); *C.F.R. 1452–61*, 132.

[87] Record of process in Chancery and in the King's Bench (P.R.O. K.B. 27/777, m. 44r); Adds. 64 is Fastolf's copy of this.

labours of Howes and Worcester and Filongley and John Crop and the others had failed; the evidence they produced was never needed because they had not produced enough. In the end Fastolf was able to rely on his power over the more obscure Thomas Wake, as in the beginning Sir Edward Hull had relied on his power over that of the retired soldier with the unfashionable politics. When the land law and the law of entail were so uncertain, when family history of a hundred years before was so obscure despite the fulness of royal archives and despite (or because of) the faltering memory of old men in the spring sunshine at Frome, there was little one could do in the law if one's title were not (as many were not) as perfect as it might be. Within those uncertainties and obscurities the opportunities for attack by powerful men on pretenced titles a little more or a little less imperfect were manifold. Without law, without lordship, there was little left for a Sir John Fastolf but luck; luck which allowed him in turn to act high-handed over an opponent now weaker than he.

On 1 April 1456 the manor of Titchwell was re-settled safely into the hands of Fastolf's feoffees.[88] The Titchwell affair was over, though the dangers inherent in the title were still alive in William Worcester's mind some fourteen years later.[89] It was a little unfair on Fastolf that land which was in no way a bargain should have given him so much trouble. But, 'glad and...feyn...to purchace a faire manoir', he had not been especially 'warre in purchasyng' and he was lucky not to have lost the land permanently. Not only the matter of Titchwell, but, according to William Worcester, those also of a dozen other estates sent his servants on many a shrewd journey for his sake.[90] But at least out of Fastolf's circle came something more enduring than titles to land which after his death were snatched out of his legatees' hands. 'The complications of the land law were a powerful incitement to historical research', and to that curious spirit William Worcester at least the training and labours of lawsuit investigation were not without their more permanent value.[91] It was perhaps as well that all the problems he dealt with were not as frustrating as those involved in Sir John Fastolf's lawsuit over Titchwell.[92]

[88] T. 68, T. 75.

[89] In a letter to Bishop Waynflete, now administrator of Sir John Fastolf's will, on 1 March 1470 he advised him to farm the then vacant manor for, he wrote, if 'som men that claymed the seid maner & disseysed my maister Fastolf vij yere & more knew yt they wold lyghtly entre yn yt vppon her holde tytle & glayme' (F.P. 96).

[90] F.P. 72; the phrase is William Paston's about Worcester's labours (*P.L.* III, 192); McFarlane, 'Sir John Fastolf', 111–14.

[91] Ibid. 113; 'William Worcester', *passim*.

[92] I am indebted for help on them to Mr P. T. V. M. Chaplais, Mr G. D. G. Hall, Dr G. A. Holmes and, above all, to Mr K. B. McFarlane.

16

FRANCE AND ENGLAND:
THE GROWTH OF THE NATION STATE

The 'Hundred Years' War', as we know, began in 1066 and did not end in 1453: that is, intermittent conflict between the rulers of France and England was a dominant feature of the political life of western Europe for half a millennium. It was a conflict, in the beginning, between a king whose existence lay very largely in myth, and a duke, formally his subject, who had conquered a kingdom in which his existence was very far from myth. Over the centuries the king of France's existence became very much more substantial; but the fortunes of both 'sides' could vary, and into the equation could come other integers.

To begin with the myth. The sovereignty of a Capetian king of France rested upon his dubious inheritance of the myth of Carolingian sovereignty, exercised effectively over the small Francia, in principle only over the larger Francia (though principle could become insidious). Why the effectively sovereign princes of the greater Francia did not simply destroy the Capetians and their inheritance is not really very clear; but it is argued that, if they had not recognised that inheritance, their own sovereignties would have been endangered by their own inferiors' view of *them*.[1] In any case, the Capetians survived, and with them France: for one must remember that without the king, without the Capetian inheritor of the Carolingian, and the Valois – or Plantagenet – inheritor of the Capetian, there is no France.

This insecurity – this nagging suspicion that perhaps after all the idea of France is not laid up in heaven, but only in the mind of a Jeanne d'Arc – seems to have evinced itself in a number of ways, by further myth-making and by propaganda, though it is hard at times to disentangle the two. The saintliness of the line – we must remember Charlemagne was a saint – was evinced not only in St Louis but arguably also in his great-grandfather;[2] saints, despite Christine de Pisan's attempt at the secular sanctification of Charles V, being rather rare on the ground amongst the kings of the later middle ages except perhaps in England, Jeanne d'Arc was a godsend. The eternal assertions of the historians – for we must remember that historiography is propaganda, and never more so that at St Denis – 'historians', as Jean Juvenal des Ursins pointed out, have it in their power to whiten or blacken kings, as king John in England knew only too well – though he was blackened by Philippe-Auguste's propaganda machine too.[3] In the later middle ages, when to the Capetian neurosis was added the Valois neurosis faced with the Plantagenet claim to the throne of France itself, the historians swung the past behind the Valois claim as in the early thirteenth century they had swung the *redditus regni Francorum ad stirpem Caroli* theme behind Philippe-Auguste's occupation of Normandy, that old Carolingian possession – and as they were to do so behind Charles VII's occupation of Normandy, and Aquitaine too, in the mid-fifteenth century.[4] Then came all the myth-mongering of the thirteenth century, all the myth-mongering of Charles V's entourage, let alone the myth-mongering around Jeanne d'Arc; and one of the most fascinating things about all this myth-mongering and about all this propagandising is that, throughout that half-millennium, very little is produced upon the other side. We may comment upon the 'pale et tardive replique' of the English to the Sainte'Ampoule as we may speculate upon the effect of the comparative poverty of English charisma upon the loss of Normandy,[5] but we may also speculate upon whether the English felt they had little need of propaganda and myth. Perhaps they felt secure enough.

But there was that greater, original myth, the myth of Capetian sovereignty itself, reinforced from the mid-thirteenth century by the assiduous attentions of the Capetian lawyers: the king emperor in his kingdom, the king only the administrator of the *imperium*, which he is powerless to alienate[6] – a theme very useful as legal cover for a king wishing to renege on his treaty obligations and one which made a final solution of what was (from the English point of view) the French problem insoluble. For we must remember that if a king is king, his lawyers are royalty; for expediency's sake a king may stray from the path of royal rectitude, but his lawyers will always 'force' him back on to it. It was against this myth that the English kings as dukes of Normandy or of Aquitaine, or in any other of their 'French' disguises, had ultimately to contend. It was this myth, made valid by Valois armies, which led on to Castillon. At this point the Plantagenet claim to France in its turn became an invalid myth; and yet it, too, was to haunt their adversaries for many years to come.

Essentially it was the inexorable if intermittent pressure of those who wished to validate the Capetian–Valois myth by force which produced the pattern of conflict. If the Capetians were on the defensive in the eleventh and earlier twelfth centuries it was the Plantagenets who had their backs at least to the sea in the later twelfth and earlier thirteenth. Accident naturally played its part: the unruly family politics of the Plantagenets, the curious incapacities of John, the readiness of Innocent III to proclaim interdict, civil war in England, the incapacities of Henry III (let alone Louis IX's apparent unworldliness). The non-fulfilment of the terms of the Treaty of Paris of 1259 led to a period of intermittent skirmishing, military, legal and diplomatic, during which English attitudes towards the last Capetians and their lawyers' interminable pressure in Guyenne hardened.[7] When Charles IV, the last Capetian of all, died in 1328, Edward III had a perfectly reasonable claim to the French throne, the title of which, at grips with Philippe VI, he assumed in 1340. Thereafter, until long after 1453, the English had two perfectly compatible claims: the throne of France, or, alternatively, part of France in full sovereignty. This latter claim, of course, answered that question begged for so long; it simply denied the myth of that Carolingian sovereignty inherent in the descendents of the Capetian line.

The details of the war need not concern us. The English tended to win the battles and the French, in a sense, the peace, in both the fourteenth- and the fifteenth-century phases of the war. And one thing we should perhaps remember. In the fourteenth century the nobility of England were French, they thought and wrote in French, they spoke in French, albeit with a peculiar accent. In the fifteenth century they spoke in English. One should above all avoid foisting too much 'nationalism' on the fifteenth century; but the war did force people – or at least the French propagandists hoped to force people – to think in terms of English and French; however half-hearted many Frenchmen seem to have been – or for that matter, in the west in the fourteenth century, some Englishmen seem to have been. But if the widow of Richard II returned sadly to France, the widow of Henry V, her sister Katharine, remained far from sadly in England – as the Tudors knew only too well.

What else did the war force? One should certainly avoid seeing it in the later middle ages as 'une simple et tragique parenthese'. To the political and social development of the twelfth and thirteenth centuries much was added. To the ancient divergences between the two countries new divergences had already been added, and they continued to be added as the pressures consequent upon later medieval warfare led to different solutions. In some sense France was a century behind England – in the development of 'national' taxation and the struggle for charters of liberties, for instance. In others a different fundamental socio-political structure predicated different development. In England the nobility was taxed from the beginning. In France, in order to raise royal taxes at all, a shoddy subterfuge exempted it.[8] In England the lack of 'provinces' and the political vitality of the community of the shire produced a community of the realm prepared to be represented in a system of territorial representation which cut across 'estates' theory – and represented fully, and in a single place. The Parliament of England, derived from the old *curia regis*, attended by a nobility quite prepared to resent taxation, was an omnicompetent, living body – though one should beware of worshiping it too much, or of seeing inanition impossible if circumstances changed. In France a central assembly with full representative powers was virtually impossible.[9] In France many regional assemblies, attended by an untaxed nobility, withered away in the periods of 'peace' in both the fourteenth and the fifteenth centuries. Essentially, in both centuries the kings of France attempted to get large assemblies only to influence public opinion when their image was tarnished by the shame of military defeat. Vital regional assemblies did survive – to the estates of Languedoc one might add those of Dauphine and Burgundy, the *Parlement* of Brittany – but these were not until very late 'royal' assemblies. As a result of the inanition of 'royal' assemblies, central and local, Charles VII could, in a fit of absence of mind, acquire the right of 'permanent, arbitrary' taxation and a 'permanent, standing' army. The king of England could not. In this sense England became the country of 'liberty', because her kings had been 'strong'; and France the country of 'servitude', because her kings had been 'weak'.

Further divergences became marked. In England local administration was in the hands of 'amateurs'; though whether these unpaid gentlemen busy in the affairs of the shire should be seen as less efficient 'players' is another matter. In

France the local civil service was 'professional'. France, at least in the earlier fourteenth century, was the country in which the pope interfered least.[10] In England the king taxed the clergy; in France he tried to, but found the pope in the way. Compromise was necessary: by the end of the fifteenth century there was very little the pope could do in England;[11] France was still under the regime of concordats. In France the *Parlement* arguably protected the benefice-holder against royal interference as much as the king's courts in England facilitated it.[12] In France the *Parlement*, and the *Chambre des comptes*, protected the king against himself: in England that 'duty' fell upon the political body, the Parliament. Bridled the king of England may have been; but were those bridles imposed by Claude de Seyssel upon the king of France – religion, his own ordinances and the control of the great offices of state – any weaker?

In England there could be 'constitutional development', in the thirteenth century ending in 'constitutional development' in Parliament. Most of these developments – the development of impeachment, say, or of the process of appeal – were the result of expediency on the spur of the moment. Much as Sir John Fortescue could laud the common law of England and the Parliament, and fear the civil law, which to him meant ruling without Parliament, one suspects he was prejudiced or *parti-pris*. Of course England was the country essentially of customary law, and of course France one in which the *droit ecrit* had long maintained or developed force. But Fortescue could not, dare not, contemn civil law; and whether English common law in its operation was all that libertarian, or even rectitudinous, is another matter. In the same way Parliament was not the be-all and end-all of politics. Politics might impinge upon it, in 1376 (when the 'Good' Parliament invented the process of impeachment) or 1378–9 (when the 'Merciless' Parliament invented that of appeal). But most 'real' politics was outside, was open: as open as real politics in France.

Of course the territorial power of the French princes was in the later middle ages still much more obvious than that of the English higher nobility. Whether their *mores*, either social or political, were very different is another matter. Their attitude to their place in the councils of the realm was the same;[13] and their reaction when, in the time of silly kings or crazy kings – Richard II, Charles VI, Henry VI, Louis XI at times, Richard III – the fountain of honour and the fountain of justice sprinkled in their view – or in the view of some of them – less than evenly, was the same: civil war which developed into dynastic war: the alternative in France the Plantagenet, in England the Yorkist, was preferred. In both countries that civil war brought disorder and ultimately, inevitably, a desire for firm and even-handed rule.

Or 'strong' rule? What is a 'strong' king? What does a king think about all day?[14] The answer is his relations with the princes his neighbours and the princes his subjects: treaties, but preferably not battles. Otherwise he presides over a patronage system working through the administrative system: an informal system working through a formal system. In France we are now beginning to see how that system works much more clearly: how someone fairly low down, or not so low down, the socio-political ladder got what he wanted out of the top, working through the court, the royal entourage, those formidable go-betweens who 'wait most upon the king and lie nightly in his chamber'.[15] In England the process is still – despite the aptness of that quotation – much more shadowy. We know about patronage in the reign of Elizabeth I; we know very little about it in the later middle ages. This is a pity; because it is the essence of 'real' politics.

About the later medieval 'affinity', that socio-politico-military joint-stock enterprise which gave the higher nobility their 'non-feudal' influence, we are much clearer in both countries. Essentially they developed under the pressures of war, 'national' and 'civil', though they could remain for the patronage purposes of peace. But whether such enterprises, or a patronage system itself, are necessarily later medieval things, is another matter. What, then, did the warfare of the later middle ages finally force? Wars need armies, and armies need pay; pay means a system of making the country disgorge. We have seen the differential response in France and England. Wars need captains and kings who are actually good in battle; unwarlike kings – unwarlike like Richard II, not like Charles V – tend to produce internal strains. But active warfare, and its thirst for cash also produce strains. In England, in the end, in both the fourteenth and the fifteenth centuries, the community simply would not stump up. Hence weakly negotiations for peace, and the disasters that led up to Castillon. In France, on the receiving end of the bid to destroy the Capetian myth, the community paid. Hence the *revanche* that led on to Castillon, and ultimately to the Italian wars, that partial fulfilment of yet another myth, the myth of the last World Emperor, called Charles.[16] That there are 'parentheses' in history, 'simples et tragiques' or not, is, of course, itself a fable, if not a heresy: things simply develop. The development from Hastings to Castillon and beyond is unbroken; things are just different at times, as they must be. They were, and they were to be.

1. R. Fawtier, *Les Capétiens et la France* (Paris, 1942), p. 65 [tr. L. Butler and R. J. Adam, *The Capetian Kings of France* (London, 1960), p. 64].
2. M. Pacaut, *Louis VII et son royaume* (Paris, 1964), pp. 33ff., 54 n. 3.
3. Cf. G. M. Spiegel, 'Political utility in medieval historiography: a sketch', *Hist. and Theory*, xiv (1975), 314–25; Jean Juvenal, *Verba Hea*, Bibliothèque Nationale, MS. Fr. 2701, fo. 111va; V. H. Galbraith, 'Good kings and bad kings in medieval English history', *History*, xxx (1945), 125ff.; Ch. Petit-Dutaillis, 'Le Déshérite-ment de Jean sans Terre . . .', *R. Hist.*, cxlvii (1924), 194ff.; cxlviii (1925), 1ff.
4. P. S. Lewis, 'War propaganda and historiography in fifteenth-century France and England', *Trans. Roy. Hist. Soc.*(1965), 1-21; above, 193-213; G. M. Spiegel, 'The *Reditus Regni ad Stirpem Caroli Magni*: a new look', *French Hist. Stud.*, vii (1971), 145–74; Bodleian Library, MS. Bodley 968, fos 185r ff.
5. J. C. Holt, *The End of the Anglo-Norman Realm* (London, 1975), pp. 32ff.
6. R. Feenstra, 'Jean de Blanot et la formule "Rex Franciae in regno suo princeps est"', *Etudes . . . G. Le Bras* (Paris, 1965), ii, 885–95; P. N. Riesenberg, *Inaliena-bility of Sovereignty in Medieval Political Thought* (New York, 1956), pp. 155ff.
7. G. P. Cuttino, *English Diplomatic Administration 1259–1339*, 2nd edn (Oxford, 1971), pp. 19–28.
8. J. R. Strayer, 'Defence of the realm and royal power in France', *Studi . . . J. Luzzatto* (Milan, 1949), i, 289–96.
9. On the French estates see P. S. Lewis, 'The failure of the French medieval estates', *Past and Present*, 23 (1962), 3–24.
10. See, for instance, B. Guillemain, *La Politique bénéficiale du pape Benoit XII* [Bibl. Ec. Hautes Etudes, cclxxxix] (Paris, 1952), pp. 129ff.
11. K. B. McFarlane, *Eng. Hist. Rev.* lxxiii (1958), 675.
12. F. Cheyette, 'Kings, courts, cures and sinecures: the Statute of Provisors and the Common Law', *Traditio*, xix (1963), 295–349.
13. See, for instance, A. L. Brown, 'The king's councillors in fiteenth-century England', *Trans. Roy. Hist. Soc* 5 Ser., xix (1969), 95–118.
14. The question is Bernard Guenée's.
15. *Paston Letters and Papers*, ed. N. Davis, i (Oxford, 1971), 617.
16. M. Reeves, *The Influence of Prophecy in the Later Middle Ages* (Oxford, 1969), pp. 354ff.

17

CONCLUSION

They were, and they were to be. Where does one go from here? There is so much to do: and not in the sense of finding New Ways in History, but of finding the old ways of the past. Pierre Charbonnier's work on Basse Auvergne, so much more significant than the emptiness of other people's work: what one needs is a sense of the concrete. Man does not, thank goodness, live by mind alone. Here, I think, one needs out of these essays to expand upon that on the crown pensions. The para-political, the efficient, the workaday: 'I never thought of them like that'. Does one bother with ideas? People had them: why they had them is another matter. Did they have them, or express them, in order to swing their interests onto other people? Or were they merely honest, or stupid? There is so much more to do, so much more discovery, and excitement.

INDEX

Adbeer (Somerset) 221n.
Agincourt, battle of 220, 223
aides see taxation
Ailly, Pierre d', cardinal 191n., 202n.
Albi 154; bishops of 154; Louis d'Amboise, bishop of 100n.
Albret, seigneurs of 18; Arnauld-Amanieu 45; Bernard Ezi II 45, 47, 64-5; Charles I 52; Charles II 51, 52, 62
'Aldroiche', Thomas 77, 88-9
Alençon, Jean, comte d' 50; Jean, duke of 200
alliance, lettres scellées d' 20ff., 33, 42ff. *passim*, 69ff. *passim*
Almain, Jacques 177
ambassadors, Italian 5, 19, 20, 22
Amboise 152, 198n.
Amboise, Jean d', bishop of Maillezais 100n.; Louis d', bishop of Albi 100n.
Amiens 163
Anjou, Charles d', comte du Maine 62; Jean d', comte de Mortain 72; Louis I, duke of 59, 177; René, duke of 39
Aprés la destruction de Troye la grant 191, 211n.
Aquinas, St Thomas 175n.
Aquitaine 86n., 208n., 218, 232, 234
Arbalestier, Guillaume 197
Arc, Joan of 153, 171n., 178, 233, 236
Arly, Jean d' 95
Armagnac, counts of 9, 59, 218; Bernard VII 44, 59; Jean I 45, 65; Jean V 21; Bernard d', comte de Pardiac 50; Jean d', bishop of Castres 163
army, royal 11, 22, 27, 153, 181ff.
Arras 200; treaty of 203
Artois 117; Estates of 107, 110, 113, 118, 125n.
Artois, Charles d' 77; Robert d' 200
Astarac, Beaumont d' 46, 49, 55, 56; Jean, bâtard d' 46, 55; Jean, comte d' 49, 55; Jean d', seigneur de Montclare 56
Aubert, Bernard 49, 55
Audite celi que loquor 202, 203, 211n.
Augustine, St 170, 171, 172n.
Austell, John 227, 228

Autrey, seigneur de 126
Auvergne, Estates of 118, 179
Avarcha, Guirault 55
Avignon 33, 38, 155
Avost, Claude d' 191n.
Avranches, bishop of 100n.
Axbridge 227

Balue, Jean 24
Bar, Charlotte de 161; Denis de 161ff, 164,; Edouard de, marquis de Pont 43, 58, 71
Barilh, Guillaume 159
Basin, Thomas 4, 6, 24, 153, 169n., 177, 179ff.
bastard feudalism 85n.
Batifol, Jean 178
Béarn 112, 117; Estates of 107, 115, 117, 125n.
Beaucaire-Nimes, sénéchausée of 8, 111, 113, 198
Beauchamp, lord 232; *see also* Warwick
Beaujolais, Estates of 116
Beaumanoir, Guillaume de 84n.; Jean de 84n.; Philippe de 106
Beaumont, Louis de 162, 164
Beauvais 23, 151ff., 164, 166; bishops of 202; *see also* Jouvenal, Jean II; Vincent of 192
Beauvaisis 151ff.
Becket, St Thomas 191n., 192n.
Beckington, Thomas, dean of the Arches 206-7n., 218
Bede 191n., 192
Bedford, John, duke of 201
Bedorede, Guillaume-Arnaud, seigneur de 54
Beighton 221n., 230
Bellay, Jean du 145n.
Belleville, Jean de, seigneur de Mirabeau 83n.
benefices 23, 161ff.
Bentes, Albert 191n.
Bernard-Aton VI, vicomte de Narbonne 83n.
Bernis, Michel du 37ff.
Berry, Jean, duke of 17, 39-40, 58, 109
Besançon, bishop of 100n.
Bialon 178

Blackford 227

Blanchefort, Jean de 72, 83n., 161

Blanchet, Gérard 155ff., 160, 164;
Guillaume 160

Blisworth (Northants.) 218, 219

Blois 171n.

Blot, Hugues de Chauvigny, seigneur de 145n.

Blondel, Robert 171 & n., 173n., 175n., 186,
190, 198, 202, 203, 211, 212; his *Oratio
historialis* 198, 203, 206

Bluet 228

Bocking, Nicholas 230, 231

Bonnay, Jean de 54

Bordeaux 153ff., 164, 218; Bordelais 113

Boucicaut, Jean 30, 31

Bourbon, dukes of 18-19, 33, 118, 184; Charles
32n., 178, 179n.; Jean I 30ff., 50, 60;
Jean II 14, 20, 179; Louis II 31, 50, 80n.;
Jeanne, de France, duchess of 198; Pierre
I 57, 68; Charles de, comte de Clermont
61; Guillaume de 57, 68

Bourbonnais 14, 124n.; Estates of 116

Bourges 155; Pragmatic Sanction of 23, 162

Brabant, Dan Thomas 226

Bracton, Henry 106

Bradwell 221n., 230

Bretagne, Gilles de 134n.

Brétigny, treaty of 205, 206

'Breuil', king of England 192

Brézé, Pierre de 56, 60

Brian, Guy 227 & n.; his wife, Alice 227n.; his
grand-daughter, Elizabeth 227n.; her husband,
Robert 228

Briçonnet, Bertrand 161

Bridgwater (Somerset) 233n.

Bridport (Dorset) 221n.

Bristol 226, 227, 228

Brit, Ralph 85

Brittany 112; Estates (Parlement) of 107, 109,
110, 113, 115, 116, 117, 121n., 125n., 133n.,
237

Brittany, dukes of: François I 30; François II 12,
19, 76, 77, 78n., 79, 80n.; François III 30n.;
Jean IV 72ff; Jean V 50, 71ff. *passim*, 80n.,
82n., 83n., 84n., 135n., 136n.; Jeanne de
Navarre, duchess of 75, 79, 80; Jean *le
roux* 81, 82n.; Pierre II 77

Bruères, Jean de 55

Bruges, Louis de, lord of Gruuthuse 198

Brusac, Mondot de 55

Bruton (Somerset) 225, 228

Bryanston 226, 229

Buch, Gaston, captal de *see* Foix

Bueil, Jean de 72, 76, 83n., 84 & n.,
146 & n.

Buffart, a Lyonnais 156

Burgundy 112, 117, 135n.; Estates of 107,
113, 115, 116, 125-6, 135n., 237n.;
Estates general of 110

Burgundy, dukes of 18, 45, 57, 109, 184; Charles
le téméraire 21, 179; Jean *sans peur* 57ff., 175;
Philippe *le bon* 21, 30, 110; Philippe *le hardi*
57ff.; Marie de 124n., 126; grande
sénéchausée of 21

Cabaret, Jean 30

Cabochien movement 8-9, 26, 181

Cadier, Jean 14

Caister (Castre) (Norfolk) 221, 231

Caparas, Ramon 55

Capetians 235, 238

Caqueran, *le borgne* 155, 156, 157

Caraman, Hughes, vicomte de 47; Jean de 47

Carcassonne, sénéchausée of 8, 111, 113

Carolingians 235, 236

Castillon, Pons de 43; battle of (1453) 233, 236,
237

Castle Cary 227

Cauchon, Pierre 151, 153

Caumont, seigneurs de 51, 53; Guillaume Ramon
II 46, 51, 52; Nompar I 46, 51, 53,
66; Nompar II 29, 33ff., 46ff., 80-1n.

Chalençon, Guillaume de, bishop of Le Puy
61; Louis de, seigneur de Beaumont 61

Chamber, Thomas 228

Champeaux, Guillaume de 24, 160; Isabelle
de 160

Chancery, court of 222, 223, 225, 231, 233

Charlemagne 23, 190, 235

Charles V, emperor 243

Charles V, king of France 4, 6ff., 23, 106,
111, 122n., 152, 160, 170, 201, 235,
236, 239

Charles VI, king of France 6, 9, 16, 23,
50, 61, 62, 69, 108, 111, 114, 125n.,
160, 180, 202, 205, 238

Charles VII, king of France 6ff. *passim*, 16,
22ff., 62, 107ff., 121n., 122n., 152ff.,
166n., 171 & n., 172n., 174n., 176, 178,
179, 181, 184 & n., 193n., 208, 210,
211-12n., 236, 237

Charles VIII, king of France 181, 209

Charles de France 163, 179ff.

Charny, seigneur de 126

Charrier 157

Chartier, Alain 15, 37, 39, 161, 194.;
Guillaume 162; Jean 211-12n.

Chartres, Regnaud de 212n.

Chastellain, Georges 16, 22, 182

Chastellux, 126

Châtagnier, Jean 156
Châteaubrient, Brient de, seigneur de Beaufort 73, 78n., 79n.
Châteaugay 155, 157
Châteauvillain, Guillaume de 125, 126
Chesnel, Even 73, 78 & n., 79n.
Chinon, Estates of 110, 111
chivalry, orders of 20, 21, 29ff., 57, 59-60, 82-3
'Chombile', Jean de 47, 48, 55
Churchill, near Axbridge 227
Cicero 216; *De Officiis* 176n.; *De Republica* 171-2n.
Clamanges, Nicolas de 171, 181
Clarence, Philippa of 211n.; Thomas, duke of 7, 60, 228
Clercq, Jacques du 182
Cleriaux, Hennotin 29
Clermon en Beauvaisis 153
Clermont (-Ferrand) 24
Clevedon, Milton *see* Lovel; Milton Clevedon
Clisson, Marguerite de 83, 84
Clisson, Olivier de 43, 56, 74, 83 & n.
Clovis 5, 23, 188, 189ff.
Cnut, St, of Denmark 191-2
Coatmen, Rolland, vicomte de 72ff., 83n
Cochon, Pierre 110
Coëtquen, Raoul[let], seigneur de 73, 75
Coeur, Jacques 24
Cognac 197
Col, Gontier and Pierre 201n.
Colinet, clerk 159
Comminges, Arnaud Roger de 46ff., 56, 67; Bernard, bâtard de 56; Jean-Roger de 49, 56; Ramon Roger de 46, 56
Common Pleas, court of 227
Commynes, Philippe de 6, 8, 16, 21, 105-6, 115, 119, 169, 177
consent 109ff., 115, 185
Conty, Etienne de 170n.
Corbie, Arnault de 15
corpus mysticum 172
Corunna 154
Couches, seigneur de 126
Coucy, monsieur de 158
Courtecuisse, Jean 173, 180n.
court 15ff., 24, 25, 160-1, 163
Couserans, Arnaud Roger de Comminges 56; Jean Roger de Comminges, vicomte de 51; Ramon Roger de Comminges, vicomte de 47, 56
Cousinot, Guillaume I 58, 171n.; Guillaume II 189
Craon (Crant) 146 & n.
Cromwell, lord 232

Crop, John 226, 227, 234
Crussol, Louis, seigneur de La Forêt 146 & n.
curia regis 133, 237
Curton, seigneur de 49, 70

Dacx, Jean 51, 54
Daillon, Jean de 56
Dalling, John, under-escheator 221 & n., 222, 230, 231
Dauphiné 112, 117, 155; Estates of 9, 107, 110, 116, 118, 124n., 125n., 237
Dax, Estates of 113
Débat des hérauts d'armes 190
Despratz, Bertrand 55
Dijon 10
Dinan, Jean, vicomte de 77; Jaques de, seigneur de Châteaubriant 79n., 84n.; Bertrand de, seigneur de Montafilant 79n., 84n.; Françoise de, comtesse de Laval 79n.
Dinham, Philippa, lady 227 & n., 228 & n.
diplomatic records 209ff.
Domesday Book 225
Dorchester 85n.
Doriole, Pierre 161, 163, 164
Dorset 218
Doyat, Jean de 14
Dubois, Jean 171n., 172 & n., 180n., 193n.
Dunois, Jean, count of 19
Duras, seigneurs de 51
Durfort, seigneurs de 53; Gaillard III 53; Gaillard IV 48, 51, 53, 54, 62
Duvergier, Denis 182

Edgar, king of England 192
Edson, of Kenn, near Bristol 228
Edward I, king of England 112
Edward III, king of England 205, 211n., 236
Edward IV, king of England 207
Egfrid, king of England 191, 192
Elcombe 228
Elfwin, king of England 191
Elizabeth I, queen of England 239
England, compared to France 235ff.; and Hundred Hundred Years War 193ff.; lawsuit in 215-34; regicidal history 191-2
Enmore (Somerset) 217
entail 219ff.
Esconchy, Mathieu d' 182
Esquerrier, Arnaud 38
Essarts, Pierre des 160
Estates *see* representative assemblies
Estissac, Amaury, seigneur d' 48, 51, 55, 56, 67
Etampes, François, comte de 202

Eton 232
Eu, Charles, comte de 60, 153
Evreux 24
exemption from taxation 10, 114, 115

Fastolf, Sir John 200, 201; his lawsuit over
    Titchwell 215-34; John, of Olton
    224, his wife, Margaret (Lovel) 224;
    Thomas 223, his wife Joan 223
Faur, Garsias du 21
Fenn, Hugh 233
Ferran, Bernard 52, 54; Jean 52
fief-rente 42ff., 71, 76, 84
Filescamps, Jacques de 163
Fillastre, Guillaume 185
Filongley, Henry 227, 228, 229, 233,
    234
Fitzwarin, Sir Ivo 85
Flanders, representation in 109
fleurs de lys 5, 171, 189ff., 213
Fleury, Aimon de 210
Fluxio biennale spacio 22
Foix, counts of: Archambaud 43ff., 53,
    80n.; Gaston III 37ff., 45ff., 53, 55,
    57, 62, 70, 117; Gaston IV 16, 19,
    38-9, 46ff. *passim*, 80-1n.; Jean I 32ff.,
    37ff. *passim*, 45ff. *passim*, 80n., 80-1n.;
    Mathieu 46, 48, 53, 66; Gaston, captal
    de Buch 45, 80n.; Yvain de Béarn, bastard
    of 37ff.; Pierre I, cardinal of 33, 38; Pierre
    II, cardinal of 56; Isabelle de 46
Folmon, Pierre de Raymon, seigneur de 147n.
Forster, Dan Thomas 226
Fortescue, Sir John 22, 27, 105-6, 109, 112,
    119, 170, 178, 185, 188, 211n., 238
Fougères 209n.
Fouquet, painter 147n.
Fouvent, seigneur de 126n.
Forez 20
Frampton 228
Fribois, Noël de 169 & n., 171n., 172n., 188,
    191 & n., 192 & n., 195, 196, 197, 201 &
    n., 202
Frome (Somerset) 226, 234

Gaguin, Robert 191n.
Gaignières 38
Galceran VI Galceran de Pinos 55
Gallicanism 5, 170
Gascony, Estates in 110
Gaucourt, Charles de 162
Gerberoy 152-3
Gerson, Jean Charlier de 171ff., 179ff., 186,
    191 & n., 202n.
Gévaudan 120n.

Girlington, Nicholas, lawyer 225
Giroult, Guillaume 197
Glastonbury, Sir Nichol of 226
Gloucester, duke of 220n.
Goldast, M. 191n., 202n.
Golein, Jean 187
Gontaud, Gaston de 55
Gordon, Marquiès of 55
Gorleston (Norfolk) 219n.
Gouge, Martin 24
Grammont, François, seigneur de 54, 61;
    Jean, seigneur de 57
Gratian 180n., 192 & n.
Great Yarmouth 219n., 221
Green, lawyer 224
Grenade 154
Guesclin, Bertrand de 83n.
Guillaume, a *juponnier* 177
Guyenne (Guienne) 112, 117, 198, 199,
    210, 213n., 236; council of 218

Hallé, François 14
Hankford, William, justice 85n.
Harcourt, Christophe d' 211-12n.
Harpenden, Jean, seigneur de Belleville
    and de Montagu 83n.
Hastings, battle of 237
Hastings, William, lord 48, 82
Henry III, king of England 236
Henry IV, king of England 57, 85-6, 142-3,
    153, 217; his wife, Joan 217
Henry V, king of England 169n., 191, 205;
    his wife, Katharine of France 237; *Vita
    Henrici Quinti* 206
Henry VI, king of England 201, 206n., 207,
    238; his wife, Margaret of Anjou 218
Henry VII, king of England 169n.
Henry VIII, king of England 169n.
Héron, Macé 160
Herrings, battle of the 217
Hesselin, Denis 162
Heydon, John, of Baconthorpe 221, 222
Historiography 193ff.
Hoby, Ralph 226
Hogshaw, Joan 220ff.; *see also* Lovel; her
    family 221n.
Holkham (Norfolk) 216
homage 41, 47
Hook 228
Howes, Thomas 222-4, 236
Hugotion, François 153ff., 164
Hull, Sir Edward 217-21, 229-34; his family
    217ff.
Hundred Year's War 193ff., 235ff.
Huntley, John 228n.; Thomas 221n., 228

Husens, Guixarnault, vicomte de 54

indentures 42ff.
Innocent III, pope 235
Ireland 229n.
Isabella, queen of England, wife of
    Edward II 205
Issoudun, Estates of 111
Italian Wars 239

Jacquerie 26
Jarlot, Colin 155
Jean II, king of France 23, 154
Jenney, councillor of Sir John Fastolf 233
John, king of England 235
Joigny, count of 126
Jonvelle, seigneur de 24
Jouvenel (Juvenal) des Ursins, family 151;
    Guillaume 15, 147 & n., 151, 161, 164,
    171n., 175n., 211n.; Jean I 58; Jean II
    1, 10, 11, 15, 23, 26, 58, 70, 106, 108,
    109, 119, 120n., 122n., 151ff., 164,
    166n., 169ff., 195, 197n., 199, 200,
    202, 203, 205, 206, 208, 209, 210, 211,
    212, 235; *Traicte compendieux de la
    querelle* 203-4, 210; Michel 15; *see
    also* Ursins, hôtel des
Juch, Jean du 73, 76, 78n.
jurisdiction, spiritual 23-4

Kerenlouët, Jean de 72
Kergorlé, Rolland de 72
Kermaon, Tanguy de 76
Kersaliou, Raoul de 72, 74, 75, 87-8;
    Rolland de 78, 84
kingship 4ff., 24, 169ff. *passim*, 235-9

La Barbe, messenger 155ff.
La Barre, Antoine de 191n; N. de 191n.
La Baume, Jean de 43, 57
La Feuillée, Silvestre de 73-4, 78n., 79n.,
    80n., 83n.
Lagny 153
La Houssaie, Eustache de 73, 75
La Marche, Olivier de 29ff.
La Mazère-en-Astarac, Jean, seigneur de
    55
Lamothe, Bertrand de 46, 54, 55; Gaillard
    de 45, 47, 66; Guillaume-Arnaud de 46ff.,
    54; Jean de 46, 51, 54
Lana, Amanieu de 52
Lancaster, Thomas, duke of 32; duchy of
    218
Lancastrians 205
Landes 113; sénéchausée of 8

Langeac, Pons de 60
language barrier 8, 112
Languedoc, Estates of 106ff. *passim*, 120n.,
    124n., 125n., 237
Languedoil, Estates of 106ff. *passim*, 155
Lannoy, Gilbert de 176, 180n.
Lanta, Guillaume-Arnaud de 46
Lanvaux, Alain de 81; Geoffroy de 81
Laon 23, 24, 151ff., 183, 202; bishop of
    see Juvenal des Ursins, Jean II
La Roche, Guy de 77
La Rochelle 158, 159, 197
La Tour, Agne III de 50
La Trémouille, Georges de 71, 86
Laval, André de 79n.; Françoise, comtesse
    de 76, 79 & n.; Guy, comte de 84n.; Jean
    de, seigneur de La Roche 76, 77; Louis
    de, seigneur de Châtillon 84n., 146
    & n.
law, English 215-34
Le Barbu, Jean 76
Le Bouvier, Gilles 152
Lectoure 21
Le Fauga, Ramonet, seigneur de 56
Le Moine, Eon 72; Prigent 73, 78
Léon, Hervé IV de 82n.
Le Preux, Poncet 191n.
Lescun, seigneur de 52
Leseur, Guillaume 39
Lesnerac, Pierre de 76
Lesparre, seigneurs de 51; Florimond de
    85-6; Guillaume-Amanieu de 86n.
Lévis-Mirepoix, Philippe de 49, 55, 80-1n.
L'Hôpital, Pierre de 79n.
'Lillington' (Bucks.) 227
Limeul, seigneur de 154
Limousin, Estates of 118
Limousin, Bas-, Estates of 113
Lisieux 24
Litcham (Norfolk) 217
livery 61, 70
Livio, Tito, his *Vita Henrici Quinti* 206
Lohéac, marshal 146 & n.
London, Clifford's Inn 215; Friday St.
    227; Tower of 225
Longueville, François, comte de 146n.
Louis IX (St Louis), king of France 23,
    81, 171, 177, 203, 235, 236
Louis X, king of France 205
Louis XI, king of France 4, 6ff. *passim*, 60
    ff., 109ff., 121n., 161ff., 169, 179ff.,
    193, 238
Louvain, Pierre de 48, 49, 51, 56
Lovel, family 216-34; family tree of
Lovels of Clevedon (for Lovels of

Titchmarsh and Titchwell *see below*) 220: Thomas I 220, 221, 225 & n., 226, 227, 228, 229, 230, his father John or Thomas 228, 229, his wife, Joan (Hogshaw) 220, 221n., her family 221n.; Thomas II 220, 221n., 224, 228, 229, his wife, Alice (Roger) 220, 221n., 229, her family 221n., thèir daughter,Margery (Hull) 217 & n., 220, 221, 222, 225, 233, their daughter, Agnes (Wake) 217, 219, 221, 222, 225, 233;

Lovel of Titchmarsh (main branch): family tree 219; John Lovel (†1287), knight 219, 220, 233; John I, lord (†1310) 219; John II, lord (†1314) 219; John III, lord (†1347) 219, 220, 227n., 229, his uncle, William 220; John IV, lord (†1361) 219; John V, lord ('Great Lord', 'the Rich') (†1408) 219, 227n., 228, 229, his daughter, Philippa (Dinham) 227n., 228, his son, Robert 227n., 229; John VI, lord (†1414) 219, 226, 227n., 228, 229; William, lord (†1455) 219, 233;

Lovel of Titchwell: family tree 219; Thomas (†1330) 219, 220, 230, his wife, Maud (or Matilda) 219, 220n., their son, Gilbert 219; Ralph I (†1362) 219, 220 & n., 223, 230, his wife, Joan 219, 220 & n., 223, her first husband, Thomas Fastolf 223; Ralph II (†1405) 219, 220 & n., 221, 224, 228, 229; William (†1415) 219, 220 & n., 223, 224, his wife, Margaret? 219, 220 & n., 224, her second husband, John Fastolf of Olton 224; Margery 216, 217, 219, 220 & n., 221, 222, 223, 224, 230, her husband, John Roys 216, 219, 220, 233

Lovel (other): James 227; Sir John, of 'Lillington' 227, 228; John 228; Maud, abbess of Romsey 228n., minoress (anonymous), of London 228n.; Sir Ralph 227; Ralph, canon of Salisbury 228n.; Richard 227; Robert 228 & n.; Roger 228

Lucé, Guillaume de 165

Lustrac, Naudonet de 54

Luxembourg, Waleran de, comte de St Pol 43, 44, 58, 62-3, 71

Lynn 231

Lyon 26, 116, 154ff., 191n.; sénéchal of, bailli of Mâcon 155

Machet, Gerard 211-12n.

Mâcon, bailli of, sénéchal of Lyon 155; Rolin de 155ff., 164, 167n.

Madaillon, Guillaume-Amanieu de 85-6, 89-90

magnates 17ff.

Mailly, M. de 148n.

Maine, comte de 179

Malestroit, Jean, sire de 78, 79n., 80n.

Malicorne, Geoffroy 159

Malmesbury, William of 192

Malsafava, foot-messenger 154

Manwood, Sir Peter 207n.

mark, royal 4, 178

Marville, Guillaume, seigneur de 77, 80n.

Masselin, Jean 116, 119, 170

Matignon, Bertrand, seigneur de 75

Maumont, Gérard de 162

Mauvezin-en-Bigorre 37ff., 80

Memore abrege grossement 210

Mendoza, comte de 38

Mer des histoires 191 & n.

Mere 228

Meschinot 172ff., 179, 185n.

Mézières, Philippe de 69ff.

Miégeville 38

Milanese ambassadors *see* ambassadors; troops 155f.

'Milglos', Arnaud de 147n.

Millau 9, 25, 116

Milstead (Kent) 221n.

Milton Clevedon *see* Clevedon; Lovel of Clevedon

Minster Lovel (Oxon.) 228, 229

Mirebeau, seigneur de 126

Mirepoix, Jeanne de Voisins, dame de 49, 55, 80-1n.; her son, Philippe de Lévis-Mirepoix 80-1n.

Mirouer historial abregie de France 201

Mistère du siège d'Orléans 193-4

mobility, social 3-4

Monstrelet, E. 175n.

Montagu, Jean de 61

Montagut, Bertrand, seigneur de 45, 65

Montauban, Guillaume, seigneur de 75, 78

Montbrun, Sampson de 54

Monteglio (Monteil), Carlo da 146 & n.

Monteils, Bruno de 55

Montereau 175

Montferrand, bailliage of 14, 19; seigneurs of 51, 53; Bertrand II 48, 51, 53; François de, seigneur d'Uza 49, 50, 53-4; Jeannot de 53-4

Montfort, Raoul, sire de 80

Montjoye, Louis, seigneur de 57

Montlaur 9
Montlhéry, battle of 11, 185n.
Montreuil, Jean de 194-8, 201, 203 & n.,
    204 & n., 205, 208, 210, 211-12n., 213n.
Mont-St.-Michel 189n.
Moorcock, of Clopton 228
Morlaas 45, 53, 54, 57, 62
Moulins 14
Mussidan, sire de 77

Nangis, Guillaume de 210, 211
Narbonne, archidiaconate of 161; bishop of
    100n.
Navarre 201
Nemours, Jacques d'Armagnac, duke of 198
Neufchâtel, Thibault IX of, marshal
    of Burgundy 126
New Hunstanton (Norfolk) 216
Nîmes 198n.
Nivernais 126
Norfolk 215-34
Normandy 117, 169n., 182, 191, 195, 199,
    207, 235, 236; Estates of 107, 110, 116,
    117, 120n., 121n., 125n.
Northamptonshire 218, 219
Northbarrow 227
Notre Dame de Paris, chancellor of 176n.;
    chapter of 162-3, 201

office 13ff.
Ordonnance cabochienne 180n.
Oresme, Nicole 201 & n.
Orgueil, Guillaume d' 55
oriflamme 5, 171, 189ff.
Orléans 8, 151, 177, 178; Estates of (1439) 108-
9
Orléans, dukes of: Charles 30, 42ff., 58, 60, 61;
    Louis 33, 39, 42ff., 56ff., 71, 80n., 175, 179,
    183n.; Valentine, duchess of 58; Jean d',
    comte d'Angoulême 163, 164, 197, his
    son, Charles 197; Guillaume le jeune 198;
    Jean, bastard of, comte de Périgord 63-4
Ormond, James Butler, 5th earl of 226n.; his
    sister, Elizabeth 226
Osred 191
Oswald 191-2
Oswin 191, 192n.

Papaillon, Jean 159; Jean *fils* 159
Papassol, Hélie de 159ff., 164
Paris 152, 154; bishopric of 162-3; cordeliers
    212n.; Estates of 112; Notre Dame *see* Notre
    Dame; Parlement of 23-4, 152, 158ff., 162,
    171, 174, 183-4, 186; treaty of (1259) 208,
    209 & n., 236; university of 6

Paris, John of 171-2n.
Parliament 105ff., 114, 185-6, 237, 238;
    'Good' 238; 'Merciless' 238
Parthenay 164
particularism, regional 3, 8
Paston, Edmund 215; John 230; William
    215, 219, 234n.; Agnes 215
Patay, battle of 232
patronage 14ff., 115
Pean, Thomas 78n., 79n.
Pellegrue, Gilbert de 85-6, 89-90
Pembroke (Pennebroc) *see* Tudor, Jasper
pensions 18ff., 49ff., 57, 71ff., 115, 179ff.
Penthièvre, Jean, comte de 77; Jean de,
    seigneur de L'Aigle 83, 84, 146 & n.
Périgord, Archambaud de 72
Périgueux 154, 159ff.
Perrier, Thibaud du 73, 74, 88; Alain 75,
    78n.
Petit, Jean 58, 175, 191n.
Philip Augustus, king of France 235
Philippe IV, king of France 23, 106, 112
Philippe VI, king of France 70, 236
Philpot, Sir John 219; his daughter,
    Margaret (Wake) 218, 219
Picquigny, Ferry de 160
Pin, E. du 191n.
Pisan, Christine de 4-5, 193, 235
Plantagenets 213, 235, 236, 238
Plymouth 154
Poitiers 156, 165; Estates of 111; Parlement
    of 155ff.
Poitiers, comte de 154; Philippe de 114,
    115, 118; bishop of 100n.
Poitou 211-12n.
Pole, Ralph, lawyer 225
Polignac, Armand, vicomte de 61
Pons, Renaud VI de 77, 80n.
Pontieu (Ponthieu) 213n.
Pot, Philippe 21, 171, 172n.
Poulglou, Jean de 72, 77, 80
Pourceque plusieurs 204, 205, 206, 208,
    209-12
Pour vraye congnoissance avoir 212
Poyanne, Arnaud-Guillaume, seigneur de 54
Praguerie 11, 178 & n.
Pré, Jean and Galiot du 191n.
Presles, Raoul de 170, 187, 190
Propaganda 193ff., 237
Provence 117, 124n.; Estates of 116
Psalms, book of 180n.
Public Weal, war of 4, 6, 11, 15, 19, 21, 22,
    179
Puycornet, Jean, seigneur de 48, 55
Puyloaut, Pes, seigneur de 52, 54

Queu, Raymond 158ff., 164
Quia Emptores 44
Quintin, Geoffroy, sire de 74
Quod omnes tangit 110

Raguenel, Jean, vicomte de Dinan 73, 75
Rampisham 228 & n.
regicide 169ff., 191-2
Reims (Rheims) 23, 151ff, 163, 202; arch-
    bishop of *see* Jouvenel des Ursins, Jean II;
    coronation at 8; duke of 176n.
Rély, Jean de 119, 169
representation 106-7
representations, backstairs 116
representative assemblies 7ff., 105ff.,
    184ff.; *see also under individual*
    Estates and Parlements
Response d'un bon et loyal François 203
Retz, Girard, sire de 74, 78n.; René de, sire
    de la Suze 78, 79n.
revenues, royal, ordinary 7; extraordinary
    7ff.
revolt, popular 25-6
Richard II, king of England 6, 174n.,
    175n., 179, 191 & n., 205, 237-9
Richard III, king of England 207,
    238
Richmond, Artur de Bretagne, earl of
    110, 155ff., 164
Ricolf, Thomas 225
Rieux, François, sire de 77
Rinel, Jean de 206n.
Riom 155; sénéchausée of 19
Roanne, maison de 155
Rochechouart, Jean de 72, 83n.
Rochefort, Guilaume de 119, 169,
    181, 191
Rodez 9, 25
Roger, Artur 220, 221n., 229; John 226
Rohan, Alain IX, vicomte de 77, 84; Jean
    I, vicomte de 74, 79n., 83n., 84-5;
    Jean II, vicomte de 78n., 80, 85
Roos, Sir Robert 218
Rouergue 8, 9, 112; Estates of 111, 116
Rovan, James 71
Roys, John 216, 219, 220, 233; his wife,
    Margery (Lovel) 216, 217, 219, 220
    & n., 221, 222, 223, 224, 230
Rue, Thomas de la 225

St Albans 232
Saint-André, Guillaume de 82
Saint-Arthémie, Bertrand de 47, 55
Saint-Blanquat, Arnaud-Guillaume de 46,
    47

Saint-Denis 180n., 211-12n., 235;
    'Religieux' de 202
sainte-ampoule 5, 171, 189ff., 236
Saint-Jean-d'Angély 158ff., 162
Saint-Martin de Seignanx, Pes, seigneur
    de 54
Saintonge 158
Saint-Papoul, bishopric of 161ff.
Saint Savin (Savigny), abbey 211n.
Saint Victor 210
Salic law 204n., 205n., 206-7n., 211
Salisbury, John of 172n.
Salmon, Pierre 173
Saluces, marquis of 146n.
Sans, Guillaume 45, 47, 64-5
Saumur 156, 157
Savoy 155
Scey, seigneur de 126
Seignouret, Aymeri 160
Seine-Yonne, généralité of 181n.
Senlis 153
Seyssel, Claude de 12, 119, 186,
    238
Sherneborne, Thomas, escheator 221,
    231
Sigibert 192
Skrene, William, justice 85n.
Sombernon, seigneur de 126
Somerset 217, 218, 225, 226
Somnium viridarii 171-2n.
Songe du verger 196, 197
Southampton 154
Southbarrow 227
Sparling, Geoffroy 222
Stafford, Sir Richard 226; his wife
    226n.; their daughter, Avice 226n.
Stoker, clerk 225
Stuart, John, constable of Scottish army
    in France 56; John 72; William 71;
    William [II] 72, 87
Surienne, François de 60
Swillington, George 218

Talbot, John, 1st earl of Shrewsbury
    217, 226n., 232, 233; his wife,
    Elizabeth (Butler) 226; his son, Lord
    Lisle 233
Talmay, Burgundian noble 126
Tancarville 146 & n.
taxation, ecclesiastical 23; royal 7ff., 25,
    27, 105ff. *passim*, 117, 152, 177, 180,
    181n.
Termes, Olivier de 81
Terre-Vermeille, Jean de 5, 12, 58, 170ff.,
    172n., 179, 206

Teulier, Jean 159
thaumaturgy 5, 170, 171, 187, 189ff.
Theopompus 175
Thil, seigneur de 125n., 126n.
Thomas, St, of Canterbury *see* Becket
Thouars 156
Tillay, Jamet du, bailli of Vermandois 183n.
Tindon, Louis 163
Titchwell (Norfolk) 215-34 *passim*
Tivarlen, Alain 73
Tolbiac 190
Toul, bishop of 100n.
Toulouse 154; parlement of 21, 25;
    sénéchausée of 8, 111, 113
Tournemine, Jean, seigneur de la Hunaudaie
    74, 75, 77, 79n.; Pierre de 75, 78
Tours 25, 111, 197; Estates of (1468) 11,
    111, 181, 189; (1484) 21, 23, 109, 111ff.,
    170, 176n., 181; truce of 151
towns 25-6, 178n.
Troyes 15; bailliage of 114, 206n.
Tuchins 26
Tudert, Jean 165
Tudor, Jasper, earl of Pembroke 146 & n.;
    his mother, Katharine of France 237
Tulle, bishopric of 161ff.
Turenne, Pierre, comte de Beaufort,
    vicomte de 56; Estates 116, 117
tyranny 169ff.

Uhtred (Obred), earl of Northumbria
    191, 192
Ursins, hôtel des 1
Uzès, Jean, vicomte d' 49, 55

Valois , house of 215, 235, 236; Charles,
    count of 212n.; his wife, Mahaut de
    St Pol 212n.; their son, Louis 212n.
Valpergue, , Théode de 156, 157, 164
Vampage, John, lawyer 225
Varye, Guillaume de 161
Vassal, Geoffroy, archbishop of Vienne
    211-12n.
Velay, Estates of 107
Vendôme, Jean de, vicomte de Chartres
    82n.
Vermandois, bailliage of 183 & n.
Vidal, R. 154
Vignolles, Etienne de, called *La Hire*
    51, 56
Villandrando, Rodrigo de 56
Villars, Guillaume de 159; Humbert,
    seigneur de 50, 80n.
Villebresme 164
Villers, *conseiller chambellan* 126
Villette, Philippe de, abbot of Saint-
    Denis 180n.
Vivarais, Estates of 107, 120n.
Vitteaux, seigneur de 126
Voluyre, Hervé de 79, 80

Wake, Thomas ('The Great Wake') 217,
    218, 219, 220, 221, 230, 233, 234; his
    father, Thomas, of Blisworth (Nhants.)
    218; his mother, Margaret (Philpot)
    218-19, 220; his wife, Agnes (Lovel)
    219, 234
Walsingham, Thomas, his *Ypodigma
    Neustrie* 206
Warwick, Richard Beauchamp, earl of
    38
Waynflete, William, bishop of
    Winchester 234
Wayt, William, clerk 215
Waxchandler, Edmund 226
Wells (Somerset) 226
Wells-next-the-Sea (Norfolk) 216
Westminster 154
Wettenhall, Sir Thomas 9
Wey, William 154
Willoughby 48, 82
Willy, William 222, 230, 231; his son 222
Wincanton 228
Windsor, Henry 225
Worcester, William 200, 201n., 207, 208n.,
    211, 216, 225-7, 228, 229n., 232, 234;
    his *Boke of noblesse* 207, 224 & n.;
    his learning 216
Worcester, sheriff of 225

Xaintrailles, Jean, seigneur de 52, 54; Poton
    de 56

Yelverton, justice 225
Yolande of Aragon, queen of France 155
Yorkists 205, 211n., 238
Ysalguier-Fourquevaux, Jacques d' 55
Yver, Jean 161